A FAITH
FOR ALL
SEASONS

A FAITH FOR ALL SEASONS

Historic Christian Belief In Its Classical Expression

TED M. DORMAN

BROADMAN
& HOLMAN
PUBLISHERS

Nashville, Tennessee

4210-74
0-8054-1074-0

Dewey Decimal Classification: 230
Subject Heading: Doctrinal Theology \ God \ Holy Spirit \
Jesus Christ \ Church
Library of Congress Card Catalog Number: 94-37019

Unless otherwise noted all Scripture is from the Holy Bible,
New International Version, copyright © 1973, 1978, 1984
by International Bible Society.

Library of Congress Cataloging-in-Publication Data
Dorman, Theodore Martin.
    A faith for all seasons: historic Christian beliefs / Ted M.
Dorman
        p. cm.
    Includes bibliographical references and index.
    ISBN 0-8054-1074-0: $27.99
    1. Theology, Doctrinal—Introductions. I. Title.
    BT65.D67   1995
    230'.044—dc20   94-37019
                                                              CIP

1 2 3 4 5 6 00 99 98 97 96 95

To my wife and children:

Lillian, Heidi, Stephen
Joshua, Aaron, Timothy

Contents

Introduction

We are like dwarves sitting on the shoulders of giants [the ancient Christian writers]. We see more than they and things that are further away—not because our sight is better than theirs, nor because we are taller than they were, but because they raise us up and add to our stature by their enormous height.

> —Bernard of Chartes (d. 1130);
> quoted by John of Salisbury,
> *Metalogicon* 3.4.[1]

It is a good rule, after reading a new book, never to allow yourself another new one till you have read an old one in between.

. . . first-hand knowledge is not only more worth acquiring than second-hand knowledge, but is usually much easier and more delightful to acquire.

> —C. S. Lewis (1898-1963),
> "On the Reading of Old Books"[2]

This is a new book about old books. It is a book written by a dwarf seated atop the shoulders of theological giants of ages past. It is about the insights and ideas of the giants, not of the dwarf.

This is a textbook which concerns itself with the principal doctrines of the historic Christian faith. It is the outgrowth of a class I teach at Taylor University, a midwestern Christian liberal arts col-

1

lege which draws students from a variety of Protestant denominations and even has a handful of Roman Catholic students. I have therefore sought to write a book which crosses confessional and denominational lines while remaining faithful to what the New Testament writer Jude calls "the faith that was once for all entrusted to the saints" (v. 3).

At the same time, the overall structure of the book testifies to the Protestant Reformed perspective from which its author writes. It is a virtual axiom nowadays that no writer can totally free himself from his ideological bias, and I make no such claim. I have tried to be fair in my descriptions of beliefs which I do not personally share. To what extent I have succeeded I shall leave for others to judge.

The title of this book, *A Faith for All Seasons*, was inspired by two unrelated twentieth-century events. The first of these is playwright Robert Bolt's 1960 production *A Man for All Seasons*, a tribute to the sixteenth-century English Christian scholar and statesman Sir Thomas More. The fact that Bolt, a self-confessed non-Christian, praised More's courage and integrity in the face of persecution and death is a testimony to the power of one life lived in obedience to Jesus Christ. The second event is an unprecedented fact of history noted by the late Bishop Stephen Neill.[3] The twentieth century has witnessed the first worldwide religion, with adherents in virtually every culture. That religion is Christianity. It is a universal faith, "a faith for all seasons."

What you hold in your hands is the result of my having taught this material for the past six-and-a-half years. It is the fruit not merely of my own research, but also—indeed, most importantly—of the questions and concerns of my students. I have written this book for them, not for the academic guild. If anyone thinks I have paid too much attention to certain subjects and not enough to others, I can only respond that I have tried to write in response to those questions which my students most often ask.

Theme

The theme of *A Faith for All Seasons* could be labeled "unity through diversity." Throughout the two-thousand-year history of the Church, Christians have articulated their understanding of the meaning of Christ in various and sometimes sharply divergent ways. Yet within this diversity an overall consensus emerges which may be termed "Historic Christian Belief." It is what one ancient writer called "that faith which has been believed everywhere, always, by all" who believe in Christ (see below, p. 299). The late C. S. Lewis referred to it as "mere Christianity."

This historic consensus constitutes a unity which approaches unanimity when it touches on the central doctrinal affirmations of the Christian Church. Among these are the doctrines of the Trinity, the Incarnation of God in Jesus Christ, and the saving death and resurrection of Christ for the sins of the world. These and other central tenets of historic Christian belief are summed up in two ancient confessions of faith to which we shall refer throughout this book, the Apostles' Creed and the Nicene Creed. The text of each appears at the end of this introductory chapter.

Purpose

The chapters which follow introduce the reader to the basic doctrines of the Christian religion as set forth by the New Testament apostolic writers and their post-apostolic counterparts, who further developed and systematized these doctrines. As we shall see, the post-apostolic writers did not always remain consistent with the apostolic witness, nor did they always agree with one another. What they did share was a heartfelt conviction that God had revealed Himself definitively in the man Jesus of Nazareth, the Messiah of Israel and Savior of the world.

It is the present writer's hope that by acquainting the reader with the testimony of both Scripture and the great thinkers of Christian history, the reader might gain a deeper understanding of the Church's theological reflection on the Person and work of Jesus Christ. Protestants especially need to become aware of the richness of the tradition which developed during the first fifteen hundred years of Christian history, prior to the Reformation. The quotations from writers such as Irenaeus, Augustine, Anselm, and Thomas Aquinas (as well as Reformation and post-Reformation lights such as Martin Luther, John Calvin, John Wesley and Jonathan Edwards) are designed to whet the reader's interest in reading some of the old books penned by conveyors of the classical theological consensus which is historic christian belief.

Methodology

The first thing to note about this book's method of presenting Christian doctrine is its trinitarian structure. After beginning with two chapters which deal with divine revelation, the format follows the order of the three persons of the Trinity: God the Father (chapters 3 through 7), Son (chapters 8 through 10) and Holy Spirit (chapters 11 through 15).

A second feature of the text which should be mentioned is its selectivity. Both the biblical and historical components by way of necessity exclude much interesting and even important information. As noted above, I have used the interests of my students as a primary indicator of what I choose to emphasize and what I choose to omit.

With regard to New Testament theology, a comprehensive treatment using the thematic approach of this volume would comprise at least twice as many pages as you hold in your hand. For example, Donald Guthrie's massive *New Testament Theology* contains over a thousand pages. In like manner, a historical theology which traced the development of all the doctrines dealt with herein would delve much more deeply into matters than an introductory book such as this one. With the exception of a few key areas of doctrine (Christology in chapter 8, for example), the present writer makes no attempt at systematic expositions of the historical development of Christian thought. Brief overviews and selective snapshots are more the order of the day, designed to introduce the student to issues she or he may wish to pursue.

Two features of this text make it a useful primer for such further research. The first is the extensive documentation of classical and post-Reformation primary sources. The second is the case studies of important people and events in the history of Christian doctrine. The biographical sketches in particular are designed to impress upon the student that Christian doctrine is not merely the result of lining up biblical proof-texts, but also of reflecting on these texts in light of not only their original contexts, but also the historical situations of the theologians who reflected upon Holy Writ.

Theological trends in the last two hundred years have for the most part been omitted here. This is by design. Great ideas are those which stand the test of time, and modern theologies springing from the Liberal Protestant tradition have not been in the saddle long enough to earn their scholarly spurs. In addition to Liberalism itself (see chapter 8, part 6) such modern departures from classical Christianity include existentialist theology, process theology, liberation theology, and feminist theology.[4]

Two modern Christian writers who do warrant significant attention are the Swiss theologian Karl Barth (1886-1968) and the British apologist C. S. Lewis, cited at the outset of this chapter. This is because each had a tremendous impact upon twentieth-century Christianity while operating within the framework of the historic trinitarian Christian confessions. The structure of Barth's massive *Church Dogmatics*, for example, is specifically trinitarian, and his theology is thoroughly centered on Jesus Christ as God's sole revelation. Whatever flaws may exist in Barth's theology from the standpoint of the historic Christian consensus (and there are several, as we shall see), he was self-consciously operating in dialogue with historic Christian belief. As for Lewis, the widespread popularity of his writings in the English-speaking world proves that classical orthodox Christianity need not be outdated.

Setting the Stage

The term "historic Christian belief" indicates that history is the stage upon which the drama of Christian doctrinal development has been carried out. A brief overview of the major periods of Church history, together with the major theologians belonging to each, will contribute to increased understanding of the Christian faith. For our purposes we may divide Church history as follows:

The Ante-Nicene Era, A.D. 100–325

During this time the Church often found itself at odds with the Roman Empire and the surrounding culture. This era includes the earliest of the post-apostolic writers, such as Ignatius of Antioch and Papias. Later writers of note include Irenaeus, Justin Martyr, Tertullian, and Origen. The Council of Nicea (A.D. 325) marks the end of this period of Church history.

The Nicene and Post-Nicene Era, A.D. 325–451

The Church came under the umbrella of the Roman Empire as Christianity eventually became the state religion. The two greatest writers of this period were Athanasius in the fourth century and Augustine in the late fourth and early fifth centuries. During this time the Church defined its belief in the triune God and the full divinity and humanity of Jesus Christ (see chapter 8).

The Early Middle Ages, A.D. 451–950

Christianity found itself in retreat as the Roman Empire collapsed and the "Dark Ages" began. The beginnings and expansion of Islam from Arabia through North Africa to Spain between A. D. 630 and 733 caused Christianity to retreat from some previously Christian areas. Writers such as John of Damascus and the Venerable Bede kept the flame of faith shining in the darkness of the age. At the same time, the stage was set for eventual resurgence on Christmas Day of A. D. 800, when the Pope crowned Charlemagne as Emperor of the Holy Roman Empire.

The Later Middle Ages and Renaissance, A.D. 950–1500

Christianity experienced both geographic expansion and intellectual and spiritual revival during the four-century interval between A.D. 950 and 1350, despite the fact that in 1054 the Eastern (Orthodox) and Western (Roman Catholic) branches of the Church finally separated from one another. Anselm of Canterbury and Thomas Aquinas, the two most significant theologians of the late Middle Ages, were men of both spiritual and intellectual greatness. Other writers of note included Peter Abelard, Bernard of Clairvaux, and Richard of St. Victor. From about A. D. 1350 to 1500 the Church experienced setbacks due to the conquest of Constantinople in the East (A. D. 1453) and the decline of the power of the Roman Catholic Papacy in the West.

The Reformation Era, A.D. 1500–1750

The Protestant Reformation shook Western Christendom to its foundations, releasing religious, political, and cultural forces which are with us to this day. Martin Luther's and John Calvin's rejection of papal authority in the early sixteenth century set the stage for theological reform and spiritual revival on the one hand, and political turmoil and intellectual freedom on the other. Two hundred years later John Wesley and Jonathan Edwards helped lay foundations for eighteenth-century religious revival and the great nine-teenth-century expansion of Christian missions. At the same time, Protestantism's emphasis on individual religious liberty helped prepare the way for the secularizing forces of the Enlightenment (eighteenth century) and theological Liberalism (nineteenth century).

The Modern Era, A.D. 1750–present

During this time the Christian Church has witnessed its greatest expansion in history. Today Christianity is the one truly worldwide religion. At the same time, the Christian faith has come under increasing attack in the very countries most influenced by the Reformation, due in large part to the subsequent effects of Enlightenment philosophy.

As the twentieth century comes to a close, many historians see the geographical center of Christianity shifting from Western Europe and North America to South America, Africa, and Asia. In these non-Western lands historic Christian belief has made unprecedented gains during the past century, even as Christians in Europe and the United States often appear to be searching for identity. To the degree that this book can help Christians rediscover their heritage and thus their historic identity, it will have fulfilled its purpose.

So What?

Even if it is true that many Christians need to rediscover their heritage, a final question is in order: Why should any Christian read this book? Those of you who are Roman Catholics have the teaching office of the Church to guide you, while you who are my fellow Protestants have the Bible. Was not the battle-cry of the Reformation *sola scriptura*, "Scripture alone"? Why all this business about the historic Christian tradition? That sounds suspiciously Catholic to Protestant ears.

Yet we live in a time when the four-hundred-year rift between Roman Catholicism and Protestantism shows signs of signficant healing, particularly among traditional Catholics and evangelical Protestants.[5] This is happening in response to what many in

Europe and North America, Christian and non-Christian alike, perceive as a crisis of cultural identity in the West.

A close look at the intellectual landscape of the historically "Christian" cultures of Western Europe and North America, and the theological crisis of authority within the mainline Protestant denominations, points to a rapidly-fading collective memory of what the third-century Egyptian theologian Origen of Alexandria called the "first principles" which until recently undergirded Western culture.[6] These first principles were forcibly overthrown in Russia at the outset of the twentieth century in favor of an atheistic ideology known as communism, which resulted in the most barbaric despotism of human history.[7] Ideas have consequences. Truth matters, as Michael Novak put it in his acceptance speech of the 1994 Templeton Prize for Progress in Religion.[8]

Jesus of Nazareth said, "I am the Truth" (John 14:6). Christians throughout the centuries have reflected on this claim, and upon the central events of His life, His death, and His resurrection. The classical interpreters of the New Testament may not have anticipated many situations we moderns encounter today, but they reflected deeply upon the first principles of Christianity. They also dealt with moral decisions common to people of all time, such as abortion and suicide.[9] Without their guidance we shall run the risk of theological amnesia, forever attempting to reinvent the wheel as we seek the meaning and significance of Scripture for our lives. But seated upon their shoulders, we shall gain a panoramic view of the Christian faith which enables us to see that what these ancients had to say does indeed relate to our present time. It is a faith for all seasons.

The Apostles' Creed
(Sixth Century A.D.)

I believe in God the Father Almighty, Maker of Heaven and earth.

And in Jesus Christ His only Son our Lord, who was conceived by the Holy Spirit, born of the Virgin Mary, suffered under Pontius Pilate, was crucified, dead and buried. He descended into Hell. The third day He rose again from the dead. He ascended into Heaven, and sits on the right hand of God the Father Almighty, from whence He shall come to judge the living and the dead.

I believe in the Holy Spirit, the holy catholic Church, the communion of saints, the forgiveness of sins, the resurrection of the body, and the life everlasting. Amen.

THE NICENE CREED
(A.D. 381)

I believe in one God the Father Almighty, Maker of Heaven and Earth, and of all things visible and invisible.

And in one Lord Jesus Christ the only-begotten Son of God, begotten of the Father before all worlds: God from God, Light from Light, true God from true God; begotten, not made; being of one substance with the Father; by whom all things were made. Who for us men and for our salvation came down from Heaven and was incarnate by the Holy Spirit of the Virgin Mary, and was made Man; and was crucified also for us under Pontius Pilate; He suffered and was buried. The third day He rose again according to the Scriptures, and ascended into Heaven, and sits on the right hand of the Father, and He shall come again with glory to judge both the living and the dead; whose Kingdom shall have no end.

I believe in the Holy Spirit, the Lord and giver of life, who proceeds from the Father [and the Son], who with the Father and the Son together is worshiped and glorified, who spoke by the prophets. And I believe one holy, catholic, apostolic Church. I acknowledge one baptism for the remission of sins. And I look for the resurrection of the dead, and the life in the world to come. Amen.

1

Our Knowledge of God

Faith and Knowledge

In what sense can we speak of faith in God as having anything to do with knowledge? Some would say we cannot. Consider, for example, the traditional Sunday School tale which includes the following dialogue:

Teacher: "Johnny, what is faith?"

Johnny: "Faith is . . . believing something you know isn't true!"

The radical dichotomy between faith and knowledge humorously set forth here is, in fact, serious business. For if religious faith has nothing to do with knowing that something is true, then theology (literally, "God-talk") is little more than a glorified form of anthropology ("man-talk").

Much modern Christian theology is based upon this sort of faith/knowledge dichotomy. God, according to this perspective, is beyond human understanding. Therefore we can know nothing about who God is in Himself. We can only speak of our *experience* of God. In the words of Rudolf Bultmann, one of the twentieth century's most influential biblical scholars, "any speaking of God . . . is only possible as talk of ourselves."[1] For Bultmann, theology is anthropology.

This, in turn, is part of modern Western culture's intellectual debt to the Enlightenment, the eighteenth-century European philosophical movement which regarded humanity as the measure of all things. In particular, the Rationalist wing of the Enlightenment tended to define knowledge in terms of statements which could be verified through an empirical process of inference from evidence to conclusion. But God by definition transcends the empirical realm, and thus cannot be known by empirical processes. On the basis of Rationalist methodology, then, we cannot have knowledge of God. Faith finds its basis in non-rational elements of human experience, not in knowledge.

Historic Christian belief, on the other hand, has generally regarded faith as an expression of knowledge, not merely an expression of emotion or experience. Such knowledge is not limited to observable or verifiable facts, of course. Faith includes a future orientation, that of hope, as well as the conviction that spiritual realities exist which transcend the scope of the scientific method. "Faith is the assurance of things hoped for; the conviction of things not seen" (Heb. 11:1, NRSV).

Note carefully what the biblical writer says: faith is assurance that certain *things* are true. Specifically, Christians confess that God has done, is doing, and will do certain things in human history, not merely in the realm of human psychological experience. At the center of this confession is the person of Jesus of Nazareth, whose life, death and resurrection are attested to by the writings of Holy Scripture.[2]

At the same time, the overall consensus of Christian theology is that God can be known to a degree apart from Christ and the Bible. This is because God has revealed Himself not only by means of Christ and Scripture, but also through His creation. The term *general revelation* refers to what God has revealed to all humanity via the created order, while *special revelation* refers to what God has revealed to a limited number of people through the events of redemptive history, especially Jesus Christ and the Bible. We shall deal with the two principal components of special revelation in chapter 2 (Scripture) and chapters 8 through 10 (Christ). The remainder of this chapter will deal with what human beings know of God by means of general revelation.

Knowledge of God
Through General Revelation

All People Know God

The Christian doctrine of general revelation teaches that all people in all places at all times know God to a greater or lesser extent, whether or not they have access to the Bible. Theologians have traditionally divided general revelation into two broad categories: outward general revelation, and inward general revelation. The former consists of the realities we perceive in the world around us, while the latter consists of the realities we sense within us as moral and spiritual beings.

Outward General Revelation

"The heavens declare the glory of God; the skies proclaim the work of his hands" (Ps. 19:1).

"Since the creation of the world God's invisible qualities—his eternal power and divine nature—have been clearly seen, being understood from what has been made" (Rom. 1:20).

The creation reveals something of the Creator, even as a work of art reveals something of the one who made it. People who do not worship the God of the Bible can nevertheless know some basic truths about the Creator. The apostle Paul acknowledged this (Acts 17:28) when he quoted two Greek poets to his Athenian audience to the effect that "in [God] we live and move and have our being" (Epimenides the Cretan), and that "we are [God's] offspring" (Aratus of Cilicia). At the same time, Paul considered such knowledge as incomplete, a fact acknowledged by the Athenians themselves, who built an altar dedicated to "an unknown God" (Acts 17:23).

What does creation reveal about God? "His eternal power and divine nature," says Paul. God's power is evidenced by the fact that something exists. God's divine nature is evidenced by the fact that this "something," the created order, is indeed a created *order* and not random chaos. This implies that God has a character which gives order and purpose to creation. We shall deal with the character of God and the purpose of creation in chapters 3 and 4.

Inward General Revelation

Christian apologist C. S. Lewis began his most famous work, *Mere Christianity*, with a chapter entitled "Right and Wrong as a Clue to the Meaning of the Universe." His argument was that our moral sentiments testify to a Supreme Moral Governor of the universe. When we tell ourselves or someone else that a particular activity is right or wrong, we are saying that people are accountable not merely to human laws or customs, but to a higher law: the Law of God. "Right" and "wrong" are words which deal not merely with values or virtues (which express personal preferences), but with morality (which expresses obligations to one another and, ultimately, to our Creator).

C. S. LEWIS

Clive Staples ("Jack") Lewis (1898–1963) was a highly-respected literary critic and Oxford don before converting to Christianity and joining the Church of England in 1929. A brilliant and prolific writer, Lewis mastered a variety of genres including novels, children's books, poetry, theology and apologetics.

Lewis used clarity of language, reasoned argumentation, and a sharp wit to articulate and defend what he called "mere Christianity" (the title of his most famous book). Lewis used this phrase to designate the doctrines which have been common to almost all Christians throughout history. In an era of theological novelty, where new ideas were consistently praised at the expense of orthodox Christianity, Lewis attempted to say nothing new.

Even the phrase "mere Christianity," which has become inextricably associated with his name, was not original. He borrowed it from the seventeenth-century English Puritan preacher Richard Baxter.

Lewis's brand of Christianity, while disowning denominational distinctives, was fundamentally in the tradition of Augustine and the Reformers. Among other things, he shared Augustine's tendency towards synthesizing biblical theology with the philosophical tradition of Plato. In an essay entitled "Myth Became Fact," for example, Lewis argued that Christianity was the unique mythology of human history in that it actually happened. All other myths were but shadows of the universal truth revealed in Jesus Christ.*

In addition to *Mere Christianity* (1943) Lewis's most famous works include *The Screwtape Letters* (1941), a delightful satire depicting correspondence between a master demon and his unfortunate nephew in the underworld, *The Problem of Pain* (1940), *The Abolition of Man* (1943), *The Great Divorce* (1946), and *Miracles* (1947). He also wrote a science fiction trilogy which set forth a Christian worldview: *Out of the Silent Planet* (1938), *Perelandra* (1943), and *That Hideous Strength* (1945). His seven-volume children's series, *The Chronicles of Narnia*, has been enjoyed by three generations of young people.

In 1956 Lewis, a lifelong bachelor, married Joy Davidman Gresham, an American Jewish convert to Christianity. When she died of cancer four years later he experienced unprecedented grief, which became the subject of his most poignant work, *A Grief Observed*. Three years later Lewis himself passed on from what he called the "Shadowlands" of this world. In spite of his popularity on both sides of the Atlantic, Lewis's death was noticed by few in the United States. For on November 22, 1963, the day Lewis died, President John Fitzgerald Kennedy was gunned down in Dallas.

---

* See Lewis's *God in the Dock*, 63–67.

In our dealings with one another as moral agents, we evaluate both how we behave towards others, and how others behave towards us. The moral faculty which judges a person's thoughts and actions towards others is commonly called the individual's *conscience*. The moral faculty which judges the acts of others towards oneself has been termed the *judicial sentiment*.[3]

Conscience. The apostle Paul viewed conscience as a person's awareness of how well he or she obeys the Law of God. In Romans 2:15 Paul speaks of conscience as both "accusing" and "excusing" an individual's behavior towards others. Paul says that even Gentiles without the Law of Moses practice (to a greater or lesser degree) the requirements of the Law, thereby demonstrating that they have God's Law "written on their hearts." Their consciences then tell them whether or not they are living up to that Law.

At the same time, however, both Scripture and everyday experience indicate that conscience is by no means an infallible guide for evaluating one's own behavior. People's consciences may condemn them for doing something which is not necessarily wrong (1 Cor. 8:7). On the other hand, one may commit heinous acts for which one feels no remorse. Paul speaks of such people as having their consciences "seared as with a hot iron" (1 Tim. 4:2). The picture here is of a person without moral feeling, much the same as when one suffers a severe burn and is left with little or no feeling on the burnt portions of the skin. It would appear that cultural factors, as well as general revelation, determine whether and to what extent our conscience functions properly.

Judicial sentiment. Such cultural conditioning does not appear to affect our judicial sentiment, however. That is to say, whereas our conscience sometimes lets us off the hook when we behave badly towards others, our judicial sentiment refuses to let others off the hook when they behave badly towards us. In this sense the judicial sentiment is virtually unerring, unlike our sometimes fickle sentiment of conscience.

In Romans 2:1-3 Paul speaks of the judicial sentiment (without using the term) when he says,

> You, therefore, have no excuse, you who pass judgment on someone else, for at whatever point you judge the other, you are condemning yourself, because you who pass judgment do the same things. . . . So when you, a mere man, pass judgment on them and yet do the same things, do you think you will escape God's judgment?

In verse one Paul is saying that all people, to a greater or lesser degree, live by a double standard. We pass judgment on others when they wrong us, yet all too often excuse the same behavior when we do it to others. We do unto others as we would *not* have them do unto us.

This sort of "do as I say, not as I do" mindset is what Jesus referred to as hypocrisy (see Matt. 23:3, 13). Such hypocrisy, Paul tells us in Romans 2:3, is deserving of God's judgment, because we are doing what we know to be wrong. So even when our conscience does not condemn us, our judicial sentiment testifies to our moral duplicity when we condemn others for the same kinds of behavior which we ourselves practice.

Cultural relativism? Some would argue that moral sentiments, whether conscience or judicial sentiment, are merely expressions of our cultural values. This sort of cultural relativism, common to much modern anthropology, sees moral judgments not as a general revelation of God's character, but merely as a revelation of our personal or social biases. No universal notion of right and wrong exists, as evidenced by the different systems of morals and ethics which different civilizations have had throughout history.

Cultural relativism, however, has trouble accounting for at least two facts of human existence which stubbornly refuse to go away. The first fact is the presence of numerous *common* elements among the different moral teachings of the world. C. S. Lewis notes that there is no morality which is *completely* different from all other moral codes, and speculates as to what a "totally different morality" would look like:

> Think of a country where people were admired for running away in battle, or where a man felt proud of doublecrossing all the people who had been kindest to him. You might just as well try to imagine a country where two and two made five. Men have differed as regards what people you ought to be unselfish to—whether it was only your own family, or your fellow countrymen, or everyone. But they have always agreed that you ought not to put yourself first. Selfishness has never been admired.[4]

The fact that no such "totally different morality" exists indicates that human beings share a common awareness of what God requires, an inward general revelation of who God is.

A second fact which makes cultural relativism problematic is that those who deny moral absolutes do not behave in accord with their professed beliefs. Lewis speaks also to this point:

> Whenever you find a man who says he does not believe in a real Right and Wrong, you will find the same man going back on this a moment later. He may break his promise to you, but if you try breaking one to him he will be complaining "It's not fair" before you can say Jack Robinson. . . . Have [cultural relativists] not let the cat out of the bag and shown that, whatever they say, they really know the Law of Nature just like anyone else?[5]

This is basically the same point which, as we have already seen, Paul makes in Romans 2:1-3. Even if our conscience permits us to act towards others as though cultural relativism were true, our judicial sentiment never allows others to act that way towards us. Deep down, we all know that we ought to behave in a certain way, and that we do not live up to the way we ought to live. In the words of Paul, "All have sinned, and come short of the glory of God" (Rom. 3:23).

Sensus divinitatis. Our moral sentiments are part of a larger reality which appears to be a universal human experience: a "sense of God" (*sensus divinitatis*)[6] which elicits not only moral codes and a sense of moral accountability, but also a need to worship the One to Whom we owe our existence. Historically, the phenomenon of religion is a ubiquitous human experience. On the other hand, religion is completely absent from the animal kingdom. Dogs and cats display no need to worship. People do.

The psalmist testifies to this universal human longing for God: "As the deer pants for streams of water, so my soul pants for you, O God. My soul thirsts for God, for the living God." (Ps. 42:1-2). Saint Augustine echoed this longing of the human heart for God with his famous dictum: "Thou hast formed us for Thyself, [O God,] and our hearts are restless till they find their rest in Thee" (*Confessions* 1.1).[7] The French philosopher Blaise Pascal spoke of humanity's desire for God as "an infinite abyss" which "can only be filled by an infinite and immutable object, that is to say, only by God Himself" (Pènsees 425).[8]

Implications of General Revelation

Knowledge of God and Knowledge of Self

General revelation makes possible not only our knowledge of God, but also our knowledge of ourselves. The writer of Proverbs states that "the fear of the Lord is the beginning of wisdom" (Prov. 1:7). We cannot understand what it means to be wise people unless we see ourselves in relationship to God.

John Calvin grasped this necessary relationship between knowledge of God and of ourselves. His *Institutes of the Christian Religion* begins by noting that "wisdom . . . consists of two parts: the knowledge of God and of ourselves." Indeed, one cannot have one without the other: "Without knowledge of self there is no knowledge of God" and "[w]ithout knowledge of God there is no knowledge of self" (*Institutes* 1.1.1,2).

In linking knowledge of God and self, Calvin was following in the tradition of Paul who believed that people fail to acknowledge

God because they do not own up to what they already know about both God and themselves. Paul spoke of the "wrath of God" coming upon people because they "hold down the truth in unrighteousness" (Rom. 1:18). Calvin, like Paul, realized that people lacked true knowledge of God because God's holiness makes sinful human beings look bad by way of comparison: "That is, what in us seems perfection itself corresponds ill to the purity of God" (*Institutes* 1.1.2). On the other hand, it is only as we become "displeased with ourselves" that we can truly begin to understand who God is, as opposed to what we would like God to be (*Institutes* 1.1.1).

Less than two centuries after Calvin, the Enlightenment poet Alexander Pope, in his *Essay on Man*, would espouse a much different view: "Know then thyself, presume not God to scan; the proper study of mankind is Man." With these words Pope assumed that knowledge of God was not possible for us because God was, by definition, beyond knowing. For Calvin and the historic consensus of Christianity, however, human ignorance of God is not due to a lack of intellect or knowledge, but to a willful rejection of what God has made known to us through general revelation.

Accountability Before God

The fundamental problem of human existence, then, is not a lack of knowledge about God, but a refusal to own up to the knowledge we already have. This in turn means that we are accountable for having rejected what God has revealed to us. Paul says in Romans 2:12 that "all who sin apart from the law [i.e., the special revelation of the Law of Moses] will also perish apart from the law," because they already know what is right and wrong due to the testimony of both conscience (Rom. 2:15) and the judicial sentiment (2:1; see our discussion in the preceding section).

Francis Schaeffer illustrates this point by setting up an imaginary scenario. "Let us suppose," he says, "that as each baby is born, a tape recorder is placed about its neck. Let us further suppose that this tape recorder works only when moral judgments are being made." Schaeffer then continues:

> Throughout one's whole life, every real moral motion is recorded upon the tape recorder. Finally, when each person dies and stands before God in judgment, God pushes a button and each person hears with his own ears his own moral judgments [against other peo-

ple] as they rolled out over the years: "You were wrong in doing this. You are wrong in doing that."

After the tape stops playing God turns and asks each person, "On the basis of your own words, have *you* kept these moral standards?" No one can reply, "Yes! I have!" Everyone is silent. No one has kept the moral standards by which he judged others. God therefore says, "I will judge you upon your own moral statements . . . even if they are lower than moral statements should be." The final, ominous question from the divine Judge is: "Are you guilty or not guilty?"

Schaeffer, like Paul over nineteen hundred years earlier, concludes: "No one will be able to raise his voice. The whole world will stand totally condemned before God. . . ." (compare with Romans 3:29). They will be judged "not upon what they have not known, but upon what they have known and have not kept."[9]

We therefore cannot beg ignorance, as Alexander Pope would have it. We judge others by the truth of God which we already know, and thereby also pass judgment on ourselves.

Common Ground Between Christians and Unbelievers

Paul's experience in Athens (Acts 17:16-34; see above, p. 13) underscores the fact that general revelation establishes a common ground between the Christian evangelist and those unfamiliar with the Gospel of Christ. The Athenian philosophers were able to understand the basic thrust of Paul's message precisely because, by Paul's own reckoning, they already knew something about God apart from biblical revelation.

Such extrabiblical knowledge of God is sometimes referred to as "natural theology," since it speaks of what nature (including human nature) can teach us about God. Others would use the term "philosophical theology," which refers to that knowledge of God which is available through human reason alone, apart from special revelation. Throughout the history of Christianity theologians have debated the extent to which God may be known by means of natural or philosophical theology.

The basic question of whether the very existence of God can be proven has been the source of much creative thought. In addition to arguments based on humanity's sense of morality and the *sensus divinitatis* mentioned above, the two fundamental types of theistic arguments are those which proceed *a priori* (logical arguments derived from self-evident propositions apart from observed facts) and those which proceed *a posteriori* (arguments derived by reasoning from observed facts). The outstanding example of *a priori* argumentation for God's existence is the "ontological argument" set forth by Anselm of Canterbury. Thomas Aquinas's five proofs for the existence of God, on the other hand, are a classic example of *a posteriori* methodology.

Anselm's ontological argument. Anselm, who served as Archbishop of Canterbury beginning in 1093, argued that the very concept of God requires that God exist. In chapters 2 and 3 of his *Proslogium* Anselm defined God as "a being than which nothing greater can be conceived."[10] He then noted that this definition of God could be thought in two ways:

(A) This definition refers to that which exists in our minds, but not in reality.

(B) This definition refers to that which exists not only in our minds, but also in reality.

Anselm went on to ask which of the two ideas, (A) or (B), is greater. The answer, he said, is (B), since idea (A) exists only in our minds, but not in reality. Thus people can conceive of a definition of God greater than (A), but not greater than (B). Therefore, God must by definition exist, since God is "that than which nothing greater can be conceived."

To some, this argument seems little more than a play on words or begging the question. It was rejected by Anselm's contemporary Gaunilo, and later by Thomas Aquinas and Immanuel Kant. Yet the notion that a proper definition of God requires God's existence persists to this day among many philosophers and theologians. For others, such *a priori* argumentation is less useful than arguments which proceed from observed facts, or *a posteriori*. Aquinas used the latter approach.

Aquinas's five proofs for the existence of God. In his *Summa Theologiae* (1. 2. 3) Aquinas set forth five variations of arguments which had been used previously by pagans and Jews as well as by Christian theologians. Briefly, they are as follows:

- *The argument from motion.* Everything which exists is in motion, i.e. is changing. Now whatever is changing obviously has the potential to change. But no potential can actualize itself; something else must actualize it (for example, wood has the potential to become fuel, but that potential must be actualized by fire). Furthermore, said Aquinas, there cannot be an infinite series of actualizers, since without a first actualizer or mover nothing can subsequently move or be actualized. Therefore, there must exist a first "unmoved Mover" (to use Aristotle's language), which is God.

- *The argument from efficient causality.* The world includes an order of "efficient causes," causes which produce other beings. But nothing can be the cause of its own being. Furthermore, no series of efficient causes can cause their own being. Therefore, there must be a first Efficient Cause which brought everything into being.

- *The argument from possible beings.* There are beings that begin to exist and cease to exist ("possible" beings). But not all beings can be "possible" beings, since what exists can come into existence only through what already exists. Therefore, there must be a "necessary" being (which neither begins nor ceases to exist), which we call God.

- *The argument from gradation of perfection.* Some things are more perfect than other things. We can know what is more or less perfect only by comparison with what is absolutely perfect. But that which is most perfect must be the cause of all the less-than-perfect things. This most perfect cause is God.

- *The argument from design.* Every agent which acts, whether a moral agent or a natural agent, acts towards some purpose or end. That which acts towards a purpose demonstrates intelligence. But natural agents have no intelligence of their own (they act towards some end by instinct, not by reason). Therefore, natural agents are directed to their end by some Intelligence, which is God. This is sometimes called the "teleological" argument (Greek *telos*, "end, purpose").

Each of Thomas's five "proofs" argues that for every effect, there must be a commensurate cause. The first three argue that the world must have had a cause, and are thus variations of what has been labeled the "cosmological" argument (Greek *cosmos*, "world"). The fourth argument argues from our sense of perfection, and may be labeled "aesthetic." The argument from design goes beyond the other four in that it says God not only created all things, and created them with greater or lesser degrees of perfection, but also that God created the world with a purpose in mind which caused Him to create it as He did.[11]

THOMAS AQUINAS

Thomas Aquinas (1224?-1274) stands as one of the three most influential theologians in the history of the Western Church, the other two being Augustine and John Calvin. He was born near the town of Aquino in southern Italy, to a relatively wealthy family. He studied at the University of Naples and became a Dominican monk around 1244, despite opposition from his family.

In 1245 Thomas began to study at the University of Paris under Albert the Great, whose desire to integrate Christian theology and the philosophy of Aristotle was passed on to his star pupil. Thomas spent long hours in silent study and prayer, which may be the reason some of his classmates gave him the nickname "dumb ox." Albert reportedly replied, "We call this lad a 'dumb ox,' but I tell you that the whole

world is going to hear his roar." This statement proved prophetic.

Thomas wrote prolifically. The most famous of his works was the *Summa Theologiae*, which remained unfinished when he died. In the *Summa* Thomas sought to demonstrate the extent to which God could be known, whether by human reason or by divine revelation. Thomas believed human reason was capable of very little knowledge of God; thus any natural or philosophical theology could serve only as a preamble for a theology based upon divine revelation.

Thomas defined human knowledge as had Aristotle, emphasizing sensory experience as the source of all we know about anything, including God. In this respect Thomas departed from the Augustinian tradition, which emphasized that direct knowledge of God was possible through intellectual illumination. For

Thomas, God was known only by the effects of his actions. This is why Thomas rejected all forms of *a priori* argumentation for the existence of God, preferring instead to argue from what God had created (effect) to the existence of God (cause). Thomas nonetheless followed in the footsteps of both Augustine and Anselm in affirming that Christian faith was a rational enterprise, making use of human reason to understand the revealed truths of Scripture. The idea that human reason might operate independently of special revelation would have been unthinkable to Thomas Aquinas.

In December of 1273 Thomas ceased writing, telling a friend that "I cannot; all that I have written seems like straw." Some attribute this to a mystical religious experience, beside which his writings appeared insignificant. Others believe Thomas suffered a physical or mental breakdown due to his rigorous daily schedule. He died on March 4, 1274.

In 1326 Thomas was canonized as Saint Thomas Aquinas, and in 1567 he was made a "Doctor of the Church." In 1879 the Pope declared Thomas to be a "Father of the Church," and his philosophy dominated Catholic education until the time of Vatican II in the 1960s. Since that time his influence has diminished in Catholic circles, but is gaining increased attention among evangelical Protestants.

What General Revelation Cannot Do

We have noted that God's general revelation, whether outward or inward, provides us with three things:

- General revelation provides the basis by which we can know not only God, but also ourselves, since as created beings we can only understand ourselves in relation to the One who created us.

- General revelation provides enough insight into both God and ourselves to hold us accountable for our actions before God. We cannot plead ignorance, even if we have never heard the gospel.

- General revelation provides a common ground for evangelism, because believers and nonbelievers alike live within a common moral and spiritual environment, as well as within the same external created order. Evidence both of God's existence and of His character provide a context for the gospel message.

What general revelation *cannot* do is give us the wisdom we need to come into a right relationship with the Divine Lawgiver whose Law we have broken. In short, divine revelation can provide us with insight into our predicament, but with no insight as to how we might deliver ourselves from that predicament. As Calvin notes (*Institutes* 1.5.14–15):

> It is therefore in vain that so many burning lamps shine for us in the workmanship of the universe to show forth the glory of its Author. Although they bathe us wholly in their radiance, yet they can of themselves in no way lead us to the right path. . . . But although we lack the natural ability to mount up unto the pure and clear knowledge of God, all excuse is cut off because the fault of dullness is within us. And, indeed, we are not allowed thus to pretend ignorance without our conscience itself always convicting us of both baseness and ingratitude.

Our brief survey of the classical "proofs" for the existence of God, as well as our reflection on the moral realities which hold all human beings, underscore what Calvin has said. Therein lies a fundamental paradox of historic Christian belief. We cannot deliver ourselves from the evil which so often besets us, yet we are held accountable by God for doing that which we cannot escape doing. We shall reflect further on this paradox in chapter 7.

For now, let us turn from the subject of general revelation to that of God's special revelation found in the Bible. For according to the consensus of Christians throughout history, human beings cannot be saved apart from the knowledge of God which comes through biblical revelation.

Points to Ponder

1. How does the Bible's view of the relationship between faith and knowledge differ from that of the Enlightenment?

2. What is general revelation? Special revelation? Be familiar with the different kinds of general revelation.

3. In your own words, define the terms *conscience, judicial sentiment,* and *sensus divinitatis.* Cite Scriptures which refer to each.

4. Summarize the three implications of general revelation discussed in part 3 of this chapter.

5. What is the difference between *a priori* and *a posteriori* arguments for the existence of God? Briefly describe an example of each.

6. What was Anselm's definition of God? Why did he believe such a definition necessitates the existence of God?

7. Briefly summarize Thomas Aquinas's five proofs for the existence of God.

8. What is general revelation not able to do for human beings? Why is this a "paradox"?

9. Why did Thomas Aquinas reject *a priori* arguments for God's existence? (See article on Aquinas)

2

The Doctrine of Scripture

The Need for Holy Scripture

In chapter 1 we spoke of general revelation as that which God has revealed of Himself through the created order to all people. We further noted that general revelation gives people enough knowledge of God to be accountable for their actions, but not enough knowledge to deliver themselves from divine judgment. It is for this reason, says the apostle Paul, that God has revealed Himself by means of Holy Scripture, that we might be made "wise unto salvation" (2 Tim. 3:15). Throughout its history the Church has agreed with Paul regarding the centrality of Scripture in the formulation of Christian belief and conduct.

The conviction that general revelation alone can lead no one to a saving knowledge of God, and must therefore be supplemented by a special revelation from God in Scripture, has to be understood in light of the first three chapters of the book of Genesis. For it is in this account of God's creation of humanity, and of Adam and Eve's subsequent rebellion and fall into sin, that our need for the Bible finds its explanation.

The first two chapters of Genesis depict a created order in which there was no distinction between "general" and "special" revelation. God's *works* and God's *words* were of a piece. The second chapter of Genesis portrays Adam as understanding God's verbal communications and appreciating what God has made (especially the woman!). What we now call "general revelation" was never designed to be complete in itself. It was part of a larger relationship between the Creator and those created in the divine image, a relationship which included open lines of communication.

The third chapter of Genesis tells how these lines of communication were severed by humanity's rebellion. Furthermore, the created order itself was placed under a curse (Gen. 3:17; see also Rom. 8:22). Thus the *works* of God no longer reflected their Creator's original design, and the *words* of God were no longer generally available to the human race. What had been a seamless garment of divine revelation was rent asunder.

Special revelation, then, is needed not because of any inherent deficiency in God's original creation; rather, the need for special revelation arose due to a deficiency brought about by humanity—sin. The situation before, at, and after humanity's fall into sin may be depicted as follows:

God's Self-Revelation		
Pre-Fall	Fall	Post-Fall
Works + Word	Works	Works (general revelation)
		Word (special revelation: the Bible, Jesus Christ)

Scripture as the Word of God

Scripture, then, is the written word of God which testifies to God's plan of salvation centered upon Jesus Christ, the Word of God incarnate. Jesus Himself affirmed the status of Scripture as "the word of God" (John 10:35), and declared that the Scripture bore witness to His work (John 5:39). The apostle Paul considered his preaching and writing to be not merely human words, but "words taught by the Spirit" (1 Cor. 2:13), so that his message and that of the other apostles was "the word of God" (1 Thess. 2:13).

Post-apostolic Christian writers seldom used the exact phrase "the word of God" to speak of Scripture. Yet the idea that the words of the Bible constitute a message from God is clearly attested by an overwhelming consensus of theologians over a period of more than a thousand years. Irenaeus, for example, used the phrase "the Holy Spirit says" when speaking of Scripture (*Against Heresies* 3.16.2), while Tertullian referred to the Bible as a "written revelation" from God (*Apology* 18). Augustine later referred to the Scriptures as "divine" and to the biblical authors as writers "who by divine assistance were enabled" (*Enchiridion* 4). Thomas Aquinas echoed these testimonies during the Middle Ages, stating that "the author of Holy Scripture is God" (*Summa Theologiae* 1.1.10).

The Protestant reformers were emphatic in their designation of the Bible as the word of God. Martin Luther used the terms "word of God" and "Scripture" interchangeably on a number of occasions. So did John Calvin, who spoke of the Bible as "having sprung from heaven, as if there the living words of God were heard" (*Institutes* 1.7.1). Reformed confessions which speak of the Bible as the word of God include the Second Helvetic Confession (1566) and the Westminster Confession (1646).

The Church's confession of the divine authorship of Scripture is closely linked to the doctrine of biblical inspiration. The term "inspiration" is derived from language used by the apostle Paul in 2 Timothy 3:16–17. This text is thus the *locus classicus* of the doctrine of the divine inspiration of Scripture, and merits close examination.

The Inspiration of Scripture

The Message of 2 Timothy 3:16–17

Paul encouraged Timothy to study the Scriptures, which are able to make one "wise unto salvation" (2 Tim. 3:15). The words which follow Paul's exhortation serve to underscore the importance of Scripture in the life of the Christian. "All Scripture is inspired by God and is profitable for teaching, rebuking, correcting, and training in righteousness, so that the man of God may be complete, equipped for every good work" (2 Tim. 3:16–17, RSV).

"All Scripture is inspired by God. The English words "inspired by God" translate a compound Greek word, *theopneustos*, which occurs nowhere else in the New Testament. The New International Ver-

sion translates it "God-breathed," since the word Paul uses comes from *theos*, "God" and *pneuma*, "breath" or "wind." Indeed, the word *pneuma* can also mean "spirit" (as in John 3:8, where Jesus uses the word twice, once meaning "wind" and once as "spirit"). All Scripture, says Paul, is a product of the work of the Spirit of God.

Note that Paul ascribes the quality of *theopneustos* to *all* Scripture. Such language mitigates against any view which would see some of the Bible as God's word, while relegating other portions to mere human ingenuity. Another New Testament text which underscores this is 2 Peter 1:20-21, which insists that "no prophecy of Scripture came about by the prophet's own interpretation. For prophecy never had its origin in the will of man, but men spoke from God as they were carried along by the Holy Spirit." Such language is consistent with the overall consensus of the Church's teaching on the divine origin of Scripture, and runs counter to modern notions of partial inspiration.

In addition, Paul says all *Scripture* is inspired by God. Inspiration extends not only to the writers of Scripture, but to the documents themselves. That is to say, the biblical authors did not merely receive a feeling of "inspiration" from God and then attempt to express their feelings in the form of language. Rather, they received a message from God which could be set forth in words. The text of Scripture, not the experience of the writers, is what matters for Paul. Indeed, Paul does not even talk about the writers. (2 Peter 1:20-21 does talk about the biblical writers, but makes it clear that *what they wrote*, and not merely a feeling of "inspiration," came from God.)

A final remark on the word "Scripture" deserves mention here. If we interpret this text strictly from its historical context, Paul is referring only to those writings which Christians call the Old Testament. This was the only Bible which he and Timothy, and indeed the entire early Church, possessed. Nevertheless, Christians have consistently applied Paul's statements here to the New Testament as well. Such an extrapolation is usually justified on grounds such as the following:

• Jesus saw His message and mission as being absolutely consistent with "the Law and the Prophets," i.e. the Old Testament (Matt. 5:17–20).

- Jesus commissioned His apostles as agents of divine revelation, inspired by the Holy Spirit (John 15:26–27).

- Jesus stated that future believers would come to faith in Christ through the apostolic word (John 17:20), of which the New Testament is a written deposit.

The message of the New Testament is therefore viewed by Christians as consistent with the message of Jesus, who in turn fulfilled the Old Testament Scriptures. Consequently, the New Testament is implicitly included in Paul's statement, "All Scripture is inspired by God."

"and is profitable for." Holy Scripture, says Paul, is useful to the believer to accomplish four things: "teaching, rebuking, correcting, training in righteousness."

- *Teaching* conveys the idea of proclaiming doctrinal truth. Paul uses a term from which we get our word "didactic." The Scripture teaches us about who God is and what He promises to do for us.

- *Rebuking* is the flip side of teaching. It refers to the activity of combatting doctrinal error. One must not only know what he or she believes; one must also be specific as to those things one does *not* believe.

- *Correction* refers to the act of leading someone away from ungodly conduct. Ethics, not doctrine, is the issue here.

- *Training in righteousness* is the positive counterpart to correction. It has to do with helping people lead godly lives. The word "training" brings to mind the picture of an athlete training for competition, or a soldier training for combat. Paul was fond of such metaphors (see 1 Cor. 9:24-27; Eph. 6:10-18).

Paul thus regards Scripture as useful for Christians in both matters of doctrine and conduct. For this reason the Bible is sometimes referred to as the Christian's "rule of faith and practice."

"so that the man of God may be." "May be" what? "Complete, equipped for every good work." The fact that Paul repeats the idea of the full sufficiency of Scripture ("complete . . . every") indicates that in his mind Scripture is all the Christian needs in the way of a written revelation from God. This is not to say that other books

may not be useful; many are. But none may claim the normative status of Scripture. This is what John Wesley meant when he said, "Let me be a man of one book."[1]

At the same time, Paul's language makes it clear that the Bible is not sufficient to equip *all* people for "every good work." Paul is speaking of the "man of God," the Christian. For Paul, this means one who is indwelt by the Spirit of God. In 1 Corinthians 2:14 he makes it clear that "the man without the Spirit does not accept the things that come from the Spirit of God, for they are foolishness to him." People who do not have Christ's Spirit reject, rather than accept, the message of the Bible because it runs counter to their view of the world and thus seems foolish to them.

For this reason the Protestant reformers emphasized the necessary link between the word of God and the Spirit of God. One may read the Bible from cover to cover and even understand its message, but will not profit from so doing unless the Spirit motivates that person to accept and follow its teachings. One may even adhere to orthodox theology but not benefit from it. Paul's admonition that "the letter kills, but the Spirit gives life" (2 Cor. 3:6) warns against dead orthodoxy.

On the other hand, biblical revelation is absolutely necessary for the Christian in discerning whether and to what extent it is the Spirit of God, and not some other "spirit," directing one's thoughts and actions. For this reason Luke, author of the book of Acts, praises those in the Macedonian city of Berea who not only received the Gospel of Christ eagerly, but also "examined the Scriptures every day to see if what Paul said was true" (Acts 17:11). Even Paul, a Spirit-inspired apostle, was subject to the teachings of Scripture.

Verbal, Plenary Inspiration

Theologians sometimes use the words "verbal" and "plenary" to describe the traditional Christian doctrine of biblical inspiration. The word "plenary" simply means "full." Hence the term "plenary inspiration" is another way of saying that *all* Scripture is inspired by God, and consequently "the Scripture cannot be broken" (John 10:35).

"Verbal inspiration" refers to the idea that the very words of Scripture are the words God desired to be written. They are, as Paul puts it, "words taught by the Spirit" (1 Cor. 2:13).

The term "verbal inspiration" has been rejected by many modern theologians, due in part to its being equated with what is sometimes called a "dictation theory" of inspiration. This theory views the biblical writers as passive scribes who wrote down words dictated to them by the Holy Spirit.

Some Christian writers, both ancient and modern, have indeed spoken of biblical inspiration in terms more or less approximating dictation, attempting to emphasize that the very words of Scripture are the words of God. The overall consensus of Christian history, however, has been to reject the notion of dictation in its strictest sense, since it fails to take into account the very different writing styles and personalities expressed by the various biblical writers. Such a dictation view of divine inspiration is closer to what Islam believes concerning the origin of the Koran than it is to what Jews and Christians believe about the Bible.

Other Christians, in their attempts to distance themselves from a dictation theory, define inspiration in terms of the experience of the writers of Scripture, who received "inspired" feelings or even ideas from God, then sought to express these inspirations in words. One modern writer views all great writings and works of art as "to some extent the work of divine inspiration." Scripture, however, is the "supreme example" of this process.[2]

Such a view does take seriously the differences in personality and style found among the biblical authors. At the same time, it defines inspiration in such a way as to make the Bible only *quantitatively* superior to, say, the writings of Plato or Shakespeare. The historic consensus of Christian theology, on the other hand, has affirmed Scripture as *qualitatively* different from any other writings. The Bible, as its name indicates, is "*the* book" (Greek *biblos*, "book"). It is unique. The difference between Scripture and all other writings is one of kind, not merely one of degree.

Modern evangelical Protestants see the Scripture as simultaneously the Word of God and the words of men. Such a view takes note of the biblical authors' differences in personality and style, affirming that the writers of Scripture were not merely passive

scribes. At the same time, it insists that the words used by the writers of Scripture were not merely human attempts to articulate their
experience of God. The words were those which God wanted written. God supervised the writing of the words of Scripture, yet not
so as to override the humanity or the individuality of the biblical
authors. This view is analogous to the orthodox Christian doctrine
of the two natures of Christ, who was at once fully God and fully
human. Like orthodox Christology, it seeks not so much to explain
as to affirm that which is ultimately a mystery.

Modern Alternatives
to Verbal, Plenary Inspiration

Karl Barth on revelation and Scripture. The twentieth-century
Swiss theologian Karl Barth affirmed that the Protestant Reformation took over and expounded upon the Church's historic doctrine
of the verbal, plenary inspiration of Scripture. Yet he himself, along
with other modern scholars, rejected the traditional notion of
inspiration and did not regard the Bible itself as the word of God.
Barth's view of the relationship between Scripture and divine revelation, along with two other current non-traditional perspectives,
needs to be distinguished from the Christian consensus we have
articulated above.

In his *Church Dogmatics*[3] Barth departs from the classical view of
revelation by refusing to acknowledge any revelation apart from the
Person of Jesus Christ. Barth thus has no place for either general
revelation or biblical revelation. "Revelation remains revelation
and does not become a revealed state. Revelation remains identical
with Christ . . ." (*CD* 1/2, 118). This means that God's self-revelation may not be confined to the past or defined as a completed
entity, which in turn means that both the created order and the
Bible fail to qualify as revelation. Instead, God's one self-revelation
is the person of Jesus.

Furthermore, since this revelation cannot be confined to the
past, it includes not only "the resurrection of Jesus Christ" (*CD* 1/2,
463) but also the risen Jesus who now "lives in Christians and they
in Him" (*CD* 1/2, 118). For Barth, divine revelation is identical
with the risen Christ who continues to live and to indwell believers.
No words about Christ, including the words of the Bible, can be
classified as "revelation" in a direct sense. Revelation does not

include ideas about God; revelation is the *person* of God who reveals Himself to us when we encounter the risen Jesus.

Thus for Barth Scripture can be called the word of God only in a secondary sense, "because by the Holy Spirit it became and will become a witness to divine revelation," to the risen Jesus who ind-wells believers (*CD I/2, 457*). In other words, the Bible "becomes" the word of God when Jesus confronts us through it. Such a view declares simultaneously that *none* of the Bible *is* the word of God, but that *all* Scripture *may become* the word of God to us. In this way the personal encounter which believers have with Christ, the living Word of God, becomes the final norm for theology. Barth himself makes this clear when he says that theology "responds to the Logos (Word) of God. . . Its searching of Scripture consists in asking the texts *whether and to what extent* they *might* witness" to Christ.[4]

Scripture and the acts of God in history. Another modern school of thought identifies divine revelation not with the Spirit of the risen Jesus, but with God's saving acts in history. The Bible is a witness to past saving acts of God, but is not itself divine revelation. Instead, Scripture consists of the ancient writers' attempts to articulate the impact God's saving acts had on their lives. The words of Scripture, according to this view, are merely human responses to God's acts in history.

While this view differs from Barth's in its definition of revelation (historical acts of God versus Barth's notion of the risen Christ), it too sees revelation as not including language, but rather as a form of "encounter." In this case, however, the biblical writers did not necessarily encounter God directly, but rather encountered the results of what God did for them. We can never know for sure just what happened, however, since their words are not descriptions of what God did, but their own impressions of the meaning and sig-nificance of God's saving activity in history. Nor are we bound to accept the biblical writers' interpretations of God's saving acts, since these interpretations are merely personal responses on their part, and not divine revelation.

Partial-inspiration theories. A third modern approach takes what may be called a two-level view of biblical inspiration. This approach takes various forms, but basically states that biblical state-ments concerning spiritual matters are inspired and therefore true,

KARL BARTH

Karl Barth (1886-1968) has been called "the one theological giant of the modern era."* Born in Basel, Switzerland, he studied under some of the great liberal scholars of his day and became devoted to theological liberalism. With the outbreak of World War I, however, he began to reevaluate his beliefs. He was particularly upset that a number of his former German seminary professors, including the great historian of dogma Adolf von Harnack, endorsed the war policies of the German government.

In 1919 Barth published the first edition of his commentary on Paul's letter to the Romans. He blasted liberal theology for assuming that people were basically in harmony with God, and that Jesus was merely the supreme model Christian and not the Savior (see chapter 8, for a brief outline of liberal christology). Barth instead stressed that God was "wholly other" from humanity, and that knowledge of God was beyond human striving. He was joined in this conviction by Rudolf Bultmann (chapter 1) and became the recognized leader of a movement known as Dialectical Theology, which emphasized that God comes to us as the One who is beyond human comprehension and who pronounces judgment on all human attempts to know Him.

In the early 1930s Barth changed direction somewhat in his thought. He broke ranks with Bultmann and insisted that God *could* be known in Himself, and not merely as an expression of our inward feelings. This is so, said Barth, not because human beings can attain knowledge of God, but because God has bridged the gap between Himself and sinful humanity in the Person of Jesus Christ. Barth then began writing his massive lifework, the multi-volume *Church Dogmatics*. In this work Barth combined historical and dogmatic theology into a trinitarian framework, drawing on both the wisdom of classical sources and the resources of modern historical-critical interpretation.

Barth's strong emphasis on Jesus Christ as God's sole revelation to humankind and the uniqueness of the Bible as God's witness to that self-revelation dominated the theological landscape in Europe and North America for several decades. On the other hand, conservative American Reformed theologians such as Cornelius Van Til and Gordon Clark saw Barth's writings as a form of theological modernism which denigrated the classical view of Scripture and was ultimately fideistic. Barth himself viewed his work as standing within the Calvinist-Reformed tradition, and regarded his initial reading of Calvin's commentaries as one of the most important events of his theological career.

---

* Thomas F. Torrance, *God and Rationality,* viii.

while statements regarding matters of history may not be historically accurate. Some interpreters hold that certain statements in
Scripture may be historically false, yet convey spiritual truth. We
may schematize such an approach like this:

Partial-inspiration Theory Of Scripture	
Spiritual (Matters of Faith)	Truth
Historical (Events)	*Some Error*

Some modern theologians use this approach to interpret the biblical affirmations that Jesus was conceived by the Holy Spirit and
born of the Virgin Mary. As we shall see later (chapter 8), Matthew
and Luke view these as historical events. A split-level view of inspiration, on the other hand, can interpret these biblical accounts as
follows: "Jesus was from the beginning responsive and obedient to
the Spirit. Where our relation to God is a broken one long before
we are conscious of it since we are born into a humanity that is
estranged from God, His relation to God is one unbroken oneness.
. . . Conceived of the Holy Spirit asserts that this was the nature of
his being from the first moment of his early existence."[5]

This sort of two-level theory of partial inspiration differs from
both the Barthian and the "God-who-acts" perspectives in that it
attempts to link divine revelation with the words of the Bible. Revelation thus includes ideas, not merely an "encounter" with the person of Christ or the saving acts of God in history. At the same time,
however, it falls short of the traditional view of verbal inspiration in
that it attributes error to some of what the biblical authors wrote
about history.

Rather than merely dispensing with such historical texts, however, the two-level view of inspiration *reinterprets* these texts as
something akin to parables or allegories. The biblical writers may
have intended to write what they thought was historical fact, but
their intended meaning is not necessarily what God desired to
communicate to us. In this way partial-inspiration theories drive a
wedge between the words of the biblical authors and the word of
God, albeit in a different manner than Barth or the "God-who-
acts" theologians.

The fact that reinterpretation of certain historical texts plays such an important role in partial-inspiration theory underscores the necessary connection between theories of biblical inspiration on the one hand, and methods of biblical interpretation on the other. We shall therefore devote our next section to a brief study of *hermeneutics* (the science of literary interpretation) and examine several theories of interpretation set forth throughout the history of the Church.

The Interpretation of Scripture

Allegorical Interpretation

A dictionary definition of allegory is "the expression through symbolic figures and actions of truths or generalizations about human conduct or experience." The notion that readers of Scripture must reinterpret many of the events recorded therein as allegories has its roots in Greek philosophical dualism. According to this dualistic worldview historical events and realities, including human language, are but images or shadows of divine realities (Plato, *Republic*, Book 6).

Ancient Judaism and Christianity, on the other hand, believed that God had acted and spoken at specific times and places in history. The preeminent example of this, declared the Church, was the life, death and resurrection of Jesus. For this reason the early Christians generally avoided allegory. Instead, they focused on the words and deeds of Jesus Christ as crucial to understanding Scripture. Jesus was the fulfillment of Old Testament prophecy, and the One of whom the New Testament spoke.

During the second century some within the Church had trouble reconciling the God of the Old Testament with the God revealed in Jesus Christ. One such man was Marcion, who moved to Rome about A.D. 140 and began teaching that the Bible revealed two gods: a warlike, judging deity in the Old Testament over against a kind, loving God in the New Testament. For this reason Marcion rejected the entire Old Testament as Holy Scripture, and sought to purge Jewish elements from the gospel tradition. We shall examine Marcion's rejection of a unified Bible in more detail in our discussion of the biblical canon below.

In the third century Origen of Alexandria sought to address this question of the relationship between the Old and New Testaments. Like Marcion, Origen considered some descriptions of God in the Old Testament as cruel and sub-Christian. Unlike Marcion, however, Origen refused to drive a wedge between the Old and New Testaments. Instead, he removed the offense from certain Old Testament passages by reinterpreting them "spiritually," that is, allegorically. Thus he said:

> Now the reason of the erroneous apprehension of all these points [including the notion that the God of the Old Testament is not the God of Jesus Christ] is no other than this, that holy Scripture is not understood by them [who deny the Old Testament God] according to its spiritual, but according to its literal meaning. Therefore we shall . . . point out . . . what appears to us, who observe things by a right way of understanding, to be the standard and discipline delivered to the apostles by Jesus Christ, and which they handed down in succession to . . . the teachers of the holy Church (*On First Principles* 4.1.9).[6]

This "right way of understanding" involved not only finding the "spiritual" understanding of the Old Testament, but also finding such spiritual interpretations in the New Testament. Furthermore, the above quote indicates that Origen did not think that every Christian was capable of finding this "spiritual" meaning. Such spiritual understanding was "delivered to the apostles by Christ," and from the apostles passed on to "the teachers of the holy Church." In this way the foundations were laid for the Roman Catholic doctrine that only the teaching office of the Church was equipped to interpret Scripture.

Origen's "spiritual" interpretation was derived from two sources. First, he was convinced that the Holy Spirit was the ultimate author of Scripture. Second, he was influenced by the Greek dualism which his Alexandrian predecessor, the first-century Jewish philosopher Philo, had used to allegorize much of the Old Testament in order to harmonize Judaism and Greek philosophy. Origen therefore considered the "literal" meaning of the biblical writers as inferior to a "spiritual" meaning which must be revealed by the Scripture's true author, the Spirit of God. Allegorical interpretation was, for Origen, the "means to trace the meaning of the Spirit of

God, which is perhaps lying profoundly buried, and the context, which may be pointing *in another direction than the ordinary usage of speech would indicate.*" (*On First Principles* 4.1.14; emphasis added).[7]

Literal Interpretation

While Origen's allegorical approach dominated the theological landscape in Alexandria, elsewhere it met with opposition. The most articulate opponents of Origen and allegory were found in Antioch of Syria during the fourth and fifth centuries. What united theologians of the "Antiochean School" was their belief that the primary meaning of Scripture was its literal, historical sense, that which the biblical writers intended to convey by means of ordinary usage of human language.

The work of Lucian (c.240-312) set the tone for Antiochean interpretation during the next century. As an exegete, Lucian encouraged a literal interpretation of Scripture and so opposed Origen's allegorical methodology. Successors to Lucian included John Chrysostom (c.344/354-407), one of the great preachers of the fourth century, and Theodore of Mopsuestia (c.350-428), regarded by some as the greatest exegete of the early Church. Like Lucian, these men sought to interpret the Bible from its own Semitic perspective, rather than imposing Greek philosophical categories upon the Scriptures. Theodore, for example, saw that when the Scriptures were interpreted literally and historically, they set forth a unified record of God's redemptive work in time, as opposed to the collection of timeless truths emphasized by the allegorical method.[8]

The Antiochean School, however, had no lasting effect on the history of interpretation. This was due in part to the fact that Lucian's view of Christ was suspect. Some see him as the true founder of Arianism, a heresy which denied the full divinity of Christ. In addition, the Antiochean school was included under the condemnation pronounced upon Nestorius in 431 at the Council of Ephesus, since Theodore was a teacher of Nestorius. (The teachings of Nestorius and the Arian heresy are discussed in chapter 8.) For the next thousand years one or another form of allegorical interpretation dominated the theological landscape.

With the onset of the Protestant Reformation came a renewed emphasis on the Hebrew background of the Bible and on literal

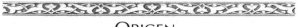

ORIGEN

Origenes Adamantius (c. 185-254) was born in Egypt and raised by Christian parents. He studied under Clement of Alexandria in the Catechetical School of that city, and eventually became the greatest theologian of his day. It may be said that Origen was the first systematic theologian in the history of Christianity, as he wrote on almost every subject that touched on matters of the Christian faith.

Origen lived in times of great tribulation for the Greek-speaking Church. His father was martyred in 202 under the persecution of Septimus Severus. Half a century later Origen himself was tortured under the persecution of Decius. He died shortly after his ordeal, following his release from prison.

While in Alexandria Origen became head of the Catechetical School, where he remained for twenty-eight years. He studied deeply both the Scriptures and the writings of neoplatonist philosophers. He wrote prolifically, though most of his works did not survive. His most famous work, *De Principiis*

(*On First Principles*), was a systematic theology which included discourses on the trinity, creation, the fall, redemption, the ongoing struggle between good and evil, and biblical hermeneutics.

Subsequent generations have looked back on Origen's career with a mixture of respect and revulsion. His work in helping to formulate the New Testament canon was crucial to the well-being of the Church. His attempts to integrate Greek neoplatonic philosophy and Christianity were deemed heretical by several Church councils and synods. His devotion to Christ was unquestioned, however. This can be seen not only by his suffering the aforementioned persecution which led to his death, but also by one of the most ironic and bizarre events of his life. This master of allegorical interpretation took quite literally Jesus's words in Matthew 19:12. In that passage Jesus speaks of those who have "made themselves eunuchs for the Kingdom of God." Origen's response to these words was to emasculate himself.

interpretation. Martin Luther was trained in the allegorical method as a Roman Catholic Augustinian monk, but later rejected it. Said Luther:

> [Scripture's] plainest meanings are to be preserved; and, unless the context manifestly compels one to do otherwise, the words are not to be understood apart from their proper and literal sense, lest

occasion be given to our adversaries to evade Scripture as a whole. This is why Origen was rightly repudiated long ago; he made allegories out of the trees and all else described in Paradise, and ignored the plain, literal sense. One might have inferred from what he said that God had not created trees.[9]

In emphasizing the "plain, literal sense" Luther did not deny that Scripture contained figures of speech and symbolic language. He simply emphasized that the writer's own words and the text's pertinent historical background should determine our interpretation of Scripture. Another name for this approach is "grammatical-historical exegesis." In this way Luther stressed what is sometimes called the *perspicuity* of Scripture. This means that the meaning of the Bible is clear enough for any reasonably informed person to understand, as opposed to being so mysterious or hidden that only the teaching office of the Church could interpret it by means of allegory.

Luther's desire to emphasize the historical nature of biblical interpretation, as opposed to a "spiritual" hermeneutic, opened new avenues of theological insight whereby the Reformation was able to articulate fresh perspectives on heretofore unchallenged dogmas of the Roman Catholic Church. At the same time, however, this newfound concern for the historical dimension of Scripture led in time to yet another hermeneutical approach which carried with it consequences unforeseen by Luther: the historical-critical method.

Historical-Critical Interpretation

During the eighteenth century biblical scholarship came under the influence of Enlightenment philosophy. Specifically, the Rationalist wing of this powerful intellectual movement defined history as a closed continuum of cause and effect which left no room for miracles.

Such a view of history, when applied to biblical interpretation, led to a "historical-critical" hermeneutic which declared that the biblical accounts of miracles were not history, but "myths." Johann Philip Gabler, for example, believed that these "myths" were a primitive way of interpreting remarkable events whose actual causes were not yet apparent in the pre-scientific age of the Bible. The interpreter must therefore go behind these myths in order to discover what "may have really happened" to Jesus which caused the Gospel writers to use miracle-language in their accounts of His life. Historical-critical scholars thus spoke of the need to tear away the mythological "husk" of the Gospel accounts in order to get at the historical (non-miraculous) "kernel" of the true gospel message of the "historical Jesus." Not surprisingly, this "historical Jesus" turned out to be a merely human teacher of ethics as opposed to a divine-human savior.[10]

Towards the end of the nineteenth century, however, such non-miraculous reconstructions of Jesus came under attack from several prominent biblical scholars who themselves were well-versed in historical-critical methodology. Their complaint was that the gospel accounts are written in such a way that it is impossible to separate a non-miraculous Jesus from a supernatural Christ.

One of these scholars, Martin Kähler, wrote a book entitled *The So-called Historical Jesus and the Historic, Biblical Christ*. For Kähler the "historical Jesus" reconstructed by historical-critical scholarship had nothing to do with what the New Testament writers were talking about. Instead, the gospels testified to a "resurrected Lord" who "is not the historical Jesus *behind* the Gospels [as reconstructed by modern scholarship], but the Christ of the apostolic preaching, of the *whole* New Testament."[11]

Historical-critical methodology, then, seeks to find the meaning of Christ *behind* the biblical texts, so to speak. By way of contrast, the allegorical approach used by Origen and others sought to find meaning *above* the text by means of a "spiritual" interpretation. Both of these hermeneutical approaches differ from the "literal" hermeneutic of the Antiochean School and the Reformers, who sought the meaning of God's self-revelation *within* the text by means of grammatical-historical exegesis.

At the same time, it is historical-critical scholars who consistently deny the traditional view that Scripture is the Word of God. Both allegorical and literal interpreters throughout Church history have affirmed that the Bible is divine revelation and therefore authoritative for matters of Christian faith and conduct. This leads to yet another question: How do Christians know that the Bible is the Word of God, and thus authoritative?

The Authority of Scripture

Christians have sought to confirm the authority of Scripture in at least four ways. These approaches may be labeled as follows: presuppositional, ecclesiastical, spiritual, and evidentialist.

The Presuppositional Approach

Those who adopt this approach say simply that we know the Bible is the word of God because it claims to be the word of God. The Scriptures are self-authenticating because God is their author. To seek any other means of confirming the authority of Scripture would be to place God under some standard of judgment other than Himself, which in turn means that God would be subject to such a standard and would thus no longer be God. The presuppositional approach is logically self-consistent, but gives no criteria by which one might distinguish the Bible's claim of divine revelation from similar claims by Islam's holy book, the Koran.

The Ecclesiastical Approach

The Roman Catholic Church holds that Christians can know Scripture to be God's word because the Church declares it to be so. The rationale for this position comes from the fact that the Church itself, through a historical process of almost three centuries, arrived at a consensus as to which books belong in the Bible. Indeed, the New Testament grew out of the very life of the Church. Since the Bible both took form within the Church and was declared Holy Scripture by the Church, we know the Bible to be authoritative because the Church says it is authoritative.

One could contrast the Roman Catholic ecclesiastical view with the presuppositionalist view as follows: The presuppositionalist says "Jesus loves me, this I know, for the Bible tells me so"; the Roman Catholic says "Jesus loves me, this I know, for the Church has told me so."

The Spiritual Approach

The Protestant Reformers believed that Rome's ecclesiastical approach to biblical authority in fact placed the Church above the Bible. For this reason John Calvin declared that "Scripture has its authority from God, not from the Church." At the same time, Calvin held that something besides the Scripture's self-designation as the word of God was needed to confirm biblical authority for the Christian: the inner witness of the Holy Spirit.

> If we desire to provide in the best way for our consciences . . . we ought to seek our conviction [of the authority of God's word] in a higher place than human reasons, judgments, or conjectures, that is, in the secret testimony of the Spirit. . . . [T]he testimony of the Spirit is more excellent than all reason. For as God alone is a fit witness of himself in his Word, so also the Word will not find acceptance in men's hearts before it is sealed by the inward testimony of the Spirit (*Institutes* 1.7.4).

Calvin did not deny that there were arguments and evidences apart from the testimony of the Spirit which could be brought forth. "Yet they who strive to build up firm faith in Scripture through disputation are doing things backwards," he added (*Institutes* 1.7.4). Human arguments and historical evidences could at best give only a high degree of probability that the Bible is God's word. Calvin desired absolute assurance, however, and believed that it could only be given by God Himself. Ultimately, then, Calvin's position could be restated: "Jesus loves me, this I know, for the Spirit tells me so."

The Evidentialist Approach

In Acts 1:3 Luke tells Theophilus that after His resurrection Jesus "showed himself to [his disciples] and gave many convincing proofs that he was alive." This is the heart of any evidentialist approach to confirming the divine authority of the Bible: that there are "many convincing proofs" that Jesus Christ rose from the dead. As one modern writer has put it, "belief in the Bible comes from faith in Christ, and not vice versa."[12]

But how can this be, if the Bible itself is our source of knowledge about Jesus? Does this not assume the truth of Scripture, the very thing we wish to prove?

The answer to this last question is, not necessarily. Although there are many "evidentialist" approaches, the following five-step argument is a rather typical one.

(1) The Bible is a generally reliable historical document. This does not mean the Bible is necessarily infallible. Rather, it merely states a

growing consensus that the Bible is what historians call "best evidence" regarding the events surrounding the person of Jesus.

(2)The evidences derived from the Bible, together with reasonable argumentation, establish beyond a reasonable doubt that Christ was crucified, dead, buried, and rose from the dead. This, of course, is the crux of the evidentialist approach. No airtight proof is possible in matters of historical evidence; it is rather like a legal courtroom case: "beyond a reasonable doubt." We shall elaborate on arguments and evidences for the resurrection of Christ in chapter 10.

(3)Jesus Christ's resurrection testifies that He is the Son of God, and therefore trustworthy in all He says. One who said He would rise from the dead, and then died and lived to tell about it, merits more than the usual amount of trust we would give to a virtuous person. His authority is total.

(4)Jesus' attitude towards Scripture was one of total trust; Jesus called Scripture "the Word of God." We covered this point earlier in this chapter.

(5)We are therefore obliged to follow Jesus, the Son of God, and place our total confidence in the Bible as God's written revelation. This is what the vast majority of Christians have done for almost two thousand years (though most of them have probably done so because of appeals to authority rather than historical argumentation!).

Fideism or Evidentialism?

The four approaches outlined above may be placed into two broader categories—fideism and evidentialism.

Fideism is a label taken from the Latin *fides*, "faith." Here the word "faith" is used in the bad sense discussed at the outset of chapter 1—belief not related to knowledge. The reasons fideists give for belief in the Bible have no common ground with what non-Christians believe or can know. For example, Calvin himself holds that the "inward testimony of the Spirit" buttresses the authority of Scripture only for the Christian, not the non-Christian. The same is true for the presuppositional and ecclesiastical approaches. All brands of fideism are ultimately appeals to raw authority, apart from arguments and evidences.

Evidentialism, sometimes called verificationism, seeks to base faith upon evidences available to all people, Christian and non-Christian alike, and to argue by means of criteria of verification agreed upon by everyone. This approach is largely a product of post-Enlightenment Protestantism, which sought to confront the rationalistic arguments against traditional Christianity set forth by philosophers and historical-critical theologians. Its main strength is that it takes with utmost seriousness the historical nature of divine revelation, refusing to confine knowledge of God to an inward, subjective experience. Its potential weakness lies in the danger of accepting anti-Christian philosophical assumptions concerning the nature of faith and knowledge before even beginning to discuss and debate the truth of Christianity with nonbelievers.

Whatever their differences in approaching the question of biblical authority, Christians have agreed that Scripture is the Church's rule of faith and practice. At this point, however, the question arises as to whether the Bible is the Church's *only* rule of faith and practice, and whether Scripture is a sufficient norm for Christian theology.

The Sufficiency of Scripture

This is perhaps the central issue which led to the split between the Roman Catholic Church and the Protestant Reformers. For Luther and his followers *sola scriptura* ("Scripture alone") became one of the watchwords of the Reformation. The Catholic Church, on the other hand, believed that certain extrabiblical teachings could also be normative for Christian dogma and conduct.

Catholic theology emphasizes that Scripture itself is a product of Spirit-inspired Church tradition, and that the same Spirit who inspired the biblical writers is at work today in the teaching office of the Church. On this basis Catholicism regards as dogma certain Church traditions not found in Scripture. Such non-biblical tradition must be "apostolic" to be authoritative, however. The label "apostolic" tradition includes Scripture, of course, but also (1) any *oral* tradition whose origin may be traced back to the apostles, and (2) the authoritative pronouncements of the ecclesiastical teaching office, whose origin (according to Catholicism) goes back to the apostle Peter. Such traditions function as a sort of parallel authority with the Bible, while in theory never being in disagreement with Scripture.

For Protestants, only Scripture deserves the name "apostolic." This is because the apostles were more than Spirit-inspired agents of divine revelation. They were also *eyewitnesses to the risen Jesus* who were *commissioned by Christ as agents of revelation*. Protestants therefore define the word "apostolic" not on the basis of what the apostles had in common with following generations (the indwelling Spirit), but on the basis of the apostles' unique eyewitness relationship with the events surrounding the life, death, and resurrection of Jesus. By definition, no subsequent generation could have such an eyewitness relationship with the central events of God's saving revelation.

The fact that both Protestants and Catholics refer to the Bible as the *canon* (Greek *kanon*, "measuring rod") is another indication that the Church intended to place all of its subsequent theological formulations under the authority of Holy Writ when it sought to determine which writings belong in the Bible. A brief historical review of the process whereby the Church defined the biblical canon will serve to underscore this point.

The Formation of the Canon

The earliest Christians considered the Hebrew Scriptures (Old Testament) as divine revelation. The need for additional canonical scripture which witnessed to the person and work of Jesus Christ became an issue around the middle of the second century A.D.

The main factor that led the Church to conceive the idea of a New Testament canon was the state of the oral tradition concerning Jesus around A. D. 150 Prior to that time collections of Paul's writings and the Gospels were circulating, but were not necessarily seen as superior to what the second-century writer Papias called the "word which remains alive" within the ongoing oral Christian tradition. But as time went on, it became more difficult to separate genuinely historical traditions concerning Jesus from those which were purely legendary.

The Church received additional impetus in its quest for a canon from Marcion (above). In his attempt to separate Christianity from Judaism, Marcion proposed a canon consisting of Paul's letters (minus the Pastoral Epistles) and a truncated Gospel of Luke purged of its Jewish elements. This was the first attempt to set forth a specific body of canonical Christian Scripture. The Church rejected Marcion's canon along with his heretical views, but did not immediately propose a list of canonical books to counter Marcion's canon. Rather, the process of formulating the New Testament went on for two more centuries.

During the first half of the third century (c. 220-240) Origen traveled extensively and recorded which books were considered as "Scripture" by the Church in various locales. He compiled the results of this survey and listed books and letters read in the Churches under three headings: undisputed, disputed, and false. The letters of Paul and the books of Matthew, Mark, Luke, and John, for example, were for Origen undisputedly Scripture, as were several other books, including Revelation. False scriptures included the so-called Gospel of Thomas. The third category, disputed books (also called the *antilegomena*, or "spoken against") included 2 Peter, 2 and 3 John, Hebrews, James, and Jude.

In the fourth century various writers set forth lists which differed somewhat as to which books belonged to the "disputed" category. Eusebius of Caesarea, for example, set forth a list in A. D. 303 which included the book of Revelation under the heading of *antilegomena*. In A. D. 367 Athanasius, the most influential theologian of his day, wrote a pastoral Easter letter which defined the New Testament canon as consisting of the twenty-seven books which today are accepted by all branches of Christendom. Thirty years later the Council of Carthage, which included Augustine among its participants, likewise endorsed the present twenty-seven books of the New Testament. The Eastern wing of the Church continued to hold the book of Revelation as *antilegomena* for six more centuries, but eventually accepted it as canonical.

During the Reformation the issue of the canon was reopened by Martin Luther, who questioned the inclusion of books such as James and Revelation. Luther nevertheless bowed to ecclesiastical tradition and included all twenty-seven books of the present-day New Testament. The Old Testament canon, on the other hand, was redefined by the Reformers to exclude the Apocrypha, a collection of books not included by the Jews in their canon but considered canonical by the Roman Catholic and Eastern Orthodox branches of the Church. The Reformers opted for the Jewish canon, because they considered it likely to be the collection recognized by Jesus and His disciples. Thus the Roman Catholic Old Testament contains nine books not found in the Protestant Old Testament (the Orthodox Apocrypha contains one less book than the Catholic version).

The fact that Protestant and Catholic Bibles differ in some respects is less important than the fundamental principle behind the fixing of a canonical body of literature. This principle is that *from the time of the fixing of the canon onward, all subsequent theological formulations must be consistent with the apostolic tradition as set forth in Holy Scripture.* Indeed, this principle was already in operation even while the exact limits of the canon were still in the process of being defined. Historic Christian belief is thus, at its root, *biblical* theology, whether one is Protestant, Catholic, or Orthodox.

At the same time, the historic Christian theological enterprise has not limited itself to words found in the Bible. The challenge confronting the Church over twenty centuries has been to articulate the "faith once for all given to the saints" (Jude 3) in ways understandable to those receiving the gospel message without going beyond the boundaries set by Holy Scripture. We shall see an outstanding example of this in the following chapter, as we survey basic Christian doctrines concerning the acts and being of the personal triune God.

Points To Ponder

1 How do the first three chapters of Genesis demonstrate why people need the Bible in order to be made "wise unto salvation" (2 Tim. 3:15)?

2. What does it mean that Scripture is "inspired by God" (2 Tim. 3:16)?

3. Why did the Protestant Reformers emphasize the relationship between the Word of God and the Spirit of God?

4. What do we mean by the phrase "verbal, plenary inspiration" of Scripture?

5. Compare and contrast the three modern alternatives to verbal, plenary inspiration discussed in this chapter.

6. Be able to distinguish between allegorical, literal, and historical-critical interpretation of Scripture.

7. How do presuppositionalists, Roman Catholics, and John Calvin differ in their response to the question, "How do Christians know the Bible is the Word of God?" How are all three of these positions nevertheless alike as opposed to evidentialism.?

8. How does the Catholic definition of "apostolic tradition" differ from the Protestant definition?

9. What respective roles did Marcion, Origen, Athanasius, and Martin Luther play in defining the limits of the biblical canon?

3

The Doctrine of God

The Names of God

"What's in a name?"

Nowadays the answer to this question is usually, "not much." The fact that someone is named Joy does not necessarily make her happy, any more than a man named Paul is necessarily small (Latin *Paulos*, "little").

When we open the pages of Scripture, however, we enter a world where names often tell us something about the one who is named. In Genesis chapter 1, for example, the first man is named "Adam" because he was taken from the ground (Hebrew *adamah*). God changed Abram's name to Abraham to signify that he would become a "father of many nations" (Gen. 17:5). And the angel told Joseph to name the virgin-born son of Mary "Jesus" (*Y'eshua*, "God saves"), "for He shall save His people from their sins" (Matt. 1:21).

In like manner, the divine names found in Scripture give insight into the character, or attributes, of God. Any discussion of the Christian doctrine of God must therefore include a survey of names by which God has revealed Himself throughout redemptive history. We shall first look at the principal Hebrew (Old Testament) names for God, then the most important Greek (New Testament) names.

God in the Old Testament

'El; 'Elohim. The Hebrew *'el* is a basic word for deity found in various forms throughout ancient Semitic languages. It is therefore more or less equivalent to the word "god," indicating one of a class of supernatural beings, or "God," the deity of the nation of Israel. The word *'el* may derive from a Semitic root meaning "power" or "preeminence."

The plural *'elohim* is the word most frequently translated "God" in the Old Testament. While this is its normal usage, it sometimes also refers to other gods (Ex. 20:3) or to angels (Ps. 8:5; compare Heb. 2:7). This plural form of *'el* is sometimes termed the "plural of majesty" to emphasize the supreme greatness of the One True God. It is the name used of God in the first chapter of Genesis, and is thus often associated with God's work as creator of heaven and earth.

'El Shaddai. This is one of several "'*el*-compounds" in the Old Testament. In such instances *'el* is used together with one other name to emphasize a certain characteristic or attribute of God. Here the word *shaddai* appears to emphasize God's supreme power, as evidenced by the Greek and Latin translations (*pantokrator*; *omnipotens*). The most common English translation is "God Almighty," which first appears in Genesis 17:1 when God uses this name upon renewing the covenant made with Abram in Genesis 12:1-3. It was probably the most common title for God used by the Hebrews between the time of Abraham and Moses.

'El 'Elyon. The second word of this title comes from a Hebrew word meaning "go up," and conveys the idea of "high, uppermost, exalted." In Gen. 14:18-21 it is the name used by Melchizedek, the king of Salem, when he refers to the God of Abraham as "God Most High." It therefore carries basically the same meaning as *'El Shaddai*, though the emphasis here may be more on God's preeminence than power.

'El Olam. Most often rendered "the everlasting God," this title is found only in Genesis 21:33. The idea of God as the "everlasting" One is found throughout the Old Testament, however. Sometimes *olam* is used of God's being (Ps. 90:2; "from everlasting to everlast-

ing you are God"); other times it is used of God's various attributes (everlasting love, everlasting mercy, and so on).

The most important Old Testament name for God is not one of the *'el*-titles, however. It is instead the name *Yahweh*, by which God revealed Himself to Moses.

Yahweh, God of the covenant. The name Yahweh is an educated guess of the original pronunciation for the Hebrew name *YHWH*. The Hebrew Scriptures were written with no vowels; these were supplied from the collective memory of the Israelite community. That collective memory has long since been lost; what remains is the four letters corresponding to *YHWH* (sometimes called "the tetragrammaton"). It is sometimes transliterated as Jahveh or Jehovah. English translations often render it "the LORD" (as opposed to "Lord," which is a title and not a proper name).

Linguists generally agree that this name is connected with a form of the Hebrew verb "to be." *YHWH* is thus variously rendered as "He who is," "He who is what He is," or "the self-existent one." In Exodus 3:13-14 God reveals Himself to Moses as follows:

> Moses said to God, "Suppose I go to the Israelites and say to them, 'The God of your fathers has sent me to you,' and they ask me, "What is his name?' Then what shall I tell them?"

> God said to Moses, "I AM WHO I AM. This is what you are to say to the Israelites: 'I AM has sent me to you.' "

Some translators render God's self-designation here as "I will be who I will be." This would indicate that Yahweh is not so much telling Moses about the inner nature of His being or essence, but rather indicating that He will reveal Himself through His forthcoming saving acts on behalf of Israel. God "will be" to them what His deeds will show Him to be. This latter translation fits the context of the Exodus account, and is consistent with the fact that the name of Yahweh is associated with God's faithfulness to His covenant with Abraham. In Exodus 3:13-14, for example, Yahweh is "The God of our fathers," the God of Abraham, Isaac, and Jacob.

Adonai. This divine name comes from a Hebrew word meaning "lord," "master," or "sir." It is sometimes used of human rulers; for example, "my lord, the king" (I Sam. 26:19). It is a name which implies God's authority or sovereign rule. Most often it is used as a modifier for the covenant name Yahweh; hence, *"YHWH Adonai"* (often written "LORD God" in English Bibles to distinguish it *YHWH 'Elohim,* "LORD God"). The name *adonai* was also used in later Judaism as a substitute for the tetragrammaton, out of reverence for the divine covenant name *YHWH.* This was done when the Scriptures were read orally, for example (apparently out of fear that one might inadvertently take God's name in vain).

God in the New Testament

Theos. This word is the generic term for deity in the Greek language. It is most frequently used in the Septuagint to translate the Hebrew *'elohim,* though it does translate other Hebrew names on occasion. In the New Testament it is the most common name for God, and is even used of the preexistent Jesus in John 1:1.

Kurios. This word is usually translated "Lord" in English Bibles, though it may also be rendered "lord" or "sir" with reference to people (as was the Hebrew *adonai*). In the Septuagint it is used to translate the Hebrew *YHWH.* In the New Testament it is sometimes used of God, though it is usually applied to the risen and ascended Jesus, sometimes in the form of the confession *Kurios Iesous* ("Jesus is Lord"; see 1 Cor. 12:3, Phil. 2:11). This in turn poses an intriguing question: Does *Kurios Iesous* mean "Jesus is *adonai"?* or "Jesus is *YHWH"?* The former interpretation would see this confession as speaking of Christ's role as lord of the Church and over all creation; the latter intepretation would speak not only of Christ's role as lord, but also of His person or essence (His divinity).

Pater. The Greek word normally translated "father" was used as a divine name by Jesus throughout His ministry. The Lord's Prayer, for example, begins with the words "Our Father," indicating how Christians are to address God. The emphasis here is on God's relationship with believers, as opposed to people in general. In other places Jesus refers to God as His Father, emphasizing that His sonship is unique (Matt. 11:27, John 6:46). God is thus called "Father" in two different senses in the New Testament: God is not the Father of Christians in the same way God is the Father of Jesus. This is borne out by the fact that Jesus never calls God "our Father" except when He tells the disciples how they should address God. The language of John 20:17 bears this out. Jesus does not tell

Mary Magdalene that He is ascending to "our Father," but rather
to "my Father and your Father."

The New Testament designation of God as "Father" goes well
beyond the Old Testament usage of the term, which is very
restrained. A few Old Testament passages speak of God as "Father"
(Hebrew *ab*; see Deut. 32:6, Isa. 64:8). Israel is sometimes referred
to as God's "son" or "first-born" (Hos. 11:1; Jer. 31:9). Jesus, on the
other hand, made the fatherhood of God central to His preaching.
At the same time, Jesus used a different form of the word for
"father" than did the Old Testament writers. Specifically, Jesus
referred to God as *abba*, an Aramaic-language diminutive form of
Ab (Mark 14:36; Aramaic had replaced Hebrew as the everyday language among the Jews of Judea and Galilee in Jesus' day).

The word *abba* could be rendered "Pappa" or "Daddy." It is what
small children called their fathers. It was never used by the Jews
with reference to God. Jesus, on the other hand, called God *Abba* in
His prayers. Furthermore, it is virtually certain that the Aramaic
abba is behind the Greek *pater* in the Lord's Prayer (Matt. 6:9), since
two decades after Jesus taught this prayer to His disciples the Apostle Paul encouraged the Roman Christians to call out "*abba, pater*
(Father)" in their own prayers (Rom. 8:15). This indicates that *abba*,
and the intimate relationship with God it represented, became such
a central feature of early Christian faith that the original Aramaic
word used by Jesus became a confession of faith even in a Greek-
and Latin-speaking environment such as Rome.

To summarize, then, the New Testament name "Father" is used
in two principal ways: of God's unique relationship to Jesus, and of
God's relationship with those who believe in Christ. It is never
applied to people in general. There is no universal "Fatherhood of
God" in the New Testament.

The Attributes of God

What Is God Like?

We have seen that the Bible responds to this question by ascrib-
ing names to God. In addition, the God of the Bible reveals Who
He *is* by what He *does*. The acts of God in Scripture begin with creation and reach their apex in the life, death, and resurrection of
Jesus Christ.

Christians therefore strive to answer the question "What is God like?" by reflecting on the divine names and acts, and what these names and acts imply regarding the character, or attributes, of God. The word "attributes" conveys the idea that we as humans *attribute* certain characteristics to God, both on the basis of divine revelation and what we deem as necessary implications of what God has revealed in word and deed.

"I Believe in One God"

These first words of the Nicene Creed echo the words of the *Shema*, the central confession of Judaism: "Hear, O Israel, the LORD our God, the LORD is One" (Deut. 6:4). This attribute of God, then, may be defined negatively: God is unique, like no other.

The first commandment of the Decalogue therefore says "You shall have no other gods in my presence," not because Yahweh is the greatest of a class of beings called "gods," but because Yahweh is in a class by Himself. "All the gods of the nation are idols, but Yahweh made the heavens" (Ps. 96:5). "I am God, and there is no other; I am God, and there is none like me" (Isa. 46:9). This is the rationale behind Yahweh's demand for exclusive devotion. Yahweh is not the greatest god of all; Yahweh alone is God.

The question remains as to what this One who is unlike all others, *is* like. Can we speak of God in any positive manner?

The Living God Who Speaks

In Judaism and Christianity God is *the living God Who speaks*. This separates God from all the so-called gods of those nations which surrounded ancient Israel.

God is the *living God*. The prophets of Israel contrast Yahweh with the gods of the surrounding nations, which are lifeless idols. In Isaiah 44:13-20, for example, Yahweh sarcastically notes how a carpenter cuts down a tree and uses half of the tree for firewood, and the other half to make an idol:

> He cut down cedars . . . it is man's fuel for burning; some of it he takes and warms himself, he kindles a fire and bakes bread. But he also fashions a god and worships it; he makes an idol and bows down to it . . . No one stops to think, no one has the knowledge or under-

standing to say, "Half of it I used for fuel; . . . Shall I make a detestable thing from what is left? Shall I bow down to a block of wood?"

Lifeless idols derive their being from human hands; the living God derives His being from no one.

The living God *speaks*, and thereby is the source of all that is. God calls all of creation into being by the divine Word ("by the word of the Lord were the heavens made. . . for he spoke, and it came to be"—Ps. 33:6, 9; see Genesis 1, "and God said"). God also calls Israel into being by promising that from a barren couple, Abraham and Sarah, "many nations" will emerge (Gen. 17:4; see Rom. 4:17). Nothing comes into being apart from the One who supremely IS ("I AM").

The living God who speaks not only calls us into being, but also calls humans to decide for God. The very tone of Scripture makes it clear that God's self-revelation is not merely to be contemplated, but to be obeyed. This point has been underscored by Erich Auerbach, a literary critic who compares the biblical narratives to one of Greek literature's classic narratives, Homer's *Odyssey*:

> The Scripture stories do not, like Homer's, court our favor, they do not flatter us that they may please and enchant us—they seek to subject us, and if we refuse to be subjected we are rebels. . . . Far from seeking, like Homer, merely to make us forget our own reality for a few hours, [the biblical text] seeks to overcome our reality: we are to fit our own life into its world, feel ourselves to be elements in its structure of universal history.[1]

Or, as Jesus put it, "He who is not with me is against me" (Matt. 12:30). We are called to choose, but are given only one option: choose God!

God, then, is the living One who is like no other, who has called all things into being, and who therefore calls us to total, exclusive obedience. What more can be said of this God? How shall we define God?

Defining the Attributes of God

In speaking of the one living God who speaks, theologians have categorized the divine attributes in various ways. One such approach is to divide God's attributes under two broad classifications: God's *incommunicable* attributes, and God's *communicable* attributes.

Incommunicable attributes. These are characteristics which are unique to God. With regard to these attributes, God is what some have called "wholly other" from us. It is hardly suprising, then, that much of the language under this heading, including the word "incommunicable" itself, is negative language which emphasizes what God is not like. For example, God may be defined by words such as:

- Infinite. God is not finite, or limited by space and time, as humans are. With respect to space, God is *omnipresent*, or present everywhere (Ps. 139:7-10), while at the same time being *transcendent* in being, above all creation (Ps. 113:4-6). With respect to time, God is *eternal*, without beginning or end (Ps. 90:2).

- Independent. God is *self-existent*, without any cause outside of Himself for His being (Isa. 43:10). God is *immortal*, not subject to death (1 Tim. 1:17).

- Invisible. "No one has ever seen God" (John 1:18), for "God is Spirit" (John 4:24). When the Bible says that the "pure in heart . . . shall see God," the reference is not to visual seeing, but to being in a proper relationship with God (compare Matt. 5:8 with Ps. 24:3–6).

- Immutable. "I the Lord do not change" (Mal. 3:6). God's character is constant and therefore reliable. When Scripture says that God "repented" or changed His mind, it means that God altered His activity to remain true to His unchanging character (see Gen. 6:6, Jonah 3:9).

- Indivisible. God's essential nature is not complex, but simple. The Christian doctrine of the Trinity does not mean that God is composed of three different parts, as we shall see later on (p. 63). "The Lord our God, the Lord is One" (Deut. 6:4).

Such language about God has been called the *via negativa*, or "negative way" of speaking of God. By way of contrast, discussion of God's communicable attributes proceeds in a somewhat different manner.

Communicable attributes. God shares certain characteristics with human beings by virtue of people being created in the divine image

(Gen. 1:26). When we speak of such characteristics as applying to God, we do so by using analogies. That is, we observe human characteristics and say that God is like that, only greater. Indeed, we attribute to God the greatest possible expression of these human characteristics. This way of speaking of God is called the *via eminentiae*, or "eminent way," since it emphasizes that God is eminently one thing or the other. For example, God is eminently:

- Personal. The God of the Bible uses the first-person pronoun "I" as a self-designation. God has personal relationships with other personal beings. God has both intellect and emotion. God speaks; God hears. God is personal in a sense which goes beyond our human experience; hence, C. S. Lewis speaks of God not merely as personal, but as "beyond personality."[2]

- Sovereign. God is eminently *free* in that God "does whatever pleases Him" (Ps. 115:3, 135:6). God is eminently powerful, or *omnipotent*, in that there is nothing consistent with His character which He cannot do (Luke 1:37). On the other hand, God cannot lie (Titus 1:2) or deny Himself (2 Tim. 2:13), two things which people all too often do.

- Holy. "Exalt the Lord our God, and worship at His footstool; Holy is He" (Ps. 99:5). "Hallowed (Holy) be Your name" (Matt. 6:9). The word "holy" means "set apart," as when valuable items such as the crown jewels of England are set apart due to their great value and glory. God is the most glorious being, perfect in all His ways, and therefore more valuable than anything or anyone else in the universe.

- Righteous. God is always living up to His own standards of moral perfection (Matt. 5:48; 1 John 1:5). The character of God is itself the highest moral standard in the universe; thus the righteousness of God is literally self-righteousness. Since God can attain to no higher standard than Himself, His self-righteousness is not a bad thing; indeed, it is necessary. Otherwise, God would be living up to a standard above Himself, which by definition would mean that He is no longer God. God therefore leads us "in paths of righteousness *for His name's sake*" (Ps. 23:3). God ultimately acts to uphold His own righteousness.

- Wise. God's wisdom consists in His designing the world with the best possible goals in mind, and choosing the best means for realizing those goals. Human thought cannot comprehend how this can be so (Rom. 11:33), due in part to the fact that we are ignorant of many things. God, on the other hand, is *omniscient*, "all-knowing." (Some define God's omniscience as knowledge of all things that have real existence; others define it as God's knowledge not only of all realities, but also of all possibilities.)

- Good. "Give thanks to the Lord, for He is good; His mercy endures forever" (Ps. 118:29). God's goodness is that aspect of His character which is demonstrated towards us in the form of mercy. Were God to act towards sinful human beings merely on the basis of His moral perfection, or righteousness, we would be without hope. "[Yahweh] does not treat us as our sins deserve" (Ps. 103:10).

- Love. "God is love" (1 John 4:8, 16). This means more than "God loves people," for Jesus speaks of the love which the Father and the Son had together within the Trinity "from before the foundation of the world" (John 17:24). Love existed in the triune Godhead prior to creation.

Taken together, the communicable and incommunicable attributes of God speak of who God is *in Himself.* They are sometimes referred to as God's *absolute attributes* because they exist "absolutely," that is, they exist apart from God's relationship with us. Other words, such as "grace," "compassion," "justice," and "mercy" speak of who God is *in relationship to people* (the word "love" is also usually used in this way). These are sometimes called God's *relative attributes.* It is debatable, however, whether or not words such as "grace" and "mercy" should be called attributes, since grace and mercy cannot come into existence until God has created a world in need of grace and mercy. We shall examine this point later under the doctrine of creation (chapter 4).

For now, let us take note of the final communicable attribute listed above: "God is love." The fact that it is linked with the doctrine of the Trinity means that we cannot adequately understand what it means to say "God is love" until we have an understanding of the Trinity.

The Triune God

Definition

The word "Trinity" is found nowhere in the Bible. The doctrine is implicit in numerous statements found in Scripture, however, particularly in the New Testament. Before we look at the biblical evidence, let us define what we mean when we speak of the Triune God: *God is one essence or substance, eternally existing in three Persons: God the Father, God the Son, and God the Holy Spirit.*

This definition of the Trinity, which sets forth the consensus of historic Christian belief, has been expressed in various forms. For example, we read in chapter 2 of the Westminster Confession of Faith: "In the unity of the Godhead there be three Persons of one substance, power, and eternity: God the Father, God the Son, and God the Holy Ghost. The Father is of none, neither begotten nor proceeding; the Son is eternally begotten of the Father; the Holy Ghost eternally proceeding from the Father and the Son." We shall have occasion to examine key terms of this definition as we proceed. For now, let us examine the biblical data relevant to the doctrine of the Trinity.

Old Testament Witness to the Trinity

Throughout the Old Testament the emphasis is on the unity of God. This is not surprising, considering that Israel consistently found herself surrounded by nations which believed in many gods. There are some statements in the Hebrew Scriptures which perhaps foreshadow the later revelation of God as triune. For example, there are frequent references to the Holy Spirit, or Spirit of God (Gen. 1:2; Judg. 13:5; Ps. 51:11). In addition, God on occasion uses the first-person plural as a self-reference: "Let *us* make man in our image" (Gen. 1:26); "The man has now become like one of *us*, knowing good and evil" (Gen. 3:22); "Let *us* go down and confuse their language" (Gen. 11:7). Indeed, as we have already noted, the Hebrew word normally translated "God," *'elohim*, is plural in form. On the other hand, the plural form of God's name may simply be a "plural of majesty" (above, p. 54), as opposed to an allusion to the Trinity.

New Testament Witness to the Trinity

God the Father. The Father is recognized as God throughout the New Testament; see for example John 6:27 ("him the Father, even God, has sealed") and 1 Peter 1:2 ("foreknowledge of God the Father"). No one has ever debated this, so we need not set forth any extended proof of it.

God the Son. We have already noted that the word "God" is used of the preexistent Jesus ("the Word") in John 1:1. This designation is repeated in John 1:18, which refers to Jesus as "the one and only God, who is at the Father's side." Indeed, the deity of Christ receives its strongest witness from the fourth Gospel (John 10:30; 20:28).

Outside of John's Gospel explicit New Testament references to Christ's deity are few, but nevertheless present. In Romans 9:5, for example, Paul refers to "Christ, who is God over all, forever praised." In addition, Paul's reference to Jesus in Titus 2:13 is probably best translated as "our great God and savior Jesus Christ." The writer of the book of Hebrews applies to Christ an Old Testament quote which states, "Your throne, O God, is forever" (Heb. 1:8; see Ps. 45:6).

Not only do New Testament writers designate Jesus as "God," but they also ascribe to Jesus the work assigned to Yahweh in the Old Testament. The outstanding example of this is the Lord's work as savior or redeemer. In Isaiah 43:11, for instance, Yahweh declares that "apart from me there is no savior." Yet God's angel declares that "Jesus. . . shall save His people from their sins" (Matt. 1:21), and Christ declares that He came "to give His life as a ransom for many" (Mark 10:45).

God the Holy Spirit. The word "Holy," used of God in the Old Testament, is applied to the Spirit of God in the New Testament. In Acts 5:3-4 Peter explicitly ascribes deity to the Holy Spirit as he upbraids Ananias for practicing deception: "Ananias, how is it that Satan has so filled your heart that you have lied to the Holy Spirit . . . . You have not lied to men but to God."

The Holy Spirit also works in ways assigned to God in the Old Testament. The Psalmist, for example, speaks of God as "a very present help in trouble" (Ps. 46:1), and God's Holy Spirit as one whom he wishes to remain with him despite his sin (Ps. 51:11). The

New Testament picks up this theme of God's presence and companionship, especially in John's Gospel, where Jesus promises that He will give to His disciples the Holy Spirit "to be with you forever" (John 14:16; see also 14:25; 15:26; 16:13).

Father, Son, and Holy Spirit. The intimate connection between the Father, Son, and Spirit is underscored in texts where they are mentioned together. For example, all three are named in the following passages:

- At Jesus's baptism (Matt. 3:16f.)
- At the Great Commission (Matt. 28:19)
- In Paul's benediction to the Corinthian Church (2 Cor. 13:14)
- In Peter's exposition of God's work of salvation (1 Pet. 1:2)
- In Paul's exposition of spiritual gifts (1 Cor. 12:4-6)

While formal trinitarian doctrine did not develop until after the New Testament was written, these and other texts show that the post-apostolic Church did not "invent" the Trinity. The Christian doctrine of the Triune God is a product of biblical revelation, not philosophical speculation.

The Trinity in Church History

Christ and the Spirit. The doctrine of the Trinity developed as part of the christological controversies which plagued the Church during its first four centuries. The most prominent of these controversies are discussed below in chapter 8 (The Incarnation).

The full deity and humanity of Jesus Christ were the central issues confronting the Church in the second, third, and fourth centuries. In the earliest debates, the person of the Holy Spirit did not figure prominently. For example, the Epistles of Ignatius (written around A. D. 110) make frequent mention of Jesus, but very little of the Holy Spirit. This is in rather marked contrast to the Apostle Paul's numerous references to the Holy Spirit. In Romans 8:1-27, for example, Paul mentions the Spirit over a dozen times.

As time went on the Church realized that the doctrines of Christ and the Spirit were inextricably connected. Thus the second-century Old Roman Creed, a forerunner of what is now called the

Apostles' Creed, contained three paragraphs which have been preserved in an early third-century formula:

Do you believe in God the Father All Governing?
Do you believe in Jesus Christ, the Son of God. . . ?
Do you believe in the Holy Spirit. . . ?
(*Interrogatory Creed of Hippolytus*, c. 215)[3]

This tripartite confessional framework became the norm for
later confessional statements, including the Nicene Creed.

God as three-in-one. The threefold Christian confession of Father,
Son, and Holy Spirit led some to believe that Christians worshiped
three gods. This was the objection of Celsus, one of the late second
century's most ardent foes of Christianity. In response to this, some
Christians went to the opposite extreme and stated that Father,
Son, and Holy Spirit were simply three names for one divine King
of the universe, who is God. One name for this teaching was
Modalism, since it viewed Father, Son, and Spirit as three modes of
the one divine Person's self-expression.

Modalism found a powerful opponent in the Latin apologist Tertullian, who insisted that such a view meant that the Father was
crucified at Calvary (see below, chapter 8, p. 175). Tertullian denied
that God was only one person, and became the first theologian to
use what would become the orthodox terminology of God as one
substance and three persons. Indeed, it was Tertullian who first
employed the word "trinity" (Latin *trinitas*) to articulate the mystery of God's three-in-oneness:

> All [Father, Son, and Holy Spirit] are of One, by unity (that is) of
> substance; while the mystery of the dispensation is still guarded,
> which distributes the Unity into a Trinity, placing in their order the
> three Persons—the Father, the Son, and the Holy Ghost: three,
> however, not in condition, but in form; not in power, but in aspect;
> yet of one substance, and of one condition, and of one power, inas-
> much as He is the one God,. . . . (*Against Praxeas* 2).[4]

The writings of Origen of Alexandria were also influential in the
development of trinitarianism. Origen, who wrote in Greek, contributed the word *hypostasis* ("substance") to trinitarian vocabulary
in order to speak of what Tertullian meant by the Latin *persona*
("person"). As time went on, *hypostasis* was used in the Eastern
Church in a manner which came to emphasize the diversity within

TERTULLIAN

Quintus Septimus Florens Tertullianus (c.155-c.220) was born in Carthage, North Africa (modern Tunisia), and raised in the cultured paganism of that great city. He was sent to Rome to study law, and was thus conversant in both Greek and Latin.

The circumstances surrounding Tertullian's conversion, which occurred around the year 185, are not known. He soon gained notoriety as an effective advocate for Christianity. About twenty years after his conversion he left the Catholic Church, apparently disenchanted with its moral laxity, and attached himself to the Montanist sect. This rigorously moralistic group believed that the teachings of Montanus, its founder and leader, were direct revelations from the Holy Spirit and signaled a third divine dispensation, following the dispensations of the Father (Old Testament) and the Son (Jesus and the early Church).

Tertullian wrote prodigiously. His Greek works have not survived, but thirty-one Latin works remain, which comprise the first significant body of Latin Christian literature. His legal training served him well in controversies against heretics such as Marcion and Praxeas. Tertullian had a penchant for memorable one-liners, such as the famous maxim that "the blood of the martyrs is the seed of the Church."

Tertullian's brilliance as a prosecutor of heretics was matched by his creative thinking in the areas of theology and Christology. His coining of the term "Trinity," along with his formula which defined God as "one substance consisting in three persons," provided the Western Church with a trinitarian model which in turn eventually formed the basis for orthodox Christology, striking a balance between the unity and diversity within the Godhead which was all too often lacking in the Eastern wing of the Church.

His most famous works include the *Apology* (a defense of Christians against slanderous charges brought against them by the Roman government), *Against Marcion* (who denied that the God of the Old Testament was the God of Jesus Christ), and *Against Praxeas* (a Modalist who denied the Trinity). His polemic against Praxeas was particularly noteworthy in that he anticipated the orthodox Christology of the ecumenical councils of Ephesus (431) and Chalcedon (451), declaring that Jesus Christ had two natures joined in one person.

the Godhead, whereas the Western Church placed more emphasis on the unity of the Godhead. Origen himself did speak of Father, Son, and Spirit as persons (*hypostases*) united in will and love as one God. At the same time, however, Origen taught a form of subordinationism—he viewed both the Son and the Spirit as subordinate to God not only in function, but also in nature.

In this way Origen's trinitarianism paved the way both for the orthodoxy of Athanasius (which emphasized the diversity of the Godhead over against Modalism) and the heresy of Arius (which subordinated the Son to the Father).[5] The debates between Arius and Athanasius will be examined more closely in our discussion of the christological debates which occurred between A.D. 325 and 451(see chapter eight, p. 178). For now, let us examine one key aspect of the Arian heresy relevant to our discussion of the Trinity.

The Son as "Begotten, not Made." In 381 the Council of Constantinople confessed the Second Person of the Trinity as "the only-begotten Son of God, begotten of the Father before all worlds. . . begotten, not made; being of one substance with the Father." In so doing the council emphasized its conviction that prior to His incarnation as the man Jesus, the pre-existent Son of God was co-equal and co-eternal with God the Father.

By way of contrast, Arius had taught that the Son was the first and most glorious created being of God's creation. The Son therefore had a beginning and was not of the same "substance" as the Father, being created rather than uncreated. Arius himself used the word "begotten" of the Son, but in the sense of "created." Furthermore, he reasoned that since a begotten son is always younger than the father who begets him, the preexistent Son must likewise be younger than the Father, and therefore must have had a beginning.

The Arian heresy's failure to distinguish between the concepts of "making" and "begetting" has been addressed more recently by C. S. Lewis as follows:

When you beget, you beget something of the same kind as yourself. A man begets human babies, a beaver begets little beavers and a bird begets eggs which turn into little birds. But when you make, you make something of a different kind from yourself. A bird makes a nest, a beaver builds a dam, a man makes a wireless set—or he may make something more like himself than a wireless set: say, a statue. If he is a clever enough carver he may make a statue which is very like a man indeed. But, of course, it is not a real man; it only looks like one. It cannot breathe or think. It is not alive.[6]

Lewis also addresses the Arian notion that if the Father has "begotten" the Son, the Son of necessity must not be as old as the Father and must therefore have a beginning:

> I asked you [in a previous paragraph] to imagine . . . two books, and probably most of you did. That is, you made an act of imagination and as a result you had a mental picture. Quite obviously your act of imagining was the cause and mental picture was the result. But that does not mean that you first did the imagining and then got the picture. The moment you did it, the picture was there . . . . If there were a Being who had always existed and had always been imagining one thing, his act would always have been producing a mental picture; but the picture would be just as eternal as the act.[7]

That "picture" in Lewis's analogy is, of course, the Son.

Augustine and the co-equal Trinity. Augustine's watershed work *On the Trinity,* written over a period of almost two decades (c. 400-416), built upon the work of his predecessors and established the framework of trinitarian doctrine for the Western Church from that time onward. Due in part to the lengthy span of time over which it was composed, *On the Trinity* sets forth some statements which seem to stress the diversity of the three divine persons, while at other times emphasizing the unity of the one God. Generally speaking, Western Christianity followed Augustine's stress on the unity of the Godhead, while the Eastern Church followed Origen's emphasis on the diversity of Father, Son, and Spirit.

Augustine, more than anyone before him, tried to probe the meaning of God's three-in-oneness. He used numerous analogies from human experience in order to understand the triune God. For example, he saw the human experience of love as "a trace of the Trinity." "But what is love . . . except the love of good? But love is *of* some one that loves, and *with* love something *is* loved. Behold, then, there are three things: he that loves, and that which is loved, and love (*On the Trinity* 8.10)."[8]

Augustine also likened God's three-in-oneness to mind, self-knowledge, and self-love; memory, understanding, and will; and memory, understanding, and love of God (*On the Trinity* 9.4, 10.11, 14.4-8).

Augustine's work was significant in that his primary emphasis was on the relationship of Father, Son, and Spirit to one another as co-equal persons. Previously, discussions of the Trinity had tended to emphasize the relationships of Father, Son, and Spirit not so much to each other as to the world. The Father, for example, related to the world as Creator, while the Son related as Reconciler and the Spirit as Redeemer or Sanctifier. Augustine shifted the focus to how Father, Son, and Spirit related to one another even before the foundation of the world. This relationship could best be summed up by the biblical witness that "God is love" (1 John 4:8, 16).

AUGUSTINE

Augustine of Hippo (354-430) was born in Northwestern Africa and spent most of his life in what is today northeastern Algeria and Tunisia. His father was a pagan converted to Christianity only shortly before his death around the year 370. His mother, Monica, was a devout Christian. The young Augustine received a classical education in rhetoric at Carthage, the major city of fourth-century North Africa. He excelled in his studies and showed great interest in matters of philosophy. Despite having received Christian catechetical teaching from his early childhood years, he was more interested in indulging his appetites for the theater and sexual activity.

Augustine's penchant for philosophy led him to embrace the teaching of Manichaeism, a dualistic worldview which taught that the principles of light and darkness, or good and evil, are co-equal and co-eternal. He regarded the Bible, par-ticularly the Old Testament, as inferior to the writings of the finest Greek and Roman philosophers and masters of rhetoric. He eventually abandoned Manichaeism, but retained some of its dualism in his own thought even after his conversion to Christianity in 386.

In 383 Augustine sailed from Carthage and traveled to Rome in order to gain greater opportunities as a teacher of rhetoric. While there he came into contact with the powerful preaching of Ambrose, Bishop of Milan. It was Ambrose who eventually baptized Augustine into the Catholic Church in Milan on Easter Day of 387, about half a year after Augustine had embraced the Catholic faith. He later attributed his conversion in great part to the unceasing prayers of his mother.

Soon after this Augustine returned to North Africa and was pressed into the service of the Catholic priesthood. In 396 he became

Bishop of Hippo, an important city west of Carthage. From that time on until his death he was embroiled in numerous theological controversies, from which sprang the greatest variety of treatises, sermons, and books written up to that time in the Western Church. His *Confessions* (c. 397-400) originated the literary genre of spiritual autobiography. *The City of God*, written between 413 and 427, began as an argument against those who argued that Christianity was responsible for the sack of Rome by the barbarians in 410 (a view later espoused by Edward Gibbon's *Decline and Fall of the Roman Empire*). The book eventually grew into the first philosophy of history, arguing that human history reflects an ongoing struggle between the forces of evil (the earthly city) and of good (the city of God).

The influence of Augustine upon the Western Church cannot be underestimated. His views on predestination, the Trinity, the sacraments, Church discipline, and sanctification set the agenda for both medieval Catholicism and the Protestant Reformation. His philosophical platonism, which emphasized knowledge of God through direct spiritual illumination, fell from favor in the late Middle Ages with the rise of Aristotle in the Western universities. Thomas Aquinas, for example, taught that God could be known only by the effects of His activity in the world. Augustine's emphasis on direct inward knowledge of God was revived by Luther and Calvin. This can be seen in Calvin's emphasis on the inward testimony of the Spirit (chapter 2, p. 44).

The social Trinity. Augustine thus laid the groundwork for what came to be called the "social Trinity." This view teaches that since "God is love," and since "love" by definition requires a plurality of persons, God must therefore consist of more than a single center of consciousness. Augustine himself did not explicitly define the Trinity in this way, however.

It was Richard of St. Victor (d. 1173), some seven centuries later, who first defined God as three "persons" bound together by love. His argument, in a nutshell, was as follows:

- The Scriptures testify that "God is love."

- Love, by its very nature, is other-directed.

- A creature would be an insufficient object for God's love.

- God therefore cannot love fully unless there are two persons in the Godhead.

- But these two persons, if they be good, would be willing to share their love with a third.

- Therefore, "In order for love to be true, it demands a plurality of persons; in order for love to be perfected, it requires a trinity of persons" (*The Trinity* 3.13).[9]

Richard's emphasis on the diversity within the social Trinity has been viewed by some as a form of tritheism (the teaching that Father, Son, and Spirit are three gods). A century after Richard, for example, Thomas Aquinas attempted a more nuanced view which emphasized that God was one essence or substance, while at the same time stating that Father, Son, and Spirit were "relationally" distinct (*Summa Theologiae* 1.28.4) and therefore three persons.

The Protestant Reformers made no significant advances on Augustine or Aquinas. John Calvin, for example, was content to insist that the terms "Father," "Son," and "Spirit" were not merely labels of God's various functions, but instead pointed to genuine diversity within the Godhead (*Institutes* 1.13.17). In this way Calvin confessed the orthodox trinitarian doctrine without attempting to go beyond the insights set forth by Augustine (see for example Calvin's final sentence of *Institutes* 1.13.19).

The social Trinity of Jonathan Edwards. Whereas Calvin did not delve deeply into the meaning of the Trinity, the American Calvinist theologian Jonathan Edwards (1703-1758) developed a finely tuned and profound philosophical apologetic for the social Trinity. He began his argument by noting that a God who is merely a single center of consciousness would fall short of perfection, in that He could not fully delight in His own glory.

> God's idea of himself [i.e., the Son] is absolutely perfect and therefore is an express and perfect image of Him, exactly like Him in every respect; there is nothing in the pattern [the Father] but what is in the representation [the Son]—substance, life, power nor any thing else, and that in a most absolute perfection of similitude, otherwise it is not a perfect idea.[10]

The Son thus shares all the divine attributes of the Father. Here Edwards's language resembles the words of Hebrews 1:3: "The Son is the radiance of God's glory and the exact representation of his being."

For Edwards, then, God must be at least two persons if He is to fully love and delight in Himself. In other words, God would not be God if He were a single center of consciousness, for He would not be able to stand over against Himself, as it were, and fully delight in His glory. "There must be duplicity [duality]" in the Godhead.[11]

The doctrine of the Trinity confesses three persons, however, not merely two. Where, then, does the Holy Spirit fit into the model set forth by Edwards?

For Edwards, the Holy Spirit is precisely the infinitely perfect and powerful love which exists between the Father and the Son from all eternity:

> The Godhead being thus begotten by God's loving an Idea of Himself and showing forth in a distinct subsistence or Person in that idea, there proceeds a most pure act, and an infinitely holy and sacred energy arises between the Father and Son in mutually loving and delighting in each other. . . . This is the eternal and most Perfect and essential act of the divine nature, wherein the Godhead acts to an infinite degree and in the most perfect manner possible. The deity becomes all act, the divine essence itself flows out and is as it were breathed forth in love and joy. So that the Godhead therein stands forth in yet another manner of subsistence, and then proceeds the third person of the Trinity, the Holy Spirit.[12]

More recently, C. S. Lewis has adopted the same line of argument, though in language a bit easier for modern readers to understand:

> God is not a static thing—not even a person—but a dynamic, pulsating activity, a life, almost a kind of drama. Almost, if you will not think me irreverent, a kind of dance. The union between the Father and Son is such a live concrete thing that this union itself is also a Person. I know this is almost inconceivable, but look at it thus. You know that among human beings, when they get together or in a family, or a club, or a trade union, people talk about the "spirit" of that family, or club, or trade union. They talk about its "spirit" because the individual members, when they are present, do really develop

particular ways of talking and behaving which they would not do if they were apart. It is as if a sort of communal personality came into existence. Of course, it is not a real person: it is only rather like a person. But that is just one difference between God and us. What grows out of the joint life of the Father and Son is a real Person, is in fact the third of the three Persons who are God.[13]

The trinitarian model set forth by Edwards and reiterated by Lewis is an advance upon the argument of Richard of St. Victor. Whereas Richard spoke of the third person of the Trinity as merely a third center of consciousness with whom the Father and the Son share their love, Edwards (and Lewis) view the Spirit as intrinsically connected with the Father and the Son, in that the Spirit is the *expression* of the love which the Father and the Son share with one another. The following diagrams represent the difference between Richard's model and that of Edwards:

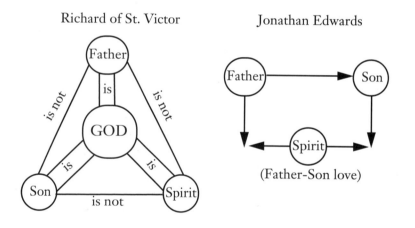

The triangular diagram used to represent Richard's trinitarian model is similar to medieval pictorial attempts to show that the three persons of the Trinity are distinct (the points of the triangle), while God is one (the entire triangle). The diagram of Edwards's model, on the other hand, attempts to show that the Holy Spirit flows out of the life and love of the Father and the Son—or, to use the words of the Nicene Creed, how the Spirit "proceeds from the Father and the Son."

It must be emphasized, however, that the social Trinity model is not identical with the orthodox trinitarian confessions of the fourth and fifth centuries. Rather, the social Trinity is one of several *interpretations* of those confessions. At present there is no ecumenical consensus affirming the social Trinity, or any other trinitarian model, as the definitive interpretation of the doctrine of the Trinity.

The doctrine itself, however, is one of the three historic essentials of historic Christian belief, without which Christianity would not be Christianity (the other two essentials are the doctrines of the Incarnation and the Atonement). As we shall see in our next chapter, the doctrine of the Trinity has important implications not only for the doctrine of God, but also for the doctrine of creation.

Points To Ponder

1. What is the significance of the divine name Yahweh (Hebrew *YHWH*)?

2. What does Jesus' use of *Abba* as a name for God tell us about God?

3. How does Erich Auerbach contrast the biblical narratives with the Homeric epics?

4. What do theologians mean when they speak of God's communicable attributes? Incommunicable attributes? Absolute attributes? Relative attributes?

5. Be able to list at least three communicable attributes and three incommunicable attributes, with scriptural references for each.

6. Define *and explain* the term "Trinity," and cite biblical evidence in support of the doctrine.

7. Know the significance of the following theologians in the historical development of trinitarian doctrine: Tertullian, Origen, Augustine, Richard of St. Victor, Jonathan Edwards.

8. How does C. S. Lewis distinguish between "making" and "begetting"?

9. What does the "social Trinity" model teach about God?

4

The Doctrine of Creation

The Biblical View of Creation

The Importance of a Worldview

A four-year-old boy was standing with his father near a construction site. They both looked on as heavy construction machinery helped the workers lift steel beams and concrete blocks into place. After a while the boy turned to his father and said, "Daddy, what kind of machine built the world?"

The little boy's question tells us that his worldview, or notion of what the world is like, was based on what he saw. Machines build buildings, football fields, and other things, so the world must have been made by a machine.

We can chuckle at a small boy's ignorance. But this story also demonstrates that what we see may lead us to erroneous conclusions. This is because we sometimes lack adequate information to figure things out.

For example, which of us was there when the world came into being (see Job 38:4)? The answer is self-evident. But if no one was there, how can we know how the world began? And even if we could know *how* the world began (if it indeed had a beginning and has not always existed), that would not necessarily answer the fundamental questions of human existence common to all of us: Who am I? Why am I here? Where am I going? Answers to such questions depend on how we view the world. For Christians, the starting-point for understanding the meaning of the world is God's revelation found in the Bible.

This does not mean that the Bible tells us everything there is to know about creation. We learn many useful truths from scientific study and common everyday experience. We would be foolish to ignore these. On the other hand, until we go beyond the realms of common sense and science and seek to understand what Scripture says about the meaning of creation, we will be ignorant as to how we should relate to God and to other people. We need a framework within which to place the facts of our existence in order to make sense of them. Otherwise we shall fare little better than the four-year-old mentioned above.

God the Father Almighty, Creator of Heaven and Earth

Question 26 of the Heidelberg Catechism (1563) asks, "What do you believe when you say: I believe in God the Father Almighty, Maker of heaven and earth?" The response—one of the finest brief expositions of the meaning and significance of God's work of creation—is as follows:

> That the eternal Father of our Lord Jesus Christ, who out of nothing created heaven and earth, with all that is in them, who likewise upholds and governs the same by His eternal counsel and providence, is for the sake of Christ His Son my God and Father; in whom I so trust, as to have no doubt that He will provide me with all things necessary for body and soul; and further, that whatever evil He sends upon me in this vale of tears He will turn to my good; for He is able to do it, being Almighty God, and willing also, being a faithful Father.

Let us now examine some implications of this statement as it relates to the doctrine of creation. (Our next chapter will deal with the doctrine of providence, or how God "upholds and governs" the world).

God created the world out of nothing. "By the Word of the LORD were the heavens made . . . . For He spoke, and it came to be; He commanded, and it stood firm" (Ps. 33:6, 9). God did not merely

THE HEIDELBERG CATECHISM

The response to Question 26 of the Heidelberg Catechism, quoted on p. 78 of this textbook, is but one example of how this sixteenth-century Reformation document combines a commitment to sound doctrine with a vital expression of personal trust in Christ. Written less than twenty years after the death of Martin Luther, the Heidelberg Catechism exudes a freshness of newly-found faith which was seldom found in even the best of the Reformed confessions of the next century.

The genesis of this catechism was a controversy concerning the Lord's Supper which arose in 1559 between Germans of Lutheran and Reformed convictions. At that time Frederic III, surnamed the Pious, became elector of the Palatinate, a country on the upper Rhine. Frederic took great interest in this controversy and studied the matter carefully. The following year, after diligent biblical and theological study, he declared himself in favor of the Reformed position. (We shall describe these positions in some detail in chapter 14). Frederic then instructed two men he deemed both devout and discerning to help him write a Reformed Catechism. Their names were Caspar Olevianus and Zacharias Ursinus.

In the spring of 1563 the first edition of the catechism was published. It begins not with orthodox pronouncements concerning God or Scripture, but with an appeal to humanity's yearning for comfort in this life and the life to come:

Question 1: What is thy only comfort in life?

Answer: That I, with body and soul, both in life and in death, am not my own, but belong to my faithful Savior *Jesus Christ*, who with His precious blood has fully satisfied for all my sins, and redeemed me from all the power of the devil; and so preserves me, that without the will of my *Father* in heaven not a hair can fall from my head; yea, that all things must work together for my salvation. Wherefore, by His *Holy Spirit*, He also assures me of eternal life, and makes me heartily willing and ready henceforth to live unto Him.

The catechism then follows the threefold division of Paul's epistle to the Romans. This is set forth in the next question:

Question 2: How many things are necessary for thee to know, that thou in this comfort mayest live and die happily?

Answer: Three things: First, the greatness of my sin and *misery.* Second, how I am *redeemed* from all my sins and misery. Third, how I am to be *thankful* to God for such redemption.

These three things correspond to Romans 1:18-3:20 (misery), 3:21-11:33 (redemption), and 12:1-16:27 (thankfulness).

The catechism received opposition from some stricter Lutherans, but Frederic persevered. He was permitted to rule his country until he peacefully passed away in 1576. His motto was engraved on his tombstone: "Lord, according to Thy will!"

The catechism was gradually introduced into all Reformed countries of Germany, into Holland, several Swiss cantons, Hungary, and Poland. In 1618 the Synod of Dort in Holland, which was composed of Reformed delegates from all countries, recognized the Heidelberg Catechism as a confession of faith of the whole Reformed Church of all languages. Immigrants from Holland and Germany later brought the catechism to America.

---

fashion the universe out of something that was already there, co-eternal with Himself, such as pre-existent matter. God created the heavens and the earth *ex nihilo* ("out of nothing") simply by calling them into being.

The Bible begins by saying that God created "in the beginning." The universe is not eternal; only God has always existed. A modern school of thought known as Process Theology speaks of both God and the universe as being eternally in development, or in process. Such a view negates the clear biblical testimony that the world had a beginning, and undercuts the fundamental distinction which Scripture makes between the creator and the created order. Since God is immutable (chapter 3, p. 60), the universe adds nothing to God's being. God has always been God: "Before the mountains were born or you brought forth the earth and the world, from everlasting to everlasting you are God" (Ps. 90:2).

The God of creation is the God of redemption. We have seen above how the Heidelberg Catechism mentions God's work as creator and redeemer in the same sentence. This link between creation and redemption has precedent from the earliest centuries of Church history.

For example, the centerpiece of both the Apostles' Creed and the Nicene Creed is the redemptive work of Jesus Christ. Yet both of these ancient formulas, though fundamentally christological, begin with the affirmation of belief in God as the Creator of all things. In this way the creeds affirm that the same deity, the one and only God, both created the world and redeemed fallen people through "Jesus Christ His only Son our Lord . . . God from God, Light from Light, True God from True God" (Nicene Creed).

The ancient Church affirmed God the Father of Jesus Christ as creator of heaven and earth in order to combat the dualistic worldview of gnosticism. The Gnostics claimed to add further insight into Christianity by means of heavenly knowledge (*gnosis*) hidden from the average person. They believed that reality was divided into two spheres: the transcendent or heavenly, and the immanent or earthly. The supreme God was by definition transcendent, but not immanent. This "two-storied" dualistic worldview may be diagrammed thus:

REALM	CONTENT OF REALM
Transcendent	Spirit; supreme God
Immanent	Matter; things of earth

On the basis of such a worldview some Gnostics assigned the work of creation to a sort of second-string deity who acted as an intermediary between the supreme God and the created order, since the supreme God by definition could have nothing to do with material creation. Some identified this inferior deity with the creator God of the Old Testament, while the Christian God was only the God of redemption. The Gnostics thus cut off Christianity from its Old Testament foundations. In response to this the Church affirmed that there is but one God, creator of heaven and earth and Father of Jesus Christ the redeemer.[1]

We have thus far affirmed that the God of Jesus Christ freely created heaven and earth out of nothing. The question remains as to *why* God created the world. Whether and how to address this question is the subject of our next section.

Why God Created the World

When people ask "Why did God create the world?" they may be asking one, or both, of the following questions:

- For what *purpose* or *end* did God create the world?
- What *caused* God to create the world as He did?

Let us examine each of these questions in turn.

For what purpose or end did God create the world? The Westminster Larger Catechism (1647) addresses this question, albeit indirectly, when it asks for what purpose God created human beings:

Question 1: What is the chief and highest end of man?

Answer: Man's chief and highest end is to glorify God, and fully to enjoy Him forever.

Creation is therefore what theologians have called a *theatrum gloriae dei* ("theater of the glory of God"), with humanity at the center. We were created for the purpose of demonstrating how glorious God is and for the purpose of enjoying God forever. The contemporary Baptist theologian John Piper has further noted that we may properly speak of one, not two, purposes for which God created us (since the catechism asks "What is the chief and highest *end*"—not "ends"—of man). That is, the chief end of humanity is to glorify God *by enjoying Him forever.*[2]

This chief end or purpose is unique to humanity. To be sure, the Bible teaches that all of creation was fashioned to show forth God's glory. "The heavens declare the glory of God; the skies proclaim the work of his hands" (Ps. 19:1). Only people, however, can "enjoy God." To put it in the language of the anthropologist or social scientist, man is the only being in all creation capable of *worship*, of praising God.

Worship and praise express the most intimate form of fellowship with, and the highest possible esteem for, another person. Joyous fellowship with God, then, is that for which we were created. God Himself is our final end: "You have created us for yourself, O God, and our hearts are restless until they rest in you" (Augustine, *Confessions* 1.1).

What caused God to create the world as He did? Some would argue that to ask this question is not proper. Augustine said, "To inquire into why God wanted to make the world is to inquire into the cause of God's will. But every cause is productive of some result, everything productive of some result is greater than that which is produced, and nothing is greater than God's will. Therefore [God's will] has no cause to be sought after" (*83 Different Questions*, Question 28).[3] In this way Augustine sought to defend the freedom of God in creation, saying in effect that God created the world because He wanted to do so.

The Protestant Reformation did not go much beyond Augustine in this regard. For example, Martin Luther reportedly answered the question "What was God doing before He created the world?" by saying that prior to creation God was cutting switches to punish those who ask such impertinent questions! John Calvin spoke in much the same way, saying (perhaps a bit tongue-in-cheek) that before He created the world God was "building hell for the curious" (*Institutes* 1.14.1).

On the other hand, the American theologian Jonathan Edwards expounded not only on God's purpose in creation, but also on what prompted God to create the world. In his essay "A Dissertation Concerning the End for Which God Created the World" Edwards held that prior to creation the triune God was delighting completely in His own glory, and was thereby motivated to display His glory to beings outside of Himself but as yet uncreated. This was not something God had to do out of necessity, however. That is, creation added nothing to God's perfection.

Here Edwards distinguished between what have been called God's *necessary work* and God's *free work*. It is *necessary* for God the Father to beget the Son and exist on the high order of Trinity in order completely to delight in Himself (see chapter 3, p. 72). Otherwise God would not be God. But God needs nothing outside of Himself in order be completely happy with who He is. Edwards said that "God's rejoicing in creation is rather a rejoicing in His own acts, and His own glory expressed in those acts, than a joy derived from the creature."[4] Thus creation was not necessary to make God happy, but is a *free* act motivated by God's very nature as the one who regards His own infinite worth, or *glory*, as the greatest thing in existence.

What motivated God to create, then, was not any needs He has, but rather what Edwards called "benevolence": a love which finds its joy in meeting the needs of others, as opposed to having one's own needs met. Edwards said,

> Indeed, after the creatures are *intended* to be created, God may be conceived of as being moved by benevolence to them . . . in His dealings with them. His exercising His goodness, and gratifying His benevolence to them in particular, may be the spring of all God's proceedings through the universe; as being now the determined way of gratifying His general inclination to diffuse Himself [in order to display His glory]. Here God acting for *Himself*, or making Himself His last end, and His acting for *their* sake, are not to be set in opposition; they are rather to be considered as coinciding one with the other, and implied one in the other.[5]

What Edwards called "benevolence" may also be designated by the biblical term *mercy*. Mercy is a love which condescends to meet the needs of the unworthy. God's acts of mercy constitute the greatest possible display of God's glory, since God is in no way obligated to show compassion towards sinners. If people were perfectly righteous, God would be obligated to treat them well. But sinful people have no right to the love of God. Thus God's acts of mercy in the forgiveness of sinners demonstrate that He is so complete and secure in Himself that He can condescend to do what He does not have to do—love the unlovely.

Mercy is therefore the most glorious display of God possible, since freely doing what one need not do is more glorious than merely doing what one must do. This is the reason, Edwards went on to say, that God chose to externalize His glory by not only creating a magnificent world, but also by ordaining a *history of redemption* wherein God forgives sinners. This history of redemption was not merely God's reaction to Adam and Eve's disobedience, but rather central to God's eternal purposes. Scripture describes Jesus as "the Lamb that was slain *from the creation of the earth*" (Rev. 13:8) in order to secure the redemption of sinful people.

God's activity of redemption is thus the "spring of all of God's proceedings through the universe" of which Edwards spoke. Furthermore, God's "benevolence" or mercy is ultimately based upon God's desire to manifest His own glory ("His general inclination to diffuse Himself"), since (1) the redemption of sinners reveals God's glory more fully than anything else, and (2) God always acts "for His name's sake"; that is, to uphold His own glory (see Ps. 23:3; 25:11; 106:8). This was why Edwards could say that God's acting for Himself to demonstrate His glory and His acting for sinners' sake to show them mercy, "are not to be set in opposition." The glory of God and the redemption of sinful people through Christ are the same end, that end for which God created the world.

Thus God's motivation for creating the world, and the purpose or end of creation, are the same: that the glory of God shall cover the world "as the waters cover the sea" (Hab. 2:14). In this way Augustine's objection to the question "What caused God to create the world?" receives an answer consistent with the biblical portrait of God. For what caused God to create the world was not something greater than God (which, as Augustine rightly saw, would be a contradiction in terms), but rather the very nature of God's own character as the one who always works to uphold His own glory.

Alternatives to the Biblical View of Creation

Greek Philosophy

Whereas Christian faith confesses that God created the world *ex nihilo*, the Greek philosophical tradition regarded as self-evident truth the phrase *ex nihilo nihil fit* ("nothing comes from nothing"). Plato held that there are two eternal, self-existent principles, God and matter. "Creation" for Plato is thus not God's act of calling matter into being from nothing; rather, it is God's activity of giving to eternal matter forms which in some way reflect God's eternal ideas. Aristotle also held that God and matter are coordinately self-existent and eternal, though unlike Plato he believed the form of the universe as we now know it had a beginning. There was also a tendency in ancient Greek philosophical and religious thought to regard the self-existent matter from which the universe sprang as intrinsically evil.[6]

For Christians, however, only God is eternal; matter had a beginning. The heavens and the earth, argued Augustine, must have had a beginning:

The very fact that they are there proclaims that they were created, for they are subject to change and variation; whereas if anything exists that was not created there is nothing in it that was not there before; and the meaning of change and variation is that something is there which was not there before. Earth and the heavens also proclaim that they did not create themselves. "We exist," they tell us, "because we were made. And this is proof that we did not make ourselves. For to make ourselves, we should have had to exist before our existence began" (*Confessions* 11.4).

Furthermore, matter is not intrinsically evil. Rather, God deemed the material world as first created "very good" (Gen. 1:31), in that it was an entirely suitable environment for the human race to inhabit in a manner which would glorify the Creator. The entry of sin into the world had nothing to do with the material nature of creation. It was the result of moral disobedience on the part of humanity.

Pantheism

The word *pantheism* comes from two Greek words which together mean "All [is] God" (*pan theos*). Pantheism is characteristic of many Eastern religions such as Hinduism, in which the world is seen as a part of, or emanation from, God. Furthermore, the word "God" has no personal connotations in a pantheistic world view; rather, "God" is equal to "all that is." Thus pantheism is what we may call *monistic*, emphasizing the unity of all things, as opposed to the dualistic tendencies of Greek philosophy.

Christians, on the other hand, affirm a fundamental discontinuity between the creator and His creation. The world is not of the same essence or substance as God. This is yet another reason, in addition to the presence of sin in the world, why human beings cannot understand who God is merely by looking at what God has made. Not only that, but we cannot even explain why the world is as it is merely by looking at the created order. This is because the world does not contain its own explanation of itself. The world depends on God both for its existence and for an explanation of why it exists.

Here we may draw an analogy between the world and God on the one hand, and a painting and its artist on the other. Consider, for example, Rembrandt's *Raising of the Cross* (1633), which depicts several men taking part in the crucifixion of Christ. The average person will see a Passion scenario set in seventeenth-century northern Europe. The person who has actually seen what Rembrandt looked like (via the artist's self-portraits) notices something more, however. The face of Rembrandt himself is among Christ's executioners. A knowledge of Rembrandt makes the painting more fully understandable. In like manner, a knowledge of God sheds light on the meaning of creation which would otherwise elude us.

Raising of the Cross. The artist (wearing the beret) testifies that his sins helped put Christ on the cross. (*Photograph courtesy of the Alte Pinakothek, Munich, Germany*).

Modern Atheistic Worldviews

Turning to more modern alternatives to biblical Christianity, we find over the past century Christianity's two most powerful adversaries have been worldviews which deny the existence of God altogether. These are dialectical materialism and what may be termed atheistic evolutionism.

Dialectical Materialism. This worldview is more widely known as Marxism, having been formulated by the German philosopher Karl Marx (1818-1883). For most of the twentieth century Marxism was Christianity's most powerful and implacable foe, at least on the political front. Indeed, many people view Marxism as basically a political or economic system. This is not the case, however.

As its name indicates, dialectical materialism is not merely a political system, but a worldview grounded upon an entirely materialistic concept of the universe. Marx followed the ancient Greek philosophers in his belief that matter was eternal. On the other hand, Marx denied that the gods or a God had fashioned the world for any purpose which might be called "spiritual." For Marx, the only goals of human history worth mentioning were material goals. A man was defined not in terms of his relationship to God, but in terms of his relationship to the means of economic production.

The mentality of Marx may be illustrated by the story (most likely legendary) of how one day Marx came rushing from his study and exclaimed to his wife, "I have found the key to the meaning of history!"

"What is it this time, Karl?" she replied.

"Economics!" he proclaimed triumphantly.

For Marx, human history was an ongoing struggle between competing economic interests which were in perpetual tension and conflict, with these conflicts continually resolving themselves and then giving rise to new conflicts. Marx believed that what he called this dialectical movement of history would reach a final resolution, or synthesis, with a pure communism wherein private property would be abolished and material goods would be owned by society rather than by individuals. Socialism is thus another name for this economic concept of a classless society.

What must always be kept in view in any discussion of Marxism, however, is that the political-economic system known as socialism or communism was not the fundamental basis of Marx's philosophy. The very name "dialectical materialism" indicates that to understand Marxism, one must understand that it is most fundamentally a worldview which makes no allowance at all for the existence of a Supreme Being. *Marxism is not basically socialism which happens to be atheistic; it is basically atheism which happens to be socialistic.*

The Bible, of course, sees human history in more than materialistic terms. God created matter for spiritual ends, not merely material ends ("economics!"). This is not to say that the Bible is unconcerned with economics. The Mosaic Law made specific provisions for the economic well-being of the poor, widows, and orphans, for example. Marxism, on the other hand, reduces human history to nothing but economic struggle. Failure to recognize the fundamentally atheistic nature of Marxism has contributed to confusion among some Christians who have sought to find common ground between Christianity and communism via "Christian-Marxist dialogue." The two worldviews are mutually exclusive.

Even before the collapse of communism in the Soviet Union in 1991, Marxism had lost its appeal to most philosophers and academics. Notable exceptions exist in North American universities, especially within English and political science departments, where resistance to the Christian worldview is fairly common and sometimes fierce.[7]

Atheistic Evolutionism. Whereas dialectical materialism is a worldview in decline, what may be termed atheistic evolutionism still holds forth as the worldview of choice among many intellectuals, particularly within the biological sciences. This worldview is sometimes referred to as Darwinism, after the British naturalist Charles Darwin (1809-1882), whose 1859 book *The Origin of Species* set the basic paradigm for biological science down to the present day.

Unlike Marx's dialectical materialism, Darwinism does not see human history as having any purpose or goal, be it an economic one such as a classless society, or any other sort of goal. Instead, this form of atheism teaches that life began billions of years ago purely by chance and out of non-living material, and has evolved from simplicity to its present complexity purely by chance.

The French philosopher Jacques Monod is a well-known proponent of this view. His book *Chance and Necessity* states,

Chance *alone* is at the source of every innovation, of all creation in the biosphere. Pure chance, absolutely free but blind, at the very root of the stupendous edifice of evolution: this central concept of modern biology is no longer one among other possible or even conceivable hypotheses. It is today the *sole* conceivable hypothesis, the only one that squares with observed and tested fact.[8]

Monod's final sentence in the preceding quote is subject to the challenge that his atheistic view of reality automatically rules out any theistic explanation of origins as inconceivable, and thus begs the question. In addition, Monod is operating on the Enlightenment assumption that a radical dichotomy exists between faith and knowledge (see chapter 1, p. 11).

The most important point Monod makes relative to our discussion here has to do not so much with origins as with the meaning of the world in general and human history in particular. If Monod is correct, if human beings are merely the result of what Francis Schaeffer has called "the impersonal plus time plus chance," what does this imply? Monod himself puts it this way:

If he accepts this message . . . then man must at last wake out of his millenary dream [that history is headed for a specific goal such as those envisioned by Christianity and Marxism]; and in doing so, wake to his total solitude, his fundamental isolation . . . . The universe was not pregnant with life nor the biosphere with man. Our number came up in a Monte Carlo game.[9]

Life has no meaning or purpose, other than those which we may assign to it, says Monod. Nothing in creation, including people, has any intrinsic value.

It goes without saying that the worldview of atheistic evolutionism runs directly counter to Christianity's affirmation that God created the world with a definite purpose in mind. At the same time, a number of modern scientists who are theists (Christian or otherwise) nevertheless believe that an evolutionary model best describes how life came to be as it is today. This leads to the question of whether and to what extent an evolutionary view of life can be harmonized with Scripture, particularly the early chapters of the book of Genesis.

Genesis and Modern Science

The spectrum of Christian opinion regarding the relationship between the Genesis creation accounts and the theory that life has evolved from simpler to more complex forms may be divided into three basic categories. These are direct creationism, progressive creationism, and theistic evolution.

Direct Creationism

This perspective views Genesis 1 and 2 as basically descriptive language of how the world in general, and humanity in particular, were created. In Genesis 1, the days of creation are viewed by some as six twenty-four hour days, and the individual elements of the creation come into being by *fiat* (that is, by God's direct command), as opposed to developing from simpler to more complex forms. In Genesis 2, the creation of humanity is seen as completely disconnected from other orders of conscious life. Adam was made from the dust of the ground, and Eve from his rib, both by special acts of creation.

Some proponents of direct creationism believe that the age of the earth should be measured in thousands or perhaps tens of thousands of years. Such advocates of a "young earth" believe that modern systems of dating fossil remains and the movements of the galaxies, which yield measurements of several billions of years, are based on flawed methodologies.

Others who espouse direct creationism believe that the universe is billions of years old, but that the world *as it presently exists* has a history of only tens of thousands of years. The vast difference in age between the original creation and the present state of creation is explained by a "gap" which ostensibly exists between Genesis 1:1 and 1:2. According to this interpretation, verse 1 speaks of the original creation, which included the very ancient life-forms left in the fossil record. Verse 2 then speaks of a great cataclysm whereby "the earth *became* formless and void," which was then followed by a further act of re-creation which occurred several thousand years ago and which produced the world as we now know it.

This "gap theory" is able to reconcile Genesis 1 with the broad scientific consensus that the earth is billions of years old. On the other hand, the theory is problematic when one looks at the lexical evidence. Specifically, the Hebrew verb *hayah* in Genesis 1:2 must be translated "was," not "became." This point is conceded even by conservative Christian Old Testament scholars.[10]

Progressive Creationism

This school of thought interprets Genesis 1 in less literal terms than does direct creationism. There are varying degrees of progressive creationism. What they have in common is a belief that Genesis 1 depicts successive stages of creation, with some *microevolution* (evolutionary development within species or kinds) during each stage of creation. The final stage is the direct creation of humanity by divine fiat.

Progressive creationism thus affirms microevolution while rejecting what is called *macroevolution*, the idea that all living beings evolved from a single simple life-form. God intervened directly at a number of stages of creation, says the progressive creationist, not merely at the outset. On the other hand, God did not create every single species by fiat. Furthermore, neither Genesis 1 nor 2 is a literal description of creation (since they record certain stages of creation in different sequences). Rather, they are culturally appropriate ways of declaring that God created everything that is.

Theistic Evolution

Theistic evolutionists accept most, if not all, of the theory of evolution as an explanation of the *mechanics* of creation. On the other hand, they steadfastly reject the underlying atheism of both Darwin and contemporary neo-Darwinian models. In addition, theistic evolutionists reject the notion that human beings are merely more intelligent versions of apes. Instead, they insist that while apes and humans are related physically, the difference between humans and apes is ultimately one of kind, not merely of degree.

Thus theistic evolution states that at some point in the evolution of primates, one branch of the primate family was specially endowed by God with what may be termed "the image of God," or a uniquely human soul. At this one point, some say, the natural chain of biological evolution was broken by God: the human soul is a fiat creation. Others would say that God so ordained the evolution of His created order that the human primate's acquisition of the divine image was programmed into creation from the outset. God thus did not have to intervene directly in the evolutionary process in order for humans to become different in kind as well as degree from their primate forbears.[11]

A Theological Assessment

Any attempt to evaluate the three approaches listed above must distinguish between assessing them as *science* and assessing them as *theology*. It is beyond the scope of this book to evaluate the scientific arguments for each view. We shall simply note here that direct creationism, progressive creationism, and theistic evolution have all been espoused by sincere Christians who share common theological convictions concerning creation while differing over certain points of biblical interpretation.

Common convictions shared by all three views, for example, include the following:

- The ultimate reality of the universe is personal: God Himself. The universe is not merely the result of the impersonal plus time plus chance.

- The world is *contingent*, or completely dependent upon God for both its origin *ex nihilo* and its continued existence. The universe did not come about merely by chance, and does not proceed merely by chance. God created the world for a purpose.

- The world, while dependent upon God, is not intrinsically connected to God's being. God created the world freely, and thus it has structures and processes of its own. God does not have to order every event directly; Christians can speak of "laws of nature and of nature's God," as does the United States of America's Declaration of Independence.

- The fact that the world exists "on its own" to a degree means that it can be investigated by scientific methodology, quite apart from biblical revelation. Since the world is rational yet not an extension of God's essence, it is neither sacrilegious nor futile to investigate it on its own terms. This biblical notion of the world's inherent rationality laid the foundations for the rise of modern science which began in the late Middle Ages.[12]

- Scientific investigation can never plumb the depths of the mysteries of heaven and earth, since the world does not contain its own explanation (as noted above, p. 86. Scientific theories therefore must never be accepted uncritically as dogmatic truth. Those who wed their theology to the latest scientific theory or fad may end up as widows.

The differences between the various Christian views of the origins of creation, as noted above, have less to do with what the Bible says than with how the Bible is to be *interpreted*. Within the history of the Christian Church a strictly literal interpretation of the language of Genesis 1-3 has by no means been universal. For example, Augustine's "literal interpretation of Genesis" (*De Genesi ad litteram*) included figurative renderings of certain words and saw the six-day structure of Genesis 1 as depicting something other than dates on a human calendar.

Yet there are limits which the text of Genesis sets upon the Christian theologian and scientist. For example:

- The Genesis accounts of creation cannot be interpreted merely as myths or parable-like stories which communicate timeless truths about the world and humanity's relationship to the rest of creation. They are instead "a faithful account of what *happened*" (Augustine, *De Genesi ad litteram* 1.1.1). They seek to tell us what the world and humanity were like "in the beginning," not to interpret what they are like now. The genealogies which connect Genesis 2 through 11 with the rest of the Bible confirm that the writer of Genesis saw himself as writing history, not mythology or allegory.

- The first chapter of Genesis cannot be harmonized with the modern evolutionary dogma that human beings are merely the end-result of biological evolution from lower forms of life. The threefold use of the Hebrew *barah*, translated "created" in Genesis 1:1, 21, and 27, witnesses to what may be called a threefold differentiation in creation:

Genesis 1:1: "God created the heavens and the earth" teaches that where once nothing existed, now something (the world) has come into existence. This radical differentiation between nothing and something is what we mean by the doctrine of creation *ex nihilo*.

Genesis 1:21: The word "created" (*barah*) does not appear again until the fifth day, when God created conscious life where previously there was none. This is the second major differentiation: from unconscious life (the appearance of plants on day three) to conscious life. The use of *barah* here is the writer's way of saying that the gap between unconscious life and conscious life is as great as the gap between nothing and something.

Genesis 1:27: The third major differentiation in creation is emphasized even more than the first two, as the writer repeats the word *barah* in a threefold parallelism: "God created man in his own image/in the image of God he created him/male and female he created them." For the writer of Genesis, the difference between humanity and the rest of creation is as great as the difference between something and nothing, and the difference between conscious life and unconscious life.

- These three major differentiations found in Genesis 1 also render problematic any attempt to "baptize" atheistic evolutionism with a theistic veneer which posits God as a first cause and then leaves God out the rest of creation's development. In any event, such a minimal expression of "theistic evolution" will gain no adherents from the guild of Darwinian evolutionary scientists, who rule out any "God-hypothesis" as unscientific.

Another aspect of the biblical view of creation which materialist philosophies view as unscientific is the notion than God's universe includes not only visible material beings, but also invisible immaterial beings. These are known as angels.

Angels: God's Secret Agents[13]

The Bible contains no systematic treatise on angels. Much Christian doctrine concerning angels stems from speculation on a rather limited base of scriptural data. Nevertheless, there are some things we can say about angels with a reasonable assurance that we shall remain within the bounds of Scripture.

Angels Are Spiritual Beings Created by God

Angels are "ministering spirits" (Heb. 1:14) who are more powerful than human beings. They are not eternal, however, as is God. The Westminster Larger Catechism speaks of the creation of angels in this way:

> **Question 16:** How did God create angels?
>
> **Answer:** God created all the angels, spirits, immortal, holy, excelling in knowledge, mighty in power, to execute His commandments, and to praise His name, yet subject to change.

The statement that angels were created "to execute [God's] commandments" is consistent with the meaning of the Greek word *angelos*, which means "messenger." Sometimes this word may be used simply of a human messenger (Matt. 11:10; see Mal. 3:1). More often it refers to the "spirits, immortal, holy, excelling in knowledge, mighty in power" mentioned in the Larger Catechism. Angels are suprahuman but not "supernatural," if by "nature" we mean the entire created order, whether material or immaterial.

Exactly when God created the angels has been debated throughout the history of the Church. Thomas Aquinas, for example, noted that while many believe God created angels at the same time He created the corporeal world, eminent theologians such as Athanasius and Gregory of Nazianzus held that angels were created prior to the corporeal world (*Summa Theologiae* 1. 61. 3). Whenever they might have been created, angels are not divine and therefore not to be worshiped (Col. 2:18; Rev. 19:10).

Angels May Appear in Bodily Form

While angels are invisible and not bodily beings, Scripture indicates that at times they may take on bodily form. In Genesis 19, for example, the angels who visited Lot in the city of Sodom appeared to be ordinary human beings (with the exception of their extraordinary power to blind the Sodomites who sought to abuse them). The angel who rolled away the stone from the empty tomb of the risen Jesus had a much more glorious appearance than those who visited Lot: "His appearance was like lightning, and his clothes were white as snow" (Matt. 28:3).

It is interesting to note that in the Bible angels never appear in female form. Whether or not this is significant is beyond the scope of our inquiry here. It is consistent with the overall Christian doctrinal consensus that angels do not marry and thus do not procreate (see Matt. 22:30). This has led some to conclude that the number of angels has been fixed from the time of their creation.

Angels Minister to God's People

As "ministering spirits" angels give comfort and strength to God's people. Angels defeated the enemies of Israel on several occasions, including the destruction of 185,000 Assyrian soldiers (2 Kings 19:35). An angel delivered the apostles from prison at least twice (Acts 5:19; 12:6-11). Angels ministered even to Jesus after His forty days in the wilderness (Mark 1:13).

The concept of "guardian angels" falls under this heading. The notion that each person (or at least each believer) has a specific guardian angel assigned to him or her is not spelled out in the New Testament. Rather, it is inferred from texts such as Matthew 18:10 (where Jesus tells His disciples that children have angels who behold God's face in heaven) and Acts 12:15 (where the servant Rhoda tells a group praying for Peter that He is at the door and they reply, "It is his angel!"). In the case of Acts 12:15 the response to Rhoda's message reflects ancient Jewish belief that the guardian angel assigned to a person resembles that person. There is too little data for a firm biblical theology of guardian angels, however.

Angels Exist in a Hierarchy

Biblical language and Christian tradition both indicate that all angels were not created equal. They appear to possess various ranks within a heavenly hierarchy.

The precise shape of any such hierarchy is difficult to determine, however. Biblical terms such as cherubim, seraphim, archangel, dominions, principalities and powers have at one time or another been ranked in various ways. In *Paradiso*, the final work of his *Divine Comedy*, Dante describes nine ranks of angelic being. Almost all such constructs are more speculative than substantive.

It does appear that in Scripture one angel is deemed of higher rank than all of the others. He is Michael the archangel (Jude 9). He is the captain of God's heavenly armies, who leads them into battle against the hosts of Satan (Rev. 12:7). He is also the one who protects the people of Israel (Dan. 12:1). Michael is the only arch-angel mentioned in the Hebrew canonical Scriptures and in the New Testament. At the same time, the Jewish apocryphal literature, which is included in the Roman Catholic and Orthodox versions of the Old Testament, mentions the names of seven archangels (Tobit 12:15 names Raphael as one of the seven). The New Testament ref-erence to "seven angels who stand before God" (Rev. 8:2) may reflect this Jewish tradition.

The only other angel mentioned by name in both the Hebrew and Greek Scriptures is Gabriel (Dan. 8:16; 9:21; Luke 1:19, 26). Like Michael, Gabriel appears to have an assigned task—to reveal God's future plan of salvation. Specifically, it is Gabriel who reveals important information regarding the coming of Messiah (Dan. 9:27; Luke 1:17, 31-33). Some interpreters regard Gabriel as well as Michael as an archangel (see Daniel 10:13, where Michael is called "*one of* the chief princes").

Angels Possess Limited Powers

Angels are "mighty in power," but that power is not absolute. It is derived from God. For example, there is no evidence that angels ever do anything except by God's command or permission. The angel who killed 185,000 Assyrian soldiers could not have acted apart from divine decree.

Neither can angels be in more than one place at a time. They are not omnipresent, as is God. In Daniel 10:12-13 an angel tells Daniel that he had come to interpret Daniel's vision, but that he was detained for three weeks by an evil angel ("the prince of the Persian kingdom"). Only when Michael came to deliver him was the angelic messenger able to come to Daniel.

Angels Are Free Moral Agents

God has granted angels have the ability either to obey or to dis-obey him. The Scripture speaks of angels who have rebelled against God and fallen from their former estate (Jude 6). These are known as Satan and the demons. Satan is also known as the devil, and was sometimes called Beelzebub (Mark 3:22). He is the most powerful and malicious of the fallen angels.

While these fallen angels can do many things, it would appear that God has prohibited them from assuming bodily form, as do the good angels at times. One indicator of this is the fact that demons are *never* depicted in Scripture as taking on human appearance. Instead, evil angels possess the bodies of humans (Mark 1:23; John 13:27; Acts 19:13-16) or the bodies of animals (Mark 5:11-13).

Unlike fallen human beings, fallen angels have no hope of redemption. Scripture speaks of some of these fallen angels as presently residing in "gloomy dungeons" awaiting their final judgment (2 Pet. 2:4; the Greek word for this abode is *Tartarus*). Many of them, however, are free enough to roam the earth and cause all sorts of trouble. Demons afflict and possess people; Satan "prowls around like a roaring lion looking for someone to devour" (1 Pet. 5:8). In the end, however, they shall all be judged and cast into hell (Rev. 20:10).

Christian tradition views Satan as originally being one of God's greatest creatures. His name was Lucifer (from the Latin translation of Isaiah 14:12; literally, "light-bearing"), a beautiful angel who fell in love with his own beauty and aspired to be like God. Some Christians have interpreted Isaiah 14:12-14 and Ezekiel 28:11-19 as referring to the pride and subsequent fall of Satan from heaven. Revelation 12:7 speaks of Michael expelling Satan and a third of the heavenly host from heaven. From this comes the tradition that when Satan fell he took one-third of the angels (who are now the demons) with him.

Satan has great power. He is so strong that on one occasion even Michael did not dare fight him, but instead said "The Lord rebuke you!" (Jude 9). Martin Luther spoke of Satan's power in his hymn *A Mighty Fortress Is Our God:*

For still our ancient foe
Does seek to work us woe
His craft and power are great
And armed with cruel hate
On earth is not his equal

At the same time, Satan's power is limited like that of any angel. Luther could thus also continue to sing:

The Prince of Darkness grim
We tremble not for him

His rage we can endure
For lo! his doom is sure
One little word shall fell him.

Satan should therefore never be seen as God's alter ego, the evil principle of the universe over against the good. Such an ultimate dualism is part of the ancient Persian religion of Zoroastrianism, but not of the Judeo-Christian worldview. Satan is the alter ego not of God, but of Michael. God alone reigns supreme.

The confidence expressed by Luther in "A Mighty Fortress is our God" was based upon this conviction that God is indeed all-powerful. Despite all the terrible evil in the world, God is firmly in control. Creation has not been abandoned by God; He is working out His purposes through all that happens. This is part of the Christian doctrine of Providence, which is the subject of our next chapter.

Points to Ponder

1. Why is it important to understand the biblical view of creation?

2. What does it mean that God created the world *ex nihilo*?

3. Why do both the Apostles' Creed and the Nicene Creed, which center on Christ, nevertheless begin by affirming God the Father as Creator of Heaven and Earth?

4. The question "Why did God create the world?" may be interpreted in two ways. State these two interpretations?

5. What is the significance of John Piper's statement that "the chief end of man is to glorify God by enjoying Him forever"? Discuss this alteration of the Westminster Catechism in light of this chapter's summary of Jonathan Edwards's essay "A Dissertation Concerning the End for Which God Created the World."

6. According to Edwards, what is the activity of God which most glorifies Him? Explain why this is so.

7. How do Greek dualism and eastern pantheism differ from the biblical view of creation?

8. What do Dialectical Materialism (Marxism) and Atheistic Evolutionism (Darwinism) teach about the nature of the world?

9. Compare and contrast Direct Creationism, Progressive Evolution, and Theistic Evolution as Christian interpretations of the Genesis accounts of creation.

10. What six basic statements about angels are made in the final part of this chapter?

5

The Doctrine of Providence

Providence as a Problem

What Is Providence?

The word "providence" is derived from the Latin *pro videre*, which literally means "foresight." God's activities in His world are neither arbitrary nor ad hoc decisions, but the result of an overall purpose based upon God's ability to foresee all possible outcomes. On the basis of this divine purpose God provides (*pro videre*) for His creatures.

The idea of God providing for His creatures, as opposed to merely allowing us to get along on our own, is central to the meaning of providence. In the Old Testament, for example, Abraham tells Isaac that "God Himself will provide a lamb" for the burnt offering Abraham is about to offer (Gen. 22:8. In the New Testament Jesus assures His followers that God will take care of all their needs, temporal as well as spiritual (Matt. 6:25-34). Paul underscores this when he says that God will supply everything we need (Phil. 4:19).

The doctrine of providence teaches that the creator of heaven and earth not only created but also sustains and governs the world. Furthermore, God's governance of the world operates not merely by means of natural laws set in place when God created the world, but also by means of God's ongoing personal involvement in the world which He has created.

The Scots Confession (1560) expresses this conviction as follows: "We confess and acknowledge one God alone . . . . By whom we confess all things in heaven and earth, visible and invisible, to have been created, to be retained in their being, and to be ruled and guided by His inscrutable providence, for such end as His eternal wisdom, goodness, and justice have appointed, and to the manifestation of His own glory" (chapter 1). The ultimate basis of divine providence, then, is the same as that of creation: the manifestation of God's own glory (see chapter 4, p. 82).

Providence also affirms that it is God *the Father Almighty* who rules and guides His creation. Providence may be "inscrutable," but it is not completely mysterious, because the God who sustains the world is God the Father of our Lord Jesus Christ. The Heidelberg Catechism thus says:

> **Question 27:** What dost thou understand by the providence of God?
>
> **Answer:** The almighty everywhere present power of God, whereby, as it were by His hand, He still *upholds* heaven and earth . . . and *so governs them*, that . . . rain and drought, fruitful and barren years, . . . health and sickness, riches and poverty, yea, all things, come *not by chance*, but by His fatherly hand.

Providence is thus a confession of faith, not of sight (2 Cor. 5:7), whereby the believer affirms: "I do not know what the future holds, but I know who holds the future." The child need not know all that is in the Father's mind in order to trust Him.

What Is the Problem?

The conviction that *all* things, both good and bad, come from the One who is called "Father" creates what may be called the problem of providence. How can one who is both a loving *Father* and *God Almighty* send bad things to His people? Did not Jesus rather speak of God giving *good* things to those who ask (Matt. 7:11)?

This is the famous "trilemma" articulated by the Greek philosopher Epicurus:

- Is [God] willing to prevent evil, but not able? Then He is impotent.
- Is He able, but not willing? Then He is malevolent.
- Is He both able and willing? Whence then is evil?[1]

The writers of the Westminster Confession of Faith felt this tension. Thus they were prompted to set forth what at first glance appears an irreconcilable paradox:

[God's] providence . . . extendeth itself even to the first Fall, and all other sins of angels and men, and that not by a bare permission, but such as hath joined with it a most wise and powerful bounding, and otherwise ordering and governing of them . . . ; yet so, as the sinfulness thereof proceedeth only from the creature, and not from God; who being most holy and righteous, neither is nor can be the author or approver of sin (chapter 5, "Of Providence").

The God who is both all-powerful and a loving Father not merely permits, but has ordained even the evil which men and angels do, yet in such a way as not to be the author of evil. How can this be? The writers of the Westminster Confession do not try to reconcile this paradox. They merely confess their understanding of what Scripture affirms. We shall summarize one theologian's attempt to resolve the problem of providence later in this chapter.

For now, suffice it to say that not everyone within the historic Christian tradition would speak so directly of God's having foreordained all that comes to pass, including evil deeds. This will become apparent as we examine what John Calvin referred to as "general" providence on the one hand, and "special" providence on the other (*Institutes* 1.16.4).

Two Categories of Divine Providence

General Providence

All Christians, together with some non-Christian philosophers both ancient and modern, affirm that God upholds the order of the universe in a general sort of way. God may not direct every detail, but He sustains creation as a whole in that He prevents it from degenerating into chaos.

The concept of "natural law" is central to general providence. For example, God does not intervene directly to cause apples to fall from trees; the law of gravity makes them fall. The universe moves in an orderly fashion because God has ordained laws of nature which govern the movements of everything from galaxies and planets to molecules and atoms.

Natural law has also been applied to matters of morality. Thomas Jefferson, though not a Bible-believing Christian, nevertheless operated from within a historic Christian consensus when he spoke of the "laws of Nature and of Nature's God." These laws in turn formed the basis for what Jefferson called the "self-evident" truth that God had endowed human beings with "certain unalienable Rights" including "Life, Liberty, and the Pursuit of Happiness" (*Unanimous Declaration of the 13 United States of America*, July 4, 1776).

Some would even see natural law as applying to divine judgment of human disobedience. Such a perspective defines the "wrath of God," which Paul says is being revealed against unrighteousness (Rom. 1:18), not as God's personal response of anger against sin, but rather as an impersonal set of consequences which befall human beings when they sin.[2] "We don't break God's laws; they break us" is one way of expressing this impersonal view of divine judgment. The Apostle Paul himself uses a "natural law" metaphor when he says, "A man reaps what he sows" (Gal. 6:7).

What humans choose to call natural law is in fact part of God's work of sustaining the created order. Providence does not operate independently of God, even when God makes use of various means and secondary causes to accomplish His purposes. "Let us therefore believe that God works constantly, so that all created things would perish, if His working were withdrawn" (Augustine, *De Genesis ad litteram* 5.20.40, commenting on John 5:17).[3]

Special Providence

God's personal and all-inclusive governance. While God's general providence in the form of natural laws has been affirmed throughout Christian history, a biblical doctrine of providence does not stop there. God is also personally involved as He acts within creation to accomplish His purposes. God is not concerned merely with the "big picture"; everything and everyone falls under the purview of His providence. Jesus said, "Are not five sparrows sold for two pennies? Yet not one of them is forgotten by God. Indeed, the very hairs of your head are all numbered" (Luke 12:6-7). To which John Wesley added:

> You say you "allow a *general* providence, but deny a *particular* one." And what is a general, of whatever kind it be, that includes no particulars? . . . What, I pray, is a whole that contains no parts? Mere nonsense and contradiction! . . . Do you mean that the providence of God does indeed extend to all parts of the earth, with regard to great and singular events, such as the rise and fall of empires, but that the little concerns of this or that man are beneath the notice of the Almighty? Then you do not consider that *great* and *little* are merely relative terms, which have place only with respect to men. . . . We may then sum up the whole scriptural doctrine of providence in that fine saying of St. Austin [Augustine], *Ita praesident singulis sicut universis, et universis sicut singulis!* [He presides over each creature as if it were the universe, and over the universe as over each individual creature.] (*Sermon 67, "On Providence"*).[4]

Wesley thus affirmed that God was personally involved at all levels of creation, with all creatures great and small. In this respect he echoed the tradition inherited from Christian thinkers such as Irenaeus, Augustine, Aquinas, Luther, and Calvin. On the other hand, Wesley did not interpret divine providence to mean that every single human act was ordained by God. In this way he made a distinction between God's *permissive will* on the one hand, and His *directive will* on the other.

JOHN WESLEY

John Wesley (1703-1791) was the founder of Methodism. The fifteenth child of Samuel and Susannah Wesley, John was educated at Oxford University and ordained in 1728 as a priest in the Church of England. With his younger brother Charles and a few Oxford undergraduates, including George Whitefield, Wesley participated in and eventually led a small group which sought spiritual improvement among the students of Oxford. This "Holy Club" became a model for the small-group meetings which years later would characterize the Wesleyan revivals.

In 1735 John and Charles sailed to the British colony of Georgia to do missionary work among the American Indians and colonists.

The venture was unsuccessful, and when he returned to England in 1738 Wesley wrote: "I went to America to convert the Indians, but, oh, who shall convert me?"

The 1735 voyage to America included a severe storm which left an indelible impression on Wesley. Terrified of death, he noticed that the twenty-one German Moravian Christians on board remained unafraid during the ordeal. When Wesley returned to London three years later he was introduced to another Moravian, Peter Boehler, who convinced Wesley that the fear he had felt on the voyage to America showed he did not truly trust in Christ. From that point on Wesley sought for the faith of Boehler and the Moravians, a faith which would give him assurance of salvation.

On May 24, 1738, Wesley attended a religious meeting at a chapel on Aldersgate Street in London. There he listened to a reading from Luther's preface to Paul's Epistle to the Romans. Wesley described his experience in his journal as follows: "About a quarter before nine, while [the reader] was describing the change which God works in the heart through faith in Christ, I felt my heart strangely warmed. I felt I did trust in Christ, Christ alone for salvation; and an assurance was given me that he had taken away *my* sins, even *mine*, and saved *me* from the law of sin and death."

From that time onward Wesley sensed that God had called him to evangelize Great Britain, which he viewed as populated with Church-going unbelievers such as he had been. In 1739 he began preaching out of doors to working-class people. When chided by Church officials for not confining his preaching to the parish pulpit, Wesley replied, "I look upon all the world as my parish!"*

Wesley's preaching, along with that of George Whitefield and the hymns written by John's brother Charles, led to the greatest revival in the history of English-speaking Christianity. The Wesleyan revival led not only to the conversion of tens of thousands, but to social reforms which included the eventual abolition of slavery in England in 1833, due in great part to the efforts of Wesley's converts William Wilberforce and John Newton. Some historians are convinced that had it not been for Wesley's preaching, England would have experienced its own version of the bloody French Revolution of 1789.

---

* Letter to James Hervey, dated March 20, 1739. Cited in Philip Watson, ed., *The Message of the Wesleys,* 27.

The Permissive will of God. Wesley viewed man as "an intelligent and free spirit, capable of choosing either good or evil." Consequently, God does not direct every human act, but rather "commands all things . . . to assist man . . . in working out his own salvation, so far as it can be done without compulsion, without overruling his liberty." Providence thus works so as "to afford every man every possible help . . . which can be done without turning man into a machine."[5] In like manner Albert Outler, writing from within Wesley's Methodist tradition, insists that "Providence does not mean the divine predetermination of historical events. It means rather the provision that such events may be affected by reason, grace, and hope."[6]

The directive will of God. Calvin, on the other hand, followed in the footsteps of Augustine, who a thousand years earlier had emphasized humanity's bondage to sin, as opposed to what Wesley called "liberty." For this reason Calvin affirmed without hesitation that under God's providential rule "nothing takes place by chance." God does not merely foreknow what will happen and thus permit it; He decrees everything that happens. This is true of human activity as well as natural events (Institutes 1.16.4). The writers of the Westminster Confession followed Calvin in affirming that even sinful deeds occur "not by bare permission," but rather by God's "governing" them (above, p. 105). To do otherwise, they reasoned, would put certain events beyond God's control and thus undermine the doctrine of God's sovereignty.

JOHN CALVIN

John Calvin (1509-1564) was born near Paris, but gained his reputation in Geneva, Switzerland. His *Institutes of the Christian Religion* was the first systematic presentation of Reformed Protestantism to be written, and set a standard unsurpassed by any of his successors.

The young Calvin first studied law, then literature, excelling at both. His first published work, a commentary of Seneca's *De Clementia*, appeared in 1532. Soon afterward he was exposed to the doctrines of Luther and other Reformation writers. Scholars know little of the circumstances surrounding his conversion from the Catholic faith to Protestantism, due to Calvin's reticence to write on the subject. We do know that Calvin helped his friend Nicolas Cop to prepare the speech Cop delivered when he was installed as rector of the University of Paris on November 1, 1533. The address included a demand for reforms such as those advocated by Luther, and led to an outburst of anti-Protestant sentiment which forced both Cop and Calvin to flee Paris.

Three years later, at the age of twenty-six, Calvin published the first of four editions of his *Institutes* (the final edition appeared five years before his death). Shortly thereafter he sought refuge from persecution in Strasbourg, but had to travel through Geneva to avoid capture by French officials. He planned to stay in Geneva only one night, but was urged by the Protestant preacher Guillaume Farel to stay and help the progress of the Reformation in that Swiss city. When Calvin demurred Farel made him an offer he could not refuse, calling down the curse of God upon him if he left Geneva.

Calvin and Farel sought to reform not only the Church, but also the notoriously immoral social climate in Geneva. For their efforts they were forced to leave the city. Calvin then went to Strasbourg, where his fame as a biblical scholar was established throughout Europe. He returned to Geneva in 1541 at the request of the city council, which sought Calvin's help in resisting the Catholic Church's attempts to return the city to papal authority. Calvin resumed his efforts to reform Geneva, this time with success, though not without opposition. His enemies viewed him as a tyrant and a theocrat. The Scottish reformer John Knox, on the other hand, considered Calvin's Geneva the closest thing to heaven on earth.

During this time Calvin held no government position, but was able to institute his reforms by moral and spiritual persuasion. He preached several times a week, wrote commentaries on almost every book of the Bible, and corresponded by letter with Protestants throughout Europe. His rigorous self-discipline eventually took its toll. Never a healthy man, Calvin developed stomach ulcers and died on May 27, 1564, six weeks before his fifty-fifth birthday.

Calvin's influence upon future generations went beyond the bounds of merely religious concerns. His emphasis on God's sovereign rule over all of human history led him and his followers to write on matters of politics, science, and history, as well as religion. The fact that the *Institutes* is the only Protestant book included in the Encyclopedia Britannica's series of *Great Books of the Western World* testifies to Calvin's ongoing influence upon Western thought and culture.

Is God therefore the author of sin? Calvin's refusal to make a fundamental distinction between God's permitting evil and ordaining evil raises the question of whether God is indeed a malevolent God, to use the language of Epicurus. As we have already seen, the Westminster divines insisted that God's absolute sovereignty did not make Him "the author of sin." They had obviously heard objections to their view of God's absolute sovereignty such as those raised earlier by Epicurus and later by Wesley and Outler.

It is apparent, however, that the phrase "the author of sin" had a special meaning for those who wrote the Westminster Confession. For God to ordain even sinful deeds must be distinguished from God's being the *author* of those deeds. This distinction has to do with the ultimate purposes of God on the one hand, and the purposes of human beings and evil angels (Satan and the demons) on the other.

Jonathan Edwards, writing a century after the Westminster Confession, made explicit this distinction between God's ordaining evil and being the author of evil. Edwards (who corresponded across the Atlantic with Wesley and greatly admired the Methodist preacher) distinguished between the purposes for which sinners do evil on the one hand, and the purpose for which God ordains men's evil deeds on the other. "God decrees that [the acts of sinners] shall be sinful, for the sake of the good that he causes to arise from the sinfulness thereof; whereas man decrees them for the sake of the evil that is in them."[7] For a human being to decree and commit sin for the sake of evil is to be an author of sin. God, on the other hand, ordains sinful acts for the sake of the greatest good in the universe, which is His own glory. Consequently the term "author of sin" is not used of God, since His ultimate purposes are good and not evil.

We may summarize the differences between the Augustinian-Calvinist view of special providence and that of John Wesley as follows:

Wesley, like Calvin, affirmed that God's providence extends to all kinds of events and creatures, whether great or small. Unlike Calvin, Wesley believed special providence includes both God's directive will (commanding that certain things happen) and God's permissive will (allowing certain things to happen). God never violates what Wesley calls the liberty of human beings.

Calvin saw no ultimate difference between God's ordaining something and God's permitting it. If God could foresee all things that would happen even before He created the world (a proposition which Wesley would not deny), then for God to permit evil deeds was equivalent to saying that God had ordained them in the first place. For did not God create the world in which these evil deeds occur? And could not God have done otherwise, had He willed to do so?

We may say, then, that Wesley and Calvin agreed on the *scope* of providence (which extends to all kinds of particular things), but not the *degree* of God's providential governance (which for Calvin places every single thing under God's directive will, but for Wesley does not).

Some view the Calvinist doctrine of providence as unduly narrow and even fatalistic. Whether or not Calvin was right, however, his teaching (along with Wesley's) must be distinguished from fatalism, as well as from other alternatives to the biblical doctrine of providence. We shall now examine three of these alternatives.

Alternatives to the Biblical Doctrine of Providence

Fatalism

"Fate" may be defined as a force which determines everything people do and experience. Ancient Greek mythology depicted the Fates as three old women who weaved the destinies of humans and even of the gods. Astrology teaches that an individual's destiny has been determined by the stars. Fatalism views the ultimate force or forces affecting our lives as impersonal and totally beyond our control.

The Greek dramatist Sophocles set forth one of the great expositions of the meaning of fate in his play *Oedipus Rex*, written around 429 B.C. The story concerns Oedipus, King of Thebes, whose parents receive a prophecy prior to his birth that the boy will kill his father Laius and marry his mother Jocasta. Laius therefore orders one of his servants to abandon his infant son Oedipus on a mountainside to die. The servant, however, gives the infant to an old man, who raises the boy. Years later Oedipus encounters Laius by chance. The two men quarrel and Oedipus kills Laius without knowing his identity. Oedipus eventually becomes King of Thebes and marries Laius's widow Jocasta—his own mother!

Some time after this a plague comes upon the city, and a prophecy attributes this misfortune to the fact that the murderer of Laius still lives. Oedipus, a righteous king concerned for his subjects, sets out to determine who killed Laius in order to stop the plague. He eventually cross-examines the servant whom Laius commanded to abandon the infant Oedipus. The servant, explaining why he did not leave the son of Laius to die, explains. "I pitied [the child], master [Oedipus], and thought [the old man] would take him away to another land, the one from which he came. If you are he [whom I gave to the old man], you were born curst by *fate.*"[8] Whereupon Oedipus blinds himself and stands in the end as a tragic figure, doomed to his destiny despite his virtue and the efforts of his parents to avoid their own fate.

At least two stark differences stand out between the Greek concept of fate found in *Oedipus Rex* and the biblical view of divine providence:

- Whereas fate is impersonal, divine providence is intensely personal. Poor Oedipus was cursed by forces beyond his control and even beyond the control of the gods, who could only execute the judgments to which fate had destined him. Jesus, on the other hand, spoke of God as a personal heavenly Father who is concerned for his children. To be sure, sinners are in the hands of an "angry God," as Jonathan Edwards said in his most famous sermon. But God's judgment is not an impersonal process; it is personal, and may be suspended by human repentance (Jon. 3:10; Acts 2:38). For Oedipus, however, repentance and forgiveness were not possible in a fatalistic universe.

- The fate of Oedipus chiefly concerned his ultimate destiny. God's providential workings are concerned not only with the end result, but also with the entire process of our getting there. Oedipus was doomed no matter what he or anybody else did; he was at the mercy of inexorable fate. Providence, on the other hand, emphasizes God's continual guidance of our lives and our responsibility to respond to

His personal care. The integrity and honor displayed by Oedipus counted for nothing. The Christian's faithful obedience counts for everything in the sight of God.

The Christian doctrine of providence, far from being fatalistic, was a liberating force in those parts of the ancient world which saw human life as being governed by the Fates, the stars, the planets, or simply random chance. "The stars . . . are not the fate of Christ, but Christ is the fate of the stars" (Augustine, *De Genesis ad litteram* 2.17.35; see also *The City of God* Book 5, chapter 1, where Augustine argues that God, not fate or the stars, brought about the collapse of Rome).[9]

Deism

This is the worldview which was held by several of the founding fathers of the United States, including Benjamin Franklin and Thomas Jefferson. It emphasizes the role of natural law in the governance of the universe.

Deism arose in seventeenth-century Europe as a result of Sir Isaac Newton's theories of mechanics. Newton was able to reduce many of the workings of nature to mathematical formulas. As a result, philosophers and theologians increasingly viewed the universe as a perfectly functioning clock that God had started and then allowed to continue running on its own. Thus God was not personally involved within the workings of the world, which were governed by laws of nature such as those which Newton had discovered.

At the heart of Deism was a philosophical dualism between spirit and matter. God is spirit; the world is material. By its very nature matter is at best fallible and at worst evil; only God can be perfectly good. When confronted with natural disasters and diseases which took countless human lives, deists defended God's perfect goodness by explaining that the world is as perfect as is possible, taking into account that it is made of finite, fallible matter. The German philosopher and theologian Leibniz declared that "among the infinite number of possible series [of events in the universe] God has selected the best, and that consequently this best universe is that which actually exists" (*A Vindication of God's Justice*, paragraph 41).[10] The phrase "best of all possible worlds" was used by Deists to explain why bad things sometimes happened to good people. Alexander Pope was later to express this perspective in his *Essay on Man* with the words "Whatever is, is right."

Deism's dualistic perspective falls short of the biblical doctrine of creation, which affirms the intrinsic goodness of the material world and flatly says that many things which are, are wrong. In addition, Deism fails to account for the sheer magnitude of evil. This was the point made by the eighteenth-century French writer Voltaire, who ridiculed the notion that this is the best of all possible worlds in his biting satirical novella *Candide*.

Pantheism

Whereas deism is dualistic, pantheism is ultimately monistic, in that it sees God and the world as being of the same essence. Since for the pantheist "all is God," it would seem to follow that everything which takes place is "the will of God." This in turn sounds much like Pope's "Whatever is, is right." Thus monistic pantheism and dualistic deism arrive at the same conclusion from radically different premises.

At the same time, however, for a pantheist to speak of "the will of God" is an exercise in what may be called weasel-wording. This is because the words "will of God" speak of a personal deity, since "will" or volition is a function of personality. But pantheism views God, the ultimate reality, as an impersonal all-inclusiveness which cannot will, purpose, or govern anything. Such distinctions presuppose the personal God revealed in the Bible.

EXCURSUS: A MODERN-DAY RABBI'S RESPONSE TO AN AGE-OLD PROBLEM

In addition to fatalism, deism, and pantheism, a more recent alternative to the historic Christian doctrine of providence is the view that God's governance of human affairs is limited to what may be termed the "spiritual" parts of our lives. Such a restricted view of divine providence is apparently held by many, considering the widespread success of Rabbi Harold Kushner's best-selling book of 1981, *When Bad Things Happen to Good People*.[11]

In addition to fatalism, deism, and pantheism, a more recent alternative to the historic Christian doctrine of providence is the view that God's governance of human affairs is limited to what may be termed the "spiritual" parts of our lives. Such a restricted view of divine providence is apparently held by many, considering the widespread success of Rabbi Harold Kushner's best-selling book of 1981, *When Bad Things Happen to Good People.*[11]

Kushner, whose son died of progeria at age fourteen, endeavors to confront the problem of suffering by reexamining the Epicurean trilemma. Like many before him, Kushner sees only two possible answers to what has been called the problem of evil: either God is able to stop suffering but does not will to do so (and is therefore cruel), or God is willing to stop suffering but is unable to do so (and is therefore limited in power).

Kushner opts for the second alternative: "God can't do everything" (113). Specifically, God is limited "by laws of nature and by the evolution of human nature and moral freedom" (134). Thus God cannot make sickness go away because natural laws which govern sickness are "inflexible" (134), and God "has set Himself the limit that He will not take away our freedom, including our freedom to hurt ourselves and others around us" (81).

The world, then, is not fully under God's control. So, why pray?

Kushner responds that some prayers are indeed inconsistent with God's nature, such as prayers for miracles (since God will not violate His inflexible natural laws). On the other hand, prayers for what may be called "spiritual" concerns are entirely proper. For example, prayer is designed to put us in touch with other people (119) and with God (122), and to give us strength to cope with problems (127), as opposed to removing them.

Kushner's God is unlike the God of Deism in that He is concerned with our daily lot. God is not aloof or unconcerned; God cares for us and gives us spiritual comfort. But such a God, in the end, can *do* very little. This is hardly consistent with the biblical affirmation that "with God nothing shall be impossible" (Luke 1:37).

In addition, Kushner's attempt to resolve the problem of evil by limiting the scope of divine providence ends up removing, rather than resolving, the Epicurean trilemma. For the problem is that God *is able* to prevent evil, but does not do so. If, on the other hand, the world merely *is* the way it is and is beyond God's control, what is the problem? Whatever exists is simply a part of a long evolutionary process, without any moral significance. The implication appears to be very much like Pope's "Whatever is, is right."

So in the end Kushner eliminates the problem of evil by eliminating moral evil itself. Yet this is precisely what the rabbi does not wish to do. He is a man whose sense of moral outrage is keen, and who very much wants to combat, and not merely accept, the evils of this world. The ultimate irony of Kushner's "spiritual" providence, then, is the he has created a god whose existence would trivialize his grief over the loss of his fourteen-year-old son.

Benefits of the Doctrine of Providence

Properly understood, the doctrine of providence can free us from all worries. This is because the Christian, in rejecting the idea of chance, places himself in the care of a heavenly Father who "so holds all things in His power, so rules by His authority and will, so governs by His wisdom, that nothing can befall except he determine it" (Calvin, *Institutes* 1.17.11). From this conviction flows a twofold assurance which responds to the anguish of Job, who suffered despite the fact that God deemed him more righteous than any man on earth (Job 1:8, 2:3). Specifically, Job's suffering prompted him to ponder two questions which have puzzled people from time immemorial: why the righteous suffer, and why the wicked prosper.

Why Do the Righteous Suffer?

The first assurance which the doctrine of providence brings to the believer is that God is in control. The believer may therefore rest in the fact that "all things come, not by chance, but by His Fatherly hand" (Heidelberg Catechism; see above, p. 104).

Strictly speaking, the conviction that "in all things God works for the good of those who love Him" (Rom. 8:28) does not explain the reason behind any particular episode of suffering. The Bible has no "theodicy of particulars" (a *theodicy* is an explanation of why God deals with people the way He does). No one can say to another person with certainty, "You are undergoing this affliction because _____." Neither does the Bible make a necessary connection between suffering and disobedience to the will of God. Scripture and everyday experience both testify that bad things do indeed happen to good people as well as to the wicked.

The testimony of Scripture indicates that God ordains or permits human suffering (depending upon one's perspective) for three reasons:

- Affliction may be the judgment of God upon evildoers. The plagues which God sent upon Egypt are the single greatest instance of this found in Scripture (Exod. 7-11).

- Affliction may be divine discipline sent by the heavenly Father upon His wayward children, or even upon those who appear to be following God more or less faithfully. In such instances, suffering is redemptive, not punitive (as is judgment). "We *must* go through many hardships to enter the kingdom of God" (Acts 14:22). "The Lord disciplines those He loves" (Heb. 12:6).

- Affliction may come to us as a result of our being caught in the middle of spiritual warfare taking place in the invisible realm of God's creation, as indicated in the first two chapters of the book of Job. The reader knows Job is neither being judged nor disciplined at this point of the narrative. Rather, God permits Satan to afflict Job as a means to a greater good: the manifestation of God's glory. For when Job refuses to curse God despite losing his wealth (chapter 1) and his health (chapter 2), he thereby testifies that God is more valuable to him than anything he possesses, despite Satan's words to the contrary (1:9, 2:4).

The Christian can be assured that the first reason for human suffering, divine judgment, does not apply in his or her case. "There is no condemnation for those who are in Christ Jesus" (Rom. 8:1). This is because Christ, "who knew no sin, became sin for us" (2 Cor. 5:21). We shall delve further into the mystery of Christ's saving death in chapter 9.

On the other hand, Christians can have no certain knowledge of the ultimate reason why any specific instance of suffering may come their way. Affliction may, or may not, be God's rod of discipline in response to specific sins. The three friends of Job, following the conventional wisdom of their day, presumed that Job's suffering was due to his having sinned against God or his fellow man. Job insisted that he had done no such thing—and Job was right.

Job went on to say, however, that since he had done no wrong, God was not being fair by allowing him to suffer. Here Job made a leap in logic, due to the fact that he was unaware of the encounter between God and Satan which preceded his suffering (Job 1-2). He presumed to know more than he actually knew, which is why God finally called him to accounts for claiming to know things he could not know (Job 38-41).

Why, then, do the righteous suffer? There is no single, all-encompassing answer to this most difficult of questions—unless one replies that in the end, God Himself is the answer. This appears to be Job's conclusion of the matter (Job 42:5-6).

Why Do the Wicked Prosper?

What troubled Job even more than His own suffering was the fact that all too often, wicked people go on their merry way through life and die full of years with a smile on their face. "Why do the wicked live on, growing old and increasing in power?" (Job 21:7). The fact that "the rod of God is not upon them" (21:9) made it appear to Job as though God were merely arbitrary in his actions towards humanity.

Divine providence, on the other hand, includes not only what God has done and continues to do, but also what God *will* do in the future. In particular, the doctrine of God's final judgment of the wicked assures us that in the end the scales of justice will be balanced. "Multitudes who sleep in the dust of the earth will awake: some to everlasting life, others to shame and everlasting contempt" (Dan. 12:2). "If anyone's name was not found written in the book of life, he was thrown into the lake of fire" (Rev. 20:15). The unrighteous shall not prevail, but will be judged "to the praise of [God's] glorious justice" (*Westminster Confession* 3.7).

In the meantime, however, suffering continues for God's people. The doctrine of providence is a reminder that from God's standpoint, the spiritual maturity forged through the fires of suffering is more important than any transitory comforts of this life.

Why Pray?

Yet another question which arises in connection with the doctrine of providence has to do with prayer. If God is totally in control of all that comes to pass, why bother to pray? God has already determined, or at least already knows, what will happen. What good are our paltry prayers in the process of providence?

Christians throughout the centuries have recognized that prayer, far from being superfluous, is "the chief exercise of faith . . . by which we daily receive God's benefits" (Calvin, *Institutes* 3.20.1). In other words, it makes no more sense to ask "Why pray for God's continued blessings?" than to ask "Why believe in Christ in order to be saved?" Prayer, as an expression of faith, is the primary *means* by which God accomplishes the goals of His providential rule. "God's providence does not always meet us in naked form, but God in a sense clothes it with the means employed" (Calvin, *Institutes* 1.17.4). If divine providence includes natural means such as the law of gravity to accomplish its ends, how much more does it include the spiritual means of prayer!

Furthermore, the assertion that God is totally in control of all that comes to pass strengthens, rather than undermines, the biblical affirmation that God answers prayer (Matt. 7:7-11; James 5:16). If God is in control of all things, then any prayer we utter may be God's means to a particular goal. Of course, we cannot know this for sure in any particular instance (since the Bible teaches no "theodicy of particulars," as we have already noted). Whether or not God will indeed use a specific prayer to achieve His ends is God's business, not ours. We are called not to know all things, but to obey in all things. And that obedience includes prayer.

On the other hand, suppose for a moment that God is *not* in control of all that comes to pass, but must wait for people to act before He can act. If this be so, how can God ever use our prayers as the means to His ends? Whether or not our prayers are answered ultimately depends not upon God's will, but upon the will of the people for whom we pray. This in turn means that *in principle* there can be no such thing as efficacious prayer. It may make us feel better to pray for loved ones who are ill or who are having trouble along life's road, but such prayers can never *accomplish* anything. Thus the conviction that God is absolutely sovereign, far from making intercessory prayer superfluous, is the basis for all such prayers.

As we have seen both in this chapter and the previous one, any discussion of God's creating and sustaining activity in the world ultimately centers itself upon what God has done and continues to do in relation to human beings. This is because, as noted in the previous chapter humanity is the crown of God's creation. The doctrine of humanity thus deserves further elaboration within the context of God's creation and providential rule. That is the subject of our next chapter.

Points To Ponder

1. Define "providence" in your own words.

2. What is the "problem of providence"?

3. How does "general providence" differ from "special providence"?

4. Compare and contrast Calvin's and Wesley's views on special providence. How are they alike? How are they different?

5. How does providence differ from fatalism?

6. Why did the deist Alexander Pope say "Whatever is, is right"?

7. Can a pantheist meaningfully say that all things which happen are the will of God? Why or why not?

8. What are the two questions asked by Job which are answered by the biblical doctrine of providence? How are they answered?

9. According to Rabbi Harold Kushner, why do bad things happen to good people?

6

The Doctrine of Humanity, Part One: Humanity as Created in the Image of God (*Imago Dei*)

The Biblical Foundation of the *Imago Dei*

The Creation of Humanity in Genesis 1 and 2

In chapter 4 we noted that the first chapter of Genesis depicts the creation of humanity as qualitatively different from every other aspect of creation. The threefold use of the Hebrew verb *barah* ("created") in Genesis 1:27 indicates that the difference between humanity and the rest of creation is as great as the difference between something and nothing (Gen. 1:1) and the difference between conscious life and unconscious life (Gen. 1:21). This fundamental difference between humanity and the rest of creation is further underscored when the biblical writer says that God created humanity in "the image of God."

At the same time, however, the text says that God *created* humanity in the divine image. Humanity is a part of creation, not a part of God. Humanity therefore may be said to consist of both natural and spiritual aspects.

Natural humanity. Scripture clearly indicates that however one interprets the phrase "image of God," it does not mean that human beings are part of God or an emanation from God. Such a teaching has more in common with pantheism and its more recent "New Age" progeny than with biblical anthropology.

Genesis 2:7 specifically states that "God formed the man from the dust of the ground." The first man, Adam, was not merely a spiritual being like the angels. On one level, he was of the same stuff as the rest of creation. Indeed, there is a play on words in the original Hebrew here: "God formed the man (*adam*; hence the name Adam) from the dust of the ground (*adamah*)."

The first chapter of Genesis likewise links humanity with the rest of God's natural creation, albeit in a more implicit manner than does Genesis 2. Specifically, the writer of Genesis 1 places the creation of humanity on the sixth day, the same day God created the animals which live on land (as opposed to birds and sea creatures, which appear on the fifth day). In this way humanity is put on the same level as the rest of the animal kingdom: a material creation fundamentally different from the Creator.

Spiritual humanity. Yet while humanity is fundamentally different from God, Genesis 1 states that in some way human beings are created like God: "God created man in his own image" (Gen. 1:27). The difference between humanity and the animal kingdom is underscored here both by the threefold use of the Hebrew *barah* ("created," as opposed to "God made the wild animals" in Genesis 1:25; see chapter 4, p. 94), and by the phrase "image of God," which is used only of humanity.

The second chapter of Genesis likewise depicts humanity as unique among God's creatures—the crowning achievement of God's creation. For example, only humanity carries on verbal communication with the Creator. In addition, the Genesis 2 narrative begins with the creation of the man and ends with the creation of the woman, with the plants and animals sandwiched in between. In this way the rest of creation is depicted as being created for humanity. The same idea is found in Genesis 1:28, where humanity is given dominion over the rest of creation.

Theological Interpretations of the *Imago Dei*

The biblical phrase "image of God" has been the subject of theological reflection throughout the history of the Church. What is it about human beings that makes us, and us alone, creatures who are like God? Let us examine several interpretations of this expression which have been articulated throughout the history of Christian doctrine.

The Human Body as the Image of God

Some have interpreted the phrase "image of God" quite literally, saying that something about the physical appearance of human beings makes us like God. This view has never been accepted as orthodox among Christians, since Scripture teaches that God is a spirit and does not have a body. The modern Church of Jesus Christ of Latter Day Saints (the Mormons), on the other hand, has no problem in defining the image of God in terms of the human body. This is because Mormons believe God is, in fact, a glorified man with a human body.[1]

At the same time, the uniqueness of the human body, over against the rest of the animal kingdom, is all too often minimized or ignored. This is due in large part to modern evolutionary theory's attempts to establish direct ancestry between humans and primates. Nevertheless, some recent biological and psychological studies have emphasized the unique features of what one writer has called "the amazing body human." Among all the members of the animal kingdom, for example:

- Only humans are designed to walk on two legs, and have both hands and feet.

- Only humans have faces which vary so greatly in appearance that we can identify one another by looking at our faces.

- Only humans can blush, showing embarrassment.

- Only humans make love face to face.

- Only humans have a brain with a speech center.[2]

It is not surprising that John Calvin said, "God's glory shines forth in the outer man . . . ." He went on to add, however, that "there is no doubt that the proper seat of his image is in the soul" (*Institutes* 1.15.3). Here Calvin was repeating the consensus handed down through over a thousand years of Church history, that the *imago dei* refers to one or more characteristics of humanity's non-physical makeup, or soul.

The Human Soul as the Image of God

Those faculties or capacities of the human soul which reflect something of who God is, and thus make humanity the "image" or "likeness" of God, are usually divided into three categories. These are humanity's *natural* capacities, *moral* capacities, and *spiritual* capacities.

Natural capacities include non-moral traits which correspond to several of God's communicable attributes (see chapter 3, p. 60). Among these would be human reason, creativity, and freedom.

Within the scientific community, for example, humanity is classified as *homo sapiens*, the thinking or reasoning being. This in turn reflects a perspective on human reason common within the philosophical tradition of Aristotle. Thomas Aquinas said "intellectual creatures alone, properly speaking, are made in God's image" (*Summa Theologiae* 1. 93. 2). This emphasis on the rational human being as most clearly reflecting the *imago dei* was most forcefully expressed in the Rationalist wing of the Enlightenment, the great eighteenth-century philosophical movement which continues to influence both Christian theology and the general culture in significant ways.

Another wing of the Enlightenment, embodied by the French philosopher Jean-Jacques Rousseau, was Romanticism. Theologies which spring from the Romantic mindset speak of human creativity and freedom as those faculties most expressive of the divine image. The creative artist, not the scientist, most clearly expresses the godlike in humanity.

Such natural capacities as reason, creativity, and freedom may also be called *self*-directed. They involve the individual acting alone, as it were, with neither other people nor God as their primary focus.

Moral capacities, on the other hand, are those exercised in relationship with other human beings. They may therefore be labeled other-directed, as opposed to merely self-directed. The moral faculties of conscience and the judicial sentiment, discussed in the first chapter of this book, are human characteristics which Christians have regarded as the image of God. Human free will, insofar as it relates to our moral behavior towards others, likewise belongs under the heading of moral capacities, since freedom of the will includes the liberty to choose between good and evil (the tree of life and the tree of the knowledge of good and evil; Gen. 2:9, 17).

Spiritual capacities are those which enable human beings, and only human beings, to think and act in relationship with their Creator. Such God-directed capacities are best exemplified in the universal human need to worship God. As noted in chapter 1, this *sensus divinitatus*, or "sense of God," is an exclusively human characteristic. John Wesley observed that we "have no ground to believe that [animals] are, in any degree, capable of knowing, loving, or obeying God. This is the specific difference between man and brute; the great gulf which they cannot pass over."[3] We therefore feel no compulsion to take our dogs or cats to worship services, nor do they feel slighted when we do not take them.

Throughout the history of Christian doctrine the majority of theologians have defined the *imago dei* as relating to faculties of the human soul common to all human beings. Whether speaking of natural (self-directed), moral (other-directed), or spiritual (God-directed) faculties, discussions of the divine image have by and large emphasized how individual human beings exhibit Godlike characteristics in their nonphysical existence.

More recently, Karl Barth has broken ranks with this tradition and proposed a model which speaks of the *imago dei* in what may be called relational, as opposed to individual, terms. Barth's view of the divine image, though somewhat unconventional, merits examination as a fresh contribution to the ongoing dialogue within historic Christian belief.

Barth's View of Human Relationships as the Image of God

In Genesis 1:27 we read: "So God created man in his own image, in the image of God he created him; male and female he created them." Barth sees the phrase "male and female he created them" as defining the previous two lines of Genesis 1:27, so that to be created in God's image is somehow connected with humanity's being created as male and female. Barth thereby defines the image of God not in terms of what humanity is or does, but in terms of the fact that God has called people to exist in personal relationship with one another (*Church Dogmatics* 3.1, 183-187).

EXCURSUS: HUMANITY AS MALE AND FEMALE

Genesis 1:27 speaks of the creation of humanity as "male and female." In Genesis 2 Adam fails to find a suitable companion among the animals. Only when God creates the woman from Adam's rib does he recognize one who can serve as a suitable companion to help him carry out God's designs for humanity.

It would therefore appear that a biblical doctrine of humanity must center itself not merely upon individual human beings with no regard to sexual identity, but upon humanity created as male and female. Karl Barth's relational definition of the divine image attempts to counter a tendency within historic Christian belief to define humanity in terms of the man, and therefore to define the woman in terms of the man, as opposed to defining both in terms of God's design for humanity as set forth in Genesis 1 and 2.

Such male-centered discussions of humanity are epitomized in Thomas Aquinas's discussion of "the production of the woman" (*Summa Theologiae* 1. 92. 1-4). Thomas echoed Aristotle's conviction that the woman was a "misbegotten male" and said that she was naturally subject to the man because "the discretion of reason predominates" in the man. The woman's deficiency of reason in turn became the basis for Satan's tempting Eve rather than Adam.

Why, then, did God create the woman? In order to fulfill nature's original intention of procreation (Gen. 1:28), said Thomas. The unmarried Thomas saw little function for the woman beyond that of procreation.

Quotations from second- and third-century postapostolic teachers take a much more nuanced view than does Thomas's Aristotelian hierarchy of the sexes. To be sure, we do not find modern notions of egalitarianism in the post-apostolic fathers (otherwise, there would probably have been a few post-apostolic mothers as well!). Nonetheless, the notion of the female as a "misbegotten male" is utterly foreign to teachers such as Clement of Alexandria. Around A.D. 200 Clement wrote: "The virtue of man and woman is the same. For if the God of both is one, the master of both is also one; one Church, one temperance, one modesty: Their food is common, marriage an equal yoke . . . . And those whose life is common, have common graces and a common salvation, common to them are love and training" (*The Instructor* 1.4).[*]

Elsewhere Clement wrote that a woman's "nature" was not the same as a man's, but only with regard to the physical functions of pregnancy and childbearing. On the other hand, "there is a sameness, as far as respects the soul, [so that] she will attain to the same virtue" (*Miscellanies* 4.8).**

The difference between Clement's perspective and that of Thomas Aquinas a millennium later may have something to do with Thomas's failure to discuss the role of the woman in relation to God's design for the family and society at large. For Thomas, the woman was defined as a "helper" to the man (Gen. 2:18), solely as a bearer of children, since in all other respects another man could have "helped" Adam as well or better than did Eve. Clement, on the other hand, saw the woman as complementing the role of the man both within the family and society at large. To be sure, the husband was the head of the household, responsible for its overall spiritual direction. The wife, on the other hand, was given primary charge of the children and the management of the household, two responsibilities prized in the early Church (if not by our modern postindustrial society).

Clement's Latin contemporary Tertullian, often characterized as a male chauvinist of sorts, nevertheless appears to have been a happily married man. He noted, for example, that Christian husbands and wives pray, work, and fast together, teach, exhort, and support one another (*To His Wife* 2.8).*** For Tertullian, the role of husband as head of the family did not rule out his receiving teaching and support from his wife. To the

contary, she was a helper in every sense of the word, as opposed to Thomas's "misbegotten male" whose only helping role was one of procreation.

Clement and Tertullian thus portray the roles of men and women in terms of their personal relationships to one another, as Karl Barth sought to do when he defined the *imago dei* as the creation of man as male and female. At the same time, the postapostolic fathers go beyond Barth in defining male and female in their relationship not only to each other, but to the family and society as well.

Barth's relational model of the image of God has something to teach us about how men and women should relate to one another. Perhaps Clement and Tertullian can take us beyond Barth's concern with how men and women should relate to each other as individuals, to how men and women should relate as partners towards the family and society. In the highly individualistic culture of modern North America, where individual rights increasingly take precedence over family and community responsibilities, this would be no small feat.

---

* *The Ante-Nicene Fathers*, vol. 2, 211.
** Ibid., 420.
*** *The Ante-Nicene Fathers*, vol. 4, 48.

Here the trinitarian emphasis which runs through Barth's theology comes to the fore. He sees human relationships in general, and the marriage relationship in particular, as an image of the fact that God exists on the high order of Trinity, three persons eternally in relationship as one essence or substance. Just as God's being is characterized by relationship (as evidenced by Genesis 1:26, "Let *us* make man in *our* image"), even so God created humanity to be in relationship. This is what Barth means by the *imago dei*: human beings, like God, exhibit diversity within unity, of which the male-female relationship is the supreme (though by no means the only) example.

While Barth's exegesis of Genesis 1:27 has been questioned by many, his relational view of the *imago dei* offers a challenging counterpoint to the aforementioned individualistic interpretations, which have dominated the theological landscape throughout most of Christian history. Human beings were not created merely as individuals with various godlike capacities. Human beings were created to be in relationship both with God and with one another.

Barth's relational view of the divine image in humanity is, despite its novel aspects, similar to the classical models in that it defines the word "image" as "resemblance." For Barth, humanity *resembles* the Creator in some way. Recent interpretations of Genesis 1:26-28, on the other hand, offer yet another alternative to both the classical and Barthian models. This alternative defines the *imago dei* not as humanity's resemblance of God, but as humanity's function as God's *representative* to the rest of creation.

A Representative View of the Divine Image

This view approaches the phrase "image of God" not as a theological problem, but a textual problem. That is, what is there in the immediate context of Genesis 1:27 that might shed light on the meaning of this phrase?

The answer lies on either side of verse 27. In verse 26 God says "Let us make man in our image," whereupon He immediately adds, "and let them rule over [the rest of creation]." Then in verse 28 God's blessing of humanity includes the command to "rule over" the rest of creation. The fact that human "rule" or "dominion" (KJV) is so closely connected with the divine image has led many Old Testament scholars to conclude that "the image of God" refers to not what people are, but what we are called to *do*: exercise dominion as God's representatives over the rest of creation. Psalm 8:5-8 is often cited as further biblical support for this view.

This interpretation of "image" to refer to humanity's function as God's representatives sees humans as called by God to exercise a role akin to that of the king's ambassador in the ancient world. Such an ambassador exercised "dominion" in the sense of having authority delegated to him by the king. As the royal representative, the ambassador was often charged with carrying the royal seal, sometimes imprinted upon a pestle or a ring. That seal often bore the image of the king. In like manner, humanity (according to this interpretation) bears the image of God in a manner analogous to the royal ambassador, who bore the image of the king as he exercised authority on behalf of his sovereign.

This view that human dominion is the content of the image of God was propounded several centuries ago by an unorthodox Protestant group, the Socinians, who followed the teachings of Faustus Socinus (see below, chapter 9, p. 206). It is included in their statement of faith, the Racovian Catechism.[4] It did not gain widespread popularity, however, since the mainline Protestant Reformed Churches condemned Socinus as a heretic.

Such a functional view of the *imago dei* does not exclude the insights of the more traditional theological formulas. For if humanity is to represent God by exercising dominion over the rest of creation, human beings must have certain capacities unique to themselves. Humanity must in some way resemble God in order to represent God as the divine ambassador who bears the image of the Lord of the universe.

At the same time, historic Christian belief confesses that the divine image in humanity was severely corrupted, if not entirely destroyed, when Adam fell from his original state of innocence. We shall examine this point more closely in the next chapter. For now, we turn our attention to the biblical testimony that the supreme example of the image of God is none other than Jesus Christ Himself.

Christ as the Image of God

In both 2 Corinthians 4:4 and Colossians 1:15 Paul refers to Christ as "the image of God." The Apostle's emphasis here is on

Christ as the One who reveals God to us. Hebrews 1:3 speaks of Christ as the "exact representation of [God's] being," thereby making the same point. When we see Christ, we see what God is like. Jesus said, "Anyone who has seen me has seen the Father" (John 14:9).

The New Testament also portrays Christ as "the last Adam" (1 Cor. 15:45), indicating that in Christ we get a picture not only of who God is, but what Adam was meant to be. This picture, or image, is also the goal of God's work of salvation in the lives of His people. The New Testament also speaks of people in general as having "been made in God's likeness" (James 3:9). Yet this likeness or image has been corrupted and is need of renewal, which prompts Paul to write that those who are in Christ are "being renewed . . . in the image of its Creator" (Col. 3:10).

During the fourth century Athanasius, in his *On the Incarnation*, likewise saw Christ's work as meeting humanity's need for the renewal of the divine image. He viewed fallen humanity as being deprived of the divine image (chap. 7). For this reason God came "to renew [to human beings] the state of being 'in the image'" (chap. 13). In one of his most famous sayings, Athanasius went so far as to say that Christ was made human "that we might be made divine" (chap. 54), by which he meant "made in the image of God." Over a thousand years later Calvin would echo the language of both Paul and Athanasius by saying that the goal of our being born again "is that Christ should reform us to God's image" (*Institutes* 1.15.4).

We noted above that Calvin, in keeping with the majority Church tradition he received, saw the image of God as pertaining to the human soul. The final part of this chapter will examine various issues surrounding the soul and its relationship to the overall constitution of humanity as originally created in the image of God.

Questions Concerning the Human Soul

What is the Soul?

Up to this point we have not taken time to define the word "soul." The reason for this is twofold. First, different definitions of the soul are usually related to issues which we shall survey in this section. The task of defining the soul ought to come after these issues have been considered. Second, and perhaps more important, there is general agreement as to what the soul is. The word "soul" refers to that animating principle (Latin *anima*) which gives life to corporeal beings. Theologians and philosophers have almost always discussed theories of the soul which distinguish it from the body, which in and of itself does not have life (since the existence of lifeless bodies is an undeniable fact).

The fact that plants have bodies and are classified as living things led Greek philosophers such as Aristotle to distinguish between three kinds of souls: vegetative (plants), sensual (animals), and rational (humans). Christian theology, on the other hand, generally reserves the word "soul" for animals and human beings. This is due to the fact that the common Old Testament word for soul (Hebrew *nephesh*) means "breath," and is used of animals and people, but not of plants. This distinction is underscored by the fundamental differentiation between unconscious life (plants) and conscious life (animals) found in the Genesis 1 creation narrative (see chapter 4, p. 95).

In this section we shall briefly survey three areas of inquiry within the history of Christian doctrine:

- How is the human soul related to our overall makeup as beings created in the image of God?
- Of what does the human soul consist?
- How do individual human souls come into being?

How is the Soul Related to Humanity's Overall Constitution?

There are three basic theories which seek to answer this question. These theories may be labeled *trichotomist*, *dichotomist*, and *unified*.

Trichotomy teaches that humanity consists of three parts: body, soul, and spirit. The first of these, the body, is common to plants, animals, and human beings. The soul, on the other hand, distinguishes animals and humans from plants, which possess unconscious life but not the animating principle which gives conscious life. Finally, the spirit is that element of human nature which distinguishes people from animals. Humanity's nature as the only moral and religious being in creation is that element which is called "spirit" by many Christians.

Scriptures cited by trichotomists include 1 Thessalonians 5:23 ("May your whole spirit, soul and body be kept blameless at the coming of our Lord Jesus Christ") and Hebrews 4:12, which speaks of the Word of God as "dividing soul and spirit." Post-apostolic writers who supported trichotomy were chiefly from the Eastern (Greek-speaking) Church. They subdivided the human constitution into *soma* (body), *psyche* (soul), and *pneuma* (spirit). Trichotomy experienced a setback of sorts in the late fourth century when it was used by Apollinarius, bishop of Laodicea, as the basis for the christological heresy which became known as Apollinarianism (see chapter 8, p. 179).

Dichotomy is the doctrine that human beings consist of two elements, body and soul. The body is the physical part of humanity, which is mortal. The soul is the immaterial part of humanity, which is not subject to death. The uniqueness of humanity is that the human soul possesses characteristics not present in the souls of animals, including that of immortality.

Dichotomist objections to trichotomy include the argument that for the most part, the terms "soul" and "spirit" are used synonymously in the New Testament. Calvin, for example, noted:

> I understand by the term "soul" an immortal yet created essence, which is [humanity's] nobler part. Sometimes it is called "spirit." For even when these terms are joined together, they differ from one another in meaning; yet when the word "spirit" is used by itself, it means the same thing as soul; as when Solomon, speaking of death, says that when "the spirit returns to God who gave it." And when Christ commended his spirit to the Father and Stephen his to Christ they meant only that when the soul is freed from the prison house of the body, God is its perpetual guardian. (*Institutes* 1.15.2)

Calvin's reference to the soul as humanity's "nobler part" and the body as a "prison house" does not mean that the body *per se* is evil. The phrase "prison house" refers to our bodily existence as fallen human beings, not human beings as originally created. The consensus of historic Christian belief is that the body, like the soul, is a creation of God and therefore good.

IRENAEUS ON THE "IMAGE" AND "LIKENESS" OF GOD

In Genesis 1:26 God says "Let us make man in our image, after our likeness." Modern Old Testament scholars generally agree that the words "image" and "likeness" are an example of Hebrew synonymous parallelism, and thus mean the same thing. Such a consensus has not always existed, however. Attempts to distinguish between the words "image" and "likeness" have led to some intriguing implications with regard to the biblical doctrine of humanity.

As early as the second century A.D. theologians began to distinguish between the words "image" and "likeness" in Genesis 1:26. Irenaeus, for example, viewed the "image" of God as humanity's natural ("fleshly") powers of reason and free will (the "soul"). On the other hand, Irenaeus viewed the "likeness" of God as a supernatural gift of God's Spirit, given at creation in addition to the image. Thus the "image" was part of the original constitution of human nature (body and soul), whereas the "likeness" was a divine grace ("the Spirit of God") added onto the image, as it were. When Adam fell, he and his progeny retained the image to some degree, but lost the likeness, which can only be regained by receiving the Spirit of God (*Against Heresies* 5.6.1).

This distinction between the image of God (nature; body and soul) and the likeness of God (grace; the Spirit) was eventually woven into the fabric of medieval Catholic theology. Among other things, it encouraged the development of natural theology and natural ethics within the Catholic tradition, apart from special revelation, since fallen humanity was viewed as retaining the image of God (though not the likeness of God).*

Both Martin Luther and John Calvin, who were well-schooled in the Catholic tradition, rejected Irenaeus's distinction between "image" and "likeness" on the basis of their exegesis of Genesis 1:26. They, along with the rest of the Protestant Reformation, concluded that the language of Genesis 1:26 was an example of Hebrew parallelism, wherein the biblical writer was merely saying the same thing in two different ways.** Luther and Calvin thereby concluded that sin had seriously damaged the *imago dei* in its entirety. For this reason Protestantism in general has been less optimistic about the possibilities of natural theology and ethics (nature) formulated apart from biblical revelation (grace).

---

* See for example Millard Erickson's discussion in his *Christian Theology,* 500f.

** See for example Martin Luther, *Lectures on Genesis,* in Luther's Works, vol. 1, 60; and John Calvin, *Institutes of the Christian Religion* 1.15.3.

The dichotomist view has been widely held throughout Church history. At the same time, some Christians view it as closer to Greek dualism (wherein the body is evil and the soul is good) than to biblical revelation, which affirms the intrinsic goodness of all creation.

For this reason a *unified* view of human nature, which refuses to make a radical distinction between body and soul, has been offered as an alternative to dichotomy. The unified view, which is the product of recent biblical scholarship,[5] appeals to what is sometimes called the "Hebrew" thought which underlies the Bible, as opposed to the aforementioned "Greek" dualism which has affected the theological vocabulary of the Church.

The unified view recognizes that Scripture does make distinctions between body and soul. Fundamentally, however, human beings are a unity. The human body as well as the human soul is what makes humanity unique in God's creation.

This unified anthropology has both strengths and weaknesses. On the positive side, it accounts for the biblical doctrine which defines salvation in terms of resurrection of the body, not merely as immortality of the soul (as did Greek neoplatonic philosophy; see chapter 10, p. 219). It also explains certain facts of human existence more adequately than does dichotomy, particularly when the latter becomes strongly dualistic. For example, bodily functions sometimes affect the soul, and vice-versa. A chemical imbalance in the brain or bloodstream (body) may affect both our thoughts and emotions (soul). Medical treatment may alter such ailments in a salutary manner, as in some cases of clinical depression. On the other hand, emotions of the soul can make us physically ill. Such illnesses are called "psychosomatic" (literally, "soul-bodily").

On the negative side, unified anthropology sometimes overstates its case, ignoring biblical statements which make clear distinctions between body and soul. Jesus speaks of those who can kill the body but not the soul, and of God who can destroy both body and soul in hell (Matt. 10:28; Luke 12:4-5). Efforts to avoid a radically dualistic anthropology need not rule out making distinctions found in Scripture itself. In addition, the unified view of humanity at times makes a virtual fetish of Hebrew thought over against Greek thought. The Bible contains no systematic treatise on anthropology, and there is nothing necessarily wrong with using Greek philosophical language to articulate biblical ideas. Paul, for example, refers to Christ as God's "fullness" (Greek *pleroma*), a philosophical term evidently used by his gnostic opponents in Colossae (Col. 1:19; 2:9).[6]

In sum, human nature is complex, yet unified. Our human constitution was originally created good by God, but our entire humanity has been adversely affected by sin. To speak of the soul as our "nobler part," as does Calvin, does not deny that the soul as well as the body has been corrupted. We shall examine this subject more closely in the next chapter.

For now, let us return our attention to the subject of the human soul. Specifically, we shall deal with the question of what comprises the soul.

Of What Does the Human Soul Consist?

Scripture does not give a specific definition of the soul or of its component parts (if indeed the soul has distinctive parts or faculties). Christian reflections on the nature of the soul have therefore frequently made use of concepts derived from the Greek philosophical tradition.

In the fourth book of *The Republic* Plato divided the soul into three parts. The first part, reason, is the faculty of thought and knowledge. The other two parts, spirit and appetite, are principles of action. The principles of action are guided by reason; hence, the need to emphasize good education. Reason, on the other hand, does not of itself produce behavior. Rather, principles of action issue forth behavior in light of the information provided by reason.

Aristotle followed Plato's basic model, further reducing the soul to two parts: "thought and sense," or the "faculty of discrimination"; and the faculty of "originating local movement" (*On the Soul*, chap. 9). The former he called "mind"; the latter, "appetite" or "will."

Christian discussions of the soul have tended to use vocabulary similar to that of Aristotle. Augustine, for example, spoke of the human soul as consisting of "understanding," "will," and "memory," thereby reflecting the Trinity and constituting the image of God (*On the Trinity* 10.12). Thomas Aquinas included memory under the category of the understanding (*Summa Theologiae* 1. 9. 7), but divided Augustine's "will" into lower and higher elements.

Thomas used the term "will" only for the higher element; the lower element he described as "sensual" and "irascible" (*Summa Theologiae* 1. 82. 3).

Calvin was reticent to subdivide either the understanding or the will, and thus defined the human soul as consisting of these two parts. In this way Calvin sought to avoid dualistic tendencies he saw in the philosophers and some Christian theologians. He noted, for example, that some believed people could live righteously by depending upon their reason (*Institutes* 1.15.6), while others such as Aquinas (whom Calvin does not mention by name) placed both understanding and will over against the sensual portion of the soul (*Institutes* 1.15.7). In either case the implication was that some portion of human nature may remain free of sin's corruption. To this Calvin replied that while Adam indeed had free will prior to the Fall, human beings are now corrupted by sin at every point in their lives (*Institutes* 1.15.8).

Thus Calvin returned to Aristotle's definition of the soul as consisting of two faculties, that of "thought and sense" (understanding) and that of "originating local movement" (will)—though Aristotle, unlike Calvin, had no doctrine of original sin and believed that people have always been the way they presently are. Calvin likewise endorsed Aristotle's notion that the understanding governs the will. That is, "the will is always mindful of the bidding of the understanding, and in its own desires awaits the judgment of the understanding" (*Institutes* 1.15.7). In other words, people make choices on the basis of what they perceive will fulfill their desires.

In this way Calvin refused to distinguish between behavior based on "sense" (one's desire for pleasure) and behavior based on "understanding" (awareness of one's duty to do that which is good or right). All people seek happiness, and there is nothing necessarily wrong with that. Problems arise when they seek happiness in the wrong way.

At this point Calvin echoes Augustine, who defined the rightness or wrongness of an act not as the desire for pleasure, but as the attempt to gain pleasure in the wrong way (*City of God* 14.6-8). A century after Calvin, the French Catholic philosopher Blaise Pascal (1623-1662) echoed this perspective when he wrote: "All men seek happiness. This is without exception. Whatever different means they employ, they all tend to this end. . . . This is the motive of every action of every man, even of those who hang themselves" (*Pènsees* no. 425).[7]

How Do Individual Human Souls Come into Being?

This is not a merely academic question. How one answers it will affect one's view of human nature, sin, and perhaps even one's christological convictions. In the history of Christianity there have been three views: *preexistence, creationism,* and *traducianism.*

Preexistence, as its name indicates, teaches that all human souls were created at the beginning of the universe, prior to the creation of matter. The most important proponent of this view was Origen, who taught that human souls existed as angelic spirits before the creation of Adam. These angelic spirits rebelled against God, however, and were consigned to bodily existence as punishment for their sins (*On First Principles* 3.5). For Origen, earthly human life is a disciplinary process through which we must go in order to be restored to our preexistent angelic state. What, then, of the Christian doctrine of the resurrection of the body? For Origen, biblical statements of the resurrection were to be interpreted allegorically by learned people, even though a literal resurrection was preached by Paul to "the simpler class of believers" so that they might be led into that better life which will in fact be spiritual and not bodily (*Against Celsus* 3.19).

Origen, by his own admission, relied heavily on Plato's dualism of body and soul in formulating his doctrine of preexistent souls (*Against Celsus* 3.81). As it turned out, with Origen the doctrine of preexistent souls had both its beginning and its end in the Church. No Christian teacher or theologian of note has held it since. Today, a different version of the doctrine of preexistent souls is taught by the Mormons.

Creationism is the view held most widely by Christians today. Like the doctrine of preexistent souls, it views each human soul as a special creation of God. This divine creation does not take place prior to the existence of the individual human body, however. Rather, the soul is created and implanted within the human body sometime between conception and birth. Scriptures such as Ecclesiastes 12:7, Isaiah 42:5, and Hebrews 12:9 are cited by creationists as evidence that the body and soul have different origins.

The creationist view dominated the early Eastern Church, and also found advocates in the Western Church, including the Italian biblical scholar Jerome (c. 345-419), who translated the Bible into Latin. Thomas Aquinas stated that what he called the "intellectual soul" (unique to humans) was created directly by God, though the "sensitive soul" (that life-principle shared with plants and animals) was transmitted biologically (*Summa Theologiae* 1. 118. 1-2). Creationism is presently the official position of both the Roman Catholic and Eastern Orthodox Churches. In addition, most Reformed theologians have held to some form of creationism (the American Calvinist Jonathan Edwards is a notable exception).

Creationists differ as to when the human body developing inside its mother receives its human soul. Some believe this occurs at conception; others, at some point after conception. In either case, the soul is viewed as having been created pure, but becoming sinful even before birth by virtue of its contact with Adam's race.

Traducianism teaches that human beings derive their souls as well as their bodies from their parents. Scriptural support for this view is found in the fact that nothing is said about the creation of Eve's soul, and that human descendants are said to be in the loins of their fathers (Gen. 46:26; Heb. 7:9-10). Paul's statements tracing the origin of sinful human nature back to Adam (Rom. 5:12-19, 1 Cor. 15:22, Eph. 2:3) were also influential in the development of traducianism.

This theory first found expression in the Western Church due to the influence of Tertullian. In supporting his view he went so far as to refer to the soul as a "corporeal substance" (*On the Soul* chap. 5) rather than an immaterial substance. Thus he linked the origin of the human soul back to Adam, stating that the soul "has been derived from Adam as its root" (*On the Soul* chap. 19).

Two centuries later Augustine claimed ignorance on the subject of the soul's origin and refused to endorse either creationism or traducianism (*Unfinished Work against Julian* 4.104). Yet, as we shall see in the following chapter, Augustine's doctrine of the origin and transmission of sin implied a traducianist anthropology. A millennium later Martin Luther, whose theological education was within the Augustinian order of the Roman Catholic Church, affirmed traducianism over creationism. This continues to be the confessional stance of Lutheranism.

As can be seen from this brief historical survey, the Christian Church has never reached a consensus on the subject of the soul's origin (other than denying its preexistence). Creationists argue that traducianism implies Jesus had a sinful human nature (since He must have inherited His soul from Mary). Traducianists, on the other hand, believe creationism fails to account for the undeniable fact that family traits such as personality, temperament, and so forth are passed on from generation to generation along with bodily traits such as physical size and appearance.

In recent years traducianism has gained adherents among those who oppose the practice of abortion. For if the fetus has both body and soul from the moment of conception, it is a human being in the fullest sense. Creationism, on the other hand, takes no position as to when the developing fetus receives a soul. Theoretically, then, creationism could allow for abortion in the early stages of pregnancy. It is worth noting, however, that while Christians have never reached a consensus on the origin of the soul, the Church has been unanimous in its condemnation of abortion from its earliest days down to the last third of the twentieth century, when its consensus against abortion began to break down among Protestants (Catholic and Orthodox teaching still proscribes abortion).[8]

As we have already noted, theories concerning the nature and origin of the human soul and its relation to the body carry with them implications for other Christian doctrines. One of these is the doctrine of sin, which we will examine next.

Points To Ponder

1. How do the first two chapters of Genesis depict the uniqueness of humanity?

2. How do the first two chapters of Genesis depict humanity's connection with the rest of creation?

3. In your own words, explain what theologians mean by humanity's natural capacities, moral capacities, and spiritual capacities.

4. How does Karl Barth define the image of God?

5. In the excursus *Humanity as Male and Female*, how do the insights of Clement and Tertullian complement Barth's view of humanity?

6. How do most Old Testament scholars interpret the phrase "image of God" within its context (Genesis 1:26-28)? Why is this view called "representative"? Why is it also called "functional"?

7. Compare and contrast the trichotomist, dichotomist, and unified views of the human soul, including arguments for and against each view.

8. Why did Calvin reduce Thomas Aquinas's threefold division of the soul into a simple twofold division of "will" and "understanding"?

9. Do you favor the creationist view of the origin of the human soul, or the traducianist view? Set forth arguments for and against each.

7

The Doctrine of Humanity, Part Two: Humanity as Fallen into Sin

The Biblical Account of the Fall of Humanity

The Human Predicament

Something is not right with the human race. We are not all that we aspire to be. As noted in chapter 1, most people fall short of what their conscience demands of them, and all people fall short of what their judicial sentiment demands of others. Since these twin moral faculties reflect something of who God is, another way of expressing this universal truth is to say with the apostle Paul: "All have sinned and fall short of the glory of God" (Rom. 3:23).

The third chapter of Genesis sets forth an explanation of the human predicament. Early in its history, the human race deliberately disobeyed God, introducing sin and death into a world which heretofore had been declared "very good" by its Creator (Gen. 1:31). The English poet John Milton (1608-1674) referred to Genesis 3 as speaking:

> Of Man's First Disobedience, and the Fruit
> Of that Forbidden Tree, whose mortal taste
> Brought Death into the World, and all our woe,
> With loss of *Eden*, till one greater Man

Restore us, and regain the blissful Seat . . .
(*Paradise Lost*, Book One, lines 1-5)

Genesis 3 and History

The Genesis narrative clearly depicts this disobedience as having occurred at a particular point in history, and as having been committed by the progenitors of the entire human race, Adam and Eve. In the New Testament, Paul underscores this point by stating that "sin entered the world through one man [Adam], and death through sin" (Rom. 5:12). This entrance of sin and death into the world via the disobedience of Adam and Eve is the Christian doctrine of *the Fall of Humanity*.

In the twentieth century a number of theologians have called into question the entire concept of a historical Fall. The American Protestant Reinhold Niebuhr, for example, speaks of the "historical-literalistic illusion" of humanity becoming corrupted by means of inheriting the fatal consequences of Adam's first disobedience.[1] Niebuhr's preference for a "representative" view of Adam, wherein Adam is a merely a symbol for the human race in general, finds precedent in Origen's attempt to allegorize the Genesis narratives. It is not as prominent in Church history as Niebuhr would have his readers believe, however. Karl Barth's treatment of Genesis 3, while insisting on the fundamental historicity of the creation accounts (*Church Dogmatics* 3/1, section 41), has also been criticized for leaving little room for a real Fall.[2]

The text of Genesis itself, on the other hand, leaves little doubt that the ancient author intended to convey the Fall as an event which occurred as a specific point near the outset of human history. This is confirmed by the *genealogies* which link Genesis 2 and 3 with the following chapters. Furthermore, the genealogical accounts of the entire corpus of Genesis 1-11 are tied together with the history of Israel, which begins in Genesis 12 with the call of Abram (see Genesis 11:10-32). From a strictly literary perspective, it is not possible to isolate Genesis 2 and 3 from the rest of the Genesis narrative.

The historical consensus of Christian theology has therefore assumed the historicity of the Fall when addressing the question of the meaning of the Fall. Granted that human disobedience fundamentally changed the human condition at the outset of history, the question remains as to why that disobedience ushered in such dire consequences. Why all the fuss about a piece of fruit?

The Meaning of the Fall

In *The Divine Comedy*, Dante's classic medieval trilogy of hell, purgatory and paradise, the author depicts Adam as saying that "the tasting of the tree [of the knowledge of good and evil] was not in itself the cause [of being expelled from the Garden of Eden], but solely the overpassing of the bound" (*Paradiso* Canto 26).[3] The act of disobedience to God's command, not the nature of the fruit, was the problem.

The nature of that disobedience hinges upon the phrase "knowledge of good and evil," used in reference to the forbidden tree and its fruit (Gen. 2:9, 17). What was this "knowledge of good and evil" which God put off-limits to Adam and Eve?

In the Old Testament "the knowledge of good and evil" refers to what may be called *moral autonomy*, or the ability to make moral decisions without being accountable to someone else. Small children, who must depend upon their parents for moral guidance, do not "know good from evil" (Deut. 1:39; Isa. 7:16). Sooner or later, however, children must grow up and arrive at a knowledge of good and evil (Isa. 7:15), since they will not always have their parents to look out for them. Within the context of human relationships, then, the knowledge of good and evil is not only desirable, but necessary.

Why, then, does God forbid Adam and Eve from seeking to obtain the knowledge of good and evil? The answer lies in the fact that in Genesis 2 and 3, Adam's "parent" is not another human being, but God Himself. To desire the knowledge of good and evil in relationship to God is to desire absolute moral autonomy, to be a law unto oneself in the same sense that God is a law unto Himself. It is to desire to be like God.

Satan's temptation of Eve spells this out clearly. He says to her that if she eats of the forbidden fruit she will "be like God, knowing good and evil" (Gen. 3:5). So when she and Adam eat the fruit of moral autonomy, it is out of a desire to be a law unto themselves rather than being accountable to God. It is a vote of no confidence in God's ability to do what is best for them.

Adam's disobedience is therefore fundamentally one of *unbelief*. God's command not to eat the fruit of the knowledge of good and evil includes a promise that the one who eats it will die (Gen. 2:17). God says in effect: "Do not try to become a law unto yourself apart from my guidance, Adam. To do so will lead to death." To which Adam and Eve reply: "Thanks, but no thanks. We believe the serpent's promise that we can become like God and get along quite well on our own."

In Romans 14:23 the apostle Paul writes that "everything that does not come from faith is sin." Fifteen hundred years later Martin Luther underscored this point in his essay "The Freedom of the Christian" when he said "what greater rebellion against God, what greater wickedness, what greater contempt of God is there than not believing His promise?"[4] Luther, like Paul, perceived that the greatest insult one person can hurl against another's reputation is to say, "I don't trust you." This is precisely what Adam and Eve said to God.

Repercussions of the Fall

"In Adam's Fall, we sinned all" begins the first lesson of *The Bay Psalm Book* of 1640, a New England spelling primer for children. This little jingle was designed not only to help students remember the letter *A*, but also to reinforce the New England Puritans' conviction that the entire human race was in some way involved in Adam's first act of disobedience. This is known as the doctrine of *original sin*.

The Scriptures testify that sin is something more than merely individual acts of disobedience to God. It is a principle which adversely affects our lives from the outset of our existence. Genesis 4 through 11 dramatizes the pervasiveness of sin in the human experience. Even a great flood which destroys almost all of humanity does not wipe away the horrible consequences of Adam's transgression. King David of Israel, described by the prophet Samuel as a man after God's own heart (1 Sam. 13:14), nonetheless writes: "Surely I have been a sinner from birth, sinful from the time my mother conceived me" (Ps. 51:5). The prophet Jeremiah echoes David's assessment of the human condition: "The heart is deceitful above all things and beyond cure. Who can understand it?" (Jer. 17:9).

The mystery of humanity's sinful nature continues as a theme running throughout the New Testament as well as the Old Testament. In Matthew 7:11 Jesus describes His listeners, who are none other than His own disciples (see Matt. 5:2), as "being evil." The apostle Paul refers to "sinful passions" (Rom. 7:5) as the driving force behind sinful behavior, and says even of himself: "I know that nothing good lives in me, that is, in my sinful nature" (Rom. 7:18).

Fallout from the Fall is not limited to the human race, however. Paul states that the entire created order "has been groaning" due to its "bondage to decay" brought about by the entrance of sin into the world (Rom. 8:21–22). This bondage will one day be broken by the redeeming work of Christ. In the meantime, all of creation is out of harmony with God's original designs as portrayed in Genesis 1 and 2. The entrance of sin into the world through Adam's fall has produced a disharmony which estranges every human being from God, self, others, and even the environment.

The Doctrine of Sin

The Nature of Sin

Sin is an aberration from God's original design. We have seen from the Genesis narrative that sin was not part of the original design of God's creation of humanity. God's declaration that His finished creation was "very good" (Gen. 1:31) belies any notion that sin is a necessary component of human existence. John Calvin underscored this point when he chastised those who view sin as something metaphysical, or inherent in nature. Such reasoning, he insisted, attempts to shift the blame for sinful acts from the sinner onto God:

> For in this excuse, impiety thinks it has sufficient defense, if it is able to claim that whatever defects it possesses have in some way proceeded from God. . . . And those who wish to seem to speak more reverently of the Godhead still willingly blame their depravity on nature, not realizing that they also, although more obscurely, insult God. For if any defect were proved to inhere in nature [as originally created], this would bring reproach upon [God]. (*Institutes* 1.15.1).

Sin is a moral problem. Furthermore, sin does not merely involve making mistakes. While it may be true that to err is human, to sin is not essentially human. Rather, it is a denial of the purpose for which human beings were created, which is to exist in a relationship of loving trust with their Creator, finding their supreme happiness in God (see chapter 4, p. 82). Sin is rebellion, a vote of no confidence in God, and not merely error. Were erroneous behavior humanity's principal problem, we would be in need of God's excusing our behavior. The Bible speaks not of God's willingness to excuse sinful behavior, however, but rather of God's desire to forgive sinners. This distinction between excusing mistakes and forgiving sins is central to a biblical understanding of the nature of sin. The old adage which says "To err is human; to forgive, divine" illegitimately links error with forgiveness.

The nature of sin is therefore not metaphysical, but moral. And since the nature of sin is moral, it has to do not with making mistakes but with deliberate disobedience to the law of God. "Sin is lawlessness" (1 John 3:4).

Sin is guilt. The definition of sin as lawlessness leads to yet another conclusion about the nature of sin. Sin includes guilt. Human beings are guilty of violating God's will for their lives, and are therefore morally responsible for their disobedience. In the first three chapters of his letter to the Church at Rome Paul emphasizes that all people are guilty before God (Rom. 3:19-20, 23).

Sin is depravity. We noted above that sin is not inherent to human nature per se. At the same time, Christianity affirms that the Fall brought about a change in the human race whereby moral pollution, or depravity, now exists where moral perfection once was. "Sin" is not merely a label for unrighteous behavior or moral guilt. Sin is an objective entity, likened to a sickness (Jer. 17:9) which produces sinful passions (Rom. 7:5), which in turn issue in sinful acts. Sinful human nature not only does not, but cannot, please God (Rom. 8:7-8). The question debated by Christians from very early on in Church history is the extent to which human nature has been polluted by Adam's original sin.

The Extent of Human Depravity

In Romans 5:12-21, as well as 1 Corinthians 15:22, Paul speaks of all human beings as being "in Adam." Here the Apostle presupposes the Old Testament's view of the *corporate solidarity* of the human race. Human beings are not merely isolated individuals;

they share a common nature derived from their original progenitors, Adam and Eve. Furthermore, the consensus of historic Christian belief is that this common human nature is not the pristine nature Adam and Eve had prior to the Fall, but rather the polluted nature which was theirs after the Fall.

At this point a debate arises within the historic Christian consensus. Is this polluted nature the sum total of who we are? Or is it merely part of who we are? Are people only partially depraved, or are they totally depraved? The two principal wings of Christendom, the Greek Church and the Latin Church, gave very different answers to this question during the first several centuries following the apostolic era. These two traditions have in turn framed the terms of this debate down to the present day.

The Greek tradition. In the Eastern portion of the Roman Empire, the Greek-speaking Churches tended to emphasize the essential goodness of humanity in order to combat gnostic teachings. Specifically, the Gnostics were metaphysical dualists who believed that evil as well as good was eternal, and that humanity is sinful by creation. This gnostic denial of the Fall in turn led to the denial that humanity was created as a free moral agent. For this reason some Gnostics taught that humanity was divided into different classes, only some of which were destined to be saved.

In response to gnostic anthropology, which denied any sort of human freedom, the Eastern Church maintained that humanity was created free, but *became* sinful by misusing the moral freedom with which God endowed the human race. In addition, the Eastern Church insisted that even as sinners men and women maintained a significant, if diminished, freedom of will. Justin Martyr (c. 100-65), for example, insisted that gnostic anthropology led inevitably to fatalism and a denial of human moral responsibility:

> Lest any should infer . . . that we are assertors of fatal necessity [as are the Gnostics], and conclude that prophecy must needs infer predestination, we shall clear ourselves as to this point also; for we learn from these very prophets that rewards and punishments are to be distributed in proportion to the merits of mankind. . . . for if it be not so, but all things are determined by fate, then farewell freedom of will; and if this man is destined to be good, and that one to be evil, then neither the one nor the other can be justly approved or condemned; so that unless we suppose that man has it in his power to

choose the good, and refuse the evil, no one can be accountable for any action whatever (*Apology* 1.54).[5]

In the third and fourth centuries the two great theological centers of the Eastern Church, Alexandria and Antioch, endorsed and elaborated upon Justin's perspective. Clement of Alexandria, for example, stated that human choices depend "on the man as being free; but the gift [depends] on God as the Lord. And He gives to those who are willing and are exceedingly earnest . . . " (*Who Is the Rich Man That Shall Be Saved?*, Chapter 10). Clement thus believed that the human will must cooperate with God's will in order for people to be saved. Clement's point of view, known as *synergism* (from the Greek *sun ergo*, "work together"), was shared by the theological school of Antioch to the north. The great fourth-century preacher John Chrysostom, for example, described the grace of God as "assisting grace." Commenting on Romans 9:16 he stated: "The phrase 'it is not of him that willeth, nor of him that runneth' does not denude man of power altogether, but indicates that the *whole* power is not of man. Assisting grace is needed from above" (*Sixteenth Homily on Romans*).[6]

The Eastern Church's emphasis on free will was shaped not only by its debate with the Gnostics, but also by its creationist anthropology (see chapter 6, p. 134). Specifically, theologians of both Alexandria and Antioch were trichotomist creationists. They held that while every person's body (physical constitution) and soul (animal instincts) were inherited from Adam and Eve, the human spirit (which includes the will) was a direct creation of God. This being the case, the original sin of Adam directly affected the body and soul of all his progeny, but not the spirit. To the extent that the human spirit is affected by sin, it is tainted by its contact with the body and the soul.

But while the human spirit may be negatively affected by the frailties of the body and the sensuality of the soul, human beings are not held guilty by God because of Adam's sin. This is because the human spirit is that part of our nature which makes us uniquely human. The Greek Church, in other words, believed in a limited sort of "original sin" (since what Adam did affects all of us to a degree), but rejected the notion of "original guilt" (since the human spirit, including the will, is a direct creation of God and thereby not guilty of Adam's sin). Gregory of Nazianzus underscored the East's rejection of original guilt when he spoke of unbaptized babies as "not sealed [by baptism] on the one hand, but not evil on the other" (*Orations*, Chap. 40).[7] Human beings inherit some of Adam's sinful nature, but are held guilty only for their own voluntary acts of disobedience.

The Latin tradition. In the Western portion of the Roman Empire most Church teachers took a more skeptical view of human moral capabilities than did their Eastern counterparts. Beginning with Tertullian at the end of the second century, the emphasis in the West was that sin's corrupting influence extended to every part of human nature. This is the doctrine of total depravity, as opposed to the Eastern Church's view of partial depravity.

The anthropological basis of the Latin-speaking Church's view of sin was Tertullian's traducianism (see chapter 6, p. 140). He believed that the human soul in its entirety (including what the Eastern Church would call the "spirit") was not directly given by God, but was passed on via procreation. This in turn means that the human will is not free in the same manner as was Adam's will before the Fall. Rather, the depravity of Adam's fallen will has been transmitted to all of his progeny. If Adam's power of choice is transmitted to us, reasoned Tertullian, so is his sin. At the same time, however, "there is a portion of good in the soul, of that original, divine, and genuine good, which is its proper nature. For that which is derived from God is rather obscured [by sin] than extinguished" (*On the Soul*, Chap. 41). Total depravity does not mean people are as bad as they could possibly be, but that every part of our being has been adversely affected by the corruption of sin.

Latin writers such as Cyprian, bishop of Carthage (d. 258), Hilary of Poitiers (d. 368), and Ambrose, Bishop of Milan (d. 397) carried forth and developed Tertullian's traducianism. In certain respects they went beyond Tertullian, gradually placing more explicit emphasis on total depravity as *guilty* human nature, not merely corrupt human nature. Unlike the Eastern Church, therefore, the Western Church spoke not only of original sin, but also of original guilt.

In addition, the Latin writers generally spoke of salvation more as a work of God's will, and less as a work of the human will, than

ORIGINAL SIN: REALISM VS. FEDERALISM

The New England Puritans, as we have seen, believed that "In Adam's Fall, we sinned all." The idea that all people participated in Adam's sin has given rise to various theories of how this could be so. The two most common theories are Realism and Federalism.

Realism emphasizes the corporate solidarity of the human race which exists due to our common descent from Adam. There is one generic human race, which was embodied in Adam. When he sinned, the entire human race was afflicted with the consequences of his sin.

As noted above, the Eastern Church defined the consequences of Adam's disobedience as corruption ("original sin") but not guilt, while the Western Church viewed the consequences of Adam's disobedience in terms of guilt ("original guilt") as well as corruption. We also noted that the Eastern Church's creationist anthropology prevented them from attributing original guilt to Adam's progeny, because they held that (1) guilt is related to the human soul, and (2) human beings have not inherited their souls from Adam. The Western Church's traducianist anthropol-

ogy, on the other hand, enabled it to view both guilt and corruption as having been passed on from Adam to his progeny. Federalism is a theory which attempts to reconcile creationist anthropology with the notion of original guilt. Federalism is a product of Reformed theology, which believes that all people are guilty as well as corrupt "in Adam." At the same time, most of those in the Calvinist Reformed tradition are not traducianists, but creationists. Reformed theology therefore views the union between Adam and his progeny as not merely biological, but also legal. Specifically, God appointed Adam as the representative, or "federal head," of the entire human race.

What Adam did when he sinned was charged to all of those whom he represented—the entire human race. All people have thus been placed on trial "in Adam," and found guilty. Federalism views original guilt not as inherited, but as *imputed* to the entire human race, in the same manner as Christ imputes His righteousness to those who are "in Christ." The Adam-Christ parallel drawn by Paul in Romans 5:12-21 serves as the biblical basis for Reformed theology at this point.

did their Eastern counterparts. That is, their tendency was towards *monergism*, the view that God's work alone makes possible our salvation, as opposed to the synergism of the Eastern Church.

This process reached its climax in the writings of Augustine. Early in his career he wrote a treatise on free will (*De Libero Arbitrio*) which held a perspective very close to that of the Eastern Church's synergism. This was due in part to Augustine's desire to refute the Manicheans, the gnostic-style sect of which he had been a member prior to converting to Christianity. He therefore emphasized free will over against the determinism of the Manicheans. As time went on, however, Augustine moved away from this position. His final major work, *On the Predestination of the Saints*, was completely monergistic, emphasizing humanity's total inability to respond to God's call apart from God's gracious predestination of some to eternal life.

Augustine's monergistic emphasis on human inability did not lead him to deny human freedom, however. Instead, the Augustinian tradition (which, as we have seen, did not begin with Augustine) defined freedom in a manner different than that of the Eastern Church. The Augustinian notion of freedom was by no means endorsed by all of the important Latin writers from Augustine to Thomas Aquinas, but it did serve as the point of departure for discussions concerning the freedom of the will within the Western Church.

Freedom of the Will

Freedom, East and West

Whereas freedom in the East (and for some in the West) was defined as *in*determination, the Augustinian definition of freedom may be labeled as *self*-determination. The two definitions may be differentiated as follows.

Indetermination emphasizes that the will is free in the sense of being indifferent or undecided by nature. The will as originally created by God is not inclined either towards good or evil. If God had created the will inclined towards either good or evil, the will would not be free but instead determined and therefore, in the view of Eastern theology, not morally accountable for its actions. One may picture this non-determined will as sitting atop a fence with no inclination to jump one way or the other, but with the ability to do either.

Self-determination views the will as always in a state of decision, as opposed to being intrinsically undecided. To will something is to decide something; hence for Augustine and the Western tradition, an undecided will is a contradiction in terms. Rather, the will is free in the sense that it does whatever it pleases. Whether the will has equal power or ability to choose two alternative choices (for example, good or evil) is quite beside the point. Augustine, for example, held that so long as the human will is not compelled or coerced from outside itself to act in a certain way, it acts freely.

Augustine further argued that the sinful human will is free, in the sense of not being forced to choose, because it delights in sin (*Against Two Letters of Pelagius*, Book 1). For example, he recalled an incident from his own youth when he stole some pears. He stole them not to enjoy the pears, "but only to enjoy the theft itself and the sin . . . . No sooner had I picked them than I threw them away, and tasted nothing in them but my own sin, which I relished and enjoyed" (*Confessions* 2.4). Nobody forced the young Augustine to steal those pears. He did so because he delighted in stealing.

Augustine spoke of sin as having its origin in Adam, and having been passed to the entire human race by propagation. Thus his anthropology appears to presuppose traducianism, even while he refused to embrace the traducianist theory explicity. This is borne out by the following quotation: "God, the author of natures, not of vices, created man upright; but man, being of his own will corrupted and justly condemned, begot corrupted and condemned children. For we all were in that one man, since we all were that one man, who fell into sin." (*City of God* 13.14). Human nature was created by God, but "vices" (sin) came into existence through Adam's free choice. Sin is therefore an acquired quality of human nature, as opposed to a created quality. We acquired sin from Adam through procreation, since "we all were that one man [Adam]." It follows that not only his corruption, but also his guilt, became our inheritance.

For Augustine, then, sin may at the same time be voluntary (delight) and inevitable (inherited). The fact that the fallen human will possesses a bias towards evil in no way excuses sinful behavior, since people always act freely in the sense of doing what they please (unless forced to do otherwise by external coercion). We are accountable for our disobedience to God despite the fact that our situation is *non posse non peccare* (not able not to sin).

The Pelagian Controversy

The Latin Church's general consensus, which placed human moral inability alongside moral accountability, was not without its opponents in the West. One of these was a British monk named Pelagius, whose sharp differences with Augustine gave rise to what became known as the Pelagian controversy.

Pelagius came to Rome around the year 383 after receiving legal training in Britain. Although he was born and lived his entire life in the western Roman Empire, Pelagius was more in line with the anthropology of the Eastern Church. He denied the Western notion of total depravity, held to the Eastern Church's creationist view of the origin of individual human souls, and believed that the soul was created neutral, with no propensity towards either good or bad. He went beyond the Eastern writers, however, by denying that there was any moral difference between Adam and his posterity. His anthropology may be summarized as follows:[8]

- Sin does not pass from generation to generation by propagation, as Augustine taught. There is no such thing as original sin, in the sense of a moral affliction which all people inherit from Adam. In his commentary on Romans 7:8 Pelagius says: "They are insane who teach that the sin of Adam comes on us by propagation (*per traducem*)."

- There is no such thing as original guilt. Adam's sin was charged to his own account, but not to his posterity. A God who charged the sin of one man to the account of someone else would not be righteous. Pelagius asked, "How can the sin be imputed by God to the man, which he has not known as his own?" (Quoted by Augustine, *On Nature and Grace* 30). For this reason unbaptized children will go to heaven if they die. Julian of Eclanum, a disciple of Pelagius and opponent of Augustine, stated: "Children, so long as they are children, that is, before they do anything by their own will, cannot be punishable" (cited by Augustine, *Unfinished*

Work 2.42). People are punishable only for the sins they themselves commit, not for any sins committed by someone else.

- Every person is thus born in just the same moral state in which Adam was first created. People do not inherit the consequences of Adam's disobedience, but rather the benefits of Adam's original righteousness as created in the image of God. This in turn means that Christ's mission was not to provide salvation for sinners, but to show essentially righteous people how to save themselves. Jesus came to educate the ignorant, not to release the captives.

Pelagius was thus a moralist, who believed that good works justified a person before God. This brought him into bitter controversy with Augustine, whose reading of the New Testament and personal battles with sin convinced him that only God's saving grace in Christ could rescue human beings from the depths of their depravity.

The Church eventually sided with Augustine. In the West the North African Church, under Augustine's leadership, led the fight against the teachings of Pelagius. In 416 Pelagianism was condemned by synods in Mileve and Carthage, a decision endorsed two years later by the bishop of Rome and thus by the Latin Church. The Eastern Church, represented at the Council of Ephesus in 431, also condemned Pelagianism.

From Augustine to the Reformation

Semi-Pelagianism. Although Augustine won his battle against Pelagius, many Christians tried to find a middle ground between the strict monergism of Augustinianism and the optimistic moralism of Pelagianism. These became known as the Semi-pelagians. They endorsed various forms of synergism, giving greater emphasis to free will than did Augustine, while at the same time denying the Pelagian notion that proper education would solve humanity's problems.

In the Eastern Church Semi-pelagianism eventually won out over Augustinianism, which never was very popular in the East (the Council of Ephesus notwithstanding). This is not surprising, since the synergistic emphasis of Semi-Pelagianism was consistent with ideas expressed earlier by the theological schools of both Alexandria and Antioch (above, p. 150). The Western Church, on the other hand, became an Augustinian institution with significant pockets of Semi-pelagianism cropping up from time to time during the Middle Ages.

The triumph of Augustinianism in the Middle Ages. In the fifth and sixth centuries Pope Leo and Pope Gregory endorsed the Augustinian notions of total depravity and monergism. Their actions in effect institutionalized Augustinian monergism in the West. In the eighth century the Venerable Bede (673-735), a British monk who was perhaps the most learned scholar of his day, followed the course set forth by Leo and Gregory.

The greatest medieval proponent of Augustine's anthropology was Anselm of Canterbury, who in the eleventh century endorsed both the notions of original sin and original guilt while arguing that human moral inability did not remove moral responsibility. In his works *On the Virgin Birth and Original Sin* and *On Free Will* he defended Augustine's view of corporate solidarity, arguing that all people were "in Adam" and therefore all sinned when Adam sinned. This in turn meant that since Adam sinned as one possessing free will, all of his descendants are not only unrighteous but also guilty before God.

Thomas Aquinas continued the Augustinian tradition by insisting that every part of human nature was affected by original sin. He spoke of "free choice" or "free will" only in the sense that people have the *liberty* to do as they please, but lack the *ability* to comply with the law of God (*Summa Theologiae* 1. 82–83). At the same time, however, he tended to define sin as a lack of righteousness rather than the presence of moral corruption. He spoke of fallen humanity as being *deprived* of all the moral ability Adam possessed, as opposed to being morally *depraved*. For this reason Thomas spoke not only of what sinful people could not do, but also what they could do, particularly in the sphere of human reason. He did not, however, believe that "the will of man was fallen, but the intellect was not," as one modern writer expressed it.[9]

Renaissance and Reformation. During the late Middle Ages and early Renaissance many Western theologians and humanist scholars drifted away from the Augustinian tradition and emphasized human ability (as opposed to inability) in ways which went beyond Thomas Aquinas. With the coming of the Protestant Reformation, however, the Western Church saw a return to the Augustinian emphasis on human inability due to total depravity. The outstanding examples of this were Martin Luther and John Calvin.

Luther's view of human depravity was, in the minds of many Catholics, too severe. The Dutch Catholic scholar Erasmus, for example, wrote a treatise entitled *On the Freedom of the Will* to counter Luther's monergism. In reply Luther wrote what he regarded as his finest theological work, *On the Bondage of the Will*. John Calvin was no less opposed to the notion of "free will" than was Luther, emphasizing that God's saving grace was not "cooperating" with human free will (synergism), but rather "operating" to release the human will from its bondage to sin (*Institutes* 2.2.6).

Within fifty years of Calvin's death, however, the Dutch Reformed Church found itself in sharp intramural debate over a number of issues surrounding the topic of free will. The catalyst of that debate was Jacobus Arminius (1560-1609), a Dutch Reformed minister who opposed the Calvinist notion that God's grace produced salvation without any cooperation of human free will. Thus

JONATHAN EDWARDS

Jonathan Edwards (1703-1758) is considered by many the greatest theologian in the history of North America. His grandfather, Solomon Stoddard, was one of the most famous Puritan preachers in colonial New England. The young Edwards showed his intellectual prowess early. He had a good knowledge of Greek, Hebrew, and Latin before he was thirteen, and was writing papers on philosophy. In 1716 he entered the Collegiate School of Connecticut, which later became Yale, to prepare for the ministry. The fledgling college, founded to counter liberal theological trends at Harvard, was firmly devoted to teaching the Puritan Reformed orthodoxy articulated in the Westminster Confession.

After stints as a pastor in New York and as a tutor at Yale, the young Edwards joined his famous grandfather in 1724 as co-pastor of the Congregational Church in Northampton, Massachusetts. After Stoddard's death five years later, Edwards remained in Northampton until 1750. During that time

Edwards, along with the English evangelist George Whitefield, became the spiritual leader of a mighty revival which began in New England in 1734 and spread throughout the American colonies. His famous sermon "Sinners in the Hand of an Angry God" was preached in 1741, towards the end of that revival which would become known as the "First Great Awakening in North America."

In 1750 Edwards was dismissed from his pastorate, due to his insistence that congregational members must demonstrate some outward signs of authentic conversion before being admitted to the Lord's Supper. The following year he became pastor of a small Church in the frontier village of Stockbridge, and a missionary to the Indians of the area. During that time he wrote his classic treatise *Freedom of the Will* in response to the increasing influence of Arminian theology throughout New England. In that book Edwards articulated and defended the Augustinian definition of freedom of the will (see above, p. 153) over against the Arminian notion of an undetermined will, at many points seeking to reduce the latter to a string of self-contradictions.

Edwards was elected president of the College of New Jersey (later Princeton University) in 1757, and inaugurated in February 1758. At that time he received a vaccination against an ongoing smallpox epidemic. Rather than protecting him, the relatively new vaccination procedure developed into smallpox, which led to Edwards's death a month after his inauguration.

The impact of Jonathan Edwards on North American Christianity and culture has been formidable. His preaching and writing, which combined a brilliance of logical precision with a profound knowledge of Scripture and theology and a heart burning with passion for Jesus Christ, established standards equaled by few. His family tree over the following century included numerous ministers as well as college professors, doctors, lawyers, and even one vice-president of the United States, Aaron Burr (who, unfortunately, was regarded as the "prodigal son" of the clan).

On the other hand, the Puritan Reformed orthodoxy Edwards advocated in *Freedom of the Will* was gradually displaced by a "New Divinity" movement which sought common ground with the Arminianism Edwards so strenuously opposed. Nevertheless, Edwards's writings remain in print two hundred-fifty years after his death, while those of his adversaries have faded into oblivion.

Protestantism, since the early seventeenth century, has been divided into two camps with regard to the issue of free will: the monergistic Calvinists, and the synergistic Arminians. We shall examine the historical background and major issues surrounding the original Calvinist-Arminian controversy in more detail below (chapter 12).

In this way the medieval debate between monergistic Augustinians and synergistic Semi-Pelagians manifested itself anew within the ranks of Protestantism. But whereas the Augustinians prevailed in the medieval Latin Church, today their Arminian Protestant counterparts appear to be prevailing over Calvinism regarding the issue of free will. In North America, for example, it may be said with little fear of contradiction that the majority of Protestants are synergists (Semi-Pelagians; Arminians) as opposed to monergists (Augustinians; Calvinists), despite Jonathan Edwards's defense of monergism in his *Freedom of the Will* (see the following article on Edwards). The fact that Western Europe and North America have been deeply influenced by Enlightenment philosophy's optimistic view of human nature has no doubt helped shape the Protestant debate on the subject of "free will."

Despite disagreements on the matter of free will within the history of Christian doctrine, the Church has reached an overall consensus that, apart from divine intervention, human beings are incapable of overcoming the deleterious effects of sin. Whether one holds that sin renders humanity morally *sick* (Eastern Orthodoxy; Semi-Pelagianism; Arminianism) or morally *dead* (Augustinianism; Reformed theology), historic Christian belief is united in condemning the Pelagian/Enlightenment notion that humanity is in a relationship of fundamental harmony with God and therefore is morally *well*.

This historic Christian consensus regarding the human predicament is reflected in the words of Jesus: "It is not the healthy who need a doctor, but the sick. . . . I have come not to call the righteous, but sinners" (Matt. 9:12-13). Christ came to deliver sinners from their moral predicament and restore them into a right relationship with God. Who Christ was and how He accomplished His mission is the subject of Christology, the next major section of this book.

Points To Ponder

1. How does the writer of Genesis 3 indicate that the biblical account of the Fall speaks of an historical event, and not a myth which merely represents the human condition?

2. What is the meaning and significance of the tree of the knowledge of good and evil mentioned in Genesis 2? What does it tell us about the fundamental essence of sin?

3. From a biblical perspective, what is wrong with the old adage that "to err is human; to forgive, divine?"

4. How did the Eastern Church's view of original sin and original guilt differ from that of the Western Church during the first thousand years of Church history? Be able to identify key thinkers in the East-West debate on this issue.

5. Define *synergism* and *monergism*.

6. In what ways did creationist and traducianist perspectives on the origin of the soul affect the East-West debate on the extent of human sin?

7. Compare and contrast the Eastern view of freedom of the will (indeterminism) with the Western view (self-determinism).

8. How did Pelagius define sin and free will? How did Augustine respond?

9. What common ground exists between Arminians and Calvinists, which distinguishes them from Pelagians concerning the issues of sin and free will?

8

Christology, Part One: The Incarnation

Definition

The term *Incarnation*, derived from the Latin *in carnis* ("in the flesh"), refers to the Church's historic conviction that in Jesus Christ God became a human being without ceasing to be God. Scripture sets forth this conviction most explicitly in the Gospel of John: "In the beginning was the Word, and the Word was with God, and the Word was God . . . . The Word became flesh, and lived for awhile among us" (John 1:1, 14). Methodist theologian John Lawson defines the Incarnation as follows: "The Christian doctrine of the Incarnation is that the divine Son, who from all eternity is God in the same full sense that the Creator-Father and the Holy Spirit are divine, completely and permanently joined Himself to our genuine human nature, so as to form one real person who was at once both fully divine and fully human."[1]

This definition summarizes the consensus of the Church following several centuries of debate ending in the year 451. As we shall see, that debate took on a form which differed somewhat from the way the New Testament itself approaches christology. We shall explore the reasons for this in due course.

For now, let us focus on Lawson's statement that the divine Son completely joined Himself to our humanity. The word *completely* indicates that Christ experienced all we have experienced—including the experience of being born. At the same time, the Church has taught from earliest times that Jesus' birth was different from ours in that His mother conceived and bore Him without the agency of a human father: "[Jesus] was conceived by the Holy Spirit, born of the Virgin Mary." This confession of the virgin birth of Jesus Christ, as set forth in the second article of the Apostles' Creed, merits further discussion.

The Virgin Birth of Jesus Christ

The Biblical Witness

Events surrounding the birth of Jesus are recorded only by the gospel writers Matthew and Luke; Mark and John, like the rest of the New Testament writers, do not deal with the subject. Matthew and Luke tell their respective stories from different perspectives, yet both agree that Jesus was conceived by the Holy Spirit and born of a virgin named Mary. (This event is not to be confused with the Immaculate Conception, the Roman Catholic dogma which teaches that Mary the mother of Jesus was conceived without original sin.)

Many modern interpreters have denied the historicity of the virgin birth. They view the biblical texts not as accounts of an historical event, but as theological interpretations of the person of Jesus set forth in story form. Such a view runs counter to the plain sense of the biblical texts, however. Specifically, neither Matthew nor Luke draws any conclusions about the meaning of the virgin birth as it relates to the person of Christ. Matthew and Luke, for example, say nothing which relates the virgin birth either to the deity of Christ or the sinlessness of Christ.

This omission of theological interpretation regarding the person of Christ is particularly noteworthy in Luke. Despite the fact that Luke was a traveling companion of the apostle Paul, nothing of Pauline influence stands in Luke's account of Jesus' birth. For example, Paul's role as apostle to the Gentiles led him to emphasize Jesus as the savior of Jews and Gentiles alike. Yet Luke records the angels' message to the shepherds as one of "good news . . . that will be for all *the* people" (Luke 2:10). In this context the definite article refers to God's covenant people, the Jews, as opposed to all people, Jew and Gentile alike.

This exclusiveness is all the more remarkable when one considers that, of the synoptic gospels, Luke's gospel most emphasizes the universal scope of Christ's salvation. The most reasonable explanation for Luke's focus on all the people of *Israel* in this text is that he is simply recording someone's account of what the angels actually said. In other words, Luke is more interested in accurate history than in promoting Paul's christological agenda.

Postapostolic Witness

Another argument for the historical nature of the virgin birth accounts is that the second-century Church accepted them as such. Around A.D. 110, for example, Ignatius of Antioch described Christ as "truly of the race of David after the flesh, and Son of God after the Divine will and power, truly born of a virgin . . . ." (*Epistle to the Smyrneans* 1.1-2).[2]

Furthermore, the virgin birth began to gain confessional status in the second century. Early confessions which mention the virgin birth include:[3]

- Irenaeus (c. 190): The Church . . . has received from the apostles and their disciples this faith: . . . [She believes in] Christ Jesus, the Son of God . . . and the *birth from a virgin* . . . of the beloved Christ Jesus, our Lord (*Against Heresies* 1.10.1).

- Tertullian (c. 200): We . . . believe . . . that the one only God has also a Son, his Word who has proceeded from himself . . . ; that this [Son] was *sent by the Father into the virgin and was born of her* both man and God, son of man and Son of God, and was named Jesus Christ (*Against Praxeas* 2).

- Creed of Hippolytus (c. 215): Do you believe in Christ Jesus, the Son of God, Who was *begotten by the Holy Spirit from the Virgin Mary* . . . ?

- Creed of Marcellus (340): I believe in God, All Governing; And in Christ Jesus His only begotten Son, our Lord, who was *begotten of the Holy Spirit and the Virgin Mary* . . . .

By the year 381 the ecumenical council held in Constantinople affirmed that "We believe . . . in one Lord Jesus Christ . . . who for us men and for our salvation came down from heaven and was incarnate by the Holy Ghost and the Virgin Mary." The doctrine of the virgin birth of Christ had attained the status of ecclesiastical dogma, a teaching which one must confess in order to become a member of Christ's Church.

Dogmatic Interpretations of the Virgin Birth

While the Bible states that Jesus was born of a virgin, it does not specify why. Throughout Church history theologians have tried to answer that question, usually by relating the virgin birth to some aspect of Christ's person or nature.

For example, many have argued that Christ had to be virgin-born in order to be divine. Tertullian (*Against Marcion* 4.10) is a case in point: "Since He is [begotten] of God the Father, He is not, of course, [the son] of a human father. If He is not of a human father, it follows that He must be [the son] of a human mother. If of a human mother, it is evident that she must be a virgin."[4]

The New Testament, however, bases Christ's divine Sonship not on the virgin birth but upon His preexistence. John 1:1 says that the preincarnate Word was already God, while Matthew and Luke draw no conclusions about the divinity of Christ in their accounts of the virgin birth.

A second widespread interpretation is that the virgin birth accounts for the sinlessness of Christ. Augustine, for example, describes Jesus as follows: "begotten and conceived without any indulgence of carnal lust, and therefore bringing with Him no original sin" (*Enchiridion*, chapter 41).[5]

More recently, theologians as diverse as Karl Barth and Millard Erickson have challenged this view.[6] Though they differ on many points, both argue that Mary alone would have passed on original sin (a sinful human nature) to Jesus. And we have stated earlier that the New Testament itself makes no link between the virgin birth and the sinlessness of Christ.

Scripture, then, sees no necessary connection between the virgin birth on the one hand, and any specific doctrine about the *nature* of Christ (such as His deity or sinlessness) on the other. Rather, these are matters of theological inference. Such inferences may be true, of course. But Matthew's and Luke's virgin birth accounts give us no direct evidence of this, since they are not dogmatic theology in story form, but rather historical narratives.

For this reason a more promising solution to the meaning of the virgin birth may lie in its role as a sign of God's grace in His history of salvation. That is to say, both Matthew and Luke may be less concerned about the *nature* of Christ than they are about His *function*, or role in salvation history.

Salvation-Historical Interpretations of the Virgin Birth

Matthew interprets the virgin birth as a sign that God had fulfilled His promise to save His people (Matt. 1:21). It is a matter of debate, however, whether or not Matthew views Jesus' birth as a *direct* fulfillment of the prophecy concerning "Immanuel" found in Isaiah 7:14. In its original context Isaiah 7:14 appears to refer to a child who would be born within a few years after the prophet Isaiah had spoken to King Ahaz of Judah (see Isaiah 7:1-9, 15-16). Some interpreters believe Isaiah was referring to the future birth of his own son (Isaiah 8:1-9). How, then, can this be a prediction of the birth of Jesus some seven hundred years later?

Many believe that Isaiah did not intend to predict the birth of Christ. Rather, the prophet foretold the birth of a child, "Immanuel," who would be a sign to King Ahaz that Judah would be saved from the impending threat of conquest by the armies of Israel and Syria (Isaiah 7:1; "Aram" refers to Syria). According to this view, Matthew has cited Isaiah's prophecy of Judah's imminent deliverance from Syria and Israel as an event which foreshadowed an even greater saving event: the coming of the true "Immanuel" to save His people from their captivity to sin (Matt. 1:21).

This sort of Jewish interpretation is sometimes called "typological." In this case the earlier saving event (the defeat of Syria and Israel) became a "type," or picture, of a future saving event which surpasses it in greatness. The future event, or "antitype," is the coming of Jesus, who offers a deliverance far greater than anything Isaiah could offer King Ahaz of Judah. In this sense the virgin birth "fulfills" Isaiah 7:14 as a sign of God's saving activity towards His people.

Luke also places the virgin birth within the framework of God's plan of salvation history. For Luke, the virgin birth of Jesus Christ was the second and greater of two extraordinary births heralding the arrival of the messianic age of salvation. The first birth, that of

John the Baptist, was a sign that the promised messianic age would come soon, within the lifetime of John.

The fact that John was born to elderly parents who had been childless makes for a striking parallel between John's birth and the birth of Isaac to Abraham and Sarah (Gen. 21). Thus the age characterized by God's promises of future blessings to all nations through the seed of Abraham (Genesis 12:3) included extraordinary births at both its beginning and at its close, just before the fulfillment of the promises in Jesus Christ.

What sort of sign, then, would signal the arrival of the messianic age? Another child born to elderly, barren parents would merely duplicate the signs of the age of promise. To put it another way, what would God do for an encore?

For Luke, God's "encore" was a sign that went beyond the amazing births of Isaac and John the Baptist: the Messiah, the fulfillment of God's promises throughout the age of the Abrahamic covenant, was born without the agency of a human father. In this way the virgin birth testifies to the fact that the age of promise is now past, and the age of fulfillment is upon us.

Taken together, Matthew and Luke testify that in Jesus God has sent a salvation greater than anything that was done during the age of promise (Matthew), thereby fulfilling the promises given during that age of the old covenant (Luke). The virgin birth of Christ is God's sign that Jesus is precisely the one whose function it is to fulfill those promises by bringing God's blessings to "all nations" (Gen. 12:3; Matt. 28:19, Luke 24:47).

The witness of the virgin birth to Christ's function within redemptive history anticipates the manner in which the entire New Testament addresses the question, "Who was Jesus Christ?" To this we now turn.

New Testament Christological Titles

In his *Christology of the New Testament*, Oscar Cullmann defines christology as "the science whose object is the person and work of Christ."[7] He then takes note of how the New Testament interprets the meaning of Christ in a manner distinct from the orthodox formulas which followed the apostolic era. The christological formulas of later orthodoxy "refer almost exclusively to the *person* or *nature* of Christ," that is, to the relation between Jesus' nature and the nature of God, and the relationship between Jesus' divine and human natures. On the other hand, the New Testament "hardly ever speaks of the person of Christ without at the same time speaking of his work." To put it another way: "When it is asked in the New Testament, 'Who is Christ?', the question never means . . . primarily, 'What is His nature?', but first of all, 'What is His function?'"[8]

New Testament christology, then, is "functional" christology. It focuses on Christ's role in salvation history as the one who has fulfilled the promises of the Abrahamic covenant. The first Christians addressed the question of Christ's function in redemptive history by means of concepts already present in Judaism. Specifically, they used *titles* from their biblical and traditional heritage to confess their faith in Jesus. The most familiar title, of course, was that of "Christ" (Messiah), which over time virtually took on the status of a proper name ("Jesus Christ" or "Christ Jesus").

Because these first Christians viewed Christ in relation to redemptive history, Cullmann divides the titles they used of Him into four categories relating to different times within that history:

- The *past* work of Christ (the Jesus of history).
- The *future* work of Christ (His second coming).
- The *present* work of Christ (the risen and ascended Jesus).
- The *preexistent* work of Christ (prior to the incarnation).

What follows is a list of eight key New Testament titles, two titles under each of the aforementioned four categories.

The Past Work of Christ: Prophet; Servant of God

Prophet. In the Old Testament, God almost never dealt directly with His covenant people Israel. Rather, he made use of mediators, or "go-betweens," to do so. The three mediatorial offices in the Old Testament were those of prophet (who spoke the Word of God), king (who governed as God's representative), and priest (who mediated access between God and the worshiping community).

The New Testament makes it clear that many Jews believed Jesus to be a great prophet (Luke 7:16, Matt. 21:46). Some even believed He was Elijah (Mark 6:15), who was regarded as "*the* Prophet" who would appear at the end of this present evil age, prior to the judgment of the nations and the deliverance of Israel (Mal. 4:5). Jesus did not regard Himself as this Elijah-style eschatological prophet, though He did describe Himself as *a* prophet (Mark 6:4, Matt. 23:37). For this reason the Church has traditionally viewed Jesus' earthly prophetic work as one of the three mediatorial offices of Christ.

Servant of God. The title "Servant of God" (Hebrew *ebed Yahweh*) was one which Jesus applied to Himself. He saw Himself as a servant who would suffer and give His life as a ransom for many (Mark 10:45). Both the words of Jesus and the testimony of the early Church in Jerusalem indicate that Jesus saw Himself as fulfilling the "suffering Servant" prophecies of Isaiah 52:13-53:12 (see Acts 3:13, 26; 4:27, 30; and especially 8:32-35). The fact that Jesus defined His messiahship in terms of Isaiah's suffering Servant stands in contrast to the messianic expectations of His Jewish countrymen, who did not expect the Messiah to suffer a vicarious death on behalf of His people (as per Isaiah 53:4-6) and therefore did not see Isaiah's suffering Servant as a messianic prophecy.

The Future Work of Christ: King; Son of Man.

King. The sort of Messiah expected by Jesus' contemporaries could rightly be called a king. The Magi who visited the baby Jesus, for example, inquired of Herod as to the birthplace of the "King of the Jews" (Matt. 2:2) showing that they were familiar with the Jewish messianic tradition at this point. Jesus' disciple Nathaniel likewise referred to Jesus as "the King of Israel" (John 1:49).

First-century Jews spoke of this royal Messiah as the "Son of David" (see Matt. 22:42). This title became part of Jewish tradition during the intertestamental period, when Jerusalem and Judea were successively under the governance of Persia, Greece, Syria, and Rome. Jews under foreign occupation came to anticipate their future Messiah as a military warrior-king, like King David of old, who would deliver Israel from her enemies and usher in the future age of righteousness ("the coming kingdom of our father David"; Mark 11:10).

In light of these militaristic messianic expectations, as well as the fact that Jesus defined His mission on earth as one of a humble suffering Servant, it is not surprising that He avoided using the royal title "Son of David" of Himself. He did *acknowledge* it when blind Bartimaeus called out to Him, "Son of David, have mercy on me" (Mark 10:47-48). But soon after that Jesus went out of His way to distance Himself from this title (Mark 12:35).

Son of Man. The title which Jesus did use of Himself most frequently was "Son of Man." Like "Son of David," this was an eschatological title pointing towards the coming of a Messiah who would deliver Israel and usher in a new age of righteousness. Unlike the former title, however, "Son of Man" referred to a heavenly being who would come down to earth from the clouds at the end of the age to judge the nations.

Jesus almost certainly used this title in the sense of Daniel 7:13. The prophet Daniel saw a vision of such a heavenly being, whom His spoke of as "one like a son of man" (who looked like a man). It is important here to stress that according to this tradition the Messiah would look human, but would be an immortal heavenly being. The fact that Jesus, who told His followers that He would die, nevertheless called Himself "Son of Man" created a conundrum for some of His listeners (as indicated by John 12:34, "Who is *this* [dying!] 'Son of Man'?").

At the same time, Jesus saw Himself as the one who would indeed come down from heaven to judge the earth at the end of the age (Matt. 24-25 and parallels). This, then, was part of the mystery of His Messiahship. There would be two advents of Messiah: the first in mundane humility; the second in celestial glory.

The Present Work of Christ: Priest; Lord.

Priest. The New Testament book of Hebrews describes the risen and ascended Jesus as presently interceding before God on our behalf as our "High Priest" (Heb. 7-9). Jesus is not idle during this present time between His first and second advents. Rather, He fulfills the role of the Old Testament priests, who served as mediators between a Holy God and sinful human beings. Jesus, however, is a greater priest than those of the tribe of Levi, in that His priesthood lasts forever (Heb. 7:23). The writer of Hebrews refers to Him not as a priest after the order of Levi, but after the order of Melchizedek, as prophesied in Psalm 110:4 (which was regarded by the Jews as messianic; see Heb. 7:17).

Lord. Perhaps the most all-encompassing New Testament messianic title is "Lord," which refers to the present invisible rule of Christ. Cullmann's *The Earliest Christian Confessions*[9] notes that the most frequent confessional statement in the New Testament is the declaration "Jesus is Lord!" (1 Cor. 12:3, Phil. 2:11). This "lordship" motif is found in one form or another in all of the New Testament confessional material.

New Testament Christianity is therefore centered not upon what Jesus has done or will do, but what Jesus is doing now. He is ruling as Lord. Furthermore, this lordship of Christ is not limited to individual Christians ("my personal Lord") or even to the Church. He is Lord over every realm of creation, "in heaven and on earth and under the earth" (Phil. 2:10-11). Belief in Christ cannot be relegated to the realm of the spiritual alone. Jesus is Lord of all.

The Preexistence of Christ: The Word; God.

Word. When the New Testament speaks of Christ's preexistence, we do indeed get glimpses of His person or nature as well as of His work. The classic example of this is John 1:1: "In the beginning was the Word [Greek *logos*], and the Word was with God, and the Word was God."

Yet even here John emphasizes the work of Christ: "Through Him all things were made; without him nothing was made that has been made" (1:3). John then goes on to say that this divine agent of creation, the Word, "became flesh" (1:14) in order to redeem sinful human beings (20:31). In this way John underscores the divine Word as the agent of both creation and redemption. So even as the nature of Christ is revealed by the Logos-title, the work of Christ remains John's primary concern.

God. Nevertheless, John does say that "the Word was God." He records Thomas's confession of Jesus as "my Lord and my God" (John 20:28). The fact that Jesus did not rebuke Thomas for worshiping Him is further testimony to the deity of Christ.

While the apostle Paul seldom refers directly to Christ as God, he does appear to do so on a few occasions. Romans 9:5, for example, describes Christ as the one "who is God over all, forever praised." And Titus 2:13 speaks of "our great God and Savior, Jesus Christ." These statements, along with the Johannine testimony, give us rare glimpses of the person of Christ as God come in the flesh, even as the New Testament speaks mainly of Christ's work in redemptive history.

Subsequent doctrinal controversies led the post-apostolic Church to respond to the question "Who is Christ?" in terms of His person rather than His work. Among the earliest controversies were struggles with the heresies of gnosticism, adoptionism, and modalism.

Christological Controversies, A.D. 100-325

Two Brands of Gnosticism

In chapter 4 we noted that Gnosticism was a worldview which presupposed a radical dichotomy between the spiritual and material realms. The spiritual realm was by definition good; the material realm, flawed or even evil. Only through secret knowledge (*gnosis*) could human beings transcend the prison-house of their earthly bodily existence and experience salvation. This radical dualism, which ran counter to the biblical doctrine of creation, spawned two dangerous christological heresies in the late first and early second centuries: Cerinthianism and docetism.

Cerinthianism is named after Cerinthus, a gnostic contemporary of John the Apostle who lived in Asia Minor. His dualistic cosmology led him to distinguish between "Jesus" and "Christ." For Cerinthus, Jesus was a normal man chosen by God to proclaim the divine *gnosis*. For this task God anointed Jesus with the Christ-spirit when Jesus was baptized by John the Baptist. This Christ-spirit departed from Jesus before He was crucified.

According to Church tradition the apostle John was Bishop of Ephesus when he wrote the following words against Cerinthus and his disciples: "Every spirit that acknowledges that Jesus Christ has come in the flesh is from God, but every spirit that does not acknowledge Jesus [the flesh-and-blood man] is not from God" (1 John 4:2-3). The Gospel of John likewise emphasizes that the divine "Word became flesh" (1:14). John refused to separate the Savior into two parts, Jesus (human) and Christ (spirit), as did Cerinthus.[10]

The term *docetism* comes from Greek verb *dokeo*, meaning "to seem" or "to appear." Docetism was a false teaching concerning the person of Christ. Specifically, it denied that Jesus Christ was truly human. Rather, He was a spirit-being who only *appeared* or *seemed* to be human.

In the early second century Ignatius of Antioch spoke out against the docetic heresy: "Be deaf, therefore, when any one speaks to you apart from Jesus Christ who . . . was truly crucified and died. . . . But if it be, as some godless men, that is, unbelievers, assert, that He suffered in semblance [phantom] only—it is they who are phantoms—why am I in bonds? (*Epistle to the Trallians* 10).[11] The problem reflected here was that some professing Christians of a Greek philosophical mindset did not believe that a divine being could suffer. God, according to their dualistic world-view, was impassible, beyond suffering. Thus Jesus, if He was divine, could not suffer. Therefore He could not be human.

The apostle John and Ignatius were engaged in no ivory-tower intellectual exercise at this point. They realized full well what was at stake. The dualistic gnostic perspective which underlay both Cerinthianism and docetism placed a gulf between God and humanity. God was spiritual and beyond suffering; humanity was material and subject to pain. If Jesus were truly God, He could not at the same time be human. But if He were not human, He could not reconcile humanity to God, since the gulf between God and man remained unbridged. The docetic *Gospel of Peter* underscored this gnostic dualism when it described Christ's crucifixion: "And they brought two malefactors, and crucified the Lord between them. But He kept silence, as one feeling no pain."[12] Such a Christ who did not suffer at all, much less for anyone else, could not save us from our sins.

Adoptionism

Whereas docetic Christians denied the humanity of Christ, other early quasi-Christian groups denied Christ's full divinity by propagating various forms of *adoptionism*. This is the theory that Jesus was by nature simply a human being who became divine in some sense by means of God's having adopted Him. The Cerinthian heresy could be described as a combination of gnosticism and adoptionism. Another version of adoptionism is found in *The Shep-*

herd of Hermes, written about A.D. 150. It taught that Jesus was a virtuous man chosen by God, and with him the Spirit of God was united.

The earliest adoptionist community was probably the Ebionites, a second-century Jewish Christian sect which, like Cerinthus, saw Jesus as having been adopted as Son of God when John baptized Him (though they did not share the radical cosmological dualism of Cerinthus). The strictly-monotheistic Ebionites no doubt felt that to regard Christ as divine in His own right could be seen as advocating the worship of two gods, the Father and the Son.

Indeed, the charge that Christians worshiped two gods was made by the pagan writer Celsus, one of Christianity's most forceful opponents in the second century. The various modalist christologies sought to counter this critique.

Modalism

This third-century movement was part of the trinitarian debate which sought to define the relationship between the preexistent Christ (the Son of God, or Logos) and God the Father. Modalism attempted to uphold Christianity's unquestioned monotheism against suspected bitheism or tritheism. This was done in several ways, all of which said basically the same thing: namely, that God's self-designations of Father, Son, and Spirit were but three modes of expression of the one God. The Godhead was not truly diverse, but was one person who had shown Himself in three different ways.

One of the earliest of these attempts to preserve the unity of the Godhead was that of Praxeas of Rome, who identified the Son with the Father and thus spoke of the Father as suffering on the cross. This brand of modalism was also known as *patripassianism.*

Such modalist attempts to preserve monotheism were swiftly rebutted. Tertullian, for example, countered the patripassianism of Praxeas with his famous line that Praxeas "put to flight the Paraclete [Holy Spirit] and crucified the Father" (*Against Praxeas* 1.5). It was Tertullian who first used what was to become orthodox terminology when he affirmed that Jesus Christ had two natures joined in one *person* (*Against Praxeas* 27).[13]

Tertullian's anticipation of the orthodox formula hardly ended the christological debate. Within two generations of Tertullian, Paul of Samosata, who was the bishop of Antioch, taught that Jesus was a mere man whom God had anointed by the Holy Spirit. This anointing conferred the divine Logos upon Jesus. Paul of Samosata interpreted this Logos as an impersonal quality of God which could be called the divine Wisdom. This Wisdom within Christ was seen as being of the "same substance" (Greek *homoousion*) with God, but not as constituting a person distinct from God the Father. Paul of Samosata was excommunicated in A.D. 268 by local Christian elders for teaching both adoptionism (Jesus was a mere man anointed by God) and a form of modalism (the Logos is not the second person of the Trinity).

The modalist, adoptionist, and gnostic heresies were early manifestations of the trinitarian controversies which culminated with the Fourth Ecumenical Council held at Chalcedon in 451. These controversies were part of the larger debate about the nature and person of Jesus Christ, with the doctrine of the Trinity emerging as a necessary implication of orthodox Christology. What follows is a brief account of key events surrounding this debate.

Christological Controversies, A.D. 325-451

Constantine Converts to Christianity

The quest for christological consensus was made all the more urgent in the early fourth century by an event which had no direct relationship to the Church's ongoing theological debates, but which changed the course not only of Church history, but of world history as well. That event was the conversion of the Roman Emperor Constantine to Christianity in A.D. 313.

Historians have debated whether Constantine's conversion was genuine. Some believe the emperor realized that the old Roman gods no longer commanded the public's allegiance, and that a new religion was needed to unite the empire. Whatever Constantine's motives, it soon became clear that his act of embracing the Christian faith would not provide a basis for uniting the empire, since the Church itself was sharply divided in its Christology. Specifically, fierce debate as to whether Christ was fully divine threatened to split the Church and therefore the empire. This prompted Constantine to call for a council of ecclesiastical representatives from all over the empire. This first ecumenical, or worldwide, council was held in the year 325 in Nicea, just south of the key Asian port city

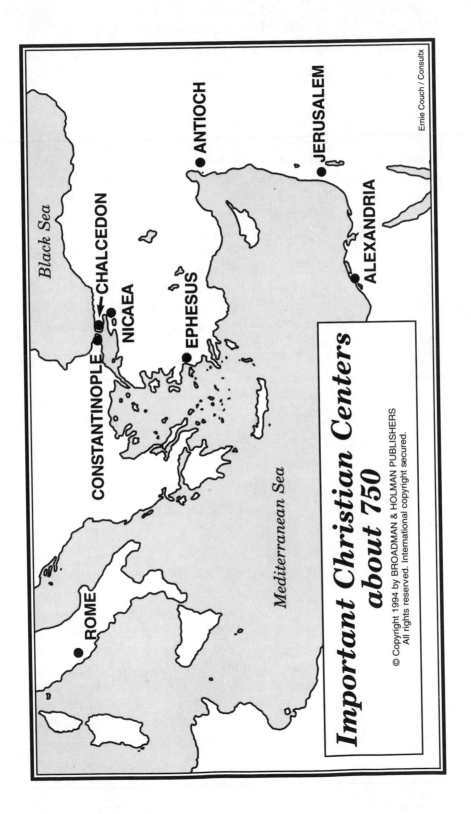

Important Christian Centers
about 750

Ernie Couch / Consultx

Black Sea

Mediterranean Sea

ROME

CONSTANTINOPLE — CHALCEDON

NICAEA

EPHESUS

ANTIOCH

JERUSALEM

ALEXANDRIA

of Byzantium (renamed Constantinople in 330; now Istanbul, Turkey).

The Council of Nicea (A.D. 325)

What became known as the Arian controversy began as a debate between Arius of Alexandria and the bishop of his diocese, Alexander. Alexander held that the Son, the divine Logos, was eternal and unchanging like the Father. Arius believed this was a form of the modalist heresy of Paul of Samosata, who had taught that the divine wisdom or Logos was of the same essence (*homoousion*) as the Father. Arius, instead held that the Son was not divine in the same sense as the Father. The Logos, Arius insisted, was the most glorious being of God's creation, but a creature nonetheless. Whereas the Father has always existed, there was a time when the Son did not exist. The Arian controversy turned out to be the most dangerous threat to orthodox Christianity in the fourth-century.

The views of Arius had gained a wide following in the East. A popular poem of that time, set to a tavern tune, tells us something of Arius's views, and perhaps of Arius himself:

Arius of Alexandria, I'm the talk of the town,

Friend of saints, elect of heaven,
filled with learning and renown;

If you want the Logos doctrine,
I can serve it hot and hot:

God begat him and before
he was begotten he was not.[14]

As noted in chapter 3, Arius and his followers used the word "begotten" in the sense of "created." Later doctrinal formulations by the Church would make a distinction between these two words (see below, p. 181, as well as the discussion in chapter 3, p. 68).

Most of those assembled at Nicea attempted to find a middle ground between Arius and Alexander. Numerous attempts at compromise were rejected, however, chiefly due to the efforts of Athanasius, chief theological adviser to the party of Alexander. Time and again the young Athanasius refused to accept any statement which left in doubt the full divinity of the Son.

Constantine himself appears to have broken the logjam by proposing that the Son should be defined as being "of the same substance" (*homoousion*) as the Father. The Arians adamantly rejected this term, which had heretofore been connected with the heretic Paul of Samosata. Yet despite its dubious theological pedigree, *homoousion* won the day and eventually became the definitive term for orthodox Christology. The fact that Constantine himself proposed the term no doubt contributed to its success at Nicea.

The Emperor's imprimatur did not guarantee the ongoing survival of the *homoousion*, however. Following the death of Constantine, the Nicean christological formula came under almost constant attack from two directions.

On the one hand, the Arians remained a powerful force throughout much of the Empire, and were able to gain the allegiance of several of Constantine's successors. On the other hand, some theologians went so far in their opposition to the Arian heresy that they affirmed Christ's full deity at the expense of His full humanity. One such man was, ironically, an ally of Athanasius against the Arians who later found himself at odds with his old friend. His name was Apollinarius.

The Council of Constantinople (A.D. 381)

Apollinarius was a strong supporter of the *homoousion* formula, affirming that Jesus was God come in the flesh. At the same time, however, Apollinarius believed that the divine Logos fulfilled the role of the human mind in Jesus, so that Jesus's humanity was not completely like ours. To put it another way: Jesus had both a human body (*soma*) and an irrational soul (*psuchealogos*) that was the inward living principle of both animals and humans, but He did not possess a human spirit, or rational soul unique to humans (*psuchelogike; nous; pneuma*).

In the language of trichotomy (see chapter 6), Jesus was human in body and soul, but not in spirit. If He had a human spirit, reasoned Apollinarius, He would be two persons, not one divine Person. This *Apollinarianism* became known as "Word-flesh" Christology, affirming as it did that the Word became flesh, even if Jesus was not fully human.

ATHANASIUS

Athanasius (*c.* 296-373) was Bishop of Alexandria from 328 until his death. He is widely regarded as the greatest theologian of his time.

His education was in the Greek classical tradition, which placed him squarely in the Alexandrian theological school and its emphasis on the divinity of Christ. For this reason he was uncompromising in his opposition to the Arian heresy. At the same time, Athanasius refused to follow the road towards Monophysitism traveled by others of the Alexandrian school, such as Apollinarius and Cyril of Alexandria. Instead, Athanasius stood firmly for the fully humanity of Christ over against his friend Apollinarius. In this way Athanasius was more in line with the "Word-Man" christological emphasis of the Antioch theological school.

Athanasius's concern for orthodox Christology was inextricably linked to his doctrine of the atonement. Specifically, he viewed Christ as God incarnate who assumed our fallen humanity in order to redeem it. "The Savior having in very truth become man, the salvation of the whole man was brought about . . . . the whole body and soul alike, has truly obtained salvation in the Word himself" (*Letter to Epictetus* 7). He even spoke of salvation as "divinization" (*theosis*) through the Spirit, though he did not mean to infer any inner deification of our human nature. Rather, he wished to emphasize that complete restoration of the divine image in humanity and full reconciliation with God could only be accomplished by our becoming united with the deity and humanity of Christ through the work of the Spirit.

Athanasius became Bishop of Alexandria three years after the Church's affirmation of Christ's full divinity and rejection of Arianism at Nicea. His tenure was marked by five periods of exile. His vigorous defense of the Nicean formula made him a target for the supporters of Arius, who were able to convince several emperors that he was unfit for office. Reports that he used physical punishment were among the charges brought against him, but whether he was the "violent man" described in Paul Johnson's *A History of Christianity* remains uncertain.*

During the years following Nicea a "semi-Arian" movement arose which preferred to call the Son of God *homoiousion* ("of *like* substance") with the Father, as opposed to the Nicean *homoousion* ("of the same substance"). While Athanasius did not like the semi-Arians' use of this word, for the sake of the unity of the Church he refused to make a big issue of it. Eventually his own view won the day, as the *homoousion* was reaffirmed at Constantinople, eight years after his death.

---

* Paul Johnson, *A History of Christianity*, 87.

Athanasius was forced to oppose Apollinarius in order to preserve the full humanity of Christ. He was joined by the so-called Cappadocian fathers (Basil the Great, Gregory of Nyssa, Gregory of Nazianzus), who carried on the battle after Athanasius died in 373. What emerged over against the "Word-flesh" formula of Apollinarius was a "Word-Man" Christology. Gregory of Nazianzus, for example, wrote: "If anyone has put his trust in [Christ] as a man without a human mind, he is himself devoid of mind and quite unworthy of salvation. For what He has not assumed He has not healed; it is what is united to His Deity that is saved." (*Epistles* 101.7)[15]

Here Gregory was following the lead of Athanasius, who had argued that Christ must be fully God and fully human in order for humans to be fully reconciled to God in Christ. But whereas Athanasius made this point to underscore the necessity of the full divinity of Christ, Gregory was attempting to show the need for Christ to be fully human, with a human mind.

What was to become regarded as the Second Ecumenical Council was convened in 381 at Constantinople, with Gregory of Nazianzus presiding over a portion of the proceedings. The influence of the late Athanasius and the Cappadocian fathers yielded two results:

- The council affirmed the "Word-Man" Christology of Athanasius and the Cappadocians over against the "Word-flesh" formula of Apollinarius.

- The council confronted the resurgent Arians by reaffirming and elaborating upon the confession adopted fifty-six years earlier at Nicea, stating that the Son was "begotten, not made; being of one substance (*homoousion*) with the Father." The formula adopted at Constantinople is what we today know as the Nicene Creed.

The Council of Ephesus (A.D. 431)

The fourth-century councils at Nicea and Constantinople had affirmed the full deity of the person of Christ, as well as confessing that Christ had both a fully divine nature and a fully human nature. In the fifth century both of these affirmations were challenged.

The *Nestorian* heresy defined Christ as not only having two natures, but also being two persons: one divine, one human. Nestorius, bishop of Constantinople, represented the Antioch school of theology and its "Word-Man" christological perspective. He therefore found it difficult to affirm Christ's full humanity without affirming that Christ was a human person who had been assumed by the divine Logos while still in the womb of His mother Mary. His statement that the one in Mary's womb "was not himself God, but God assumed him" also left Nestorius open to charges of adoptionism.[16]

Nestorius therefore refused to refer to Mary by the currently-popular title of "Mother of God" (*theotokos*; literally, "God-bearer"). Instead, Nestorius called her the "Mother of Christ." To call a human being the "Mother of God," he felt, would be to call into question the full deity of the Logos and revert to Arianism. In his own way, then, Nestorius sought to preserve the divinity as well as the humanity of Christ.

On the other side of the coin was *Monophysitism* (from the Greek *mono physis*, "one nature"). This view, represented by Cyril of Alexandria and others who carried the "Word-flesh" Christology of Apollinarius to an extreme, denied any distinction between Christ's divine and human natures. Jesus was not God and Man, or even God and two-thirds Man. Instead, the Monophysites saw Jesus as what may be termed "God-Man" in the sense that His two natures were so intermingled that all real distinctions between His divine and human natures were overcome in the incarnation. Cyril propagated his perspective fiercely, attempting to have Nestorius branded as a heretic.

On the day of Pentecost, A.D. 431, the Emperor Theodosius II convened in Ephesus what turned out to be a highly contentious council (due by some accounts to the thoroughly unsavory personality of Cyril). What finally emerged two years later was a compromise between the Nestorian and Alexandrian parties, which asserted two distinct natures of Christ against Cyril, and the title "Mother of God" (*theotokos*) against Nestorius. The text reads in part:

> We confess, that our Lord Jesus Christ, the only begotten Son of God, is perfect God and perfect man, . . . of the same substance [*homoousion*] with the Father as to his Godhead, and of the same substance [*homoousion*] with us as to his manhood; for two natures are united with one another. Therefore we confess one Christ, one

Lord, and one Son. By reason of this *union*, which yet is *without confusion*, we also confess that the holy Virgin is *mother of God*, because God the Logos was made flesh and man, and united with himself the temple [humanity] even from conception; which temple he took from the Virgin.[17]

Nestorius and Cyril both ended up losing their respective positions of authority (Nestorius during the Ephesus council; Cyril soon after). Ironically, modern research has discovered a book written by Nestorius, *The Book of Heracleides*, in which he explicitly denies the heresy for which he was condemned. Whether he recanted or was misunderstood is beyond the scope of our survey.

In any event, the Nestorian movement went its own way and made no challenge to the orthodox faith reaffirmed at Ephesus. The Monophysites, on the other hand, sought to capture eccesiastical power to further their theological agenda. They very nearly succeeded.

The Monophysites and the "Robber Synod" of A.D. 449

The consensus obtained at Ephesus in 431 did not last long. Eutyches, an otherwise obscure monk who appeared with Cyril at Ephesus, soon declared that Christ has only one nature, and that this nature is divine. Jesus' humanity was assimilated into the divine Logos so that even His body, though real, is not of the same substance as ours. This extreme form of Monophysitism became known as Eutychianism, and was vigorously opposed by Leo I, Bishop of Rome, who argued for the orthodox formula of two distinct natures united in one divine person.

Leo, however, was outmaneuvered by Cyril's successor in Alexandria, Patriarch Dioscorus, who in 449 persuaded Emperor Theodosius II to convene another council in Ephesus. This gathering, reinforced with armed soldiers, eventually went down in history as the "Synod of Robbers." The 135 assembled bishops condemned the orthodox one person-two natures formula and excommunicated all who embraced it, including Leo I.

The following year Theodosius II was dead, and Marcian succeeded him upon the imperial throne. To Leo and others of the orthodox persuasion, this must have seemed nothing less than providential.

The Council of Chalcedon (A.D. 451)

Leo was able to convince Marcian to convene a new council in the year 451, which first met in Nicea, but soon after adjourned to nearby Chalcedon in order to insure better riot control by the imperial government. This fourth ecumenical council was more largely attended than any other of antiquity. The approximately six hundred bishops gathered were almost all Greeks and Easterners. Yet when representatives of Leo, Bishop of Rome, set forth his *Epistola Dogmatica* for adoption, the other bishops heartily proclaimed, "This is the true faith!" After further consultation, the orthodox formulas dating from 325 (Nicea) to 431 (Ephesus) were reaffirmed. Specifically,

- The *homoousion* was affirmed with relation both to Christ's divinity and His humanity.

- The terminology which had first been articulated by Tertullian over two centuries earlier—one divine person with two distinct natures, one divine and one human—was reaffirmed.

- The doctrine of the hypostatic union—that Jesus Christ is *vere Deus, vere homo,* "truly God, truly man"—became the norm for all major branches of Christendom from that time onward.

This is not to say that Monophysitism died out. To this day, the national Churches of Egypt (Coptic), Syria (Jacobite), and Armenia are Monophysite. But they have gone their separate way, having no fellowship with either the Orthodox patriarchs of the East or the Roman pontiff in the West.[18] Protestantism has likewise rejected Monophysitism.

Thus, for all of their divisions, ecclesiastical bodies of Protestant, Catholic, and Orthodox persuasions confess the same Jesus Christ. This common christological confession is best summarized by the second article of what has become known as the Nicene Creed.

CHRISTOLOGIES: Orthodox and Heretical
(A.D. 325–451)

Christologies	Views of Christ	Proponents	Councils
Orthodox	God / Human One divine person; Two distinct natures, divine and human	Athanasius Pope Leo I	Nicea (325) Constantinople (381) Ephesus (431) Chalcedon (451)
Arian	God-like / Human Fully human nature; *not* fully divine nature	Arius	Nicea, Constantinople
Apollinarian	God / Human Body/Soul Fully divine nature; 2/3 human nature	Apollinarius	Constantinople
Monophysite	God-Human One nature (mingling of divine and human)	Cyril of Alexandria Eutyches	Ephesus Chalcedon
Nestorian	God / Human Two distinct *persons*	Nestorius	Ephesus

Some Later Christological Developments

Communion of Attributes vs. Communication of Attributes

The ecumenical council held at Ephesus in 431 A.D. concluded its christological confession as follows:

> But concerning the words of the Gospel and Epistles respecting Christ, we know that theologians apply some which refer to the one [divine] person to the two natures in common, but separate others as referring to the two natures, and assign the expressions which become God to the Godhead of Christ, but the expressions of humiliation to his manhood.[19]

The term "communion of attributes" (*communio idiomatum*) has been used with reference to this confession. Specifically, it refers to the belief that Christ's divine attributes (such as His immutability or omnipotence) may be applied to the man Jesus, and that His human attributes (such as mortality) may be applied to His divine person. Thus the ecumenical council of Ephesus did not refrain from calling Mary the "Mother of God." In so doing it was not attempting to deify Mary; it was affirming the full divinity of Jesus. On the other hand, the hymn writer Isaac Watts can praise Christ with the words "God, the mighty Maker, died." What is true of the divine Son is true of the man Jesus, and vice-versa. He is the one divine Person.

During the Protestant Reformation both Luther and Calvin affirmed the notion of a communion of attributes. Luther went one step further, however, and affirmed a "*communication* of attributes" (*communicatio idiomatum*).[20] According to this view the attributes of Jesus are not merely in communion, or relationship, with one another. Rather, Christ's human nature participates in the divine attributes by virtue of the hypostatic union. That is to say, there is an *interpenetration* of the human nature of Christ by the divine.

Lutheranism views the communication of attributes as affirming that in Jesus Christ we become partakers of the divine nature (see 2 Pet. 2:14), and that the risen Christ indwells believers both in His divinity and His humanity. Reformed theology, on the other hand, has tended to affirm only a communion of attributes, in order to avoid the danger of Monophysitism, in which the two natures of

Christ become confused and His humanity eventually becomes lost (as in the Eutychian form of Monophysitism).

Kenosis Christology

In Philippian 2:6-7 we read, "[Christ], though He was in the form of God, did not count equality of God a thing to be grasped, but emptied [*ekenosen*] Himself, taking on the form of a servant." The principal christological issue here is the meaning of Christ's "emptying" himself. Of what does this "emptying" (*kenosis*) consist?

Numerous theories have been advanced. Some argue that during His incarnation the Son gave up some of His divine attributes ("emptied Himself of all but love" wrote Charles Wesley in his hymn *And Can It Be That I Should Gain?*). Others believe the Son turned over all of his divine duties to the Father, so that Jesus' entire ministry was done not under His own power, but the power of the Spirit of God. Still others say Christ gave up none of His power, but "emptied Himself" in the sense of choosing not to use His divine power. Variations exist on each of these theories.

Any consideration of the numerous *kenosis* theories must take into account what we noted in our discussion of New Testament Christology: The biblical perspective on Christ is almost totally functional. It is therefore unlikely that in his letter to the Philippians Paul had any theory of Christ's divine attributes in mind. It is more likely that Paul is describing the role Christ played in redemptive history; i.e., He fulfilled His mission by "taking on the form of a servant." This phrase modifies the verb *ekenosen* ("emptied"), and probably contains an allusion to the "suffering Servant" passage in Isaiah 53.

The Sinlessness of Jesus Christ

The Church has been unanimous in confessing that Jesus, in the words of Hebrews 4:15, was "tempted in every way, just as we are, yet was without sin." There has been some disagreement, however, on the meaning of the phrase "without sin." Two issues which have been subject to debate are:

- Was Jesus sinless in the sense that He was untainted by the pollution of original sin? Or was He sinless by virtue of His perfect obedience to the Father, even though He shared in our fallen human nature?

- Was Jesus peccable (capable of sinning), by virtue of His true humanity? Or was He impeccable (incapable of sinning) because He was God?

With regard to the sinlessness of Christ, historic Christian belief is virtually unanimous in declaring that Christ was free from original sin. More recently, Karl Barth has insisted that Christ took on the human nature of His mother, Mary, and was thus in His humanity no different from us. Barth argued that Jesus committed no sin, yet had to assume our fallen nature in order to become the mediator between God and sinful humanity (*Church Dogmatics* 4/1, 91).

Barth's view may find a precedent in Athanasius. It is unclear, however, whether Athanasius believed that the Son of God bore a sinful human nature during His incarnation (as Barth insists), or whether that sinful human nature was purged of its corruption due to its union with the divine Logos by the Holy Spirit of the virgin Mary, so that Christ did not bear a sinful nature while on earth (*On the Incarnation* 20.4). Later writers, including Augustine, Anselm, and Aquinas, all taught that Christ lived among us as a genuine human being, yet with a human nature unpolluted by sin.

Concerning the peccability or impeccability of Christ, even Barth argues that by virtue of His divinity Christ could not sin. Jesus was not merely "able not to sin" (as was Adam prior to the Fall); Jesus was "not able to sin."

Christology in the Liberal Protestant Tradition

Since about 1750 Enlightenment philosophy has exercised a tremendous influence upon Protestant (and more recently, Roman Catholic) Christology. The anti-supernatural bias of this intellectual movement has tended to reduce Jesus to a mere man. To understand Liberal Christology, however, one must begin not with the Enlightenment prejudice against miracles, but rather the anthropology which undergirds all Enlightenment philosophy.

Basic to the Enlightenment's view of humanity was its insistence that the fundamental relationship between God and humanity is one of *continuity*. Humanity and God were viewed as being in basic harmony with one another. The Rationalist wing of the Enlightenment saw human reason as the link between God and us; the Romantic movement saw human feelings as the point of common ground. Representatives of each camp include Immanuel Kant (Rationalism) and Jean-Jacques Rousseau (Romanticism).

Within this intellectual framework Jesus was no longer viewed as one who saved people from sin, since there was no sin problem in the first place (at least in the sense of original sin). Liberal theology instead viewed Jesus as the model Christian, the supreme example of human attainment of the divine ideal for humanity. Whereas orthodoxy had viewed Jesus as different in *quality* from other humans by virtue of His divinity, Liberals saw only a *quantitative* difference between Jesus and other people. It was a difference merely of degree, not of kind.

Liberals thus viewed Christianity as the religion *of* Jesus rather than a religion *about* Jesus (one which worships Him). Johann Gottfried Herder, for example, wrote in 1776, "[T]he so-called religion *about* Jesus must necessarily change . . . into a religion *of* Jesus . . . His God, our God; His Father, our Father! . . . Whoever contributes to bringing back the religion of Jesus from a meretricious slavery and from a painfully pious Lord-Lording to that genuine Gospel of friendship and brotherliness . . . he himself has taken part in Christ's work and has advanced it."[21] For Herder, to deny the lordship of Christ was to advance Christ's work.

Since the Liberal Jesus was merely one of us, and humanity is not by nature in bondage to sin, Liberalism denied any saving value in the death of Christ. Rather, one gained salvation through ethical behavior. Many Liberals considered the Sermon on the Mount as the epitome of such behavior. German historian Adolf von Harnack, for example, stated that "the whole of Jesus' message may be reduced to these two heads—God as the Father, and the human soul so ennobled that it can and does unite with him."[22]

It is little wonder, then, that American theologian J. Gresham Machen, in his 1923 book *Christianity and Liberalism*, argued that Liberal theology was not another form of the Christian religion, but was a different religion altogether. For in denying the orthodox doctrine of the person of Christ, Liberalism ultimately cut the heart out of historic Christian belief, which centers around the conviction that "Christ died for our sins according to the Scriptures" (1 Cor. 15:3). The meaning of this confession will be examined in our next chapter.

Points To Ponder

1. How does John Lawson define the Christian doctrine of the incarnation?

2. What theological implications concerning the person of Christ do Matthew and Luke draw from their accounts of the virgin birth?

3. How do Matthew and Luke, respectively, link the virgin birth to previous events in God's history of salvation?

4. Know the significance of the eight titles of Jesus which refer to His past, future, present, and preexistent work.

5. Why were Cerinthianism and docetism such threats to the Christian faith?

6. What was the basic teaching of modalism? How did Tertullian argue against it?

7. What were the issues and who were the principal persons involved in the ecumenical councils of Nicea, Constantinople, Ephesus, and Chalcedon?

8. What do theolgians mean by the term "hypostatic union" (Chalcedon, A.D. 451)?

9. What is the difference between "communion of attributes" (Reformed Christology) and "communication of attributes" (Lutheran Christology)?

10. Be able to summarize the various interpretations of "kenosis Christology."

11. In what two senses do Christians speak of the sinlessness of Christ?

12. What is the fundamental assumption of Liberal Protestantism? How does it affect the Christology of Liberalism?

9

Christology, Part Two:
The Atonement

Definition

The term *atonement* can be understood by dividing it into syllables: at-one-ment. Etymologically, it communicates the idea of bringing together ("at one"). Theologically, it refers to the work accomplished by Jesus Christ through His suffering and death on the cross. What Jesus accomplished, according to historic Christian belief, was "at-one-ment," or reconciliation between the Holy God and sinful human beings.

The doctrine of the atonement lies at the heart of Christian faith, for the divine Son, the second person of the Trinity, became incarnate to reconcile people to God. The mere fact that God became human in Christ did not accomplish "at-one-ment," however. Jesus Himself stated that He came "to give His life as a ransom for many" (Mark 10:45). The *death of Christ* therefore stands at the center of the atonement. In no other major religion is the death of its founder the most important aspect of that religion.

Why did God use the death of Christ to secure the salvation of His people? What caused God to ordain the atonement? Did Christ have to die in order for God to forgive sinful people? These questions touch on a certain paradox regarding the atonement: The saving work of Christ was both a *free* act and a *necessary* act.

191

The Freedom and the
Necessity of the Atonement

The Atonement as God's
Free Act of Salvation

God's work of salvation, as we have already seen, is inextricably linked to His work of creation (chapter 4). Just as God did not have to create the world in order to make up for some deficiency in the Godhead, even so God is in no way obligated to save people who rebel against Him. Salvation, like creation, is a *free* act of God's mercy.

In one sense, then, we can say that there is no ultimate cause for the atonement, if by "cause" we mean something which compelled God to redeem sinners. If this were the case, that "something" would be greater than God, which in the view of historic Christian belief would be absurd. "Our God is in heaven; he does whatever pleases him" (Ps. 115.3). God is sovereign, accountable to none but Himself.

At the same time, to say that God has chosen to redeem sinners for no reason at all would be tantamount to making salvation an arbitrary decree. But the God of the Bible does not act arbitrarily. Scripture consistently speaks of God as working with a purpose, towards a goal. In other words, something motivated God to show mercy to sinners. In chapter 4 we noted that it was God's own glory which motivated Him to create not only a world, but a world which includes a history of redemption. The bottom line, then, is that God ultimately saves sinners not for our sake, but for His sake (Ps. 23:3). The atonement is the central saving act of God by which He upholds and displays His glory (Eph. 1:6, 12, 14). Historic documents bearing witness to this include the Westminster Confession of Faith (chapter 3) and the Baptist New Hampshire Confession of 1833 (chapter 9).

The Atonement as God's Necessary
Act of Salvation

But while the atonement is a free act in that its motivation comes from within God Himself, there is another sense in which we can speak of the *necessity* of the atonement. The historic consensus of the Church is that Christ *had to die* in order for people to be saved. That is to say, *once God had freely decreed to save sinners, the death of Christ was the necessary means by which that salvation was accomplished.*

This necessity is brought about by the character of God Himself. The Lord, says Scripture, "does not leave the guilty unpunished" (Ex. 34:7). God's righteousness demands that divine judgment fall upon sinners (Rom. 1:18, 32). At the same time, the Lord is "compassionate and gracious" (Ex. 34:6), a God who has no pleasure in the death of the wicked (Ezek. 18:23). Instead, God "wants all men to be saved and to come to a knowledge of the truth" (1 Tim. 2:4). That which is closest to the heart of God is not judgment, but mercy.

How, then, can God exercise mercy while at the same time upholding His character as the one who judges sin with perfect justice? How can God remain both "just, and the one who justifies" [one who forgives sinful people], as God is described in Rom. 3:26? The answer is found in the previous verse, Rom. 3:25: "God presented [Christ] as a sacrifice of atonement, through faith in his blood." (NIV). There is something about the death of Christ which brings about "at-one-ment," or reconciliation between a Holy God and sinful people.

Throughout Church history theologians have set forth theories which seek to explain what that "something" is. They have sought to interpret the vocabulary Scripture uses when it speaks of the meaning of Christ's death. We shall first examine some important biblical concepts which refer to the death of Christ, then do a survey of the prominent theories of the atonement promulgated throughout the history of the Church.

Biblical Concepts of the Atonement

Sacrifice

The New Testament consistently speaks of Christ in terms of the Old Testament sacrificial system. Jesus, for example, spoke of His blood being shed "for the forgiveness of sins" (Matt. 26:28), an allusion to the blood sacrifices mandated in Leviticus 4-5, as well as the Yom Kippur (Day of Atonement) ceremony described in Leviticus 16. Paul makes a connection between the death of Christ and the Passover lamb (Ex. 12) when he says "Christ, our Passover

Lamb, has been sacrificed" (1 Cor. 5:7). The writer of Hebrews likens Christ both to the high priest and the sacrificial animals of the Yom Kippur ceremony, emphasizing that "without the shedding of blood there is no forgiveness" (Heb. 9:22). The word "sacrifice" thus conveys the notion of one whose death makes possible the forgiveness of sins.

Some theologians have preferred to use the word "sacrifice" in a different sense. Rather than speaking of Christ's sacrificial death, they focus on what may be called His sacrificial *life*. Jesus sacrificed Himself in that He continually offered His life to God in total dedication. Augustine, for example, wrote: "Thus a true sacrifice is every work which is done that we may be united to God in holy fellowship. . . . Thus man himself, consecrated in the name of God, is a sacrifice insofar as he dies to the world that he may live to God. . . . True sacrifices are works of mercy to ourselves or others, done with reference to God" (*The City of God* 10.6). According to this view Paul's statement that Christ "became obedient to death" (Phil. 2:8) is more concerned with Jesus' obedient life than with His death. The death of Jesus was the conclusion of a totally sacrificial life, not a sacrifice in and of itself.

Expiation and Propitiation

These two words have to do with the forgiveness of sins. "Expiation" conveys the idea of the removal of sin or religious defilement, while "propitiation" has to do with placating the righteous anger of someone who has been offended by another's unrighteous behavior.

Some scholars believe the Bible does not include the notion of blood sacrifices as the means of appeasing the wrath of an angry deity. C. H. Dodd, for example, argues that in the Bible the "wrath of God" refers not to God's personal and angry response to sin, but rather to an impersonal process of cause and effect whereby disaster follows sin (people "reap what they sow"). On this basis Dodd insists that the Greek words normally translated "propitiate" and "propitiation" carry the meaning of "expiation" in the Bible.[1] The death of Christ brings about the removal or forgiveness of sin, but not by means of placating an angry God.

Leon Morris and others have found Dodd's impersonal notion of "wrath" unconvincing, and thus argue for the traditional understanding of Christ's death as a propitiatory sacrifice.[2] That is to say, the death of Christ brings about forgiveness (expiation) by means of satisfying God's righteous anger against sin (propitiation). Propitiation is the means towards the end of expiation. To put it another way: the death of Christ as "expiation" refers to how the death of Christ affects *sinners* (the procurement of forgiveness), while the word "propitiation" refers to how Christ's sacrificial death satisfies the righteous demands of *God*.

It must be added here that the biblical picture is not one of an angry God who was prepared to damn sinners until the loving Jesus intervened on our behalf. To the contrary, Paul says in Romans 3:25 that "*God* presented [Christ] as a sacrifice of atonement." God the Father is the architect of the plan of salvation. The Son did not have to beg the Father to forgive sinners. This was the Father's desire all along.

Romans 3:25 also draws an analogy between Christ's death and how God forgave sins under the Old Covenant on the Day of Atonement. The phrase "sacrifice of atonement" in Romans 3:25 is a translation of a single Greek word, *hilasterion*. In the Septuagint this same word refers to the lid, or covering, on the Ark of the Covenant (Lev. 16:15). Leviticus 16:15-16 tells how the blood of the sacrificial goat was sprinkled atop the lid of the ark in order to make atonement for the people of Israel. In like manner, the death of Christ makes atonement for God's people of the New Covenant.

One can view the two goats of Yom Kippur (the sacrificial goat and the scapegoat) as signifying propitiation and expiation, respectively. The blood of the sacrificial goat "propitiates," or placates, the wrath of God against His people on account of their sin. Once God sees the goat's blood atop the Ark of the Covenant, He considers the goat's death as payment for the sins of the people, and His judicial sentiment is satisfied. This clears the way for God's further action of removing, or expiating, sin. This expiation is symbolized by the second goat, which is led outside the camp bearing the sins of the people (Lev. 16:22). Expiation (forgiveness of sins) takes place on the basis of propitiation (the turning away of God's wrath); hence the offering of the sacrificial goat *before* the release of the scapegoat.

This interpretation sees Christ fulfilling the roles of both the sacrificial goat and the scapegoat. In Romans 3:25, however, the reference is only to the sacrificial goat, or propitiation, as evidenced by the fact that Paul refers to "faith in [Christ's] *blood*." Thus the context of the word *hilasterion* in Romans 3:25 and Leviticus 16:15, as well as its normal usage in the Greek language, indicate that it refers to propitiation, not merely to expiation.

Redemption and Ransom

Scripture speaks of salvation not only as forgiveness of sins, but also as deliverance from the bondage of sin. Such deliverance is often referred to as redemption, which is accomplished through the payment of a ransom. At times the verb "redeem" is used in the sense of "pay a ransom," thereby referring both to the payment and the deliverance (Gal. 3:13).

The term "redemption" is language of the marketplace. In ancient Israel both property and life could be redeemed by making an appropriate payment, or ransom. For example, if a man sold himself into slavery to pay off debts, he could be redeemed if a relative came forward to provide the redemption price, or ransom (Lev. 25:47-54). God's deliverance of Israel from Egypt is spoken of as a redemption (Ex. 6:6; 15:13; Ps. 78:35), as is Judah's release from Babylon (Jer. 31:11). The psalmist speaks of the Lord as He who "redeems your life from the pit" (Ps. 103:4). The Old Testament does not always specify the payment of a ransom as the means of redemption, however.

The New Testament sometimes speaks of redemption without a specific reference to a ransom. Furthermore, where the word "ransom" is used, it does not always specify to whom the ransom is paid. The outstanding example of this is Mark 10:45, where Jesus notes that He came "to give His life as a ransom for many." Paul sometimes uses the word "redemption" both in the sense of forgiveness of sins which Christians already possess (Col. 1:14), and of our future deliverance from the power of sin (Rom. 8:23; see Eph. 4:30). When redemption refers to forgiveness of sins, the price of redemption is the blood of Christ (Eph. 1:7; 1 Pet. 1:18-19). Paul's focus is on the great cost of our salvation—the death of Christ— and not on the recipient of the ransom. Indeed, nowhere does the New Testament say to whom Christ's ransom was paid.

Reconciliation

We have noted that "atonement" and "reconciliation" are virtually synonymous terms. This being the case, reconciliation is the most all-encompassing New Testament term for the saving work of Christ. For it is the one great end towards which God was working in Christ: "God was reconciling the world to himself in Christ" (2 Cor. 5:19). All of the other concepts we have examined—sacrifice, expiation, propitiation, redemption, ransom—are various *means* by which God in Christ has accomplished His one great *end* of reconciliation. This reconciliation does not occur in people's lives as a matter of course, however. Paul's message is that people must respond to Christ's work; hence his appeal: "Be reconciled to God" (2 Cor. 5:20).

Paul then returns to what Christ has done for us, and why Christ did it: "God made him who had no sin to be sin for us, so that in him we might become the righteousness of God" (2 Cor. 5:21). Here the apostle refers to two aspects of the atonement which have been called the *passive* work of Christ and the *active* work of Christ.

The phrase "to be sin for us" speaks of Christ's passive work of receiving upon Himself the sin of the world (John 1:29) and being put to death on account of our sins (Rom. 4:25). The suffering Servant of Isaiah 53 was almost certainly in view as Paul wrote to the Corinthians. "Surely He took up our infirmities . . . He was pierced for our transgressions . . . the Lord has laid on him the iniquity of us all" (Isa. 53:4-6).

Christ did all of this, says Paul, "in order that we might become the righteousness of God in Him." This is the active obedience of Christ. Christ not only "passively" allowed His enemies to kill Him; He also actively fulfilled the righteous requirements of God's law on our behalf. This righteousness becomes ours when we are "in Him,"—in union with the risen Christ (2 Cor. 5:17; see Rom. 4:25; 5:15-16; Gal. 3:14).

The passive and active work of Christ are closely connected with the concept of *imputation*. Our sins have been credited, or "imputed," to Christ's account, and His righteousness has been imputed to our account. Paul's language in 2 Corinthians 5:21 is seen by many, especially those in the Reformed tradition, as teaching this sort of double-imputation. Christ receives that which is properly ours (sin); we receive that which is properly Christ's (righteousness).

The fact that Paul's principal theme in this context is reconciliation makes it likely that the "righteousness of God" of 2 Corinthians 5:21 refers not to ethical righteousness, but rather to a right relationship with God. Christ has removed the barrier of sin which stood between God and humanity, and has brought people into a right relationship with God. "God was in Christ, reconciling the world to Himself."

But precisely how did Christ's death accomplish this reconciliation? Theologians have proposed various theories in response to this question. We shall examine some of these in the following section.

Six Theories of the Atonement

There are two ways to examine the different theories of the atonement. The first is chronological, discussing them in the order in which they appeared in history. The second is topical, listing them according to category. We shall use the latter approach.

Generally speaking, interpretations of the atonement have been divided into two categories, "objective" theories and "subjective" theories. Those in the objective category insist that the work of Christ was needed in order to overcome some sort of objective barrier or hindrance which prevented reconciliation between God and humanity. Subjective interpretations, on the other hand, reject the notion that God had to remove any barrier between Himself and humanity in order to forgive sins. Such subjective theories view the death of Christ as merely demonstrating something about the love or justice of God, or the meaning of true obedience to God.

We shall first examine three objective theories, known respectively as the "classical" view, the "Latin" view, and the "Reformed" view. In addition, three subjective interpretations will be examined: the "moral influence" view, the "moral example" view, and the "governmental" theory of the atonement.

Objective Theories of the Atonement

The classical view (Christus Victor). The earliest interpretation of the atonement emphasized that by His death Christ overcame the power of the devil, which had heretofore held humanity captive to sin. It was an objective interpretation in that the devil was viewed as a real enemy who had to be conquered in order to free people from his bondage.

The death of Christ was seen as part of the larger drama wherein Satan had first tempted Adam to rebel against God. This in turn led to humanity's enslavement to the demonic powers of the devil. Adam's disobedience and bondage to sin proved the undoing of his descendants. For this reason God Himself entered into human history in the person of Jesus Christ, the "last Adam" (1 Cor. 15:45), through whom deliverance comes from sin and death (Rom. 5:12-21; 1 Cor. 15:21-22).

Christ's work was twofold. He succeeded where Adam had failed, and He redeemed us from Satan's power. Christ succeeded in living in obedience to God and overcoming the temptations of the devil (Matt. 4:1-11), and He redeemed us by means of giving His life as a ransom (Mark 10:45).

Christ's obedience to the Father was His active work on our behalf. Specifically, Christ, the second Adam, succeeded where the first Adam did not, thereby reversing the effects of Adam's transgressions on the human race. Therefore all those who are in Christ share in Christ's conquest of the power of the devil. Irenaeus (c. 130-200) appears to have been the first to formulate this theology of "recapitulation," whereby God in Christ abolished the enmity which existed between Himself and humanity by reversing the effects of the fall of Adam:

> [God] had pity on men, and flung back on the author of enmities [Satan] the enmity by which he had purposed to make man an enemy of God; He took away His enmity against men, and flung it back and cast it upon the serpent. So the Scripture says: I will put enmity between thee and the serpent, and between thy seed and the seed of the woman; he shall bruise thy head, and thou shalt watch for his heel. This enmity the Lord recapitulated in Himself, being made man, born of a woman and bruising the serpent's head. (*Against Heresies* 4.40.3)[3]

The fact that "the Lord recapitulated in Himself" the error of Adam indicates that for Irenaeus there was an inextricable connection between the Incarnation and the atonement. God did not merely decree the effects of Adam's sin to be undone; God undid them in the person of Jesus. Here Irenaeus includes the notion of Christ's giving Himself as a ransom for us:

> He who is the almighty Word, and true man, in redeeming us rea-sonably by His blood, gave Himself as the ransom for those who had been carried into captivity [by the devil]. And though the apostasy had gained its dominion over us unjustly . . . He redeemed that which was His own [by right of His having created humanity] not by violence, but by persuasion . . . in order that the ancient creation of God might be saved from perishing, without any infringement of justice. (*Against Heresies* 5.1.1)[4]

God would not allow Satan to retain dominion over us. At the same time, however, God would not use force to rescue us. This is because Adam had sold himself and his posterity over to the devil, thereby giving the devil property rights over the human race. Hence, Christ gave Himself as a ransom paid to the devil for humanity's deliverance. In this way God saved us in a manner con-sistent with justice.

Nevertheless, the emphasis in the *Christus Victor* view is not legal, but dramatic. Satan has enslaved us; God in Christ has set us free by giving His life as a ransom. Some went so far as to say that Christ tricked the devil into killing Him by hiding His divinity under His human nature. Jesus was thus God *incognito*, so that Satan and the demons, the "rulers of this age," did not recognize Him; "if they had, they would not have crucified the Lord of glory" (see 1 Cor. 2:7-8).

The notion of God paying a ransom to the devil did not meet with universal approval, however. Uneasiness with this idea, as well as growing attention to the notion that the atonement was neces-sary to satisfy divine justice, eventually led to what came to be called the "Latin" theory of the atonement.

The Latin view (vicarious satisfaction). In 1098 Anselm, Arch-bishop of Canterbury, authored what is arguably the most brilliant book ever written on the atonement. In *Cur Deus Homo (Why God Became a Man)* he confronted a problem which had been set forth by pagan philosophers during the Middle Ages: "For what reason and on the basis of what necessity did God become a man and by His death restore life to the world (as we believe and confess), seeing that He could have accomplished this restoration either by means of some other person (whether angelic or human) or else merely by willing it?" (*Cur Deus Homo* 1.1).[5]

Anselm's goal was not to synthesize the biblical data on the atonement, but to give a rationale for the necessity of both the incarnation and the death of Christ. Like theologians throughout the history of the Church, he saw an inextricable connection between the incarnation and the atonement (as the title of his book indicates). At the same time, however, he departed from the *Christus Victor* tradition in at least two respects:

- Anselm rejected the notion that the death of Christ was a ransom paid to the devil. "The devil has no just claim on man" (1.7); to the contrary, the Son of God "offered Himself to Himself," not to the devil (2.18).

- Anselm emphasized the legal necessity of the atonement in a way heretofore not done. He felt compelled to do so because he did not believe that God needed to become a man in order to defeat the devil; He could have dealt with the devil directly, without an incarnation (1.7). Rather, God needed to become a man in order to satisfy the requirements of divine justice against sinful people (2.6). The main parties in Anselm's theories were therefore not God and the devil, but God and Jesus.

Anselm viewed the relationship between God and humanity as that between the lord of a medieval estate and his vassals. When a vassal fails to obey or pay what is due the lord of the manor, the vassal dishonors the lord. In like manner, a person who sins dishonors the Lord God. Two things are then required of the disobedient vassal/sinner: a return to obedience, and a repayment of the debt incurred (1.20).

Disobedience against the infinite God, however, constitutes a debt of infinite proportions, which no man can repay. God cannot merely cancel such a debt, lest the moral order of the universe and God's own honor be debased (1:11-12). Yet God is merciful and wants to forgive human beings. Here Anselm confronts the dilemma mentioned by Paul in Romans 3:25-26: How can God be both just and forgiving? But whereas Paul merely states that

Christ's death resolves the dilemma, Anselm seeks to explain why God had to become a man in order for His justice to be satisfied.

Anselm defines the divine dilemma, and its solution, as follows (2.6):

- Only God Himself can satisfy divine justice; no man can do this.
- Only a man ought to make this satisfaction.
- Therefore, a God-man must make this satisfaction.

Jesus, the God-man, is able to offer such a satisfaction for two reasons (2.18):

- He is sinless and thus does not have to die; hence His self-sacrifice is purely voluntary.
- Since He does not have to die, His obedience unto death goes beyond what God requires of Him, and therefore provides a satisfaction of divine justice which can be credited to the account of others.

Indeed, the God-man's sacrifice is of infinite value, since His life is of infinite worth. Thus it is sufficient to cover the sins of all people, even those who put Him to death (2.15).

Anselm's theory of the atonement is called "Latin" for good reason. Throughout its history the Western, Latin-speaking Church, consistent with the traditions of Roman jurisprudence, has tended to emphasize the legal aspects of the Christian faith. Tertullian, for example, set forth the concepts of satisfaction and merit (*On Penance* 6). And we have already noted that Augustine spoke of sacrifice in terms of a life which pleases God (above, p. 194). What we see in Anselm, then, is a synthesis of this Latin tradition which speaks of the death of Christ in terms of Christ's obedient life which, by virtue of His divinity, provides infinite merit for Christ's people and thus satisfies divine justice.

The label "vicarious satisfaction" has been applied to Anselm's theory that Christ has satisfied the just requirements of God's law on our behalf. This theory has also been labeled the "representative" view of the atonement, since Christ in His humanity acts as our representative, doing for us what we cannot do for ourselves.

The Reformed view (penal substitution). Whereas Anselm emphasized Christ's life as vicarious satisfaction, with His death seen as a

ANSELM OF CANTERBURY

Anselm of Canterbury (1033-1109), Archbishop of Canterbury and author of *Cur Deus Homo* (*Why God Became a Man*), was born in northern Italy and educated in northern France. At age twenty-seven he became a monk in the Le Bec Abbey in Normandy. There he lived a monastic lifestyle of contemplation and scholarship, serving in turn as the monastery's prior (1063-78) and abbot (1078-93) before moving to Canterbury to become Archbishop. His tenure in Canterbury was marked by two exiles due to political debates with the Church hierarchy. He nevertheless wrote with such profound effect as to become one the greatest theologians of his day.

Anselm's theological method was shaped by the Augustinian tradition. He used reason not to arrive at religious truth, but rather to elucidate and further understand the faith already delivered to him through the Church. Reflecting upon Augustine's remark *credo ut intelligam* ("I believe in order to understand"), Anselm wrote an argument that God must by necessity exist and entitled it *fides quaerens intellec-*

tum ("faith seeking understanding"). This little book, later entitled the *Proslogion*, argued for God's existence on the basis of defining God as "that Being than which no greater can be thought" (see above, chapter 1 p. 21).

But while Anselm followed Augustine's model of faith seeking understanding (as opposed to reason seeking faith), Anselm departed from Augustine and most medieval monks by making little use of Scripture. In *Cur Deus Homo*, for example, Anselm argues for the necessity of the incarnation and Christ's death as a vicarious satisfaction for sin not on the basis of the biblical witness, but on the basis of logical necessity.

Despite this lack of biblical exposition, *Cur Deus Homo* remains one of the great expositions of the atonement ever written. In rejecting the notion that Christ paid a ransom to the devil, but rather satisfied the demands of divine justice, Anselm set the agenda for both Catholic and Protestant theology down to the present day.

giving of His life to God, some later theologians put more emphasis on Christ's death as such. In his *Summa Theologiae*, for example,
Thomas Aquinas spoke of Christ's sufferings on the cross (*passio
Christi*) as that which takes away sin (3.48.1-2), and of Christ as
being punished for the sins of humanity (2.ii. 87.8). Martin Luther
and John Calvin laid particular emphasis on this latter idea of
"penal substitution," stressing that Christ took upon Himself the
punishment for sin which we deserve. Luther, for example, wrote in
his commentary on the book of Galatians:

> Jesus Christ the Son of God died upon the cross, did bear in His
> body my sin, the law, death, the devil and hell. . . . Christ was deliv-
> ered for my sins, and was made accursed for me, that I might be
> delivered from everlasting death. . . . These words of Paul are not
> spoken in vain: "Christ was made a curse for us;" "God made Christ
> which knew no sin, to become sin for us, that we in Him might be
> made the righteousness of God," 2 Cor. 5[:21]. (comments on Gal.
> 2:19-20)[6]

Calvin likewise spoke of Christ's death not merely as a sacrifice
done on our behalf, but as divine punishment which He took upon
Himself in our place:

> In order to accomplish a full expiation, [Christ] made his soul *asham*,
> i.e., a propitiatory victim for sin (as the prophet says, Isa. 53.5, 10),
> on which the guilt and penalty being in a manner laid, ceases to be
> imputed to us. The Apostle declares this more plainly when he
> teaches: "For our sake He who knew no sin was made sin by the
> Father, so that in Him we might be made the righteousness of God."
> [2 Cor. 5:21]

> The cross was accursed, not only in human opinion but by decree of
> God's law [Deut. 21:23; see Gal. 3:13-14]. Hence, when Christ is
> hanged upon the cross, he makes himself subject to the curse. It had
> to happen in this way in order that the whole curse—which on
> account of our sins awaited us, or rather lay upon us—might be
> lifted from us, while it was transferred to him. (*Institutes* 2.16.6)[7]

In this way Calvin, along with Luther, abandoned Anselm's
notion that satisfaction for divine justice made punishment unnec-
essary. Sin demanded *both* satisfaction *and* punishment. For this
reason Calvin spoke of "propitiation" not as Christ's righteous life
satisfying God's justice on our behalf (as our representative), but

rather as Christ's experiencing the divine curse in our stead (as our substitute).

Note that both Luther and Calvin cited 2 Corinthians 5:21 as crucial to their view of penal substitution. In this way they alluded to the sort of double-imputation which we discussed above (p. 197) in relation to the passive and active work of Christ. In addition, both Luther and Calvin incorporated the classic motif of *Christus Victor* into their views of the atonement. Calvin, for example, taught that "Christ, by dying, conquered Satan, who had 'the power of death,' and triumphed over all his forces, to the end that they might not harm the Church" (*Institutes* 1.14.18). And Luther loved to speak of Christ's victory over the devil and demonic powers, frequently citing Colossians 2:15 to that effect. His hymn *A Mighty Fortress Is Our God* likewise rejoices in the devil's demise:

> The Prince of Darkness grim,
> We tremble not for him;
> His rage we can endure,
> For lo, his doom is sure,
> One little word shall fell him.

The Reformers thus saw the atonement in starkly objective terms. Christ's death was necessary in order to overcome the power of the devil, satisfy the righteous requirements of God's law, and pay the penalty for our sins. Until these obstacles were overcome, forgiveness of sins and freedom from the bondage of sin were impossible.

Subjective Views of the Atonement

The moral influence theory of Abelard. Peter Abelard (1079–1142) is generally associated with the teaching that Christ's death accomplished nothing objective, but was designed to demonstrate the greatness of God's love towards wayward humanity. His views on the atonement were closely linked to his ethical theory. Specifically, he believed that the goodness or wickedness of an act depended only on the intent of the one performing that act.

Such a theory left little if any room for Anselm's notion that the goodness or evil of any action depended upon its conformity to the law of God. Thus for Abelard, God was free to violate His own rules if He intended to do good to people. If God wished to forgive sinners, He was not prevented from pardoning them by any necessity that His justice first be satisfied.

Abelard's starting place was the love of God. He held that God loved people and desired to forgive them, but that people would not repent because they did not realize that God loves them. Abelard saw people as being estranged from God not by anything in God, but by their own ignorance and refusal to accept God's forgiveness. Since for Abelard the barrier between God and humanity exists only subjectively in our minds, and not objectively in the mind of God or the order of divine justice, his theory has been labeled "subjective."

Abelard viewed the death of Christ as the outstanding demonstration of God's love. It shows to what lengths God will go in order to win our love for Himself. Abelard spelled out this theory most systematically in his *Exposition of Romans*. For Abelard, Paul's statement that we are "justified freely" (Rom. 3:24) meant exactly that: Justification is free. There is no price involved, such as the price of Christ's death as a ransom. Christ's death accomplishes our redemption because it shows us how much God loves us, so as to convince us how much we ought to love him.

Christ's death on the cross, then, is designed to produce godly sorrow in the human soul. Such godly sorrow in turn influences us to repent and love God; hence the name "moral influence theory." This teaching was strenuously opposed by Abelard's contemporary Bernard of Clairvaux, who argued that Christ died in order to wash away our sins. Abelard was condemned at the Council of Sens in 1141, one year before he died.

The example theory (Socinianism). Faustus Socinus (1539-1604) was an anti-trinitarian contemporary of the Reformation. Like Abelard, he rejected the notion that God's justice presented an obstacle to God in His desire to forgive people. He thus joined Abelard in condemning any notion of vicarious satisfaction: "If we could but get rid of this [idea that God's] justice [requires Him to punish sinners], even if we had no other proof, that fiction of Christ's satisfaction would be thoroughly exposed, and would vanish" (*de Jesu Christi Servatore* 3.1).[8]

Even as Socinus shared Abelard's "subjective" view of sin, his perspective on Christ's death was different. Whereas Abelard saw the death of Christ as a demonstration of God's love for humanity, Socinus taught that Christ suffered in order to leave us an example to follow. He found support for this view in 1 Peter 2:21, which says in part: "Christ suffered for you, leaving you an example, that you should follow in his steps." For Socinus, Jesus was the model Christian.

Undergirding the Socinian view of the atonement lay an anthropology which was fundamentally Pelagian. Socinus and his followers denied the historic doctrine of human depravity, teaching instead that people were morally capable of doing God's will. In addition, they viewed Jesus as merely a godly man, not the God-man of Anselm and the Nicene Creed. In this way Socinus went beyond even what Abelard had taught and laid the foundations for Unitarianism and Protestant Liberal theology. His views were rejected by all the main branches of the Reformation, including the Lutheran, Calvinist, and Armininan traditions.

The governmental theory of the atonement. One such man who rejected the Socinian doctrine of atonement was Hugo Grotius (1583-1645), a Dutch Reformed theologian who became an Arminian. Grotius saw the law of God as something which could not be disregarded, as Socinus had done. For this reason he wrote a tract (*Defensio fidei catholicae de satisfactione Christi adversus Faustum Socinum*) in which he set forth what has been called the "governmental" theory of the atonement.

Grotius tried to steer a middle course between the Reformed doctrine of penal substitution and a merely subjective view of the atonement. His theory is called "governmental" because it lays stress upon the righteous governance of God over the universe. Under the divine government, or indeed any righteous government, punishment is a good thing, for it acts as a deterrent to unlawful behavior. According to Grotius, "all punishment presupposes some common good—the conservation and example of order."[9] The death of Christ served this common good by displaying in starkest terms the seriousness of sin.

Grotius thus interpreted Christ's death not as satisfying God's requirement that people perfectly obey the divine law, but as satisfying our need to take seriously God's role as moral governor of the world. Although he used the Reformed term "penal substitution,"

Grotius did not mean that Christ suffered the penalty of sin which we deserve. Instead, Christ suffered death as a substitute for any penalty whatsoever. Christ did not come under the divine curse of God's wrath, as Luther and Calvin had taught. Rather, He died to demonstrate the high price of violating God's law.

On what basis, then, did God forgive sins? Here Grotius sided with Abelard, insisting that God was free to forgive people whenever He pleases. God is like a governmental magistrate, granting clemency to lawbreakers who repent and subsequently display a proper regard for the law. At the same time, Grotius saw Christ's death not as an example of the depth of God's love, but as an expression of His justice. The message of the cross is that those who persist in sin will most surely run afoul of the divine tribunal, with catastrophic results. The cross therefore acts not as a punishment of sin, but as a deterrent against further sins. As such, it functions to uphold the moral government of God's creation.

Grotius sought to set forth a view which took sin seriously while avoiding the Reformed notion of penal substitution. He was particularly concerned that the Calvinist emphasis on Christ becoming a curse in our place would lead to a disregard for the law. If people are taught that Christ has paid the penalty for all of one's sins, Grotius reasoned, they will not feel compelled to continue obeying God. The deterrent against sin will be gone.

The governmental theory appears at first glance to contain an objective element, in that Christ had to die in order to uphold the moral government of the universe. In the end, however, it is more subjective than objective, emphasizing how Christ's death affects our attitudes towards God by providing a deterrent against breaking God's law.

The Multifaceted Nature of the Atonement

No one theory of the atonement can encompass the meaning and significance of the saving death of Christ. Each theory we have examined (with the possible exception of the governmental theory) can point to specific biblical texts for support. At the same time, the historic consensus of the Church has been that the crucified Christ overcame an objective barrier which was impeding reconciliation between God and humanity.

Six Views Of The Atonement

Objective Views			
View	1. Classical	2. Latin	3. Reformed
Proponent	Irenaeus	Anselm	Luther, Calvin
Object of Christ's Work	Satan	God	God
Humanity's Problem	Satanic captivity due to sin denies access to God	Lack of righteousness dishonors God	Disobedience to God requires divine punishment
Meaning of Christ's Death	A ransom from captivity to Satan; undoes effects of Adam's Fall (*Christus Victor*)	Satisfies the righteous demands of God's law on our behalf (vicarious satisfaction)	Pays the penalty of sin in place of Christ's elect (penal substitution)

Subjective Views			
View	4. Moral Influence	5. Moral Example	6. Governmental
Proponent	Abelard	Socinus	Grotius
Object of Christ's Work	Humanity	Humanity	Humanity
Humanity's Problem	Failure to understand how much God loves us	Need of a role model to show us how to obey God	Need to understand the seriousness of continuing to violate God's law
Meaning of Christ's Death	Shows us the love of God; influences us to repent and follow God (Jesus = God)	Ultimate Example of true human obedience to God (Jesus = Humanity)	Demonstrates how serious sin is, thereby deterring us from sinning (penal example)

For this reason subjective views such as those of Abelard and Socinus have been deemed heretical not because of what they teach, but because of what they do not teach. Abelard, for example, could support his moral influence theory by citing the apostle Paul's statement that "God demonstrates his own love for us in this: While we were still sinners, Christ died for us" (Rom. 5:8). But is this *all* that Christ accomplished in His death? The Church's collective response to this question has been a firm "No." The historic confession that Christ died for sinners must include objective concepts such as victor, representative, and substitute in order to do justice to the biblical data.

The Design and Purpose of the Atonement

Theologians who debate the "design and purpose" of the atonement attempt to answer two questions:

- For whom did Christ die? (Design)
- For what reason did Christ die for these people? (Purpose)

This debate has been carried out within the context of "objective" views of the atonement, in particular the vicarious satisfaction and penal substitution theories. It is a controversy generally connected with the seventeenth-century debate between the Calvinist and Arminian wings of the Reformation. We shall summarize the main points of this debate in chapter 12.

For the time being, let us examine three different perspectives on this issue. They may be termed general atonement (the Arminian position), particular atonement (held by many in the Calvinist tradition), and the christocentric interpretation of Karl Barth.

General Atonement

This view holds that Christ died in order that all persons *might* be saved. The language of 1 John 2:2 is taken at face value: "[Christ] is the atoning sacrifice for our sins, and not only for ours but also for the sins of the whole world." Christ desires that all people be saved (1 Tim. 2:4), but His death in and of itself does not accomplish their salvation. Unless they believe, they will not benefit from His saving grace. Arminians hold that the reason some do not believe lies not in the will of God, but in the free will of the unbeliever. Lutherans do not share the Arminian notion of free will, but do believe that Christ died for all persons (as do some Reformed theologians).

General atonement may therefore be characterized as follows: The *scope* of Christ's sacrifice of atonement is unlimited ("the whole world," meaning every individual); the *efficacy* of that sacrifice, however, is limited. That is, Christ did not die in order to save anyone in particular, but to make salvation *possible for everyone*. But the death of Christ only removes the barrier between God and humanity; it does not in and of itself reconcile us to God.

Adherents of general atonement usually reject the notion of Christ dying as a penal substitute. The phrase "Jesus paid the penalty for our sins," while used by some Arminians, is seen by others as amounting to a sort of spiritual "double-jeopardy." If Jesus died for all, and by His death has already paid the penalty for all of our sins, how can God punish anyone for rejecting Christ? This would be tantamount to penalizing someone twice for the same offense. For this reason the notion of penal substitution is more consistent with particular atonement than with general atonement.

Particular Atonement

Adherents of particular atonement believe that Christ's death purchased the salvation of those whom God predestined to salvation in Christ from before the foundation of the world, that is, the elect. According to this view, the scope of Christ's sacrifice is limited (hence the more common label "limited atonement"), but its efficacy is *un*limited. Christ laid down His life for "His sheep," the elect (John 10:11), and in so doing gave them eternal life. This theory thus sees Christ's sacrifice as a *saving act* in and of itself. The benefits of salvation—new birth, faith, forgiveness, reconciliation— all are gifts of God which come through Christ, the Lamb slain from before the foundation of the world on behalf of His elect.

Although this view is often called the "Reformed" or "Calvinist" position, its origins go back to Augustine's doctrine of predestination. The form in which it is generally taught today, however, derives neither from Augustine nor Calvin, but from the generation of Reformed theologians who followed Calvin. Most notable of these was Theodore Beza, Calvin's successor in Geneva.

Some Reformed theologians avoid the term "limited atonement." They argue that the Arminian view, general atonement, could just as easily be called "limited," since it limits the efficacy of Christ's death. The term "particular atonement" is therefore more accurate in describing the Reformed position, conveying the idea that Christ died for particular people, and that His death actually accomplished their salvation.

Karl Barth's Christocentric View of the Atonement

Although in the Reformed tradition, Barth departed from the classic Reformed view of particular atonement. For while Barth followed the reformers in affirming the full efficacy of the atonement, he also saw Christ as dying for all humankind. Thus in Barth both the scope and the efficacy of the atonement are unlimited.

Barth's doctrine of the atonement is a necessary implication of his doctrine of election, which we shall examine more closely in chapter 12. Here we need only note that Barth sees Christ not merely as our penal substitute (as did the Reformers), but as our substitute in every respect. Furthermore, it is Christ *as God* who has accomplished everything for us, including taking upon Himself our rejection as sinners. In *Dogmatics in Outline* Barth writes concerning Christ's sufferings:

> The life of Jesus Christ is not a triumph but a humiliation, not a success but a failure, not a joy but suffering. For that very reason it reveals man's rebellion against God and God's wrath against man which necessarily follows; but it also reveals the mercy in which God has made His own man's business and consequently his humiliation, failure and suffering, so that it need no longer be man's business.[10]

For Barth, the life of Jesus is as important as His death for our reconciliation with God. Throughout His life Jesus suffered in our place, not merely as our representative but as our substitute ("so that [suffering] need no longer be man's business"). But Barth uses the language of substitution not only of Christ's suffering and death, but of His righteous life. In Jesus Christ God took our place not only as the One judged for sin, but also as the One who acted justly.[11]

Barth's notion that in Christ God has replaced sinners in every respect has convinced many that Barth teaches universalism—that all people will be saved. Barth has denied this, but has also refused to deny the possibility that this might be the case. Thus Barth's affirmation that both the scope and the efficacy of the atonement are unlimited, while it contains elements of both the Calvinist and Arminian positions, implies a universal salvation which both Calvin and Arminius denied.

Design And Purpose Of The Atonement

View	Scope For Whom Did Christ die? (Design)	Efficacy To What End Did Christ Die? (Purpose)
General Atonement (Arminian)	Unlimited Christ died for all people. . .	Limited so that they *might* be saved.
Particular Atonement (Calvinist)	Limited Christ died for His "elect" only . . .	Unlimited so that they *shall* be saved.
Karl Barth's View of the atonement	Unlimited Christ died as a penal substitute for all people;	Unlimited therefore, all are "elect" in Christ.

"He Descended into Hell"

The Apostles' Creed confesses that Christ "was crucified, dead and buried; He descended into hell." The meaning of Christ's descent into hell is as ambiguous as it is controversial.

To begin with, this phrase was not universally confessed by the post-apostolic Church. Between the second and seventh centuries most prominent theologians omitted it (Irenaeus, Tertullian, Marcellus, Augustine), and the Nicene Creed does not include it. Even today some Churches refuse to include this phrase when reciting the Apostles' Creed.

As to its meaning, no one is sure exactly what its original author intended to convey, since the origins of the phrase are clouded in obscurity. One man who did use the phrase, Rufinus (A.D. 390), evidently understood "descended into hell" to mean simply that Christ was buried. Subsequent Church tradition has usually interpreted Christ's descent into hell with reference either to His triumph over the devil, or His suffering the punishment for our sins.

The earliest exposition of the descent into hell appears to have been late in the fourth century. The word "hell" in this case referred to Hades, the realm of the dead. Jesus descended into Hades, preached to the spirits imprisoned there, and departed on the third day when He rose from among the dead. The message Christ proclaimed in Hades was of His victory over the powers of sin, death and the devil. Biblical texts such as 1 Peter 3:18-19 and Colossians 2:15 may have been in view here.

The medieval Roman Catholic doctrine of "the harrowing of hell" interpreted Christ's descent into hell as an invasion of the devil's realm. Christ, who has already bound Satan (Luke 11:21-22), descends with His angels into Hades to release Old Testament saints who were confined there in *limbus patrum* ("limbo of the fathers"). This form of the *Christus Victor* motif was popularized in medieval plays and religious art.

The Reformers affirmed the confession that Christ descended into hell. Some interpreted the phrase metaphorically rather than literally. Calvin, for example, saw the phrase as referring to Christ being "tortured" with the punishment which we deserved, thereby connecting the creed with penal substitution (*Institutes* 2.16.10). Luther, on the other hand, interpreted Christ's descent into hell in terms of *Christus Victor*. Christ with both body and soul went to hell in order to destroy it for believers, "and has redeemed them from the power of death, of the devil, and eternal damnation of hellish jaws" (*Formula of Concord, Solid Declaration* 9.4).

Whatever one makes of the confession that Christ "descended into hell," it is a valuable witness to the objective nature of the atonement, and the extent to which God in Christ has loved His Church and worked for her salvation. To be sure, what Christ did between His death and resurrection remains a mystery. For Christians, however, what matters most is not what Christ did during those three days, but what He did afterward: "The third day He rose again from the dead." That is the event upon which the truth of Christianity depends, and which we shall examine next.

Points To Ponder

1. What is the basic meaning of the word *atonement?*

2. In what sense was the atonement a *free* act of God? In what sense was it a *necessary* act of God?

3. What are the two theological meanings of the word *sacrifice?*

4. How do *expiation* and *propitiation* differ? How are they related to one another?

5. What is the connection between the concepts of *redemption* and *ransom?*

6. In what way is the concept of *reconciliation* different from the five concepts mentioned in questions 3, 4, and 5 above?

7. What did Irenaeus mean by "recapitulation"? How does this concept fit into the classical (*Christus Victor*) view of the atonement?

8. What was the philosophical problem Anselm confronted with his "Latin" view of the atonement? What was Anselm's solution to this problem?

9. How does "penal substitution" differ from "vicarious satisfaction"?

10. What was the significance of Christ's death for Abelard? for Socinus? for Grotius?

11. Why do advocates to "general atonement" usually reject the notion of penal substitution?

12. In what various ways has the creedal phrase, "He [Christ] descended into hell" been interpreted?

10

Christology, Part Three: The Risen Savior

The Resurrection of Jesus

The Centrality of the Resurrection

In the previous chapter we saw how Christians, in a variety of ways, have consistently viewed the death of Christ as the central event which made possible the salvation of God's people from the guilt and bondage of sin. The disciples of Jesus did not believe this after their Master was crucified and buried, however. Had Jesus remained in the tomb, there would have been no theories concerning the significance of Messiah's death. Indeed, there would have been no Christian Church.

But Jesus did not remain in the tomb. The unanimous witness of the New Testament writers is that on the third day following His burial Jesus returned to the land of the living. Furthermore, it was not merely Jesus' "soul" or "spirit" which appeared to His flabbergasted disciples. "It is I myself! Touch me and see; a ghost does not have flesh and bones, as you see I have" (Luke 24:39). The Easter faith is that Jesus rose bodily from the dead, vanquishing death and the power of the devil.

It is therefore impossible to speak of the saving death of Christ without in the same breath speaking of His resurrection. "[Christ] was delivered over to death for our sins and was raised to life for our justification," wrote the apostle Paul to the Church in Rome (NRSV, Rom. 4:25). John Calvin likewise saw the two events as inseparable. "Let us remember that whenever mention is made of [Christ's] death alone, we are to understand at the same time what belongs to His resurrection. Also, the same synecdoche applies to the word 'resurrection:' whenever it is mentioned separately from death, we are to understand it as including what has to do especially with His death" (*Institutes* 2.16.13).

Christ's resurrection must therefore be placed alongside His crucifixion as the central event in God's history of salvation. As Oscar Cullmann has expressed it, "No other point of time in the entire process [of God's history of salvation], either in the past or in the future, can have so central a significance as this one does for men who are convinced that Jesus Christ has risen in bodily form as the first-born of the dead!"[1]

When Cullmann refers to "the entire process" of redemptive history, he makes it clear that while the resurrection of Jesus caught His disciples by surprise, it did not occur in an intellectual or historical vacuum. To the contrary, it was consistent with the Jewish expectation that God would one day raise His chosen people from the dead. At the same time, Christ's resurrection did catch His disciples unawares precisely because it occurred in a manner different from their expectations.

It is therefore appropriate to examine how the resurrection both fulfilled and exceeded Jewish expectations. To this end, we shall first examine the historical background of the resurrection of Christ. We shall then see how Christ's resurrection stands both in continuity with and contrast to the ancient Jewish doctrine of resurrection.

Judaism and Resurrection

We noted in chapter 6 that the Jewish doctrine of humanity rejected the radical division of body and soul common to Greek Platonic dualism. The contrast between the Jewish and Greek perspectives is nowhere more clearly seen than in Acts 17:16-34, where Luke recounts Paul's encounter with the philosophers of Athens.

Paul begins his presentation of the Gospel by appealing to ideas which he and the Athenians hold in common: God has created all things, and God sustains all things; therefore, we owe our allegiance to God. The apostle even quotes two Greek poets to buttress his position (v. 28). But when he moves on and speaks of the judgment of God, Paul leaves this sort of common-ground argumentation and states that God has declared His intentions for humanity by raising Jesus from the dead (v. 31).

Luke records what happened next: "When they heard about the resurrection of the dead, some of them sneered, but others said, 'We want to hear you again on this subject'" (v. 32). The sneers were understandable from the standpoint of Greek dualism. The body is a prison-house of the soul, and salvation consists of the soul's escaping or transcending mortal bodily existence and thus continuing to live on in a state of immortality. So why would God bother to raise up someone's body? (The words "we want to hear you again" in verse 32 carry some ambiguity. Were some of the Athenians sincerely interested in talking about the idea of a resurrection? Or was it a polite brush-off, in the same category as "don't call us; we'll call you"?).

The Jews, on the other hand, believed that God's elect would be saved not merely as disembodied souls, but as entire persons, body and soul. The Greek hope of immortality of the soul would seem to the Jews anemic at best, given the Jewish unified view of human nature. Such a disembodied soul would be seen as a mere shadow of the whole man. Only a resurrection of the entire person, body and soul, could be seen as full salvation in the Jewish view of humanity.

The origins of the Jewish doctrine of bodily resurrection are obscure. The theme of life after death is not developed significantly in the Old Testament, and clear statements of a future resurrection of the righteous are found late in the history of the canon (Dan. 12:2). Jewish literature written between the time of Malachi (c. 400 B.C.) and Jesus, on the other hand, develops the resurrection theme more fully. Second Maccabees, for example, views resurrection as the reward of the faithful (7:36), including a physical restoration of their bodies (14:36). It is here that the Greek *anastasis* is first used as a term for resurrection of the righteous dead (7:14, 12:43). The books of Enoch (second century B.C.) and 4 Ezra (c. A.D. 100) expect a resurrection of the just and unjust. In each case the resurrection was connected with the *eschaton*, the end of world history as we know it.

This link between resurrection and the hope of eschatological salvation is clearly seen in John 11:17-27. Jesus has come to raise Lazarus from the dead, and assures Lazarus's sister Martha that her brother will rise again. She replies, "I know he will rise again in the resurrection at the last day." Martha thereby echoes the Jewish hope of salvation at the end of the present age. She is probably also expressing no small exasperation with Jesus, saying in effect, "Don't tell me something I already know. What can you do for Lazarus *now?*" Whereupon Jesus answers her question by calling Lazarus forth from the tomb.

The raising of Lazarus was not an eschatological event, however. It was but a harbinger of the eschatological resurrection which would signal the end of the age—a resurrection which occurred long before most people in Israel expected it.

The Resurrection and the Kingdom of God

We have seen that first-century Jews regarded the future resurrection as the end of history. Thus when Jesus rose again from the dead, the inescapable conclusion for His followers was that *the end has already come*. The Kingdom of God, the messianic age, has begun. Yet this has occurred *even as this present evil age continues*. The future has invaded the present.

The significance of the resurrection of Jesus can be seen more clearly by contrasting the Jewish and Christian expectations of how Messiah's coming was to relate to the rest of world history. The Jewish view of history may be pictured as follows:

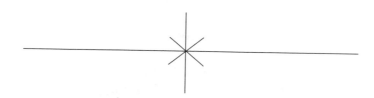

Here the vertical line represents the division of history into "the present evil age" and "the age to come," while the 'X' represents the coming of Messiah. The two coincide at what may be called the mid-point of history. Messiah's coming will usher in the resurrection of the just and unjust, the final judgment, and the age of righteousness. Another name for this event is "the Day of the Lord." The basic orientation is therefore future.

The resurrection of Christ, without changing the underlying structure of the Jewish timeline, introduces a new element: the *shifting of the midpoint of history from the future to the past*. This midpoint is the historical life, death, and resurrection of Jesus. The Christian view of history thus looks like this:

As in the first sketch, the vertical line represents the division between the present evil age and the coming age of righteousness, while the 'X' represents the coming of Messiah.

What this means is that with the life, death, and resurrection of Jesus Christ the long-anticipated Kingdom of God has already come. Jesus already defeats the powers of the devil, prior to the Day of the Lord and the final judgment: "But if I drive out demons by the Spirit of God, then the kingdom of God has come upon you" (Matt. 12:28). Yet while God's Kingdom *rule* has already been definitively established in Jesus Christ, the coming of the Kingdom as the *realm* wherein dwells God's perfect righteousness has not yet arrived. The Kingdom of God is therefore already here by virtue of Christ's resurrection, but is not yet consummated until the return of Christ (Matt. 24-25 and parallels).

Oscar Cullmann has likened this "already-not yet" tension to the situation which existed towards the close of World War II. Writing in the immediate aftermath of that war, Cullmann compared it to the New Testament view of the Kingdom of God, "*The decisive battle in a war may already have occurred in a relatively early stage of the war, yet the war still continues.* Although the decisive effect of the battle is perhaps not recognized by all, it nevertheless already means victory. But the war must be carried on for an undefined time, until "Victory Day." Precisely this is the situation of which the New Testament is conscious . . . *that event on the cross, together with the resurrection which followed, was the already concluded decisive battle.*[2]

The resurrection of Christ may thus be compared to "D-Day," June 6, 1944, when the Allied military forces invaded Europe. It was the beginning of the end of Nazi Germany. But fierce battles remained, and casualties continued until "V-Day" (Victory Day) almost a full year later. In like manner Christ conquered death and the power of the devil when He rose from the grave. Since that time Christ's kingdom rule in the hearts and minds of His people has extended itself throughout the world in a way unprecedented in the history of Israel. During this interval, to be sure, the devil continues to resist his inevitable defeat and inflicts casualties upon humanity. Yet Satan's demise is inevitable, and will occur at world history's spiritual equivalent of "V-day"—the return of Christ.

Another sign of the inauguration of God's kingdom rule on earth may be seen in the nature of Christ's resurrection. Jesus' return from the dead was unlike the raising of Lazarus, for example. Lazarus, like other people raised from the dead in the Old and New Testaments, remained mortal and eventually died. His was a resuscitation, not a resurrection. Jesus, on the other hand, rose from the grave in a transformed and glorified body which will never again taste death (1 Cor. 15:35-55). At the same time, it was not a different body from that which died on the cross: "He arose from the dead with the same body in which He suffered" (*Westminster Confession*, chap. 8). This demonstrates that the risen One and the crucified One are the same person, so that death has truly been conquered in Jesus Christ, even as the final universal conquest of death, "the last enemy to be destroyed," still lies in the future (1 Cor. 15:26).

The Meaning of Christ's Resurrection

The primary meaning of the resurrection, then, is that in Jesus Christ God has inaugurated His kingdom rule on earth, a rule which shall be consummated in the future when the knowledge of the Lord covers the earth as the waters cover the sea (Isa. 11:9). In addition to this, the New Testament sees the resurrection as significant in several other ways.

- The resurrection of Christ is *God's declaration of Jesus' divine Sonship*. Paul tells us that Jesus "was declared with power to be the Son of God by his resurrection from the dead" (Rom. 1:4). This powerful *event*, and not mere words, testified supremely to Christ's divine authority.

- The resurrection confirmed that Jesus was *perfectly righteous and therefore an appropriate representative and substitute for sinful human beings,* as Paul portrays Him in 2 Corinthians 5:21. Had Christ not been raised, we would have no reason to believe this and would still be in our sins (1 Cor. 15:17).

- The resurrection *demonstrated Christ's victory over death and the power of the devil.* The risen One now rules as Lord, His victory over all other spiritual forces guaranteed (Phil. 2:9-11; Col. 2:15).

- The resurrection of Jesus *anticipates the final resurrection and glorification of believers.* He is the "first fruits of those who have fallen asleep" (1 Cor. 15:20), a guarantee of His people's eventual resurrection, even as the first fruits of a crop indicate what the final harvest will eventually look like. For this reason 1 John 3:2 states that "when he appears, we shall be like him."

- The resurrection not only witnesses to the final salvation of God's people, but may be called the *cause* of believers' *justification, regeneration* (new birth), and *final resurrection.* Jesus "was raised to life for our justification" (Rom. 4:25). God has given Christians "new birth into a living hope through the resurrection of Jesus Christ from the dead" (1 Pet. 1:3). Paul wants to share in "the power of [Christ's] resurrection" in order that he himself might "attain to the resurrection from the dead" (Phil. 3:10-11).

- The resurrection brings *redemption* not only to the people of God, but *to the entire order of creation.* "The creation waits in eager anticipation for the sons of God to be revealed . . . in hope that the creation itself will be liberated from its bondage to decay and brought into the glorious freedom of the children of God" (Rom. 8:19-21). "For God was pleased to have all his fullness dwell in [Christ], and through him to reconcile to himself all things, whether things on earth or things in heaven" (Col. 1:19-20). "Then

I saw a new heaven and a new earth . . . . He who was seated on the throne said, 'I am making everything new'" (Rev. 21:1, 5).

Every saving act of God comes to us through the resurrection of Christ. This is the unique message of the gospel. As Thomas Oden has observed: "There is no direct parallel in the history of religions of a founder whose bodily resurrection from the dead confirms and ratifies his life and teaching and enables followers to enter eternal life."[3]

The Historicity of the Resurrection

The centrality of the resurrection to Christian faith, as well as the extraordinary nature of a dead man coming back to life, have prompted many to question whether Jesus in fact rose bodily after He had been crucified, dead, and buried. Denials of the resurrection of Jesus generally have taken two forms, philosophical and historical. Philosophical objections argue that a bodily resurrection could not be part of God's means of saving humanity, while historical objections usually argue that miracles such as a resurrection do not happen.

Immortality versus resurrection. The apostle Paul confronted philosophical objections to the very idea of bodily resurrection when he preached in Athens (above, p, 218). The dualistic mentality which looked down on bodily existence and defined salvation merely as the immortality of the human soul caused some in Athens to reject Paul's message that salvation consists in resurrection.

The same sort of mentality was present in Corinth as well, causing the Apostle to write an extended treatise on the resurrection to the Christians there. Paul wrote to combat the teaching that Christ could not have risen from the dead because nobody is raised from the dead (1 Cor. 15:12). In his rebuttal to the false teachers Paul argued from the lesser realities of plant life to the greater reality of human life. If God can "raise" plants to a higher level of bodily existence than they had as seeds, why should it be unreasonable for God to do the same with human beings? Indeed, this is precisely what God has done in Jesus Christ, and will do for all who are in Christ (1 Cor. 15:35-55).

The radical body/soul dualism present in Athens and Corinth continued to plague the Christian Church long after Paul had gone on to his reward. In *The City of God*, for example, Augustine had to deal with self-styled Platonists such as Porphyry, who identified the eternal bliss of salvation with a bodiless soul. To this notion of bodiless immortality Augustine replied, "To obtain blessedness, we need not quit every kind of body, but only the corruptible, cumbersome, painful, dying—not such bodies as the goodness of God contrived for the first man, but such only as man's sin entailed" (Book 13, chapter 17).[4]

The impediment to salvation is not bodily existence *per se*, but bodily existence as we know it, corrupted by sin. Here Augustine echoes Paul's remark that "the perishable [body] must clothe itself with the imperishable, and the mortal with immortality" (1 Cor. 15:53).

Augustine further states that Plato himself did *not* equate eternal bliss with bodiless existence. To the contrary, "Plato said that souls could not exist eternally without their bodies." In other words, Porphyry the Platonist does not follow Plato! On the other hand, Augustine agrees with Porphyry's statement "that the purified soul, when it returned to [God], shall never return to the ills of the world," that is, be affected by sin and death. Augustine therefore concludes:

> Consequently, if Plato had communicated to Porphyry that which he saw to be true . . . ; and if Porphyry, again, had communicated to Plato the truth which he saw . . . I think they would have seen that it follows that the souls return to their bodies [as per Plato], and also that these bodies shall be such as to afford them a blessed and immortal life [as per Porphyry's emphasis on eternal bliss unburdened by sin] (Book 22, chapter 27).[5]

Plato and Porphyry thus each had half of the truth, so to speak. Eight centuries later Thomas Aquinas found it necessary to argue in much the same manner as Augustine, due to the renewed influence of classical philosophers such as Porphyry (whom Aquinas mentions by name). Like Augustine, Thomas sought not so much to prove the resurrection as merely to respond affirmatively to the question, "Is the resurrection reasonable?" His philosophical arguments are given in reply to this question. When Thomas seeks to establish the truth of the resurrection, he does not argue, but instead cites Scripture (*Summa Theologiae* Supp. to Part 3, Q. 75 Article 1).

Historical evidences for the resurrection. The first evidence that Jesus had risen from the dead was the empty tomb. One of the earliest explanations of Jesus's missing body was that the disciples stole the body while the soldiers guarding the tomb were asleep (Matt. 28:13). The absurdity inherent in this explanation was not lost on Augustine, who sardonically remarked, "You bring forward as witnesses men who were sleeping. Truly, it is you who have fallen asleep, you who have failed in examining such things. If they were sleeping, what could they have seen? If they saw nothing, how are they witnesses [to the disciples having stolen the body of Jesus]?" (*Exposition on Psalm 64* 13).[6]

Twentieth-century Liberal theologian Kirsopp Lake argued that in their grief the women lost their way, went to an empty tomb in the same general area where Jesus was buried, and jumped to the conclusion that Jesus had risen from the dead. This ignores two facts:

- First, the tomb in which Jesus was buried belonged to Joseph of Arimethea, a prominent member of the Jewish Sanhedrin who had not consented in Jesus' execution (Mark 15:43 and parallels). Had Jesus' enemies wanted to disprove the disciples' claim that He rose from the dead, they would have known just where to find the body. The most reasonable explanation for why they failed to do so is that they were unable to do so.

- Second, the tomb which the women and, later on, Peter and John discovered was not *completely* empty. John's Gospel tells us that the graveclothes were still there, not strewn around haphazardly, but still wrapped up. It was as though the body of Jesus had "dematerialized," leaving the graveclothes as an empty shell. It was not merely the empty tomb, but the appearance of the graveclothes, which first caused one of Jesus' disciples to believe that He rose (John 20:8). For why would anyone who wished to steal the body go to all the trouble to unwrap the graveclothes from around the corpse, then put them back into place?

The *many eyewitnesses* who saw the risen Jesus (Paul numbers them at over five hundred; 1 Cor. 15:6) constitute the second major evidence of His resurrection. Some have attributed these sightings, including Paul's Damascus road experience in Acts 9, to hallucinations. Such a "mass-hallucination" theory demands belief in a miracle almost as amazing as a resurrection, in that it has no analogy in history. Paul's vision of the risen Christ is particularly difficult to explain, since people who hallucinate usually see visions of things they have already seen. Paul had never seen Jesus, and by his own account had no desire to see Him (Acts 22:4).

Another explanation for the widespread eyewitness testimony to the resurrection is that Jesus never really died. This "swoon theory" says that Jesus was placed in the tomb unconscious, was revived by the cool air inside, arose, and departed. Later He appeared to His disciples, who thought He had died, and they viewed Him as risen from the dead. This theory founders first of all on the extensive eyewitness testimony that Jesus *died*; indeed, that He died prior to the two thieves with whom He was crucified (Mark 15:44; John 19:33-35). It also fails to explain the disciples' conviction that Jesus had triumphed over death. The Jesus of the "swoon theory" would hardly have given anyone that impression, even if He could have made it out of the (sealed!) tomb in the first place. John Stott asks whether it is credible to believe:

> That after the rigours and pains of trial, mockery, flogging [which of itself sometimes killed the prisoner] and crucifixion He could survive thirty-six hours in a stone sepulchre with neither warmth nor food nor medical care? That He could then rally sufficiently to perform the superhuman feat of shifting the boulder which secured the mouth of the tomb, and this without disturbing the Roman guard? That then, weak and sickly and hungry, He could appear to the disciples in such a way as to give them the impression that He had vanquished death? . . . Such credulity is more incredible than Thomas' unbelief.[7]

The explosive growth of the early Church, due to the *transformed lives* of Jesus's disciples, is a third witness to the resurrection. They proclaimed not merely a master teacher, but a risen Savior. The fact that the Church grew in the face of stiff persecution underscores this witness. Had the earliest disciples had doubts about the resurrection, sooner or later at least some of them would almost certainly have renounced their faith in Christ.

One could compare the rapid expansion of Christianity to that of Islam six centuries later, and thereby conclude that the resurrection of Jesus was not necessary for the growth of the religion He taught. Such a comparison ignores the nature of these two religions, however. Islam was founded by a prophet who lived to see his teachings triumph; Christianity was founded by a prophet who died an apparent failure and whose teachings spread abroad only after His death. In addition, the rapid growth of Islam was of a completely different sort than that of Christianity. Mohammed conquered by the sword; Christ conquered in spite of the sword.

To sum up, then, there are three principal strands of evidence for the resurrection of Jesus:

- The tomb of Jesus was empty three days after He had been laid in it.

- Many people testified that they saw Jesus alive after the discovery of the empty tomb.

- The disciples were transformed from a frightened band of fugitives into fearless witnesses of the risen Jesus, so that their testimony spread as far as the center of the Roman Empire within a quarter of a century.

Such evidences beg for an explanation. As one modern writer notes, "In a rational world an effect requires a sufficient cause."[8] The three strands of evidence mentioned above constitute an effect which has convinced many that the only sufficient cause is that "on the third day He rose again from the dead."

Life, death, and resurrection. Reasonable objections to such historical evidence are hard to come by unless one assumes *a priori* that miracles cannot happen. Such an assumption is based on philosophical naturalism rather than evidence, however. Thus some modern non-Christians do not even try to refute the resurrection. Instead, they argue that even if Christ did rise from the dead, it does not prove His claims. Such an assertion, based on existentialist philosophy, sees the universe not as rational, but as arbitrary. The resurrection is therefore but one more trivial event in a meaningless world. John Warwick Montgomery speaks to this issue:

WHERE DID JESUS RISE FROM THE DEAD?

Christians believe that the resurrection of Jesus Christ was an event which took place not merely in the minds of His disciples, but within the framework of space and time. But whereas the approximate time of Christ's resurrection is well known, the location of history's most momentous event is less certain.

The traditional site of the resurrection is now located within the Church of the Holy Sepulchre, located in the Christian quarter of the Old City of Jerusalem. Within the walls of the Church, less than fifty yards to the east and down a flight of stairs, stands a great rock which many believe to be the biblical Golgotha ("place of the skull") where Jesus was crucified.

In the early fourth century Queen Helena, mother of the Roman Emperor Constantine, took a pilgrimage to Jerusalem and claimed to have found the locations of Christ's crucifixion and resurrection. Her son thereupon tore down a temple to Aphrodite which stood on the spot and erected the Church of the Holy Sepulchre. This traditional site was long opposed by historians on the grounds that it probably stood inside the city walls during Jesus's time, whereas

Scripture testifies that Christ was crucified and buried outside of the city (Heb. 13:12). More recent excavations have indicated that the Church of the Holy Sepulchure stands just *out*side of the western wall which stood when Jesus died. Several years later an outer wall was built, which stood until the Romans destroyed the city in A.D. 70.

In the nineteenth century an alternative site north of the Old City was dubbed "the Garden Tomb." It is near a hill called "Gordon's Calvary," named after General Charles Gordon, who in 1885 noted the resemblance of the hill to a human skull. It was later determined that the skull-like formation of this hill was due to human excavations only a few hundred years old. For this reason most historians rule out the Garden Tomb as the place where Jesus rose from the dead.

It is therefore reasonable, though by no means certain, that Jesus rose from the dead at or near the location now occupied by the Church of the Holy Sepulchre. In the end, however, precisely *where* Jesus rose is not important. The *fact* that He rose from the dead is the cornerstone of Christianity.

In a recent public discussion I delivered at Roosevelt University, I was informed by a philosophy professor that Christ's conquest of death was no more significant qualitatively than a medical victory over pattern baldness. To which I offered the inevitable reply: "A knock comes at the door. It's the faculty secretary with a message that your wife and children have just been killed in a traffic accident. Your comment would of course be: 'Oh well, what's death? Just like pattern baldness'." In point of fact, we all recognize the overarching significance of death.[9]

Christian faith presupposes this universal human recognition that death is the enemy of all things we hold dear. It is because no one actually behaves in accord with an existentialist worldview that the Christian message of Christ's triumph over the grave holds out the greatest hope ever proclaimed to the human race.

Inside the Church of the Holy Sepulcher, traditional site of Jesus' burial (tomb of Joseph of Arimathea). *Credit: Thomas V. Brisco, Southwestern Baptist Theological Seminary*

The Garden Tomb is one site offered by tradition as the burial place of Jesus' body. *Credit: Thomas V. Brisco, Southwestern Baptist Theological Seminary*

The Ascension

Following His resurrection Jesus appeared to His disciples for a period of forty days, teaching them about the Kingdom of God in preparation for the time when He would depart from them (Acts 1:3). When the time came for His departure, it was as dramatic as His resurrection: "He was taken up before their very eyes, and a cloud hid them from their sight" (Acts 1:9).

The ascension has been defined as "the visible ascent of the Mediator, according to His human nature, from earth to heaven: a going from one place to another."[10] Such a definition confesses two things. First, the divine Son, the second person of the Trinity, was still present in the Trinity during the incarnation. Christ ascended according to His human nature, not His divine nature. Second, the incarnation did not cease to exist with the ascension. There is a man in heaven. Humanity has forever been joined with God, yet not so as to be confused with the Godhead.

Christ ascended into heaven to accomplish several purposes. These include:

- To further demonstrate the Lordship of Christ. When Paul says that God "*highly* exalted" Christ (Phil. 2:9) in order that He might be called "Lord," he was almost certainly referring not merely to the resurrection, but also to the ascension of Christ.

- To inaugurate Christ's ministry as our Great High Priest. (Heb. 4:14). In order to intercede before God on our behalf (Rom. 8:34), Christ has gone from the earthly realm into the presence of the Father.

- To make possible the coming of the Holy Spirit. "It is for your good that I am going away. Unless I go away, the Counselor [Holy Spirit] will not come to you; but if I go, I will send him to you" (John 16:7).

- To prepare a place for us in heaven. "In my Father's house are many rooms . . . . I am going there to prepare a place for you" (John 14:2). Paul speaks of those who are in Christ as already being "seated with him in the heavenly realms in Christ Jesus" (Eph. 2:6). Because He ascended, we shall also ascend to heaven.

- To assure His followers that He will return visibly and gloriously. Jesus was taken up to heaven in a cloud, reminiscent of the cloud which appeared to Moses in the tabernacle of God and represented the glory of God (Ex. 40:35). No sooner had the disciples witnessed this that two men dressed in white stood beside them and said, "This same Jesus, who has been taken from you into heaven, will come back in the same way you have seen him go into heaven." (Acts 1:11). Groups which teach that Christ will return secretly, or has already returned in some hidden fashion, contradict the words not only of the divine messengers, but of Jesus Himself: "As the lightning comes from the east and flashes to the west, so will be the coming of the Son of Man" (Matt. 24:27).

The Session

The creedal statement that the risen Christ "sits at the right hand of God the Father Almighty" is referred to as the Session. The term "right hand" is a metaphor denoting authority. In popular parlance, for example, we speak of one to whom authority has been delegated as someone's "right-hand man."

Paul speaks of God the Father having delegated authority to the risen and ascended Jesus: "[God] has given [Jesus] *the name above all names*, so that at the name of Jesus every knee should bow . . . and every tongue confess that Jesus Christ is *Lord*, to the glory of God the Father." Jesus rules as co-regent with God the Father. To be seated is not to be at ease; it is a sign that the King is on His throne, and thus the heavenly tribunal is in session. "Thus 'to sit' means nothing else than to preside at the heavenly judgment seat" (Calvin, *Institutes* 2.16.15).

Christ is thus at work between the time of His ascension and His return. Specifically, He does the following:

- He sends the Holy Spirit to indwell believers. Before He died Jesus told His disciples that He would send the Holy Spirit, "who will be in you" (John 14:17). And before He ascended into heaven the risen Jesus promised that His followers would "receive power when the Holy Spirit comes upon you" (Acts 1:8).

- He intercedes for us before God's throne. On the Day of Atonement in ancient Israel the high priest entered the "holy of holies," or inner sanctuary of the tabernacle, in order to "make atonement . . . for the uncleanness and rebellion of the Israelites" (Lev. 16:16). Jesus, as our Great High Priest, has, in like manner, entered the heavenly sanctuary to make atonement for His people (Heb. 7-9). For this reason those who are in Christ are urged to view the throne of God not merely as the divine tribunal, but as the "throne of grace" (Heb. 4:16).

- He rules over His Church. Paul refers to Christ not only as "Lord," but also as "Head" of the Church (Eph. 1:22; 5:23). The metaphor of Christ as "head" of the "body of Christ" indicates that He does not merely rule *over* the Church but also *through* the Church, by means of spiritual gifts (Eph. 4:11; see also 1 Cor. 12:27).

- He rules over all of creation. The Lordship of Christ is not merely spiritual. He is more than the Christian's "personal Lord and Savior," and even more than the Lord of the Church. He is Lord of *all*. He exercises this universal lordship even now, albeit invisibly, having conquered the kingdom of Satan and his demons (Col. 2:15). Christ is the one who even now holds all things in the universe together (Col. 1:17). He will complete His work of reconciling all things to Himself when He returns (Col. 1:20; 1 Cor. 15:24; Rev. 20-21).

The Return of Christ

In Titus 2:13 Paul speaks of the Christian's "blessed hope" that Christ will return. This blessed hope is likewise expressed in the third part of an ancient threefold confession which is preserved in many liturgies to this day:

Christ has died;

Christ is risen;

Christ shall come again.

The twofold advent of Messiah was part of the "mystery of the Kingdom of God" to which Jesus referred (Mark 4:11 and parallels). The Jews did not expect two advents of Messiah, and thus did not expect an interval between these two advents which would include a mission to the Gentiles.

To be sure, the early Christians did not anticipate an interval of at least two thousand years. Peter's urgent calls to repentance in Acts 2 and 3 indicate that he believed Jesus would return within a matter of a few months or years. For the early Christians, however, the important thing was not the length of time between Christ's advents, but the fact that Messiah had granted people a period of time to repent and believe prior to His return.

The early Christians believed the return of Christ would occur in conjunction with "The Day of the Lord," that point in history which would divide this present evil age from the glorious age to come, the Kingdom of God. Paul refers to this event as "the day of the Lord" (2 Thess. 2:2), the "day of Christ Jesus" (Phil. 1:6), and the "day of our Lord Jesus Christ" (1 Cor. 1:8). Messiah will judge the world and establish His reign visibly.

Speculation concerning the time of the Kingdom's arrival was present not only among early Christians, but also among their Jewish counterparts. For example, the second-century Rabbi Eliezer taught that Messiah would come and set up the Kingdom of God when the nation of Israel had repented. Another school of thought, represented by one Rabbi Joshua, stated that the Kingdom would come at a fixed time (A.D. 240), whether or not Israel repented.

Some early Christians followed Rabbi Joshua's approach and believed that a fixed period of time would intervene between the first and second comings of Christ. The Epistle of Barnabas, for example, posited a six-thousand-year gap between the creation of Adam and the coming of the Kingdom of God. More frequently, however, post-apostolic Christian writers followed Rabbi Eliezer's approach by renouncing the calculation of dates and establishing the moral attitude of people as the condition for the coming of the Kingdom. The Second Epistle of Clement is typical of this tendency.

The problem with both of these approaches was that they limited God's sovereignty. Eliezer and Second Clement made the coming of the Kingdom contingent upon human behavior, while the Joshua/Barnabas approach subjected the Kingdom's arrival to human calculations (which in addition to limiting God's freedom could eventually be proven wrong). For God to remain sovereign, however, the coming of His Kingdom must be viewed as occurring both when and how He pleases, independent of either our will or our knowledge.

This was precisely the sort of solution offered by the New Testament writers. Specifically, they tied the return of Christ to the *completion of the Gentile mission:* "And this Gospel of the kingdom will be preached in the whole world, as a testimony for all nations, and then the end shall come" (Matt. 24:14). In this way no specific date was set, nor was the return of Christ made dependent on the Gentiles' response to the gospel message. For this reason Jesus could say, "No one knows that day or hour. . . . Therefore keep watch, because you do not know on what day your Lord will come" (Matt. 24:36, 42).

Until Christ does return, Christians believe that He rules in their midst through the presence of the Holy Spirit. The person and work of the Holy Spirit will therefore be examined in our next chapter.

Points To Ponder

1. How did the Greek hope for life after death differ from the Jewish hope?

2. How did the ancient Jewish view of history differ from that of the early Christians? What caused this difference?

3. To what crucial event of recent history does Oscar Cullmann compare the resurrection of Jesus? Why does Cullmann make this comparison?

4. What is the "primary meaning" of the resurrection? In what six other ways is the resurrection significant?

5. How did Augustine argue against Porphyry's view that eternal bliss required a disembodied existence?

6. Be able to identify and expound upon the "three principal strands of evidence" for the resurrection of Jesus.

7. Define the ascension. What are two implications of this definition?

8. What did Christ accomplish when He ascended into heaven?

9. What is the meaning of "the Session"?

10. How did the early Christian expectation of the arrival of the Kingdom of God differ from the two major Jewish schools of thought mentioned in this chapter?

11

The Holy Spirit:
Who He Is and What He Does

The Person of the Holy Spirit

The third and final article of the Nicene Creed confesses belief in "the Holy Spirit, the Lord and Giver of life." It goes on to speak of the relationship of the Spirit to God the Father and to Jesus Christ, as well as to the Old Testament prophets. The Creed then concludes by speaking of the Church, forgiveness of sins, the resurrection of the dead, and eternal life in the world to come.

In this way the Nicene Creed, together with the Apostles' Creed, makes a connection between the person of the Holy Spirit and the application of Christ's work of redemption to the lives of believers. It is by the power of the Spirit that the Church of Jesus Christ exists and performs its ministry. It is by the power of the Spirit that Christians will be raised from the dead at the end of the present age. It is by the power of the Spirit that God will create the world to come, the dwelling place of Christ's redeemed people.

This first section of chapter 11 will therefore deal with the person of the Holy Spirit, while the second section will deal with the work of the Spirit. Our discussion will examine both the biblical witness and issues raised in the history of Christian doctrine.

Biblical Witness to the Holy Spirit

The Spirit is personal. The Holy Spirit is not merely an impersonal spiritual "force," as groups such as Jehovah's Witnesses teach. This can be seen both in the grammar and vocabulary of the Greek New Testament, and in the Bible's descriptions of what the Spirit does.

In John 16:13 we find grammatical evidence that John regards the Spirit as personal rather than impersonal. The text begins as follows: "But when he, the Spirit of truth, comes, he will guide you into all truth." The first occurrence of the word "he" translates the Greek *ekeinos*, a masculine singular pronoun. Yet the noun to which it refers, "Spirit" (*pneuma*), is not masculine, but neuter in gender. The rules of Greek grammar dictate that a pronoun and the noun to which it refers must agree in gender. In this instance, however, the evangelist uses the masculine pronoun, apparently to emphasize the personality of the Holy Spirit. The Spirit is "he," not "it."

John further underscores the personality of the Spirit by comparing Him with Jesus. In John 14:16-17 Jesus tells His disciples that after He has left earth, God the Father "will give you another Advocate, to be with you forever. This is the Spirit of Truth . . . ." In referring to the Spirit as "another" Advocate, Jesus indicates that He Himself is an Advocate, or Comforter, or Helper (Greek *parakletos*) to the disciples. Jesus Himself, of course, is personal. The Spirit is therefore likewise personal, since He is another Comforter of the same kind as Jesus. This is the precise meaning of the Greek word *allos* ("another"), as opposed to the word *heteros*, which John would have used had he viewed the Spirit as different in kind from Jesus. The significance of John's reference to "another" Advocate was noted as early as the fourth century by Gregory of Nazianzus (*Orations* 41.12).

The Scripture also testifies to the personal nature of the Spirit by speaking of His doing personal deeds. In John's Gospel, for example, the Spirit teaches the disciples (14:26), bears witness to Jesus (15:26), gives guidance, hears, and speaks (16:13). Paul speaks of the Spirit's performing intercessory prayers on behalf of God's people (Rom. 8:26). He also notes that the Spirit can be grieved (Eph. 4:30).

The New Testament, then, portrays the Spirit as a person who teaches and guides Christians, as opposed to an impersonal spiritual "force" who merely provides power to Christians. This in turn carries with it an important implication: the Holy Spirit is not at our disposal. The Spirit is not merely a power source we use to further our own purposes. Rather, the Holy Spirit sets the agenda for God's people. Christians are called not to use, but to follow, the Spirit.

The Spirit is God. The phrase "Spirit of God," which first appears in Genesis 1:2, is used so often in Scripture that one need not cite specific references to belabor the point. One such reference does merit attention, however. In Romans 8:9 Paul states: "You, however, are controlled not by the sinful nature but by the Spirit, if the Spirit of God lives in you. And if anyone does not have the Spirit of Christ, he does not belong to Christ." Here the terms "Spirit of God" and "Spirit of Christ" are used synonymously. God, Christ, and Spirit all share divine status.

The writer of Hebrews speaks of "the eternal Spirit" through whom Jesus offered Himself to God (9:14). Eternality is one of the incommunicable divine attributes, belonging only to God (Ps. 90:2). The eternal Spirit must therefore be no less than God.

The name "Holy Spirit" likewise points to the divinity of the Spirit, since God is holy. The apostolic Church considered this to be the case. Recall, for example, the apostle Peter's remarks in Acts 5:3-4, which have already been mentioned in our discussion of the Trinity (chapter 3, p. 64). In this text we see Peter chiding the duplicity of Ananias, who sold a piece of land and pretended to give all of the proceeds of the sale to the apostles, while in fact keeping back a portion for himself. Peter says to him: "Ananias, how is it that Satan has so filled your heart that you have lied to the Holy Spirit and have kept for yourself some of the money you received for the land? Didn't it belong to you before it was sold? And after it was sold, wasn't the money at your disposal? What made you think of doing such a thing? You have not lied to men but to God." For Peter, to lie to the Holy Spirit was to lie to God (which in this case turned out to be a capital offense!).

Finally, the New Testament mentions the Holy Spirit alongside God the Father and Jesus Christ as worthy of honor and glory. The

baptismal formula of Matthew 28:19 ("Make disciples of all
nations, baptizing them in the name of the Father and of the Son
and of the Holy Spirit") is the outstanding example of this, along
with texts such as 1 Corinthians 12:4-6 and 2 Corinthians 13:14.
These statements were forerunners of the trinitarian formulas
developed in the postapostolic era, which confessed the full divinity
of the Holy Spirit alongside the Father and the Son.

Classical Statements Regarding the Holy Spirit

The testimony of the New Testament notwithstanding, widespread recognition of the full personhood and divinity of the Spirit
did not come immediately within the postapostolic Church. The
early christological controversies, which centered on the person of
Jesus Christ, tended to relegate pneumatology (the doctrine of the
Spirit) into the background.

Subordinating the Spirit. Early attempts to relate the Holy Spirit
to God included statements which seemed to depict the Spirit as a
lesser god than the Father and the Son. Irenaeus, for example, subordinated both the Son and the Spirit to God when he likened
them to the hands of God which created the human race (*Against
Heresies* 4.20.1). Origen further widened the gap between the Spirit
and God when he stated that "all things came into being through
the Word, and that of all these things the Holy Spirit is the most
honorable, ranking first of all that have been brought into being by
God through Jesus Christ" (*Commentary on John* 2.10.6.).[1] Origen's
words found an echo a century later when Arius used similar language to describe the relationship of Christ to the Father. Indeed,
Arius not only subordinated Christ to the Father, but also the Spirit
to Christ, so that each was essentially unlike the other.

Separating the Spirit. Others in the post-apostolic Church sought
not merely to subordinate the Spirit to the Father and the Son, but
to separate the work of the three members of the Trinity. Perhaps
the most radical attempt to separate the work of the Spirit from
that of either the Father or the Son was set forth by the Montanists.
These late second-century sectarians saw the Spirit as taking over
the work of revelation and salvation which had previously been
done by the Father and the Son.

According to Montanus, founder of the sect, God's history of salvation was divided into three dispensations or ages: the age of the Father (Old Testament), the age of the Son (Incarnation), and the age of the Spirit. Montanus believed that the Spirit had given him and some of his disciples a sort of hotline to heaven, whereby they were enabled to utter inspired prophecies in addition to those given by the Old Testament prophets and Christ and His apostles. The Church eventually condemned Montanism as a heresy, not because it depicted the Spirit as a lesser god than Christ, but because it drove a wedge between the prophecies of Christ and those of the Spirit, claiming that the latter superseded the former.

The triumph of trinitarianism. Attempts to subordinate or separate the person and work of the Spirit from God and Christ were defeated at the Councils of Nicea and Constantinople. Athanasius and his followers convinced the Church to affirm that the Holy Spirit, like the Son, was of the same substance or nature (*homoousion*) as the Father. "If the Spirit were a creature," said Athanasius, "he would not be included in the Trinity; for the whole Trinity is one God. Nothing alien is mingled in the Trinity, it is indivisible and of the same nature" (*Letters to Serapion* 1.17). In this way the doctrine of the Trinity, first articulated by Tertullian (see above, chap. 3p. 66), eventually found expression in the Nicene Creed. The revised version of the creed adopted in 381 at Constantinople spoke of the Spirit as "the Lord and Giver of life, who proceeds from the Father, who with the Father and the Son together is worshiped and glorified." This formula gradually became the accepted orthodoxy of all branches of Christendom.

The filioque controversy. In the late sixth century the Western Church, at the Spanish Council of Toledo (589), inserted the phrase "and the Son" (Latin *filioque*) at the end of the Nicene confession that the Spirit "proceeds from the Father." The *filioque* was declared dogma by the Western Church in 1017, despite strong opposition from the Eastern Church. The East appealed to John 15:26, where Jesus states that the Spirit "proceeds from the Father." The West, on the other hand, pointed out that John 15:26 depicts Jesus Himself as sending the Spirit, thereby testifying to a twofold procession. Attempts to adopt a compromise formula stating that the Spirit "proceeds from the Father through the Son" were rejected by the West. In 1054 the *filioque* controversy became one of several issues which led to the official split between the Eastern (Greek Orthodox) and Western (Roman Catholic) Churches.

The diagrams below depict how the Eastern and Western views, as well as the attempted compromise view, differ from one another:

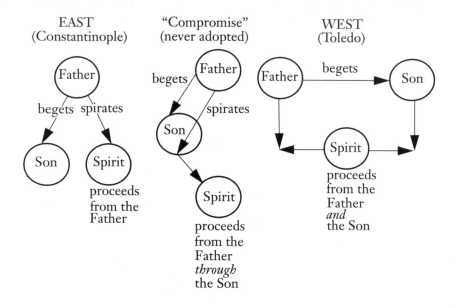

If the diagram on the right looks familiar, it is because we have already seen it in chapter 3 under our discussion of the "social Trinity." This is not to say that the *filioque* phrase demands adherence to the social Trinity. It does, however, provide a basis for it which is lacking in the other two models.

In addition, the *filioque* of the West implies a necessary intrinsic relationship between Father, Son, and Spirit which is not evident in either the Eastern or "compromise" models. Note, for example, that the Eastern model sees both Son and Spirit as relating to the Father, but not to one another by way of necessity. The Western view, on the other hand, sees the Spirit as necessarily proceeding from both Father and Son as the infinitely dynamic and joyous expression of their mutual love and delight in one another. The language of Romans 8:9, which refers to the Holy Spirit both as

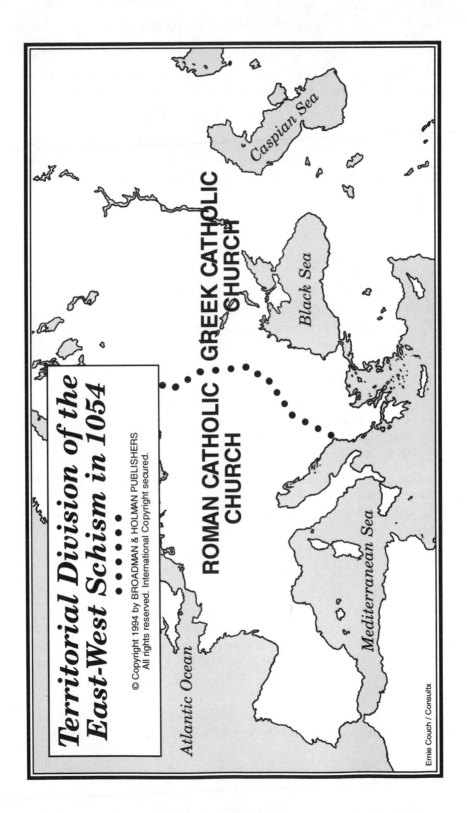

Territorial Division of the East-West Schism in 1054

© Copyright 1994 by BROADMAN & HOLMAN PUBLISHERS
All rights reserved. International Copyright secured.

GREEK CATHOLIC CHURCH

ROMAN CATHOLIC CHURCH

Caspian Sea

Black Sea

Mediterranean Sea

Atlantic Ocean

Ernie Couch / Consultx

"the Spirit of God" and "the Spirit of Christ," finds a theological basis in the *filioque* which is lacking in the other two models.

The Significance of Classical Pneumatology

The biblical witness to and historic affirmation of the full personhood and deity of the Holy Spirit carries with it important implications for Christian faith and conduct. Among these are the following:

- The fact that the Spirit is a person and not an impersonal power or force means that Christians are called to obey the Spirit, as opposed to using the Spirit as a power-source to accomplish their own ends.

- The full deity of the Spirit assures Christians that when the Holy Spirit comes into their lives, they receive nothing less than the full presence of God, thereby becoming partakers of the divine nature (2 Pet. 1:4).

- The intimate connection between Father, Son and Spirit serves to remind Christians that the Spirit will neither command nor do anything contrary to the will of God the Father and Jesus Christ as revealed in Scripture, just as Jesus Himself does nothing but what the Father commands (John 14:31).

This last reference to the commands and deeds of the Spirit brings us to the second section of our study of the third person of the Trinity. What role does the Spirit play in God's work of salvation?

The Work of the Holy Spirit

Karl Barth employed a trinitarian structure when writing his massive *Church Dogmatics*, dividing the work of God into three parts: creation, reconciliation, and redemption. While the entire Trinity is involved in all three aspects of salvation, Barth followed the traditional Christian consensus which links creation with the Father, reconciliation with the Son, and redemption with the Holy Spirit.

The redeeming work of the Spirit may likewise be defined in a threefold manner. The Holy Spirit bears witness to Jesus Christ, applies Christ's saving work to our lives, and works moment-by-moment in the lives of Christians.

The Spirit Bears Witness of Jesus Christ

We have already noted that John 15:26 refers to the Spirit's work of bearing witness to Jesus Christ. What the Spirit does is an extension of the work of Christ, since Jesus referred to Him as *allos parakletos*, "another Advocate" (John 14:16). During His earthly incarnation Jesus was uniquely the bearer of the Spirit. Since Pentecost, the Spirit dwells within the Church as a whole. For this reason Jesus said to His disciples shortly before His death, "The Spirit of truth . . . lives with you and will be in you" (John 14:17). Luke therefore speaks of Jesus' earthly ministry not as that which Jesus did and taught, but rather as "all that Jesus *began* to do and to teach" (Acts 1:1). Luke's second treatise, the book of Acts, is an account of all that Jesus *continued* to do and teach through the Holy Spirit within the Church.

In all He does, then, the Spirit works to glorify not Himself, but Jesus Christ. Jesus is the object of all truly Spirit-filled worship. Attempting to divorce the workings of the Spirit from the worship of Jesus Christ, as Montanus did, drives a wedge between the two which is foreign to the testimony of Scripture and the classical trinitarian formulas. A danger similar to that of Montanism arises when Christians so emphasize extraordinary or miraculous manifestations of the Spirit that people pay more attention to the gifts of the Spirit than to the Giver of the Spirit, who is Jesus Himself.

The Spirit Applies Christ's Salvation to His People

All of the benefits of Christ come to His people by the Holy Spirit, since He is "the Lord and Giver of Life." A Christian without the Holy Spirit is a contradiction in terms (Rom. 8:9), for it is by the Spirit that we are adopted into God's family, so that we may call God our heavenly Father (Rom. 8:15).

The apostle Paul uses the ceremony of baptism as a metaphor to speak of the Spirit's activity of incorporating Christians into the realm of Christ's saving grace. "We were all baptized by one Spirit into one body"—the body of Christ—at conversion (1 Cor. 12:13). This baptism by the Spirit is sometimes referred to as the "first fruits" (Rom. 8:23) of salvation. This phrase may be an allusion to the Jewish Feast of Weeks, when the first fruits of the harvest were brought before God in anticipation of the final ingathering of the entire crop (Deut. 16:9-12). In like manner, the gift of the Holy Spirit is a promise of even greater things to come. It is therefore not surprising that the initial giving of the Spirit to Christ's Church came during the Feast of Weeks, on the day of Pentecost (Acts 2:1).

At the same time, however, the New Testament also refers to the Spirit as bringing the "fullness" of Christ to all Christians at conversion, even though that fullness does not manifest itself immediately. "From the fullness of His grace we have all received . . ." (John 1:16). ". . . you have been given fullness in Christ . . ." (Col. 2:10). How, then, does one explain the relationship between "first fruits" and "fullness"?

Jesus' own use of agricultural metaphors in His parables may offer a clue. He often spoke of the Word of God and the Kingdom of God as seeds. A seed, though very small, gradually develops into a fully-grown plant (Mark 4:26-32). There is a sense, then, in which the fullness of the plant is already contained within the seed. Jesus' seed-parables are ancient versions of a modern proverb: "Great oaks from little acorns grow."

The indwelling Spirit may therefore be seen as the first installment of our full redemption in Christ, which will be revealed at His second coming (Rom. 8:22). For this reason Paul speaks of Christians as having been "sealed [by the Holy Spirit] for the day of redemption" (Eph. 4:30). During the interim between Christ's first and second comings even as mature a Christian as Paul could say: "Now I know in part; then I shall know fully, even as I am fully known" (1 Cor. 13:12). The fullness of Christ's redemption is already here in seed form, but will not be manifested until a future date. This is another instance of the "already-not yet" tension which characterizes the Christian life between the first and second comings of Christ (chapter 10, p. 221).

On the other hand, a few New Testament passages speak of Christians being "filled" with the Spirit at specific points of time following conversion to Christ. Peter and John were "filled with the Spirit" on more than one occasion (Acts 4:8, 31). Such texts indicate that the Holy Spirit is working in the lives of God's people during the interval between Pentecost and the return of Christ. The following section will deal with the ongoing work of the Spirit in the lives of Christ's followers, including the problem of understanding the repeated "fillings" of Acts 4 in light of the once-for-all "fullness" mentioned in John 1:16 and Colossians 2:10.

The Spirit Works Moment-by-Moment in the Lives of Christians

To live the Christian life is more than imitating Christ. It is living in the power and under the guidance of the Spirit.

The unbreakable connection between life in Christ and life in the Spirit finds its strongest biblical foundation in the eighth chapter of Paul's letter to the Church at Rome. Paul begins by reaffirming that those who are "in Christ" are no longer under the condemnation of God's judgment (v. 1). This being the case, those in Christ are free to live "according to the Spirit" (v. 4). Paul's overview of the Christian life takes up the next twenty-three verses, ten of which mention the Holy Spirit. If repetition is the first law of learning, Paul's lesson is obvious: one cannot live the Christian life apart from moment-by-moment reliance upon the Holy Spirit.

The work of the Spirit includes moral transformation, intellectual illumination, priestly intercession, assurance of salvation, spiritual gifts, and binding believers together in the life of the Church, the Body of Christ. Without the Spirit of Christ, none of these things are possible for Christ's people (John 15:5).

Moral transformation comes to Christians not by mere imitation of Christ, but by the power of the indwelling Spirit. In Galatians 5:22-23 Paul speaks of Christian virtues such as love, joy, and peace as the "fruit of the Spirit," contrasting these to "deeds of the flesh" such as immorality, idolatry and envy (Gal. 5:19-20). The word "deeds" indicates what the efforts of sinful human nature bring forth, while "fruit" points towards virtues which find their source in God's Spirit as opposed to human effort. This does not, however, rule out active obedience on the part of the Christian. Rather, it points to the biblical witness that spiritual growth is ultimately a gift from God: "Work out your own salvation with fear and trembling, for it is God who works in you to will and to act according to his good purpose" (Phil. 2:12-13).

Luke's references to the apostles being "filled with the Spirit" in the fourth chapter of Acts (vv. 8, 31) also speak of this transforming power of the Spirit. These verses are linked to the apostles' bold proclamation of the gospel in the face of persecution. Here we see the apostle Peter, a former coward who denied Christ three times, now proclaiming the truth without regard to the consequences. These "fillings" of the Spirit indicate that God gave Peter and his companions courage to face particular situations at a specific time and place. On the other hand, they in no way indicate that the Spirit had somehow left the apostles at times during the interval between Acts 2 and Acts 4. The Holy Spirit does not come and go; He is the Spirit who, as Jesus promised, "will remain with you forever" (John 14:16). The ongoing presence of the Spirit provides a foundation for special endowments of power and boldness.

Intellectual illumination is given by the Spirit in conjunction with the ministry of the Word of God. Like a lamp which is lit in a darkened room, the Spirit sheds light upon God's Word which comes to God's people through the reading and preaching of Scripture, thereby "enlightening" those who hear the Word (*Westminster Larger Catechism* Q. 155). This notion of "enlightening" or illumination has been interpreted in two very different ways in the history of the Church.

In chapter 2 we noted how Origen viewed the Holy Spirit as the final interpreter of Scripture, which in turn led him to use allegory to find "spiritual" meanings which go beyond the literal meanings of biblical language. Origen saw the Spirit as actually adding revelatory information beyond that found in the words of the biblical text. This in turn opened the door for the notion that the Holy Spirit could grant to the Church, via its teaching office, new revelations beyond those found in Scripture.

The Protestant tradition departed from Origen's allegorical method and saw the illuminating work of the Spirit as one wherein God gives insight as to how the message of Scripture might be applied to our lives. Illumination in this sense adds nothing to the literal meaning of the biblical text, in much the same way that light adds nothing to a dark room. John Calvin, for example, insisted that the illuminating work of the Spirit does not grant Christians new revelations beyond those found in the Bible, but rather consists in "sealing our minds" with the teachings of the gospel (*Institutes* 1.9.1).

The intercessory work of the Spirit enables Christians to "approach the throne of grace with confidence" whenever we have needs to place before God (Heb. 4:16). This is true even when we do not know what to pray for, says Paul, because "the Spirit Himself intercedes for us" as we pray (Rom. 8:26). The prayers of God's people are heard by the heavenly Father not because of their worthiness, but because the Spirit intercedes on our behalf.

Assurance of salvation is imparted to the believer by the Holy Spirit, both in an objective sense and a subjective sense. Objectively, the Spirit "seals" Christians "unto the day of redemption" (Eph. 4:30), thereby ensuring that those who are in Christ will be brought through life's tribulations to their hope of final salvation (see also Phil. 1:6). Subjectively, the Spirit provides an inward witness to Christ's people that they are indeed children of God (Rom. 8:16).

This inward witness of the Spirit, said John Wesley, expresses itself as a subjective feeling of confidence that one does indeed trust Christ for one's salvation and is therefore a child of God (*Journal* 1, p. 424).[2] Objective assurance, on the other hand, goes beyond the conviction that one is *now* a child of God to the assurance that one *will persevere* by virtue of the Spirit's power until one dies or Christ returns. Calvin viewed such objective assurance as a necessary element of saving faith (*Institutes* 3.2.16). Another way of distinguishing between these two aspects of assurance is as follows: Wesley speaks of the *assurance of faith*, while Calvin speaks of the *assurance of hope*.

The gifts of the Spirit (Greek *charismata*) are given to Christians for the purpose of equipping God's people for the work of ministry, in particular for building up the Christian community referred to by Paul as the "Body of Christ" (Eph. 4:12). Paul mentions eighteen gifts in the New Testament (see 1 Cor. 12:8-10, 29-30; Rom. 12:6-8; Eph. 4:11). There is no reason to believe that the New Testament list of spiritual gifts is all-inclusive.

Paul's discussion of spiritual gifts in 1 Corinthians 12 stresses two points: (1) No Christian is without a spiritual gift or gifts, and (2) no Christian possesses all the gifts. In this way, as John Chrysos-

PENTECOSTALISM—AZUSA STREET

Pentecostalism is a twentieth-century phenomenon which began in North America. It is an outgrowth of the nineteenth-century Holiness Movement, which in turn grew out of John Wesley's emphasis on the need for holiness in the Christian life in order to combat what Wesley saw as the morally and spiritually dead state of the eighteenth-century Church of England.

Pentecostalism defines "Spirit baptism" as an experience different from conversion, in a manner similar to Wesley's definition of "sanctification" as a post-conversion crisis experience. In Wesley's case, however, the post-conversion experience was evidenced by inward and outward holiness, which Wesley termed "Christian perfection" (see chapter 12). Pentecostalism, on the other hand, viewed the outward manifestation of "speaking in tongues" (Acts 2:1ff.; 1 Cor. 14) as the definitive evidence of the "baptism of the Spirit."

The movement began in 1901, but gained nationwide attention in 1906 when William J. Seymour, an African-American revivalist, founded the Apostolic Faith Gospel Mission on Azusa Street in Los Angeles. The movement became international soon after this when Thomas Ball Barratt, an Englishman who pastored a Methodist Church in Norway, came to the United States and experienced the "baptism of the Spirit" at a Pentecostal meeting in New York. He returned to Norway a convert to Pentecostalism and in 1916 founded the Filadelfia Church, which became the largest dissenting Church in Norway. Other English-speaking Europeans eventually spread the Pentecostal faith to England, Germany, Brazil, Chile, and India.

The two largest Pentecostal denominations are the Church of God in Christ (an African-American denomination) and the Assemblies of God. Pentecostalism includes numerous smaller denominations as well, but is not confined to these. In the 1960s the Pentecostal doctrine of "Spirit baptism" and the practice of speaking in tongues began to manifest themselves within mainline Protestant Churches, most notably Presbyterians, Episcopalians, and Methodists. This trans-denominational brand of Pentecostalism became known as the "charismatic movement," and has forced mainline Protestants and even Roman Catholics to reassess their views concerning the gifts of the Spirit, which have heretofore tended to be cessationist.

In South America and Africa, indigenous Pentecostal Churches have been the fastest-growing Christian groups on their respective continents during the past thirty years. Some experts in Church growth believe that this rapid expansion of Pentecostalism in the southern hemisphere will eventually shift the center of worldwide Christianity from its present location in Europe and North America. On the other hand, the single largest Christian congregation in the world is located neither in Africa nor in South America, but in the city of Seoul, South Korea. It has three-quarters of a million members—and is Pentecostal.

tom pointed out in his *Homily on 1 Corinthians*, no member of the Church is self-sufficient, and no member of the Church fails to contribute to the ministry of the Church.[3]

The role of spiritual gifts in the life of the Church has received increased attention within Protestantism and the Roman Catholic Church in recent years. This is due in large part to the worldwide phenomenon of Pentecostalism, which emphasizes God's continuing miraculous intervention within the life of the Church (see p. 250). Pentecostalism in turn was in part a reaction to nineteenth-century "cessationist" theology which taught that most, if not all, of the miraculous gifts of the Spirit mentioned in the New Testament ceased operations after the close of the apostolic age (around A.D. 100).[4]

Whatever faults modern mainline Protestants and Catholics may find in the Pentecostal tradition, it is difficult to defend the cessationist notion that God has suspended certain gifts of the Spirit in our time. There is simply no biblical evidence that this is the case. When Martin Luther wrote in the sixteenth century that "the Spirit and the gifts are ours" (from his hymn "A Mighty Fortress is our God"), he was not speaking in the past tense.

Life in the Body of Christ is the context within all of the previous ministries of the Spirit take place. Life in the Spirit is not primarily individual, but rather corporate. Christians have been baptized by the Spirit not merely to relate to Christ as individuals, but to relate to one another as members of Christ's Body called to worship God and serve one another in community. This is the point Paul makes in 1 Corinthians 12:13 when he speaks of Christians having been baptized into the Body of Christ. Spiritual gifts (1 Cor. 12:4-11, 27-31; 14:1ff.) are given by the Spirit not merely to strengthen Christians as individuals, but to build up the Body of Christ in love (1 Cor. 13).

Jesus spoke of the love Christians have for one another as the primary evidence of Christian discipleship. Miraculous gifts such as tongues, prophecy and miracles count for nothing without love (1 Cor. 13:1; Matt. 7:22). On the contrary, people will know Christ's followers by their love for one another (John 13:35), a love which in turn will give evidence before a watching world that God has sent Jesus (John 17:21). Such loving unity within the body of Christ is what Francis Schaeffer referred to as the "final apologetic" for the truth of Christianity.[5]

To sum up the second half of this chapter: Union with Christ through the Spirit is the foundation for the Christian life, both individually and corporately. The following chapter will therefore deal with how the Spirit brings Christ's salvation to individuals, while chapter 13 will relate the work of the Spirit to the Church, the Body of Christ.

Points To Ponder

1. How does the grammar and vocabulary used in John's Gospel testify to the full personhood of the Holy Spirit?

2. In what ways did Irenaeus and Origen subordinate the Holy Spirit (as well as the Son) to God the Father?

3. What did Montanus believe about the Spirit? Why was Montanism condemned as a heresy?

4. How does the Eastern version of the Nicene Creed differ from the Western version? What are the theological implications of the *filioque* clause?

5. What are the three major activities of the Holy Spirit's work of redemption?

6. What does Acts 1:1 teach us about the relationship between Jesus and the Spirit?

7. How can the New Testament speak of the Spirit both as the "first-fruits" of salvation, and also as the bearer of the "fullness" of Christ?

8. Be able to identify and expound upon five ways in which the Spirit works moment-by-moment in the lives of Christians.

9. What is the primary purpose for which God has given the gifts of the Spirit to His Church?

10. Compare and contrast the Pentecostal and cessationist perspectives on the gifts of the Spirit.

12

The Doctrine of Salvation

━━━

Receiving the Grace of God

In [Jesus Christ] was life, and the life was the light of men. . . . He came to His own, and those who were His own did not receive Him. But as many as received Him, to them He gave the right to become children of God, even to those who believe in His name, who were born not of blood, nor of the will of the flesh, nor of the will of man, but of God. . . . For of His fullness we have all received, and grace upon grace (John 1:4, 11-13, 16, NASV).

Salvation refers to that event in the life of an individual human being whereby the grace of Jesus Christ enters into that person's life, overcoming the estrangement between God and that individual which previously existed on account of human sin. As we saw in chapter 9, the Christian Church has historically viewed this estrangement in starkly objective terms. Human beings are in spiritual bondage to the power of Satan, have failed to live up to God's righteous standards, and are under a divine death sentence due to their disobedience to God. The classical, Latin, and Reformed perspectives on Christ's atonement seek to articulate, insofar as is humanly possible, how Jesus Christ has solved this threefold human predicament.

The doctrine of salvation, or *soteriology*, addresses the question of how the benefits of Christ's work are applied to the lives of God's people. These benefits have already been identified in our discussions of the resurrection and ascension of Christ, and the work of the Holy Spirit. A question now arises: How do these benefits come into the lives of individuals? What does it mean, in the words of the John's Gospel, to "receive" the grace of Jesus Christ?

How one answers that question depends a great deal upon one's anthropology. As we saw in chapters 6 and 7, throughout the history of Christianity there has been more division on issues of human nature and the extent of human sinfulness than has been the case with the doctrines of God, Christ, and the Holy Spirit. The Church has reached a general consensus (albeit at times a tenuous one) on the question of who God is in Himself. There is less consensus in matters of anthropology.

It is therefore not surprising that when we address the question of how human beings receive God's salvation in Christ, we find significant divisions among Christians throughout history. Consider, for example, the text from John's Gospel cited at the outset of this chapter, which speaks of those who "received" Christ and "believe" in His name. What is the relationship between *receiving* Christ and *believing* in His name? Are these two words which speak of the same human activity? Or does the phrase "those who believe"[1] identify those who have already "received"?

Christians have failed to come to an overall agreement on this matter. Those who argue for the former view have tended the emphasize the free will of the human being who responds to the grace of God. Those who hold to the latter view interpret the word "receive" as emphasizing God's prior giving of grace, which in turn issues in a new life of faithful obedience. This latter group speaks of God's choosing us (John 15:6); the former group, of our choosing to believe God (John 3:16). For this reason these two groups also have very different ways of interpreting New Testament language concerning God's activities of "election" and "predestination" unto salvation.

Divine Election

Biblical Testimony

In Romans 8:29 the apostle Paul tells his readers that "those God foreknew he also predestined to be conformed to the likeness of his Son." In like manner Ephesians 1:4-5 says that "God chose us in

[Christ] before the creation of the world . . . in love he predestined us to be adopted as his sons through Jesus Christ." The words "predestined" and "chose [elected] before the creation" have occasioned great debate and even anxiety among Christians throughout the history of the Church (as noted, for example, by Calvin, *Institutes* 3.21.1).

Yet Paul's desire in the New Testament is to affirm that the Christian's salvation is not merely the result of social or psychological factors, but is firmly grounded in the deepest intentions of God. As such, the doctrine of divine election seeks to assure Christ's followers that God is in control of the eternal destiny of His people, come what may (Rom. 8:28-39).

Despite the apostle's assurances in the eighth chapter of Romans, his further exposition of divine election in Romans chapter 9 has led to sharp disagreements among sincere followers of Christ. While some common ground can be found as to what the words "elect" and "election" mean in the ninth chapter of Romans, the question of whether and to what extent God decides human destiny has divided Christians for almost two thousand years.

Common Ground Concerning Election

Paul's discussion of God's election of Israel in Romans 9-11 emphasizes that throughout the history of the Old Testament covenant community, only a small portion were actually faithful to God. These Paul terms the "elect" (Rom. 11:7). The question is, what was God's "purpose in election" (Rom. 9:11).

Paul's argument in Romans 9:6-18 indicates that God's purpose in election includes His choosing certain individuals or groups of people through whom He would carry out His plan of redemption in history. As one modern Methodist theologian defines the term, "election" refers to the fact that "God chooses some persons and some nations to play a particular role in history."[2] Thus God's promise of redemption was given to Abraham and his posterity, but was carried out only through Isaac and Jacob, thereby excluding Ishmael and Esau (Rom. 9:7, 11-13), even though they also were descendants of Abraham.

This definition of election, which may be labeled "election in history," deals with the *historical* destinies of certain individuals or nations, as opposed to the *ultimate* destinies of individuals (that is, salvation or damnation). No one disputes that Paul means at least this much in Romans 9. On the other hand, the most prominent theologians in the history of Western Christianity (Augustine, Anselm, Aquinas, Luther, Calvin) have also used the word "election" as a virtual synonym for the "predestination" of particular individuals to salvation or perdition. Calvin, for example, spoke of "eternal election, by which God has predestined some to salvation, others to destruction" (*Institutes* 3.21, title). This is the doctrine of particular election, or predestination.

Particular Election (Predestination)

In chapter 7 we saw how the Western Church's anthropology led Augustine and his followers to a monergistic view of God's saving grace, whereby salvation was defined as solely the work of a sovereign God, given the total moral inability of the spiritually-dead human will. Augustine's final work, *On the Predestination of the Saints*, sets forth the concept of particular election which would later become the foundation for what Protestants refer to as "Calvinism."

Augustine laid great weight on God's sovereign freedom in election. God's reasons for choosing some for salvation do not depend upon anything people do, but solely on God's mercy, which is beyond human comprehension (*Enchiridion* 98-99). Here Augustine spoke out against his adversary Pelagius, who taught that God knew before He created the world who would be holy "by the choice of [human] free will." To the contrary, said Augustine, Pelagius has it backwards. God does not elect us because we are holy; God predestines us unto holiness (*Predestination* 35-37). God elects without regard to anything present in our human condition. Divine election is therefore *unconditional*.

Augustine's notion of unconditional election eventually became known as the "second point of Calvinism" (the total depravity of sinful humanity is the first point), since the French reformer and his successors followed Augustine in this regard. At the same time, however, some within the sixteenth-century Reformed Church challenged the Augustinian-Calvinist tradition on this matter of predestination. Most prominent among them was a Dutch preacher named Jacobus Arminius.

Corporate (Conditional) Election

The Dutch Reformed Church of the late sixteenth century further systematized Calvin's doctrine of election, which became known as "double predestination." According to this view, God's first decree from before the foundation of the world was to predestine some to salvation (election) and others to destruction (*reprobation*). God's decree to send Christ to save sinners was, according to this second-generation Calvinism, logically secondary to the decree of predestination, a point not found in Calvin's discussion of the subject.

Arminius was born four years prior to Calvin's death and was educated in the intellectual environment of Dutch Reformed orthodoxy. He was not comfortable with the notion that God's first decree included reprobation. To Arminius, this made God equally willing to damn as well as to save. Rather, Arminius viewed God's first decree as appointing His Son, Jesus Christ, as the savior of sinful humanity by virtue of His life, death and resurrection. The second decree, according to Arminius, was the election of the Church unto salvation.[3] In this way Arminius reversed the decrees of Dutch Reformed orthodoxy.

Arminius went beyond this, however, to define God's election of His people as corporate rather than individual. God elects a class of people, defined by Arminius as those who repent and believe in Christ. In this way election is not only corporate, but conditional. God elects not particular individuals, but a corporate entity—the Church—unto salvation. Individuals are deemed "elect" not on the basis of an unconditional decree, but on the basis of their faith in Christ (*not* their meritorious works, as with Pelagius!), which God foresees from before the foundation of the world. In this way Arminius sought to harmonize the biblical language of election with his conviction that people must have free will in order to be accountable before God.

The interpretation of Romans 8:29 is a crucial distinction between Arminians and Calvinists. "Whom God foreknew, did He predestine" means, for the Arminian, "whom God *foresaw* [i.e., God foresaw their faith in Christ], did He predestine." For the Calvinist, Romans 8:29 should be rendered, "whom God *foreordained*, did He predestine." Here Reformed theologians refer to the Old Testament concept of "foreknowledge" found in Jeremiah 1:5, where

God says to Jeremiah: "Before you were formed in the womb I knew you." God then defines His foreknowledge of Jeremiah as follows: "Before you were born I set you apart; I appointed you as a prophet to the nations." In this context, "foreknowledge" is more than foresight. It is foreordination of Jeremiah's individual destiny.

The Calvinist-Arminian debate over predestination echoes the debate carried on one thousand years earlier between the Eastern and Western Churches concerning the relationship between divine sovereignty and human free will, a debate we have already surveyed in chapter 7. Calvinists, coming out of the Western Augustinian tradition, emphasize God's sovereign choice of human beings for salvation. Arminians, more in accord with semi-Pelagianism than with outright Pelagianism, emphasize the human being's free choice of Christ as savior. Calvinists are monergists; Arminians are synergists.

Karl Barth's Christocentric Doctrine of Election

Like Arminius, Karl Barth rejects the notion of a divine decree of particular election prior to God's decree to elect Jesus Christ. At the same time, however, Barth wants nothing to do with synergism. He thus develops a doctrine of election which is thoroughly Christocentric (as Arminius sought to be) and monergistic (in the Augustinian-Reformed tradition).

According to Barth, Jesus Christ is both the Electing God and the Elect Man. This sort of language was used by Augustine in chapter 31 of his *On the Predestination of the Saints*. But Barth refused to follow Augustine's notion that God had decreed to elect or reject particular individuals to salvation in Jesus Christ. Rather, in Jesus Christ are found all the decrees of God, including both election and rejection: "The election of grace is the eternal beginning of all the ways and works of God in Jesus Christ. In Jesus Christ God in His free grace determines Himself for sinful man and sinful man for Himself. He therefore takes upon Himself the rejection of man with all its consequences, and elects man to participation in His own glory" (*Church Dogmatics* 2/2, 94). Jesus Christ alone is at once the object of God's election and rejection. In Christ God elected to undergo rejection for us on the cross, and to elect us into fellowship with Him.

The question thus arises as to whether there is room for any notion of reprobation in Barth's theology. Here, as in his doctrine of the atonement, Barth appears to be a universalist (see chapter 9, p. 212). In Barth's doctrine of election, no one is "determined by God merely to be rejected" (*Church Dogmatics* 2/2, 506), as in the double-predestination of Reformed orthodoxy. At the same time, Barth does not say flatly that all will be saved. Concerning Judas, for example, Barth writes: "we must be careful not to draw . . . the conclusion that his determination [i.e., Judas's fate] is ultimately positive" (*Church Dogmatics* 2/2, p. 504). On the other hand, neither must we assume that Judas's fate is ultimately negative.

The Foundation of the Christian's Salvation

For all of their differences, the three perspectives on election which we have examined share a common conviction: Jesus Christ is the first and final cause of the Christian's salvation ("the author and perfecter of our faith," Heb. 12:2). The Gospel of Christ proclaims that God's redemptive work in Jesus Christ is not an *ad hoc* activity done in response to God's being frustrated by humanity's disobedience. To the contrary, God's people are those whom He chose in Christ before the creation of the world, and predestined in His love to both holiness and adoption as children of God (Eph. 1:4-5).

Predestination should therefore not be considered as an abstract theological problem, as though it were something which has no practical value in the Christian life. Predestination relates to the entire Christian life, including our relationship with God (adoption) and our day-to-day walk with God (holiness). It also provides hope. As Paul says, "those [God] predestined, he also called; those he called, he also justified; those he justified, he also glorified" (Rom. 8:30).

Words such as adoption, holiness, justification, and glorification take us out of the realm of "before the foundation of the world" and bring us into the realm of daily living. This in turn leads us to our next major topic in the doctrine of salvation: the *ordo salutis*, or "order of salvation."

The Ordo Salutis

The Answer to Life's Biggest Question

In the book of Acts we read of Paul and Silas being imprisoned in Philippi because they preached the gospel. During their imprisonment the jailer asked them the question which lies at the heart of all religions: "What must I do to be saved?" Paul and Silas responded with the uniquely Christian answer: "Believe in the Lord Jesus, and you will be saved" (Acts 16:30).

The simplicity of the apostles' answer to the jailer's query belies the complexities which lie beneath it. Specifically, Paul and Silas's statement defines neither belief nor salvation. The letters of Paul, as well as the rest of the New Testament, must be read in order to give meaning to these and other terms which speak of how one begins, continues and finishes what Paul calls the "good fight" or "race" which leads to the "crown of righteousness" which Christ's followers will receive when He returns (2 Tim. 4:7).

We defined salvation at the outset of this chapter. How one attains to this salvation—how one finishes the race, if you will—is the question which various formulations of the *ordo salutis* seek to answer. What is the order of events which must be realized in our lives in order to obtain salvation?

The concept of faith is central to any discussion of the order of salvation, as may be seen by Paul and Silas's response to the Philippian jailer. The watchword of the Protestant Reformation, for example, was *sola fide*, "faith alone." Yet the presence of the word "alone" (*sola*) indicates that the Reformers were reacting to a Roman Catholic *ordo salutis*, which placed significant emphasis on activities done in addition to faith. That this was the case may be seen as we briefly examine the Catholic version of the *ordo salutis* which existed at the outset of the sixteenth century, and which remains essentially intact to the present day.

The Roman Catholic *Ordo Salutis*

Catholicism views salvation not merely as one's relationship with the person of Christ, but also as one's relationship to Christ's Church (which for Catholics means the Church of Rome). The Church, as Christ's Body, mediates salvation to the world. The principal means by which this is done is through institutions which

Catholics (as well as Eastern Orthodox and some Protestant Christians) refer to as *sacraments*. The Catholic *ordo salutis* may therefore be called sacramental.[4] We shall elaborate further on sacramental theology, especially with relation to baptism and the Lord's Supper, in chapter 14.

For now, let us identify those institutions which Catholicism regards as sacraments. They are *baptism, confirmation, eucharist, penance, extreme unction, holy orders*, and *marriage*. Of these seven sacraments, the first five constitute the Catholic *ordo salutis*, in the order listed above. The final two, holy orders (the consecration of priests) and marriage, are not part of the Catholic order of salvation, since they are not mandated for all Catholics; indeed, they are mutually exclusive (priests do not marry).

The word "sacrament" comes from the Latin *sacramentum*, meaning a sacred or holy thing. For Catholics, sacraments are not merely symbols of God's grace (as is the case with many Protestants who use the term). They are "effective signs of grace instituted by Christ" which actually *give* grace.[5] The efficacy of the sacraments depends, in the final analysis, not upon the faith of the one receiving it, but upon the proper administration of the sacramental rite. Grace comes to the recipient not by the recipient's inward attitude, but *ex opere operato*, "by the power of the completed sacramental rite."[6]

The word "grace" in Catholicism receives a different emphasis than in Protestantism, especially the grace which is given in the sacraments. For Protestants, "grace" is connected primarily with God's benevolence, demonstrated in the forgiveness of sins, or what Luther and Calvin called "justification." Catholics, on the other hand, speak of grace in terms of "sanctification" or holiness, the actual practice of moral virtue. Indeed, for historic Catholicism "justification" consists in becoming increasingly sanctified. This is because Catholics interpret the notion of justification (Latin *justificare*) as a person's being *made* righteous (holy), as opposed to merely being *declared* righteous (not guilty) on the basis of Christ's vicarious sacrifice. "[Justification is] not that by which the Lord is just, but that by which He justifies those who from unrighteousness He makes righteous" (Augustine, *Sermon 131*).[7] In other words, justification does not merely impute righteousness (see below p. 264), but *infuses* righteousness.

The Roman Catholic order of salvation, then, consists of an ever-increasing measure of grace as actual righteousness given to the Church member via the sacraments. A different level of grace is given in each sacrament.

Baptism removes the taint of original sin from the one receiving the sacrament and regenerates that person in the power of the Spirit. "[Christ] saved us through the washing of rebirth and renewal by the Holy Spirit" (Titus 3:5). This is the beginning of the Christian life. Anyone who is not baptized will not enter heaven. "Unless he is born of water and the Spirit, he cannot enter the Kingdom of God" (John 3:5). Infants are therefore baptized as soon as possible after they are born. On the other hand, baptism alone is no guarantee of entering the Kingdom of God. One must continue on to the next sacrament of the *ordo salutis*.

Confirmation is logically, though not always chronologically, the second stage of the Catholic order of salvation (some Catholics receive their first communion, or eucharist, before being confirmed). It is that sacrament in which, by the laying on of hands together with anointing and prayer, a baptized person is filled for the inner strengthening of the supernatural life and for bold outward confession of faith. Aquinas defined it as a sacrament of the fullness of grace, "that sacrament in which strength is conferred on the regenerate" (*Summa Theologiae* 3. 72. 2). It is generally given following a period of instruction in the Catholic faith. Confirmation, unlike baptism, is not necessary for salvation, though it adds to the quality of one's salvation.

The Eucharist is the central means of grace in the Roman Catholic order of salvation. Catholics view the eucharist as a sacrifice wherein Christ, truly present in the bread and the wine of the sacrament, offers Himself to the heavenly Father and gives Himself to the faithful as ongoing nourishment for their souls. Unlike baptism and confirmation, the eucharist is not once for all, but is a part of every Roman Catholic service of worship. Indeed, it is the central event of the Catholic Mass. We shall examine the Roman Catholic doctrine of eucharist, including the notion of transubstantiation, in chapter 14.

Penance is a word derived from the Latin *poenitentia*, which in turn was used to translate the Greek *metanoia* (see Luke 24:47 in the Latin Vulgate), usually rendered "repentance" in English. This sacrament deals with post-baptismal sins, and is tied to the Catholic practice of the confession. Once a baptized Catholic sincerely and contritely confesses his or her sins to a priest duly ordained by the Catholic Church (holy orders), the priest pronounces absolution, the forgiveness of sins. In addition, the priest usually prescribes a "sacramental satisfaction," which consists of works of penance imposed by the priest on the penitent. Such works are done in atonement only for the temporal punishment of sins, which remain after the guilt of sin and its eternal punishment have been forgiven.

Extreme unction is the sacrament whereby a sick or dying believer, by the anointing of oil and the prayer of the priest, receives the grace of God for the supernatural salvation of the soul, and sometimes also for the natural healing of the body. It is sometimes referred to as "last rites," since it is the final sacrament one receives prior to death. Catholics who receive extreme unction prior to death obtain remission of both venial sins (less serious transgressions) and mortal sins (grievous transgressions such as murder and adultery), and thus go directly to heaven. Catholics who die with venial sins unremmited go to purgatory. If one dies in mortal sin, hope of salvation is lost.[8] Since suicide is a mortal sin according to Catholic doctrine, Church members who take their own lives are assumed to have damned themselves and are thus not granted a Church burial on sacred ground.[9]

The classical Roman Catholic *ordo salutis* thus views the Church itself as God's channel of sanctifying grace, which comes to Church members in the sacraments properly administered by a duly ordained priest. For this reason the Church itself has been referred to in Catholic tradition as God's "means of salvation," though the Second Vatican Council in 1965 changed that designation to one of a mystery or sacrament, "a reality imbued with the hidden presence of God" (Pope Paul VI).[10] In any event, Catholicism emphasizes the giving of grace by God in the sacraments through the priest to the Church member. It is a hierarchical, or "top-down," perspective. When we enter the world of Protestant thought, a different perspective emerges.

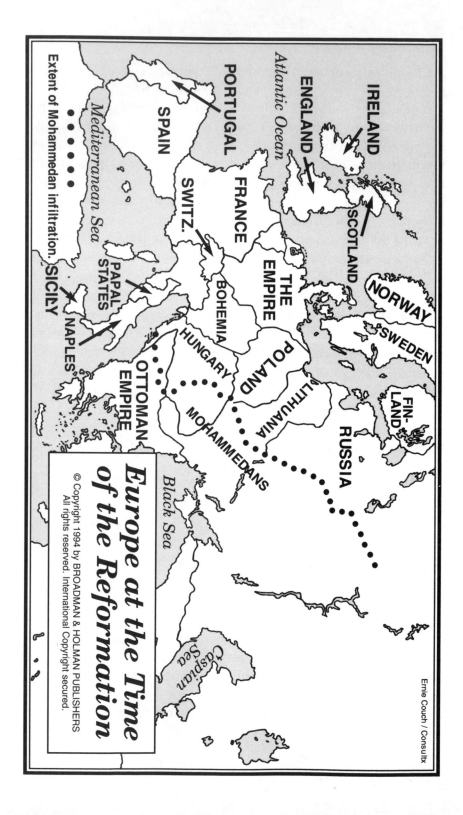

Europe at the Time of the Reformation

Extent of Mohammedan infiltration. • • • • • •

IRELAND

ENGLAND

SCOTLAND

Atlantic Ocean

PORTUGAL

SPAIN

Mediterranean Sea

FRANCE

SWITZ.

PAPAL STATES

SICILY

NAPLES

BOHEMIA

THE EMPIRE

NORWAY

SWEDEN

FIN-LAND

POLAND

LITHUANIA

RUSSIA

HUNGARY

OTTOMAN EMPIRE

MOHAMMEDANS

Black Sea

Caspian Sea

Ernie Couch / Consultx

MARTIN LUTHER'S NINETY-FIVE THESES

Historians generally cite October 31, 1517 as the beginning of the Protestant Reformation. On that date Martin Luther (1483-1546), a Roman Catholic priest, nailed a document on the door of the faculty of theology at Wittenberg University. That document consisted of ninety-five theses, or points of debate, which Luther articulated in order to begin a process of discussion with the Catholic Church concerning the subject of "indulgences."

Indulgences were one form of the sacrament of penance. Specifically, an indulgence was permission to relax the temporal satisfaction required of a contrite sinner following confession and absolution (see p. 264). In the sixteenth century such indulgences could be granted in exchange for financial contributions to the Church. This notion of paying for penance ran counter to Luther's growing conviction that forgiveness of sins came solely through faith in Jesus Christ.

The indulgence which offended Luther was granted by the Pope in order to raise money to help pay for new construction at St. Peter's Cathedral in Rome.

The Vatican's representative in Germany, John Tetzel, went so far as to say that people could buy indulgences not only for their own sins, but for those of their relatives who had died and gone to purgatory. Tetzel's slogan as he went from village to village has been quoted as follows: "For every coin that in the coffer lies/ Another soul from purgatory flies!" For this reason Luther's twenty-seventh thesis stated: "They preach only human doctrines who say that as soon as the money clinks into the money chest, the soul flies out of purgatory."

Luther merely intended to start an in-house theological debate, and not a religious and political revolution, by posting his Ninety-Five Theses. This is demonstrated by the fact that Luther wrote the theses in Latin, the language of the Catholic religious hierarchy. Someone, however, translated Luther's document into German. Numerous copies were then printed and circulated, thanks to a technological marvel invented less than seventy years earlier: the printing press. The Reformation had begun.

Protestants and the *Ordo Salutis*

Martin Luther's revolt against sacramentalism. The sacrament of penance, together with the Catholic doctrine of purgatory, was the occasion for Martin Luther's "Ninety-Five Theses" which launched the Protestant Reformation (see the following article on Luther). Luther's differences with Rome went beyond individual issues, however. He rejected the entire sacramental notion of grace. As we have already noted, the sacramental *ordo salutis* viewed grace as ethical righteousness infused or imparted by the sacraments. Luther, building upon his studies of Paul's letters to the Romans and the Galatians, defined grace as God's free declaration of pardon of sinners by virtue of the saving death of Christ. "God spreadeth over them an infinite heaven of grace, and doth not impute unto them their sins for Christ's sake" (*Commentary on Galatians* 5:19).[11] Rather, God *imputes* (credits to their account) the righteousness of Christ, as noted in chapter 9 in our discussion of 2 Corinthians 5:21 (p. 197).

For Luther, then, grace is not a quality of ethical righteousness imparted in various stages via the sacraments. Rather, grace comes completely ("an infinite heaven of grace") in the form of imputed righteousness. For Luther the righteousness of God of which Paul speaks in Romans 1:17 is not a righteousness which we actually perform. It is instead what Luther termed an *alien* or *passive* righteousness which properly belongs to Christ, but which is credited to our account.[12] This imputed righteousness is not moral transformation, but a right relationship with God given to sinners by God Himself through Christ. It is not righteousness in the sense of justice, but rather of mercy.

This in turn means that *justification* is not a process of ever-increasing actual righteousness, as in Catholicism, but a free gift of God's imputed righteousness which brings us into a right relationship with God. Such righteousness in no way depends upon our adding something to God's gift by way of our own efforts. Rather, it is received solely by trusting in what God has done, is doing, and promises to do on our behalf in Jesus Christ. This attitude of total confidence in God's resources, as opposed to our own, is what Luther termed *faith* (Rom. 1:17; 3:21).

For Luther, faith was not something done in addition to obedience to the commandments of God. Rather, Luther defined such obedience solely in terms of faith. "What commandment is there that such obedience [of faith] has not completely fulfilled? . . . Therefore God has rightly included all [evil] things, not under anger or lust, but under unbelief" (*A Treatise on Christian Liberty*).[13] Good works were thus not excluded by faith, but necessarily included within Luther's definition of faith. On the other hand, any works which placed confidence in one's own ability to merit God's forgiveness or satisfy God's demands for justice were viewed by Luther as the essence of unbelief. Such works reject God's offer of salvation in Christ and instead place confidence in oneself. "Nothing makes a man good except faith, nor evil except unbelief."[14]

Luther's emphasis on faith as an inward confidence in the promises of God was a shift from medieval Catholicism's tendency to define faith in terms of assent to ecclesiastical dogma and obedience to the sacramental order of salvation. To use Latin terminology common in his day, Luther emphasized *fiducia*, while Rome stressed *assensus*. This is not to say that Luther despised doctrine; his voluminous theological writings belie any such notion. What it does say is that Luther's answer to the question, "What must I do to be saved?" laid stress upon the believer's inward attitude of trust in God (*fiducia*), as opposed to objective doctrines which must be believed (*assensus*) or outward deeds which must be done.

To be sure, Luther viewed faith as a confidence in the objective person and saving work of Jesus Christ. But his emphasis on justification by faith set a precedent for Protestants by focusing on the subjective response of the believer to God's grace. In this way Luther, although a firm believer in the Augustinian doctrine of predestination, nevertheless became the spiritual godfather not only of Calvin and the Reformed Protestant tradition, but also of non-predestinarians such as Arminius and John Wesley. The latter, by his own account, was converted to genuine faith in Christ by hearing someone read aloud Luther's *Preface to the Epistle to the Romans*.

The Reformed ordo salutis. John Calvin followed Luther's lead by emphasizing faith in Christ as the sole means by which Christians are justified before God, and by defining justification in legal terms (being declared not guilty on the basis of Christ's sacrificial death) rather than ethical terms (being made ethically virtuous by ever-increasing amounts of divine grace). He also shared Luther's conviction that justification must be distinguished from sanctification.

For Calvin, justification refers to a once-for-all event issuing in forgiveness of sins and a right relationship with God. Sanctification, on the other hand (which Calvin often referred to as "repentance" or "mortification of the flesh"), is a process whereby one gradually grows in what Luther had termed "proper" righteousness, which is personal holiness (Luther, *Two Kinds of Righteousness*).[15] Calvin spoke of sanctification as "the fruit of faith," in that one cannot have any serious motivation for living a godly life "without knowing himself to [already] belong to God" (*Institutes* 3.3.1-2).

Such knowledge, Calvin went on to say, comes from placing one's confidence in Christ's offer of free justification as revealed in the Word of God, as opposed to placing one's hope in whatever the Church might teach (*Institutes* 3.2.1-2). This is the meaning of saving faith. It is trust in the person and work of Christ, not in a system of doctrine or a sacramental *ordo salutis*, which in Calvin's view leaves one unsure of one's final salvation.

Faith, then, is the means by which one receives justification, which in turn provides a sure foundation for continuing in sanctification. In addition, faith for Calvin is ultimately a work of God, not ourselves: "Now we shall possess a right definition of faith if we call it a firm and certain knowledge of God's benevolence toward us, founded upon the truth of the freely given promise in Christ, both revealed to our minds and sealed upon our hearts through the Holy Spirit" (*Institutes* 3.2.7). Faith is indeed something that we do. We bank our hope on God's promises in Christ. But this trust ("a firm and certain knowledge of God's benevolence") is given by God ("revealed . . . and sealed . . . through the Holy Spirit").

Calvin's definition of faith demonstrates his desire to strike a balance between the "top-down" *ordo salutis* of Rome, which emphasized grace coming from God to the one receiving the sacraments, and Luther's "bottom-up" emphasis which laid its greatest stress on the believer's acts of obedient faith.

Calvin's successors in Geneva, Holland, and England further systematized Calvin's ideas in the area of the *ordo salutis* much as they did with the doctrine of predestination. Indeed, the Reformed expression of the order of salvation is based upon the doctrines of predestination and total depravity. While absolute unanimity does not exist in Reformed circles, the following items are typical of the *ordo salutis* in the Reformed tradition: *effectual calling, regeneration, conversion, justification, adoption, sanctification,* and *glorification.*

- *Effectual calling* is Reformed theology's interpretation of Paul's statement in Romans 8:30 that those whom God predestined He also "called." This divine call is labeled effectual because it is always successful; no one who is effectually called fails to receive salvation. "Whom He called, He also justified" (Rom. 8:30). Effectual calling is not to be confused with God's "general call," to which Jesus referred when He said that "many are called, but few are chosen" (Matt. 22:14). The gospel message is proclaimed to all, but only God's elect, those who are "chosen," embrace it.

- *Regeneration,* or new birth, is the Holy Spirit's gift of new life in Christ. The tenth chapter of the Westminster Confession of Faith links regeneration with effectual calling. Such a call therefore consists of two elements: the outward preaching of the gospel, and the inward regenerating work of the Spirit which consists of "enlightening their minds . . . taking away their heart of stone, and giving unto them an heart of flesh; renewing their wills . . . and effectually drawing them to Christ; yet so as they come most freely, being made willing by His grace."

- *Conversion* is the human response to the divine initiative of effectual calling and regeneration. It consists of repentance (turning from sin) and faith (embracing Christ as Savior). Conversion is a free decision made possible by the prior work of God's saving grace of effectual calling and regeneration, without which the human will remains in bondage.

- *Justification* is a once-for-all event whereby God freely declares His elect righteous, "not by infusing [ethical] righteousness in them, but by pardoning their sins" so that "they can never fall from the state of justification" (*Westminster Confession,* chap. 11). The Reformers thus opposed the Catholic notion that justification was not merely forgiveness of sins but also a process of increasing holiness, so that works complete justification (*Canons and Decrees of the Council of Trent*, chap. 7; chap. 16 canon 24). To put it another way: Whereas sixteenth-century Catholicism said godliness was a necessary part of justification, the Reformers took literally Paul's affirmation that God "justifies the *ungodly*" (Rom. 4:5). The Christian is what Luther called *simul justus et peccator:* simultaneously righteous "in Christ", yet sinful in and of himself (*First Lecture on Galatians* 2:18).[16]

- *Adoption* is a legal term signifying that all who are justified "enjoy the privileges of the children of God." They "receive the Spirit of adoption, have access to the throne of grace with boldness, . . . are pitied, protected, provided for, and chastened by [God] as by a father, yet never cast off, but sealed to the day of redemption, and inherit the promises, as heirs of everlasting salvation" (*Westminster Confession*, chap. 12). Paul's statement that Christians have received "the Spirit of adoption" (Rom. 8:15) may refer to the laws of ancient Rome, whereby an adopted son enjoyed all the rights and privileges of a natural-born son. Even so, those who are "in Christ" have a relationship with God akin to that of Jesus Himself, with respect to His humanity (*not* His divinity!).

- *Sanctification*, as noted earlier, is a process whereby the Christian grows in what Luther called "proper righteousness." It is distinct from justification ("alien righteousness"), but may not be divorced from justification. Both are given at the time of regeneration (*Westminster Confession*, chap. 13). For this reason Calvin states that good works may be viewed as "signs of the divine benevolence toward [the Christian]," while at the same time insisting that one's assurance of salvation depends not upon one's good works, but by depending entirely upon God's free promise of justification (*Institutes* 3.14.18). Christians are not saved *by* good works, but neither are they saved *without* good works. These good works of sanctification, though bringing substantial spiritual healing and growth, nevertheless remain "imperfect in this life" (*Westminster Confession*, chapter 13). In Reformed theology, this imperfection is overcome only in the final stage of the *ordo salutis*, which is glorification.

- *Glorification* refers to the resurrection of the body to everlasting life mentioned in 1 Corinthians 15:42-57 and at the close of the Apostles' and Nicene Creeds. It is the final link of Paul's unbroken chain of salvation found in Romans 8:29-30 ("God foreknew . . . predestined . . . called . . . justified . . . glorified"). All whom God has justified, God will glorify. The fact that Paul uses the past tense, "glorified," underscores this. Glorification is, from the divine perspective, already accomplished, since it is based on justification, not sanctification. At the same time, this does not rule out the need for human perseverance in faith. Rather, it assures such perseverance. This is why Calvin taught that one could have assurance not only that one is presently a Christian, but that one would persevere to the end.

The fact that Reformed theology's order of salvation is based upon an Augustinian view of predestination eventually led to a rift in the Reformed Church. We have already seen that it was Jacobus Arminius who challenged the Reformed doctrine of double predestination. It was therefore inevitable that sooner or later he would challenge other elements of the Reformed order of salvation.

The ordo salutis in the Arminian tradition. Arminius must have felt himself in somewhat of a bind as he opposed the Dutch Reformed Church. On the one hand he rejected predestination, believing that God's election of individuals was based upon His foreseeing who would freely accept Christ. On the other hand, Arminius was no Pelagian. He viewed human nature as having been adversely affected by Adam's sin, so that all people are "devoid of that original righteousness and holiness (Rom. 5:12, 18-19)" which was Adam's prior to the Fall.[17]

Arminius also believed that the will of sinful humanity was incapable of performing the spiritual good necessary to gain salvation. He believed Adam had free will prior to the Fall, but that since the Fall the human will "has no powers whatsoever except such as are excited by divine grace. For Christ has said, 'Without me ye can do nothing.'"[18]

This "divine grace" of which Arminius spoke was the call of the gospel of Christ to salvation, accompanied by the work of the Holy Spirit. Any positive response to the call of the gospel, for Arminius, is a work of divine grace. This divine grace, however, does not inevitably lead to salvation. Here Arminius denied the Reformed distinction between Christ's "general call" to salvation, and the "effectual call" which inevitably leads to saving faith via regeneration. "Is the grace of God a certain irresistible force? . . . I believe that many persons resist the Holy Spirit and reject the grace that is offered."[19]

In this way Arminius opposed the Reformed doctrine of irresistible grace. It violated his notion of free will, which defined human freedom as freedom from necessity. If a person inevitably does something, it is not a free act. A free will must be an undetermined will. As we saw in chapter 7, this echoes the Eastern Church's view of free will, as opposed to the Western notion of freedom as self-determination. To affirm that regeneration precedes faith, as did Reformed orthodoxy, would affirm that God's work made faith necessary or inevitable. This would not be inconsistent with the Augustinian notion of freedom as self-determination, which sees freedom as compatible with necessity (i.e., people necessarily act according to their nature) but not with coercion (Calvin, *Institutes* 2.3.5). Arminius, on the other hand, made no distinction between necessity and coercion. God's grace calls people to believe, and makes it possible for all to believe. But not everyone does believe.[20] Saving grace can be resisted.

Arminius further believed that those who are truly regenerate may eventually resist the grace of God and fall away from salvation. It was not a position with which he was totally comfortable, but he felt compelled towards it both by biblical passages and actual experience which indicate that true Christians do fall away from faith in Christ.[21] It was also consistent with his definition of free will. In this way Arminius denied yet another point of Reformed orthodoxy, that of the perseverance of the saints.

For Arminius, then, the order of salvation is based not on the predestination of particular "elect" individuals, but upon God's desire to save all who come to Christ. In human experience, therefore, the Arminian *ordo salutis* could be expressed as follows: general call, saving grace offered, faith, regeneration, justification, sanctification, glorification. Unlike Reformed theology, however, the Arminian order of salvation has no necessity to it. Human free will may interrupt the chain of events, Paul's language in Romans 8:30 notwithstanding.

Arminius was thus more concerned with salvation from the human being's perspective than from the standpoint of immutable divine decrees. In this way his perspective on the *ordo salutis*, if not his actual doctrinal stance, was more akin to the early Luther than to Calvin. Arminius emphasized the human response to the gospel ("bottom-up") rather than the sovereignty of God ("top-down").

John Wesley's Contribution to Arminianism

More than a century after Arminius John Wesley found himself attracted to the Dutch scholar's theology over against the Calvinism of his day. Yet Wesley was not an ideological clone of Arminius. He endorsed the Reformed doctrine of total depravity, and did not shy away from speaking of original sin. On some points he described himself as a "hair's breadth" from Calvinism.[22]

The brand of Arminianism which is most popular today is Wesleyan Arminianism. Three important areas in which he clarified or expanded upon Arminius are divine grace, justification, and sanctification.

Prevenient grace is an expression which can be traced back to Augustine, but which gained new meaning in Wesley's thought. The word "prevenient" means "to come before." Wesley viewed this as an elemental form of grace present in everyone. This prevenient grace works in such a way that "there is a measure of free-will supernaturally restored to every man, together with that supernatural light which 'enlightens every man that cometh into the world'[John 1:9]."[23] In this way Wesley was able to maintain that humans are by nature incapable of faith, but by prevenient grace given enough ability to respond to God's saving grace which comes in the gospel (*The Twenty-Five Articles of Religion*, Art. 8).[24] That saving grace, however, may be rejected just as freely as it may be accepted.

Justification by faith was central to Wesley's preaching as it was for both Luther and Calvin. Wesley spoke of the "merits of Christ" whereby one was "reconciled to God" (Sermon 11, "The Witness of Our Own Spirit").[25] He followed Arminius, however, in rejecting the Reformed doctrine of penal substitution as being inconsistent with his conviction that Christ died for all, and not merely for the elect (see chapter 9, part 5). He also followed Arminius in denying the Lutheran and Reformed doctrine that God imputes the righteousness of Christ to Christians. Rather, Wesley stated that our "faith is imputed to us for righteousness."[26] In his sermon "Justification by Faith" Wesley declared:

> Least of all does justification imply . . . that [God] accounts [Christians] to be otherwise than they are. . . . Neither can it ever consist with His unerring wisdom, to think that I am innocent, to judge that I am righteous and or holy, because another is so. He can no more, in this manner, confound me with Christ, than with David or Abraham ("Justification by Faith" II.4).[27]

Wesley was apparently concerned that the Reformed doctrine of Christ's imputed righteousness would lead to antinomianism, or flagrant disregard for the Law of God. Antinomianism was, of course, also a concern of the apostle Paul (Rom. 6:1, "Shall we go on sinning, that grace may increase? By no means!"). Thus Wesley, like Arminius, denied that justification assured the believer's ultimate glorification. Rather, Wesley took pains to define justification as the forgiveness of *past* sins, but not future sins.[28]

Wesley's notion of the "merits of Christ" therefore seems closer in certain respects to the Augustinian-Catholic notion of *infused* righteousness than to the Reformed doctrine of justification. As one Methodist theologian put it, Wesley set forth "a Protestant doctrine of original sin *minus* most of the other elements in classical Protestant soteriology, *plus* a catholic doctrine of perfection *without* its full panoply of priesthood and priestcraft."[29] This is further reflected in Wesley's concern for sanctification, which included his unique contribution to Arminian theology: the doctrine of Christian perfection.

Sanctification for Wesley was a process of growth in actual righteousness, as it was for the Reformers. Unlike Luther and Calvin, however, Wesley also taught that sanctification might be completed in this life through a second work of grace which he called entire sanctification, or "Christian perfection."[30] Sanctification, like justification, could become a status, not merely a process.

Wesley's view of perfection was based on his reading of texts such as Philippians 3:12 and 1 John 5:18. In his sermon entitled "Christian Perfection"[31] Wesley carefully qualified the term. By "perfection" he did not mean sinlessness in the sense of "freedom from ignorance, or mistakes, or infirmities, or temptations." Nor did he merely mean freedom from sinning "willfully" or "habitually" (II.6). Christian perfection is, negatively speaking, freedom from outward sin, evil thoughts, and evil tempers. Positively speaking, said Wesley, Christian perfection consists of the fact that "Christ liveth in me" (II.25) so that the Christian be like Christ not only after death, but also "*in this world*" (see 1 John 4:17). Expressions such as "holiness" and "perfect love" are other Wesleyan synonyms for entire sanctification.

Common Ground Between Calvin and Wesley?

Differences between the Calvinist Reformed and Wesleyan-Arminian traditions are significant. Yet Wesley, as noted above, described himself as a "hair's breadth" from Calvin in certain respects, and worked together with the English Calvinist George Whitefield during the Wesleyan revivals in England. A Protestant consensus which seeks to encompass Calvin and Wesley would include the following points, among others:

- Human beings are sinful, separated from the love of God by nature and by choice, without hope of reconciliation to a holy God unless God takes the initiative (*Westminster Confession* 6, 9; *Twenty-Five Articles* 7, 8).

- God has taken the initiative to save sinful human beings. The death and resurrection of Jesus Christ provided the basis for both justification and sanctification, and the Holy Spirit gives grace to sinners which enables them to come to faith in Christ (*Westminster Confession* 8, 10; *Twenty-Five Articles* 8, 9).

- Justification and sanctification cannot be separated. The good works which flow from sanctification do not save anyone, but neither can anyone be saved without significant progress in sanctification (*Westminster Confession* 13; *Twenty-Five Articles* 10).

Both Calvin and Wesley also held that the Christian life cannot be lived in isolation from one's fellow believers in Christ. Rather, Christians are called into the life of God's new covenant community, the Church. The next two chapters will examine what the Church is and is not, and what it means to live the Christian life within the context of the Church.

CALVINISM VS. ARMINIANISM

In 1618 the Reformed Church in Holland convened a theological conclave, or synod, in the city of Dordrecht. What became known as the Synod of Dort concluded the following year when the Dutch Reformed hierarchy declared as unorthodox the teachings of Jacobus Arminius and his followers, known as the Remonstrants. The Dutch Reformers also set forth the five doctrines which became known as the "five points of Calvinism."

The acrostic TULIP is sometimes used to identify these doctrines, which are: **T**otal depravity, **U**nconditional election, **L**imited atonement, **I**rresistible grace, and **P**erseverance of the saints. These five points, and their Arminian counterparts, are briefly depicted on the following chart, together with Scripture texts each group uses to bolster its point of view. (No endorsement of either group's use of these texts is intended or implied.) The Synod of Dort became a watershed event in the history of Reformed theology, setting forth double predestination and limited (particular) atonement as standards of doctrinal orthodoxy. It is an irony of Christian history that these same views were condemned almost one thousand years earlier. In 848 the Synod of Mainz (Germany) condemned the Saxon monk Gottschalk for teaching double predestination and particular atonement. Double-predestination had also been rejected in 529 by the Second Council of Orange (France). For the Calvinist delegates at the Synod of Dort, the third time was the charm.

Five Points (T.U.L.I.P.)	Propositions debated at the Synod of Dort	Calvinist response	Arminian response
Total depravity	Sinners are incapable of faith apart from God's saving grace	Yes (Eph. 2:8-9)	No (John 1:9)
Unconditional election	God chooses His elect apart from anything they do	Yes (Acts 13:48)	No (Rom. 8:29)
Limited atonement	Christ died for His elect, and for no others	Yes (John 10:11, 15)	No (1 John 2:2)
Irresistible grace	God's saving grace always leads to the sinner's conversion	Yes (Eph. 2:1,10)	No (Luke 7:30)
Perseverance of the saints	All who have been born again will persevere to the end and be saved.	Yes (Rom. 8:30; Eph. 4:30)	No (John 15:6; Heb. 6:4-6)

Points To Ponder

1. What are the two historical interpretations of what it means to "receive" Christ?

2. Why is the doctrine of particular election sometimes called "unconditional" election?

3. In what sense do Arminians see election as "conditional"?

4. According to Arminius, what was God's first decree in His plan of salvation? What is the first decree for Calvinism?

5. How is Karl Barth's doctrine of election similar to both Calvinism and Arminianism? How does it differ from both?

6. Identify and explain the five elements of the Catholic *ordo salutis*.

7. How did Luther's view of justification differ from that of Roman Catholicism?

8. According to Luther, what is the relationship between faith and works?

9. Identify and explain the seven elements of the Reformed *ordo salutis* discussed in this chapter.

10. Why did Arminius oppose the Reformed *ordo salutis*? What is the Arminian version of the order of salvation?

11. Be familiar with Wesley's three contributions to Arminian theology.

12. What are "indulgences"? Why did Luther oppose them? (See article on Luther's 95 Theses)

13

The Church:
The People of God

The Meaning of *Church*
in the New Testament

Ekklesia in the Ancient World

The word *Church* translates the Greek *ekklesia*, a combination of the prefix *ek* ("out") and the verb *kaleo* ("to call"). For this reason the Christian Church is sometimes referred to as God's "called-out" community, called out of the world to serve God.

The New Testament authors probably did not choose the word *ekklesia* because its etymology or root meaning enshrined a theological concept of the Church being called out of the world. They used it because it was already available in the Greek translation of the Hebrew Scriptures, the Septuagint. On over one hundred occasions the Septuagint uses *ekklesia* to translate the Hebrew *qahal* ("congregation"). The word *qahal* has at least three shades of meaning.

- *Qahal* can refer to an assembly of Jews, including the entire covenant community of Israel. In Deuteronomy 9:10 and 10:4, for example, it refers to all the people of Israel gathered to confirm the covenant at Mount Sinai. In this sense *qahal* and its Greek counterpart *ekklesia* refer to the people of God.

- *Qahal* can refer to a political or judicial assembly, gathered together to render decisions on matters of law (Judg. 21:8). The Greeks used *ekklesia* in the same manner as early as the fifth century B.C. to refer to what today might be called a town meeting.

- *Qahal* can refer to a group of people assembled for worship (Ps. 22:23, 89.6). The Greeks never used *ekklesia* in this way, but the Septuagint does. By the time of Jesus, however, the word *synagoge* ("synagogue") was the term of choice among Greek-speaking Jews for a religious assembly. Thus the early Christians, in choosing to use the word *ekklesia* of their gatherings, distinguished themselves from their Jewish counterparts.

Ekklesia in the New Testament

The apostolic writers use the word *ekklesia* to refer to people who profess faith in Jesus Christ. Within this general definition one sees in the New Testament the following threefold distinction, going from the narrowest to the broadest sense of the term *Church*:

A Christian assembly. In Romans 16:5 Paul refers to the "Church," or congregation, gathered in the house of Priscilla and Aquila for worship. Paul also speaks of Christians gathered together "as a Church" (*en ekklesia*) to celebrate the Lord's Supper (1 Cor. 11:18).

Christians living in one locale. Paul's letters generally begin with salutations which include the formula "to the Church in [name of city]" or words to that effect. The epistle to the Galatian Christians appears to break this formula, as Paul writes "to the Churches in Galatia" (Gal. 1:2). In point of fact, however, Paul remains consistent. This is because Galatia was not a city or town, but a widespread region encompassing several cities which Paul had visited (Iconium, Lystra, and Derbe, for example; Acts 13:13-14:20). In Paul's mind, the Christians living in one relatively small locale, such as a town or city, were not merely part of the Church. They were the Church, and as such experienced the fullness of Christ in their midst.

The Church universal. The word *ekklesia* is sometimes, though not always, capitalized in translation ("Church") when referring to all Christians living everywhere in the world. This concept of the universal company of believers is found in Acts 9:31 and Ephesians 1:22.

A common modern usage of "Church" is absent in the New Testament: the word *ekklesia* is never used for a building. It refers to the people of God. In addition, not all groups of God's people are Churches. Mission agencies and ministry organizations such as Campus Crusade for Christ, InterVarsity Christian Fellowship, and the Navigators are sometimes called "paraChurch" groups because they work alongside (Greek *para*) the Church. They are not Churches because they do not accept into their organizations anyone who professes faith in Christ. They are exclusive, accepting only those who sense God's call to a particular ministry and who meet their particular requirements of membership. The Church, on the other hand, is by definition inclusive of all who confess Jesus as Lord.

The Church as the Body of Christ

Union with Christ

The New Testament views the Church as more than a collection of individual Christians. The Church is the "body of Christ," an organic whole wherein its individual members are united in Jesus Christ through the Holy Spirit (1 Cor. 12:13; see chap. 11, p. 251). The Church as a whole is greater than the sum of its individual members.

Paul employs the body-of-Christ metaphor in three discussions of spiritual gifts and ministries in the Church: Romans 12:3-8, 1 Corinthians 12:12-28, and Ephesians 4:4-16.

- *Romans 12:3-8* emphasizes that the members of Christ's body are united not merely for fellowship, but also for ministry. Not everyone can serve others in every way; each should endeavor to do that ministry to which God has called him or her. "We have different gifts, according to the grace given us" (v. 6).

- *1 Corinthians 12:12-28* sets forth a strong argument against spiritual pride. The Corinthian Christians were divided into factions, each claiming to be more spiritual than the other (1 Cor. 1-2). Such factionalism manifested itself in the area of spiritual gifts, where some claimed superiority to others on the basis of which gifts they possessed. Paul's response to this sort of spiritual "one-upsmanship" is that even the so-called lesser parts of the human body are necessary in order for it to function properly. Even so, the body of Christ can function properly only if all of its members are working together in love. For this reason Paul follows this discussion of spiritual gifts with the famous "love chapter," 1 Corinthians 13.

• *Ephesians 4:4-16*, written several years after Paul's Roman and Corinthian correspondence, reflects a matured perspective on the relationship between Christ and His Church. Whereas in 1 Corinthians various parts of the head were included as the body of Christ, in Ephesians Christ Himself is the "Head" over the body, which is His Church. (v. 15; see also 5:23).

Recently, scholars have debated whether the word "head" in this context means "authority" (the traditional interpretation) or "source." Whatever conclusions one draws from a grammatical-historical exegesis of the text, from the standpoint of historic Christian belief Christ is "head" both as the supreme authority over the Church (as the brain governs the rest of the human body) and as its "source" (the Church not only gets her marching orders from Christ, but derives her very being from Christ).

The principal goal of the ministries of the body of Christ is to build up the body of Christ. While one of the gifts Paul mentions here is "evangelism," the New Testament contains no systematic treatise on the subject of how to preach the gospel to those outside the Church. Rather, the primary emphasis of spiritual gifts is the "building up of the body of Christ" (v. 12). For Paul the gift of evangelism, like all other gifts, must operate within the context of the Church.

This is the way Paul himself operated. It would have been unthinkable for him to do the work of evangelism without being accountable to a local body of believers (see Acts 13:1-3, 14:26-28; Rom. 15:23-29). A healthy local Church is essential to all ministries of outreach. The world will know that God sent Jesus not merely

DID JESUS INTEND TO CREATE THE CHURCH?

In Matthew 16:18 Jesus says "I will build my Church." Two chapters later He again envisions a community He calls "the Church" which will exercise spiritual discipline among the disciples of Jesus. These are the only two times the four Gospels record the word *Church* on the lips of Jesus.

Some modern critical scholars, on the other hand, argue that Jesus had no intention of founding a community which would continue to meet together and minister in His name after He was gone. They base their conclusions on either of two assumptions, which are as follows:

- Jesus believed that He would establish the Kingdom of God in the very near future, thereby bringing this present age to an end. This view was espoused in 1906 by Albert Schweitzer in his book *Vom Reimarus zu Wrede* (English translation *The Quest for the Historical Jesus*, 1910).

- Jesus did not view the end as imminent, but neither did He view His mission as setting up a new covenant community. His primary purpose was to call Judaism to repentance and reform. He therefore told His disciples to go "only to the lost sheep of Israel" (Matt. 10:6).

Only later, when a renegade Pharisee named Paul of Tarsus began telling Gentiles that they did not have to become Jews in order to receive salvation from God's Messiah, did the followers of Jesus eventually split from Judaism.

Schweitzer's theory assumes that Jesus failed in his true mission and died as a deluded apocalyptic fanatic. The problem with this view is similar to that we examined in chapter 10, regarding those who deny the resurrection of Jesus. Specifically, Schweitzer has to deal with a historical effect (the Christian Church which worships Jesus as Lord) which in his view has no commensurate cause in history. Schweitzer's denial of Jesus' intention to establish a Church leaves him with no explanation of how the Christian Church came to be.

The notion that Paul corrupted the simple message of Jesus and turned a Jewish prophet into the Lord of history fails to account for the fact that from its earliest recorded history the community of Jesus' disciples not only follow His teachings, but *worshiped Jesus as Lord*. In addition, the basic institutions of Christian worship (apostolic teaching and authority, baptism, Lord's Supper, giving to the needy, appointment of deacons and elders) did not evolve gradually as the Church moved beyond Jerusalem into Gentile territory. They were part of the early Christian worship in Jerusalem.

This is not to deny that certain aspects of Christian worship and Church governance evolved as time went on. To say that Jesus intended to found a community of disciples does not mean that He prescribed everything they were to do. Rather, He promised to send them the Holy Spirit, who would continue His minis-try on earth and guide the disciples into all truth (John 14-16; Acts 1:1).

The historic conviction of Christians regarding the origin of the Church is properly expressed in the words of the hymn *The Church's One Foundation*:

The Church's one foundation is Jesus Christ her Lord.

She is His new creation, by water and the Word.

From heaven He came and sought her to be His holy bride;

With His own blood He bought her, and for her life He died.

by hearing the Christian message, but by observing the love Christians have for one another (John 17:21-24).

Old Testament Images Applied to the Church

The metaphor of the Church as the body of Christ is part of the "mystery" of the gospel message, which Paul described as "Christ in you, the hope of glory" (Col. 1:27). The notion that the Spirit of Messiah would indwell His chosen people was a mystery in that it was not part of the Jewish messianic expectation. At the same time, the New Testament writers employ numerous Old Testament images which originally referred to Israel, but which the writers now apply to the Church. These include terms such as the bride, the flock of God, the vine, the royal priesthood, and the temple of God.

The Bride of Christ

In Isaiah 54:4-9 God speaks of Himself as Israel's husband who keeps faith with Israel despite her unfaithfulness. The book of Hosea repeats this imagery (2:19-20) and even dramatizes it, as the prophet Hosea is commanded by God to take a harlot for his wife (1:2). This demonstrates how God has espoused Himself to Israel not because of her faithfulness, but in spite of her spiritual adultery of departing from the Lord.

In 2 Corinthians 11:2 Paul tells the Corinthians, "I promised you to one husband, to Christ." Paul further develops this analogy between the marriage union and union with Christ in Ephesians 5:31-32, where the "great mystery" of marriage becomes a living parable of the relationship between Christ and His Church.

In the book of Revelation John speaks of the marriage of Christ and His Church not so much as a present reality, but as a future event. The "marriage supper of the Lamb" (19:7) coincides with the return of Christ, and the "bride" is the "new Jerusalem," symbolizing the final redemption of God's people (21:9). At the same time, John also appears to speak of the bride as a present reality (22:17). The New Testament imagery of the Church as the bride of Christ thus speaks of both a present and a future reality, reflecting the "already-not yet" tension of Christian eschatology (chapter 10, p. 221).

The Flock of God

The most widely-loved of the Psalms depicts Yahweh as the shepherd of His people. God leads His sheep to green pastures and quiet waters, and protects them from danger (Ps. 23:1-4). Isaiah 53:6 likewise views Israel as the flock of God, albeit an unfaithful flock. "We all, like sheep, have gone astray."

Jesus told His disciples, "Do not be afraid, little flock, for your Father has been pleased to give you the kingdom" (Luke 12:32). In this way He singled out His disciples from among the rest of Israel as those who would receive the blessings of the Kingdom of God. They, not Israel as a whole, comprise the flock of God. In John 10:16 Jesus identifies His followers as "my sheep," and later excludes the religious leaders of Jerusalem from His flock (10:26). The apostle Peter picks up Jesus' terminology at this point when he admonishes Church elders to "be shepherds of God's flock that is under your care" (1 Pet. 5:2).

The Vine

Jesus told His disciples, "I am the true vine" (John 15:1). He was probably alluding to imagery used by the prophet Isaiah (5:1-8), which spoke of Israel as God's vineyard. For Isaiah, however, Israel was an unfruitful vineyard which produced "wild grapes" which tasted sour, as opposed to sweet grapes. Jesus, on the other hand, is God's true and fruitful vine.

For Jesus, the word "vine" refers to the central stalk of the plant, from which the branches shoot forth and from which they obtain the life-giving nourishment that enables them to bear fruit. The disciples are the branches, but are fruitful only insofar as they remain attached to the vine. Apart from Jesus, they can do nothing and have no hope of salvation (15:5-6). This imagery, found only in John's Gospel, corresponds to Paul's metaphor of the Church as the body of Christ, with Christ being the Head of the Church.

A Royal Priesthood

In Exodus 19:6 God speaks to the nation of Israel from Mount Sinai as He establishes His covenant with them: "You will be for me a kingdom of priests and a holy nation." The function of a priest is to be an intermediary between God and humanity, bringing divine blessings from God to one's fellow human beings. Even so, God here calls Israel to be a nation which shows forth the mercy of God to surrounding nations. In this way Israel's call from God was to fulfill the last promise of God's covenant with Abraham: "All the peoples of the earth will be blessed through you" (Gen. 12:3).

The apostle Peter picks up this priestly imagery when he says of Christ's followers, "You are a chosen people, a royal priesthood, a holy nation, a people belonging to God, that you may declare the praises of Him who called you out of darkness and into His wonderful light" (1 Pet. 2:9). Most historians believe that Peter's audience was primarily Gentiles. If this be so, then Peter here sets forth Christianity's historic conviction that God's saving activity in history has shifted from ethnic Israel to the multi-ethnic Church. The fact that Peter also says "once you [Gentiles?] were not a people, but now you are the people of God" (2:10) is often cited as support for this view, which sees the Church as "the Israel of God" (Gal. 6:16).

The apostle Paul, while setting forth the same basic perspective, does not make an absolute dichotomy between Israel and the Church. Instead, he sees the Church as growing out of the promises and blessings God gave to Israel, in much the same manner as a branch grafted into a tree gets its life from that tree (Rom. 11:11-24). There is one people of God, though under the new covenant that people of God is not limited to a single nation or culture, but includes both Jews and Gentiles.

The Temple of God

In ancient Israel the tabernacle, and later the temple, symbolized the presence of God among His people. "The Lord is in His holy temple; let all the earth be silent before Him" (Hab. 2:20). Prior to the destruction of Jerusalem in 586 B.C. the nation of Judah assumed that so long as the temple stood, God would be in their midst. The prophet Jeremiah warned them to rely on God, not on the temple (Jer. 7:4, 14). During Jesus' ministry the Jews held the temple in the same sort of high esteem, and Jesus delivered the same message as Jeremiah did six hundred years earlier (Matt. 24:2). The temple which stood in Jesus' day was destroyed by Roman armies, along with the rest of Jerusalem, in A.D. 70.

Even prior to the destruction of the temple, Paul spoke of the Church as "God's temple," the dwelling place of God's Spirit (1 Cor. 3:16). In this way he echoed the language of Stephen, whom Paul himself helped put to death for uttering blasphemy against the temple (Acts 7:48-8:1). The true temple of God is not a building of stone, but is comprised of "living stones," the people of God (1 Pet. 2:5).

The Church as Organism, Not Merely Organization

As we review the New Testament images of the Church, we find that they have an important common denominator. They are *organic*. They refer to living things or relationships. This in turn underscores the nature of the Church as more than an organization. The Church has organizational features, to be sure; we shall examine these more closely in our next chapter. But the Church is a living organism in vital union with Jesus Christ. This is further underscored when Peter adds an organic element to the one non-organic metaphor we examined, the temple. The Church is a temple built of *living* stones.

The Church and the Kingdom of God

In chapter 10 we saw how the resurrection of Christ bore witness to the coming of the Kingdom of God. We further noted that the term "Kingdom of God" in the New Testament refers primarily to God's saving *rule* in the lives of His people. In this sense the Kingdom is already here. The manifestation of the Kingdom as a *realm* in which sin will be eradicated and righteousness will dwell, has not yet arrived.

The Church may therefore be seen as the locus of God's saving rule at the present time, but the Church is not the Kingdom of God. Rather, the Church is a creation of the Kingdom of God, a result of God's saving rule. The Church and the Kingdom of God are therefore related to one another, but are never equated with one another in the New Testament. Rather, the Church is called to proclaim the coming of the Kingdom.

The Mission of the Church

The Call to Discipleship

The Church's mission is one of proclaiming the good news of the Kingdom of God. But it is more than that. It is what Paul called a "ministry of reconciliation" wherein people are called to "be reconciled to God" on the basis of the fact that "God was in Christ, reconciling the world to Himself" (2 Cor. 5:18-20).

Proclaiming the gospel to all people is a necessary means towards the goal of divine-human reconciliation, according to Mark 16:15: "Go into all the world and preach the gospel to every creature." It is not the sole means, however. The New Testament text which may best summarize the mission of the Church is Matthew 28:18-20, where Jesus articulates specific instructions which go beyond the proclamation command found in Mark. The last will and testament of Jesus, known as "The Great Commission," says, "All authority in heaven and on earth has been given to me. Therefore go and make disciples of all nations, baptizing them in the name of the Father and of the Son and of the Holy Spirit, and teaching them to observe everything I have commanded you. And surely I am with you always, to the very end of the age."

At first glance there appear to be two commands in this text: "go" and "make disciples." There is, in fact, only one. The word "go" translates a Greek participle, not a finite verb, and should be rendered "as you are going." The one command is "make disciples of all nations." Whatever else Christians may be about, whether individually or corporately; whatever may be one's occupation; wherever one may live or travel ("as you go")—the bottom line is that Jesus calls His followers to "make disciples of all nations."

The word *nations* here bears examination. It translates the Greek *ethne* as better rendered "peoples" or, to use the language of modern missionaries, "people-groups." A people-group is a unit of people characterized by common language and culture. The word "nation," on the other hand, usually connotes a geopolitical entity such as a country. From a political standpoint, for example, the United States is one nation. But from the standpoint of Matthew 28:19, many "nations" exist within her borders, each characterized by different languages and/or customs. The mission of the Church is to reach people "from every nation, tribe, people, and language" (Rev. 7:9).

And to what end does the Church reach out to these people-groups? To "make disciples." A disciple is one who follows the teachings and way of life of another. Here Jesus commands His eleven disciples (Judas having already hung himself) not merely to preach to people, but to recruit them so that they also might follow Jesus.

The Meaning of Discipleship

Following this single command, Jesus uses two more participles to expound on what it means to make disciples: "baptizing them in the name of the Father and of the Son and of the Holy Spirit," and "teaching them to do all" that Jesus has commanded.

Baptism in the New Testament is both a witness to conversion and a rite of initiation into God's covenant community. It testifies to human realities such as repentance and faith, and to the divine gifts of forgiveness of sins (justification), and receiving the Holy Spirit (Acts 2:38; 10:44-48). It dramatizes the reality of believers being "baptized into one body," the body of Christ (1 Cor. 12:13). It is, outwardly speaking, the beginning of the Christian life. We shall examine the subject of baptism more thoroughly in our next chapter.

Teaching encompasses everything involved in living the Christian life following conversion. Disciples are to be taught "to observe all [Christ has] commanded." To enumerate and expound upon all of Christ's commands would require a much larger book than this one! We shall therefore attempt to summarize the way of Christian discipleship under a few general categories.

Perhaps the most all-encompassing way to summarize the commandments of Christ has been set forth by Martin Luther. In the previous chapter we read the following quote from his *Treatise on Christian Liberty*: "What commandment is there that such obedience [of faith] has not completely fulfilled?" For Luther, every commandment is God's way of saying: "Trust me. Take my word for it."

But just what does faith involve? What does it mean to trust someone? Christian faith encompasses several concepts, including *commitment*. Commitment, among other things, involves the three great virtues Paul mentions at the end of 1 Corinthians 13: faith, hope, and love. In addition, Christian commitment has a threefold focus, or objects towards which it is directed. These may be identified, in order of priority, as: commitment to Christ, commitment to the body of Christ, and commitment to Christ's work in the world. This threefold commitment is a useful (though by no means the only) perspective on what it means to be a disciple of Jesus Christ.

Commitment to Christ expresses itself supremely in worship. Jesus said that God seeks one thing: those who will worship God "in Spirit and in truth" (John 4:24). Commitment to Christ is not first and foremost duty, but praise. "Shout for joy to the Lord . . . Worship the Lord with gladness; come before Him with joyful songs" (Ps. 100:1-2). Worship, by definition, involves gladly proclaiming the value or worth ("worth-ship") of the one being praised. To worship God is to experience the joy of God's presence and God's promises, thereby glorifying Him. This is the chief end for which humanity was created (*Westminster Larger Catechism* Q. 1). For this reason worship is the foundation for everything else that Christ calls His Church to do.

Commitment to the body of Christ involves what Calvin called the "communion of saints" or Christian fellowship, and education of Church members. In this way Calvin agreed in principle with his Catholic adversaries that "you cannot have God for your Father unless you have the Church for your Mother" (*Institutes* 4:1:1-5; quotation from Cyprian, *On the Unity of the Catholic Church* 6).

Paul spoke of the "fellowship of the Holy Spirit" (2 Cor. 13:14). John wrote that "our fellowship is with the Father and with his Son, Jesus Christ" (1 John 1:4). God gives His people fellowship with Christ through the Spirit in order that they might have fellowship with one another (1 John 1:3). The word "fellowship" translates the Greek *koinonia*, which has to do with more than Sunday morning "fellowship" hours which consist of coffee and polite conversation. It is the sort of "meeting together" (Heb. 10:25) which includes moral and spiritual accountability, including mutual encouragement against unbelief (Heb. 3:12-13) and confessing our sins to one another and praying for one another (James 5:16). John Wesley sought to encourage such *koinonia* by what he called "class meetings," or small groups of a dozen or so Christians from within the larger congregation which met during the week between Sunday worship services.[1] Such small-group meetings are increasingly common throughout the world today, particularly in large Churches where it is impossible to know everyone well if one merely attends on Sunday morning.

Christian nurture which takes place through the fellowship or communion of God's people is based upon "the ministry of the Word" (Acts 6:4), or Christian education. In Ephesians 4:11-15 Paul emphasizes that it is "pastors and teachers" whom God has given to the Church in order that the body of Christ might be built up. Mature discipleship, both individually and corporately, is grounded in what the Reformers referred to as the twofold ministry of the Word and the Spirit. Without the Spirit, preaching and teaching the Word of God can lead to dead orthodoxy. Without the Word, Christian fellowship can degenerate into religious or psychological enthusiasm void of reference to objective truth.

Commitment to Christ's work in the world, like commitment to the body of Christ, is ultimately based upon worship. If one does not have a zeal for the all-encompassing worth and glory of God, there will be little motivation for the arduous task of making disciples of all peoples in all parts of the world.[2] Commitment to Christ's work in the world is also inextricably linked with commitment to the body of Christ. A healthy Church is, by definition, engaged in ministry outside of its own community. The diagram below illustrates the relationship between the threefold commitment inherent in the Great Commission.

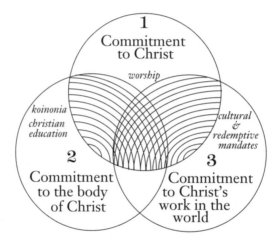

Modern missiologists sometimes speak of two components of Christ's work in the world. These are the *redemptive mandate* and the *cultural mandate*. The first is God's unique command to the Church; the second consists of commands which God requires of all people as bearers of God's image.

The redemptive mandate consists to the preaching of the gospel to all people in order "to open their eyes and turn them from darkness to light, and from the power of Satan to God, so that they may receive forgiveness of sins and a place among those who are sanctified by faith in [Christ]" (Acts 26:18). Evangelism and missions come under the heading of the redemptive mandate.

The cultural mandate includes ministries of mercy such as giving of one's time and money to alleviate the suffering of the poor, to combat injustice, and to maintain civic order. The giving of alms to the poor, for example, was a central element in the first-century Christian community (1 Cor. 16:2; see also Acts 2:45; 11:27-30). Faith demands deeds as well as words; faith without deeds is dead (James 2:17, 26).

Christ's work in the world is incomplete without both its redemptive and cultural components. At the same time, the redemptive mandate and the cultural mandate must be distinguished. To say, as some modern theologians do, that everything the Church does is evangelism or mission is to blur the necessary distinction between the two mandates (and in actual practice usually involves the neglect of evangelism). The necessity of distinguishing the two mandates can be seen when we consider the opposition of many Christians to abortion, for example. In obedience to what they see as a divine mandate, these Christians forge coalitions with Mormons, orthodox Jews, and even Muslims and an occasional agnostic. On the other hand, can anyone imagine a Mormon, a Jew, and a Muslim sharing the platform with Billy Graham at one of his evangelistic crusades? This illustrates the point made three paragraphs above. Two mandates are given to the Church, but the redemptive mandate is unique to the Church. It is not given to any other community, nor to civil government.

In the Power of the Spirit

The Great Commission is founded on the authority of Jesus Christ (Matt. 28:18). Jesus does not send His Church out alone with its marching orders, however. Instead, He promises that He will be with His people until the close of the age (28:20).

The presence of Jesus within His Church is none other than the presence of the Holy Spirit, as we saw in chapter 11. God does not merely command; He also empowers. This in turn means that evangelism is more than convincing people to join the Church. It is first and foremost calling them into a saving relationship with Jesus Christ (Rom 1:16-17; Acts 26:18). Evangelistic programs which emphasize Church membership without calling people to a specific commitment to the person of Christ betray an attitude which regards the Church as a club or organization rather than what it is: the body of Christ.

What the Church is, and what she is called to be, may also be expressed by speaking of those characteristics which have historically been labeled the marks of the Church. We conclude this chapter with a brief survey of these.

Marks of the Church

Within the post-apostolic tradition both the Apostles' Creed and the Nicene Creed confess "one, holy, catholic, apostolic Church." These four defining characteristics of the people of God have been termed the *marks of the Church*. We shall examine each in some detail.

The Unity of the Church

During the apostolic age the unity of the Church was a fundamental assumption of its existence. Paul spoke of "one body and one Spirit, one Lord, one faith, one baptism, one God and Father of us all" (Eph. 4:4-6; also Irenaeus, *Against Heresies* 1.10.2). The individual Churches found throughout the Roman Empire were all part of the one Church of Christ. The Church in Jerusalem functioned as a sort of first among equals, because it was founded and governed by the original apostles of Jesus (see Acts 15).

Following the destruction of Jerusalem in A.D. 70, other important centers of Christian activity arose, including Alexandria and Carthage in North Africa, Antioch in Syria, Constantinople in Asia Minor, and Rome. Of these, Rome and Constantinople ended up struggling for the right to be regarded as the spiritual center of Christianity. The final split between East (Constantinople) and West (Rome) occurred in A.D. 1054. The visible unity of the Church had been broken.

Five centuries later the Protestant Reformation resulted in further fragmentation of the visible unity of the Church. The Reformers not only disagreed with the Bishop of Rome, but also among themselves. The seemingly endless variety of Protestant denominations which exists today grew out of those disagreements.

It is therefore not surprising that the Reformers defined the unity of the Church in spiritual, rather than organizational, terms. Specifically, Protestantism stressed the distinction between what

Calvin called the visible Church and the invisible Church (*Institutes* 4.1.7).

The *visible Church* consists of all those who profess faith in Christ and participate in the life of the local congregation. It is a mixed company, consisting both of regenerate and unregenerate people. The *invisible Church*, on the other hand, consists of God's elect who are truly regenerate. The invisible Church is "one" in that all of God's elect are in union with Christ through the Spirit (*Westminster Confession* 25.1). In his own day Calvin compared the invisible Church to the seven thousand faithful in ancient Israel who had not joined the majority of their countrymen in the worship of Baal (1 Kings 19:18; *Institutes* 4.1.2).

At the same time, Calvin insisted that the *visible* Church, and not merely the invisible Church, was the "mother of believers" through whom Christians receive spiritual nurture. Indeed, "away from her bosom one cannot hope for any forgiveness of sins or any salvation" (*Institutes* 4.1.4). Thus Calvin affirmed the Roman Catholic tradition that "outside of the Church there is no salvation" (*extra ecclesiam nulla salus*; Cyprian, *Epistles* 73.21). The English Calvinist Puritans, on the other hand, stated that the visible Church is "the house and family of God through which men are *ordinarily* saved and union with which is essential to their *best* growth and service" (*Westminster Confession* 25.2; emphasis added). In this way English Calvinists allowed that in extraordinary cases some might be saved and nurtured apart from the visible Church.

The Holiness of the Church

The Church is "holy" in that it derives its life and sustenance from the Holy Spirit. In everyday experience, the visible Church should give outward evidence of the fruit of the Spirit in its midst through holy living (Gal. 5:22-23). The mark of holiness does not refer to the actual moral righteousness of its members, however, but to the source of whatever righteousness they exhibit: the Spirit of Christ. Even a congregation with as many problems as the first-century Church in Corinth is referred to by Paul as "those sanctified in Jesus Christ." At the same time, the apostle describes the Corinthians as people who are "called to be holy" (1 Cor. 1:2). The mark of holiness ("sanctified") is the basis for acts of holiness ("be holy").

In the fourth and fifth centuries a movement arose in North Africa which sought to define the visible Church as "holy" in a moral as well as a spiritual sense. This movement became known as *Donatism*, named after the North African bishop Donatus (d. c.355). The historical setting was the final great persecution of the Church by the Roman Empire, undertaken by the Emperor Diocletian in 303.

The issue which gave rise to Donatism was whether or not Christians who had denied their faith and cooperated with the Roman government during the persecution should be readmitted to the Church. In 312 one such Christian, Caecilian, was ordained bishop of Carthage. Many North African Christian leaders objected that Caecilian had betrayed the Church and should not be accepted back. These leaders elected a man named Majorinus in place of Caecilian. Majorinus in turn was succeeded in 313 by Donatus.

Throughout the fourth century and into the fifth, the Donatist movement gained enough adherents so that it became a rival to the Catholic Church. The Donatists stressed that the Church must be holy, consisting of righteous people. Those who committed apostasy under persecution, or in other ways failed to maintain personal holiness, were to be excluded. The Catholic Church, on the other hand, emphasized that the Church must be unified, and thus condemned the Donatists as schismatics (people who were dividing the Church), though not necessarily heretics (advocates of false doctrine).

In 395 Augustine was consecrated by the Catholic Church as Bishop of Hippo, North Africa. He immediately found himself in the middle of the Donatist controversy. Over the next several years he wrote a number of letters and tracts advocating the Catholic point of view that the visible unity of the Church took priority over its outward holiness. For Augustine, the Church was defined not as a pure company of saints, but a mixed company which included sinners. He stressed that the Church should not turn away those who fall away from the faith and then return, provided they exhibit sincere repentance. Augustine's view of the Church was somewhat analogous to Martin Luther's description of individual Christians over a thousand years later: simultaneously righteous and sinful (*simul justus et peccator*; chapter 12, p. 271).[3] The Church, though its members be sinful in themselves, are holy in Christ, the Holy One of God.

The Universality of the Church

The word "catholic" in the creeds means "universal." It does not refer specifically to the Roman Catholic Church. Those who confessed the "catholic" Church at fourth-century Nicea and Constantinople were, after all, primarily Greek-speaking bishops from the East. Rather, "catholic" refers to the entire visible Church throughout history in all parts of the world.

The earliest expression of the Church's catholicity is found in Paul's letter to the Churches of Galatia. "There is neither Jew nor Greek, slave nor free, male or female, for you all one in Christ Jesus" (Gal. 3:28). Membership in the Church is not restricted by one's sex, ethnicity (including culture), or social standing. "Whoever believes in [Christ]" is welcome (John 3:16).

A second aspect of catholicity finds expression in the Synoptic tradition. Matthew, Mark and Luke all speak of Jesus' mandate to preach the Gospel to all people everywhere (Matt. 28:18-20, Mark 16:15, Luke 24:47; Acts 1:8). The Church is universal in that it finds expression all over the world. This distinguishes the New Covenant community from the people of the Old Covenant and, as we saw in the previous section, provides the impetus for the worldwide Christian mission.

In the post-apostolic era catholicity began to focus on what is believed concerning Christ as well as who believes in Christ. This increasing interest in sound doctrine was a response to the rise of heretical movements within the Church. Around A.D. 200 Clement of Alexandria stated: "The one Church is violently split up by the heretics into many sects. . . .[On the other hand] we say that the ancient Catholic Church is the only Church" (*Miscellanies* 7.16.107).[4]

What, then, constitutes doctrinal "catholicity" or universality? Vincent of Lérins, writing in the fifth century, defined it as "that faith which has been believed everywhere, always, by all" (*Commonitory* 2.6).[5] The various christological formulas which we examined in chapter nine were attempts by the Church to gain universal consent to certain doctrines. For Vincent and the Catholic Church, universal consent did not always mean unanimous consent, but rather broad agreement which lay somewhere between a bare majority and unanimity.

The Apostolicity of the Church

In Ephesians 2:20 Paul speaks of the Church as being "built on the foundation of the apostles and prophets, with Christ Jesus himself as the chief cornerstore." Jesus Himself, according to John 17:20, stated that people would come to faith in Christ through the preaching of His apostles. The apostle Paul clearly believed that not only his oral preaching, but also his writings, constituted an authoritative message from God (1 Thess. 2:13, 2 Thess. 2:2).

The Church has therefore regarded both the Old Testament (prophets) and the New Testament (apostles) as the canon, or standard of measurement, by which subsequent doctrinal formulations shall be measured. Roman Catholics and Protestants take different views of the relationship between the biblical canon and post-canonical theological formulations. Whereas Protestants confine the word "apostolic" to the biblical canon, Catholics define "apostolic" tradition and authority as including dogma articulated by the teaching office of the Church.

Catholics view the ecclesiastical teaching office as originating with Peter, the first Bishop of Rome, who was given authority whereby whatever he "bound on earth" would be "bound in heaven" (Matt. 16:19). This apostolic authority was passed on by Peter when he ordained successors prior to his death. These successors in turn ordained others, and so on throughout the history of the Church, so that Catholics speak of the priesthood and the teaching office as being endowed with the authority of *apostolic succession*.

Protestants, on the other hand, believe apostolic authority is inextricably tied to the eyewitness testimony of the original apostles of Jesus and their closest associates (Luke would be an example of such a close associate, being Paul's traveling companion on many occasions). For this reason Peter's role as an apostolic *founder* of the Church cannot be passed by on ordination, although his role as a *leader* can and was passed on.[6] The New Testament applies words such as "foundation" and "pillar" to both Christ and the apostles, but never to bishops, who were merely leaders. In addition, Protestants find insufficient historical evidence to support Rome's claim that Peter was the first Bishop of Rome.

The Catholic Church has pointed to what it calls the "rule of faith" as evidence that Christians who lived after the death of the apostles viewed ecclesiastical tradition as a norm equal in authority to Scripture. The term "rule of faith" may be defined as the core of beliefs which found expression in early formulas such as the Apostles' Creed and the Nicene Creed. We have already seen that these early creeds were indeed considered authoritative standards of orthodoxy within the Church.

At the same time, however, the concept of a "rule of faith" did not include the notion of a continuous, ongoing, ever-widening tradition within the Church. Rather, the rule of faith was seen as a summary of core New Testament doctrines, a summary whose text was *fixed* rather than subject to expansion. The fact that this rule of faith was circulating in various forms from the second century onwards does not change the *principle* of a fixed, apostolic creed which was to be accepted as normative over against all later creeds. The "rule of faith" can therefore provide no precedent for regarding ongoing dogmatic formulas of the Church's teaching office as having apostolic authority.[7]

Protestant Marks of the Church

The Protestant Reformers saw themselves not as separatists, but as members of the one, holy, catholic, apostolic Church seeking to institute reform from within. When they spoke of "marks of the Church" in addition to the four we have examined, they were not seeking to overturn the historic Christian consensus but rather to expound on it by clarifying what ought to be happening within the life of the visible Church.

Primary among the Reformer's marks of the Church was the *preaching of the Word of God* (Calvin, *Institutes* 4.1.10). This was a direct challenge to the sacramental *ordo salutis* of Rome, which placed the eucharist as the central event of Catholic worship. It was also a challenge against the notion of apostolic succession. The Church is not founded upon Peter and his successors, argued Calvin, but upon the Word of God (*Institutes* 4.2.4), a Word which in his view had been both ignored and corrupted by the sixteenth-century Church of Rome.

The second Protestant mark of the Church was the *administration of the sacraments* (*Institutes* 4.1.10), which for the Reformers numbered two: baptism and the Lord's Supper. The Reformers' removal of five of the seven Catholic sacraments was yet another expression of their desire to dismantle the Catholic order of salvation. At the same time, neither Luther nor Calvin challenged the notion that baptism and the Lord's Supper should be called sacraments. As Protestantism grew and divided, certain groups did object to the term "sacraments," preferring the word "ordinances" to refer to baptism and the Lord's Supper. Today, Baptists comprise the single largest Protestant group which uses the language of ordinances rather than sacraments.

Protestants sometimes add a third mark, *Church discipline*, alongside baptism and the Lord's Supper (*Scots Confession* 18). Calvin wrote at length on the subject in the *Institutes* (4.12.1-13). Discipline includes private admonition (Matt. 18:15), public admonition (Gal. 2:14), and even excommunication ("Expel the wicked man from among you," 1 Cor. 5:13; see also Deut. 17:7; 19:19). The purpose of discipline is not to punish, but to preserve purity of faith and conduct within the Church and to motivate the transgressor to repentance and restoration to fellowship.

These three Protestant marks of the Church—preaching, sacraments, and discipline—speak not so much of what the Church is as they speak of what the Church does in matters of doctrine and conduct, or what some have called "Faith and Order." The following chapter goes into matters of Faith and Order in more detail.

Points To Ponder

1. What are the three meanings of "Church" (*ekklesia*) in the New Testament? Cite texts to support each.

2. How do spiritual gifts contribute to the health of the body of Christ?

3. What is the significance of each of the five Old Testament images of Israel which the New Testament applies to the Church? What do these images have in common?

4. What is the relationship between the Church and the Kingdom of God?

5. What is the mission of the Church, according to Matthew 28:19?

6. What threefold commitment is involved in Christian discipleship? Elaborate on each point.

7. How did John Wesley encourage believers to grow in their faith and Christian fellowship?

8. Identify and explain the twofold mandate involved in Christ's work in the world.

9. What are the four traditional marks of the Church? Discuss each.

10. What three "marks" did the Reformers add to the four traditional marks of the Church? Which of these three was central to the Protestant Reformation?

14

Faith and Order in the Church

Life in the Early Christian Community

In Acts 2:42 Luke tells us that the first Christians in Jerusalem "devoted themselves to the apostles' teaching and to the fellowship, to the breaking of bread and to prayer." These were the people who responded to Peter's command in Acts 2:38 to "repent and be baptized, every one of you, in the name of Jesus Christ for the forgiveness of sins." In this way Luke identifies the following practices as central to the earliest Christian worship and community life:

- Apostolic preaching (v. 38).
- Baptism (v. 38).
- Apostolic teaching (v. 42).
- Fellowship (v. 42).
- Common meals ("breaking of bread," v. 42).
- Prayer (v. 42).

The Christian congregation in Jerusalem was called into being even prior to Peter's first sermon. The coming of the Holy Spirit "like the blowing of a violent wind" on the day of Pentecost created the Church, which at first consisted only of the eleven apostles and their close associates (Acts 2:1-4). Within the first hour of its existence this new community called out of the world by God, this *ekklesia*, added three thousand new members who were baptized in response to Peter's call to repentance and faith in Jesus. The apostolic preaching and baptism were thus the foundational institutions of the early Church.

The continuing life of the early Church centered around worship. The earliest disciples, being Jewish, had not yet forsaken association with the temple in Jerusalem (Acts 2:46). Their main activities, however, are described by Luke as devotion to the teaching of the apostles and to the fellowship (*koinonia*) of believers. The Greek text of Acts 2:42 indicates that the phrase "to the breaking of bread and to prayer" does not describe two activities done in addition to *koinonia*, but defines the content of that *koinonia*. The fellowship of believers prayed with one another and shared a common meal, identified elsewhere as "the Lord's Supper" (1 Cor. 11:20; see vv. 17-34). As time went on situations arose within the life of the Church which necessitated elementary administrative organization (Acts 6:1) and the need for some sort of governing authority for the Church at large (Acts 15:1).

In this chapter we shall examine those practices which became central institutions in the life of the first-century Church. These include the preaching and teaching of the apostolic message, prayer, baptism, the Lord's Supper (also known as the Eucharist or Communion), and Church offices such as elder and deacon. We shall pay particular attention to how various Christian groups throughout history have interpreted the meaning of baptism and the Lord's Supper.

The Ministry of the Word

In Acts 6:4 Peter tells the Jerusalem disciples that he and the other apostles must devote themselves to "prayer and the ministry of the Word," and not be distracted with everyday administrative matters. We shall look at the subject of prayer in the following section. Here we consider "the ministry of the Word," the preaching and teaching of the Gospel message as handed down to the Church by Christ through His apostolic spokesmen.

In Romans 10:17 Paul says that "faith comes by hearing, and hearing by the word of Christ." The preaching and teaching of the apostolic witness of Christ was the foundation of the early Church.

The New Testament uses the Greek verbs *kerysso* and *didasko* when it speaks of preaching and teaching, respectively. These two activities both center on Christ, but have different functions within the overall ministry of the Word.

The word *kerysso* means "to proclaim." The New Testament writers use it of evangelistic preaching which calls people to believe in Christ for salvation (Acts 8:12; 14:21; 15:35; 1 Cor. 15:1, Gal. 1:8, to mention only a few such texts). Modern biblical scholars sometimes refer to the gospel message as the *kerygma*, or "proclamation" of salvation through Christ.

The apostolic *kerygma* or preaching is to be distinguished from teaching, which may be referred to as *didache* (from *didasko*, "to teach"). The English word "didactic" comes from this Greek expression. Whereas *kerygma* emphasizes the initial preaching of the good news of salvation through Christ, *didache* refers to systematic exposition of the words and deeds of Jesus and their implications for Christian discipleship. Preachers call sinners to faith in Christ; teachers build them up in their newly-found faith by explaining the meaning and significance of Christian doctrine (Eph. 4:11-12; 1 Tim. 4:11). This does not mean that the two activities are mutually exclusive. Paul calls on Timothy, a pastor and teacher, to "preach the Word" and "do the work of an evangelist" as a part of his pastoral ministry (2 Tim. 4:2, 5).

For several centuries following the apostolic era the Church continued to view the Word of God as central to Christian faith and practice. The New Testament canon was a product of the Church's focus on the apostolic preaching and teaching as the norm for both doctrine and conduct. Biblical exposition became a prominent feature in the preaching and teaching of men such as John Chrysostom and Augustine, due to the Church's conviction that Scripture was the divinely-inspired Word of God (2 Tim. 3:16; see chapter 2, part 3).

Between the sixth and fifteenth centuries the Eucharist gradually replaced the preaching of the Word as the most prominent aspect of Christian worship. By the time Luther was born in 1483 the Roman Catholic Church not only featured the Eucharist at the center of the Mass, but celebrated the Mass in Latin rather than in the language spoken by those worshiping. The Word of God had all but disappeared from Christian worship in the West.

The centrality of the ministry of the Word to Christian faith and worship was recovered by the Reformers. Luther and Calvin insisted that the preaching of the Word, the sermon, should be the principal activity of the Christian pastor during corporate worship. They viewed the Word of God preached, rather than the sacraments, as the principal means whereby God's grace comes to His people. It was for this reason that Luther translated the Bible from its original languages into German. During his ministry in Geneva Calvin preached several times a week and wrote commentaries on almost every book of the Bible. Heinrich Bullinger, who succeeded Ulrich Zwingli as the most prominent theologian of the Swiss Reformation, wrote in 1561 that "the preaching of the Word of God is the Word of God" (*Second Helvetic Confession* chap. 1). For this reason the Reformed branch of Protestantism has laid great stress on educating its preachers and teachers in the original languages of the Scriptures as well as in the discipline of theology.

The Word of God is sometimes referred to as one of God's "means of grace" whereby He builds up His Church (*Call to Unity*, 1927 Faith and Order Conference).[1] The other principal means of grace, according to the Protestant tradition, is prayer.

Prayer

The disciples of Jesus asked Him many questions. They only asked Him to teach them how to do one thing, however: "Lord, teach us to pray" (Luke 11:1). Prayer was central to Jesus' ministry. He prayed all night before choosing His disciples (Luke 6:12). He was at prayer when His disciples asked Him to teach them to pray. He prayed in the Garden of Gethsemane prior to His arrest and crucifixion (Mark 32-40 and parallels; John 17). He prayed while on the cross (Luke 23:34, 46).

Peter regarded prayer as of primary importance in the apostolic ministry (Acts 6:4). In the first five chapters of the book of Acts Luke records that the apostles prayed to God for wisdom and courage when they were in trouble with the religious authorities in Jerusalem.

Paul opened almost all of his letters with references to his praying on behalf of his readers. He also asked for their prayers at the close of several of his epistles (Rom. 15:31; Eph. 6:19; Col. 4:3). Paul directed his young protégé Timothy to "first of all" command that people pray for rulers in government (1 Tim. 2:1).

Prayer includes adoration or praise of God (see for example many of the Psalms), confession of sin (Matt. 6:12, 14-15; Luke 18:9-14; 1 John 1:9), thanksgiving (Phil. 1:3), and supplication, which includes both personal requests of God and intercession for others (Matt. 7:7; 2 Thess. 3:1). Sometimes this fourfold definition of prayer is represented by the acrostic ACTS: Adoration, Confession, Thanksgiving, Supplication. The singing of "psalms and hymns and spiritual songs" also comes under the heading of prayer (Eph. 5:19; *Institutes* 3.20.31-32). The chief end of prayer is the same as the chief end of humanity: the glorification of God (Matt. 6:9; John 14:13; *Westminster Shorter Catechism* Q. 1).

Calvin called prayer "the chief exercise of faith" in the Christian life, and devoted seventy pages to prayer in the final edition of his *Institutes* (3.20.1-52). Prayer is the chief exercise of faith because it is the one thing we are called to do which, from a human perspective, can accomplish nothing. The one who prays must depend entirely upon God to fulfill His promises.

Karl Barth spoke of prayer as "the most intimate form of Christian action" (*Church Dogmatics* 3/3, 264). God gives prayer not merely as a means to get things done, but first and foremost as the chief means of intimate fellowship with Christ.

Prayer must never be carried out in a vacuum, however. It must constantly be informed by the Word of God, even as the Word is energized by prayer. "Prayer and ministry of the Word" (Acts 6:4) are inextricably linked in the life of both the individual Christian and the worshiping community.

The designation "means of grace" has been used not only of the Word of God and prayer, but also of baptism and the Lord's Supper. On this point, however, there is a significant measure of disagreement among Christians in the various Protestant traditions. Why this is so will become apparent as we examine the institutions of baptism and the Lord's Supper.

Baptism

Baptism in the New Testament

Historical background. The word "baptism" comes from the Greek *baptizo*. The word generally meant to dip something in water, usually (though not always) totally immersing it. At times it referred to death by drowning, a usage which Paul may have in mind in Romans 6:2.

The religious meaning of baptism in antiquity had to do with purification. In the Septuagint translation of 2 Kings 5:14, for example, *baptizo* is used of Naaman the Syrian's sevenfold immersion in the Jordan River to purify him from leprosy. The Jews of Jesus' day practiced baptism as a rite of initiation for proselytes, that is, Gentile converts to Judaism. The waters of baptism demonstrated the purification of the proselyte from his former way of life outside the covenant community of Israel, and entrance into new life among the people of God. Jews, on the other hand, were already members of the covenant community. For this reasons Jews did not practice baptism among themselves as a rite of initiation. Ritual bathings for religious purification were part of Judaism, but these were done repeatedly, not once for all time.[2]

So when John the Baptist came and exhorted his fellow Jews to repent and be baptized, he was treating them like Gentiles. John was telling them that their Jewishness would give them no advantage over anyone else when the Kingdom of God came (Matt. 3:9). Peter made the same point in his Pentecost sermon when he urged his all-Jewish audience to "repent and be baptized in the name of the Lord Jesus" (Acts 2:38), though he may not have realized the full implications of baptism until later on, when he told his fellow Jews that "we believe that we [Jews] are saved by the grace of the Lord Jesus, just as they [Gentiles] are" (Acts. 15:11).

The meaning of Christian baptism. To be baptized in the name of Jesus means to be identified both with Christ Himself (Rom. 6:2-4) and with His Church, the body of Christ (1 Cor. 12:13). The book of Acts shows that the early Church linked baptism with repentance, faith in Jesus Christ, forgiveness of sins, and the gift of the Holy Spirit (2:38; 8:15-17; 10:44-47; 19:5-6). In Titus 3:5, and possibly John 3:5, baptism is associated with regeneration in conjunction with the work of the Holy Spirit. Peter states that Christians are saved through the waters of baptism like Noah and his family were brought through the waters of the flood (1 Pet. 3:20-21).

Since baptism places the recipient within the body of Christ, Gentiles who are baptized need not receive circumcision. They have already been "circumcised with a circumcision made without hands, having been buried with [Christ] in baptism" (Col. 2:11-12).

Baptism also testifies to the universality of Christ's saving grace (Gal. 3:28) in at least three ways:

- Even Jewish believers in Jesus must undergo baptism in order to gain entrance into the Church. Circumcision, the old covenant rite of initiation, is of no spiritual value whatsoever (Gal. 6:15).

- Baptism, unlike circumcision, is applied to all members of the new covenant community, not merely to its male half.

- Baptism contains no cultural stigma for those outside of Judaism, as did circumcision among some of the ancient Greeks and Romans, who regarded circumcision as a mutilation of the body.

Baptism also has an enormous practical advantage over circumcision as a rite of initiation: It does not hurt. The pain associated with circumcision, as well as its cultural stigma for many Gentiles, accounts for the mention of many "God-fearing Gentiles" in the pages of the New Testament (Acts 13:26). These God-fearers were Gentiles who believed in the God of Israel, but refused to become full Jewish proselytes due to the deterrent effect of circumcision. It is unlikely the Gentile mission could have gone forward with great success had the Council of Jerusalem (Acts 15) decided that Gentile Christians must become Jews in order to be saved.

Infant Baptism? The New Testament always speaks of baptism in connection with the conversion of adults to the Christian faith. There are, to be sure, a few references to entire households being baptized (Acts 16:15, 31-34; 1 Cor. 1:16, 16:15). Such household formulas need not include infants and small children, however. Adults, older children, and servants who have exercised faith in Jesus may be all that is in view. Even advocates of infant baptism concede that the New Testament gives no direct evidence that the first-century Church baptized infant children of Christian parents.

The first Christian witness to infant baptism does not appear until near the end of the second century A.D.

Baptism in the Post-Apostolic Church

Who receives baptism. Around the year 180 Irenaeus spoke of infants and children as being among those who are "born again to God" through baptism (*Against Heresies* 2.22.4; 3.17.1). This is the first explicit post-apostolic reference to infant baptism. The practice must therefore have been going on from the early to mid-second century onward.

It is even possible, though not demonstrable, that infants were being baptized before the end of the first century. For example, the New Testament lacks any trace of evidence that baptism was administered to *adult children* of parents who were already Christians and who brought up these children in the Christian faith.[3] The implication, say supporters of infant baptism, is that these adult children of believing parents had already been baptized as infants. In the end, however, it is an argument from silence, as is the lack of explicit New Testament statements that infants were baptized.

By the fourth and fifth centuries infant baptism was widespread, due in large part to the conversion of the Roman Emperor Constantine and the ensuing christianization of the Empire. The issue of infant baptism would not arise again in the Church for over a thousand years. The *meaning* of infant baptism, and of baptism in general, was quite another matter.

Interpretations of baptism. In the fourth and fifth centuries the meaning of baptism became a point of controversy due to division in the Church concerning the notion of original sin. The Western Church, as we saw in chapter 7, included the notion of original guilt within its definition of original sin, while the Eastern Church did not. Consequently, different interpretations emerged regarding the meaning of baptism in general and infant baptism in particular.

In the West, Augustine and Jerome saw baptism as the sacrament which removed the guilt which Adam had passed on to his progeny. This view developed into the Roman Catholic doctrine of baptismal regeneration already mentioned in chapter 12 in connection with the *ordo salutis*. Eastern theologians, on the other hand, were reluctant to attribute guilt to newborn infants, due to their notion of human free will (chapter 7, p. 150). Gregory of Nazianzus, for example, argued that infants should be baptized not to remove original guilt, but to become sanctified and dedicated to the Spirit from earliest infancy. He spoke of infants being initiated into the Christian faith by receiving the "seal" of baptism.[4] This sort of language was picked up by the Reformers in their debate with Rome a millennium later.

The post-apostolic Church fathers of both East and West defined the benefits of baptism in ways which echo the language of the New Testament. Baptism brings with it blessings such as the gift of the Holy Spirit, the new birth, renewal of the divine image, union with Christ and the triune Godhead, justification, adoption into the family of God, and spiritual illumination.[5]

All of these benefits were later connected with the Roman Catholic view of baptism. In addition, Catholicism gradually placed less emphasis on the faith of the recipient of baptism and more emphasis of the actual rite of baptism. The fact that infant baptism was now widespread was almost certainly one factor in this shift. This in turn contributed to the sacramental mentality mentioned above in chapter 12. According to this sacramentalism the blessings associated with baptism do not come merely by faith, but are imparted *ex opere operato* through the holy waters of the sacrament. The Catholic Counterreformation reaffirmed the notion of the sacramental *ex opere operato* in 1563 at the Council of Trent (*Canons on the Sacraments in General* canon 8).[6]

Protestant Views of Baptism

The necessity of faith. The various branches of the Protestant Reformation did not agree on all aspects of the doctrine of baptism. On one matter, however, they were in unanimous accord: Baptism will be of no ultimate benefit to its recipient if that person does not exercise faith in Christ. This view is a logical outgrowth of the Reformation's insistence on *sola fide*, justification by faith alone.

Luther's threefold view of baptism. In his 1521 essay "The Holy and Blessed Sacrament of Baptism"[7] Luther opposes the *ex opere operato* by insisting that faith is the third and "most necessary" part of the sacrament, without which the baptized person gains no benefit (par. 12). The first part consists of the "sign," the water of baptism, which for Luther means immersion (par. 1-2). The second part is

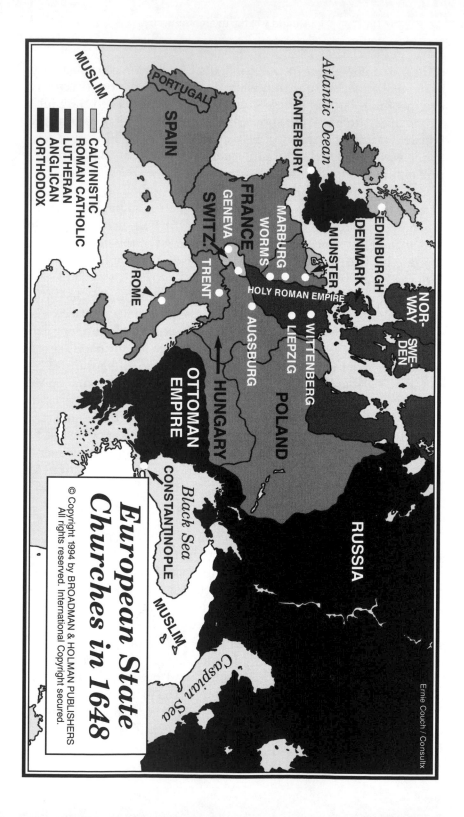

European State Churches in 1648

MUSLIM

CALVINISTIC
ROMAN CATHOLIC
LUTHERAN
ANGLICAN
ORTHODOX

PORTUGAL

SPAIN

ROME

SWITZ.

GENEVA

FRANCE

TRENT

WORMS

MARBURG

MUNSTER

DENMARK

EDINBURGH

Atlantic Ocean

CANTERBURY

NOR-WAY

SWE-DEN

HOLY ROMAN EMPIRE

AUGSBURG

LIEPZIG

WITTENBERG

POLAND

HUNGARY

OTTOMAN EMPIRE

CONSTANTINOPLE

Black Sea

MUSLIM

Caspian Sea

RUSSIA

Ernie Couch / Consultx

that which is signified. For Luther, the primary significance of baptism is dying to sin and rising again to new life. Christians are immersed in water and come forth again from the water, signifying that "sins are drowned in baptism, and in place of sin, righteousness comes forth" (par. 3). The faith which is the third and most necessary part of baptism is not faith in the sign itself, but in that which it signifies.

Luther's view of the relationship between faith and baptism would at first glance appear to exclude infant baptism. Yet Luther affirmed the practice, comparing infants to the paralytic whom Jesus healed after He had seen the faith of the sick man's friends (Luke 5:20): "Infants are aided by the faith of others, namely, those who bring them for baptism. For the Word of God is powerful enough, when uttered, to change even a godless heart, which is no less unresponsive and helpless than any infant" (*The Babylonian Captivity of the Christian Church*).[8]

Anabaptist objections to infant baptism. Three years after Luther wrote his treatise on baptism, Conrad Grebel, a follower of the Swiss Reformer Zwingli, challenged the practice of infant baptism. While he was in basic agreement with Luther on the meaning of baptism, he believed Luther's emphasis on faith in Christ ruled out infant baptism, since infants cannot exercise faith. Grebel also made Luther's distinction between the sign of baptism and what it signifies into an outright dichotomy. Outward baptism does not confirm or increase faith, as Luther taught. Only the inward experience of Spirit baptism, or new birth, does that.[9]

Menno Simons (1496-1561), founder of the Mennonite movement, went further than Grebel and denied that baptism was even a sign of God's grace. In his *Foundation of Christian Doctrine* Simons argued that baptism is a sign of what takes place in the believer. It is a sign of human faith and obedience, not of forgiveness or new birth. Baptism is an expression of our response to God's grace, not a sign of that grace, and must therefore be administered only after one believes in Christ.[10]

The opponents of infant baptism became known as Anabaptists (from the Greek *ana baptizo*, "to baptize again"). This is because they baptized adults who had already been baptized as infants (which included everyone in sixteenth-century Catholic Europe).

Their rejection of infant baptism set a precedent followed by the English Baptists in the seventeenth century. It is not certain there is any direct historical connection between the sixteenth-century Anabaptists and the English Baptists, who were part of the Puritan movement which sought reforms in the Church of England (Anglican). For example, the Baptist requirement of total immersion was not set forth until the 1640s in England.

Baptism and covenant in Reformed theology. In 1525 Zwingli wrote a response to the Anabaptist movement entitled *On Baptism.*[11] In it he emphasized the connection between baptism and circumcision, noting that both are signs of the covenant between God and His people. Baptism, the sign of the new covenant, replaces circumcision for Christians. Zwingli did not deny a connection between baptism and faith, but his focus lay with baptism as the sign of the new covenant. He also affirmed the practice of infant baptism. For Zwingli, faith must accompany baptism in order for the rite to be efficacious, but faith need not precede baptism. It may follow in due course as the child grows within the fellowship of the covenant community.

Calvin added little that was new to Luther's and Zwingli's insights. His contribution was to set forth the Protestant Reformation's most complete systematic presentation of baptism. His principal argument for infant baptism was that infants were circumcised under the old covenant, and that baptism differs from circumcision only in its outward form as sign of the covenant. Circumcision pointed ahead to the promise of Christ; baptism points backwards to the fulfillment of that promise (*Institutes* 4.16.3-6).

John Wesley followed the Reformers in regarding baptism as a sacrament. He advocated infant baptism as the means by which original sin is washed away and the one baptized is admitted into Christ's Church. He also taught that a "principle of grace is infused" with baptism. Such grace is not saving grace, however, but rather a form of prevenient grace which may be taken away if the one baptized perseveres in wickedness.[12] Most of Wesley's spiritual descendants in the Holiness tradition limit baptism to believing adults, however. For this reason they avoid the term "sacrament" when referring to baptism. They instead join with the Baptist tradition in calling baptism an "ordinance," since it was ordained by

Four Views Of Baptism

View	Summary of Main Points and Scripture References
Roman Catholic	Baptism is a sacrament which is efficacious *ex opere operato*, by virtue of the rite itself. It is the means of grace which brings regeneration, washing away the taint of original sin (Titus 3:5). Baptism is the first step of the way of salvation (Acts 2:28). Infants as well as adults must receive baptism in order to be saved.
Lutheran	The sacrament of baptism consists of three parts: the sign (water), the thing signified (death to sin and new life in Christ; Rom. 6:3-4), and faith in the thing signified. Faith is normally exercised prior to baptism, but may be exercised afterward in the case of infants. The faith of the parents who bring infants for baptism likewise aids those infants (Luke 5:20). Without faith, baptism is not efficacious.
Reformed	Baptism is the sign of the new covenant, replacing the old covenant rite of circumcision (Col. 2:11-12) as it points back to Christ's having fulfilled the promises of the old covenant. Baptism may be called a sacrament in that it incorporates the one baptized into Christ's new covenant community, the Church (1 Cor. 12:13). John Wesley viewed baptism as the means whereby God's prevenient grace comes to the recipient. Baptism must be accompanied by faith (whether before or after the rite is administered) in order to be efficacious.
Baptist	Baptism is an ordinance, not a sacrament. It is the immersion of a believer in water in the name of the Father, the Son, and the Holy Spirit. Baptism symbolizes death to sin and resurrection to newness of life (Rom. 6:3-4). It is also a testimony to the faith of the one baptized (Acts 8:12). One must be baptized before becoming a member of a local Church.

Christ (Matt. 28:19; see the 1859 Baptist *Abstract of Principles*, sections 15 and 16).[13]

The Ongoing Debate over Baptism

Protestant disagreements on the subject of baptism have been sharply and at times violently contested since the outset of the Reformation. Some of the early Anabaptists were martyred for their beliefs. Over the centuries, Protestants have gradually agreed to disagree on whether or not infants should be baptized.

What is apparent from our brief survey here is that baptism is defined differently by the two Protestant factions. Those who support only believers' baptism define baptism as a sign of one's faith in Christ. Those who support infant baptism define baptism as a sign of one's being incorporated by God into His covenant community. Each group can quote Bible verses to back up its interpretation of the meaning of baptism, since both concepts are present in the New Testament. All too often people who debate whether or not infants should be baptized use the word *baptism* in these different senses, thereby resembling the proverbial pair of ships which sail past one another in the night.

The Protestant controversy over baptism is part of the larger debate as to whether baptism and the Lord's Supper are sacraments and thus means of grace, or should instead be referred to as ordinances, which are merely symbolic. We shall now examine the second element of that debate, the institution of the Lord's Supper.

The Lord's Supper

The Twofold Meaning of the Supper in Early Christianity

In Acts 2:42-46 we read that the first Christians in Jerusalem shared common meals in their homes amid an atmosphere of joyful fellowship. When we turn to 1 Corinthians 11:20-26, however, a different ambiance emerges. Paul's attitude is one of solemnity as he focuses on the Passover meal Jesus shared with His disciples the night before His death on the cross.

Each of these texts refers to the early Church's custom of meeting together on a regular basis to share a common evening meal separate from morning worship. Paul refers to this meal as the

"Lord's Supper" (1 Cor. 11:20). In both Acts 2 and 1 Corinthians 11 a full meal appears to be in view, as opposed to merely bread and wine. The disciples of Jesus met to give thanks to God and to celebrate their fellowship with the risen Christ. For this reason this common meal came to be designated as Eucharist (Greek *eucharisto*, "give thanks") and Communion (Latin *communio*, "fellowship").

Why, then, does Paul interject a somber reference to the crucified Christ into this celebration of thanksgiving to the risen Lord? It appears that the reason lies in excessive exuberance on the part of wealthy Church members at Corinth. Paul notes that these wealthy Christians, who could afford to bring food for the entire congregation, would arrive early and end up eating and drinking everything before the poorer Christians (who had to spend the entire day working) arrived on the scene. The death of Christ was a reminder to these rich Christians of the sacrifice Jesus had undergone for them. Could not they in turn make the small sacrifice of waiting for their brothers and sisters (1 Cor. 11:21-22, 33-34)?[14]

Paul therefore wrote 1 Corinthians 11:23-26, familiar to Christians worldwide as the eucharistic "words of institution," in order to balance the exuberance of the Corinthian Christians with a reminder of the death of Jesus. The sacred meal the Corinthians were eating, which Paul called the "Lord's Supper" in verse 20, was a celebration of the presence of the risen Christ in the midst of His Church. It sprang not from the final meal Jesus ate with the apostles before He died, but from the disciples' recollections of meals they ate together with Jesus *after* He had risen from the dead. Paul's admonitions in 1 Corinthians 11 presupposes this joyful "Lord's Supper," even as he interjects the solemn note of Jesus's last supper *prior to* His death (vv.23-26; see also 1 Cor. 10:15-17).

This twofold tradition of "Lord's Supper" (joyful meal with the risen Christ) and "last supper" (bread and wine signifying the death of Christ) is found in postapostolic liturgies of the late first and early second centuries. Furthermore, these two liturgical traditions do not have a common source.[15] This is further evidence that the earliest meals were indeed "eucharist" and "communion." They were the giving of thanks for fellowship with the risen Christ.[16]

The Two Traditions Combine

The eucharistic celebration of the early Church underwent a crucial change in the second century. It became part of the morning order of worship which included the preaching of the Word. The first witness to this combining of preaching and the Lord's Supper (literally, "eucharisted things") is found in Justin Martyr around the year 150 (*First Apology* 67).[17] As a general rule the preaching portion of the service was open to non-Christians, who were then asked to leave before Church members celebrated the Eucharist.

Another change was the reduction of the Eucharist from a full meal to merely the partaking of the bread and wine. The emphasis was not so much on the death of Christ, however, as it had been with Paul. Rather, the bread and wine were viewed as spiritual food and drink, the body and blood of Christ, which imparted *life* to the faithful. Justin Martyr, for example, described the meal as follows:

This food is called Eucharist [thanksgiving] with us, and only those are allowed to partake who believe in the truth of our teaching and have received the washing for the remission of sins and for regeneration [baptism]. . . . . We do not receive these gifts as ordinary food or ordinary drink. But as Jesus Christ our Saviour was made flesh through the word of God, and took flesh and blood for our salvation; in the same way the food over which thanksgiving has been offered through the word of prayer . . . is, we are taught, the flesh and blood of Jesus who was made flesh (*First Apology* 66).[18]

What has happened here is an intermingling of the two traditions mentioned above. The earliest eucharistic tradition celebrated the congregation's eating together with the Spirit of the risen Christ. As time went by, however, the Pauline tradition centering on the body and blood of Christ became part of the Eucharist. This was probably because only the "last supper" tradition was preserved in the New Testament canon, while the "Lord's Supper" tradition was not. Justin's remarks witness to this intermingling of two traditions, wherein the earlier eucharistic notion of eating *with* Christ now became one of *eating Christ*.

The New Testament itself contains passages open to this sort of sacramental interpretation. Paul spoke of the bread and wine as a "participation" (*koinonia*) in the body and blood of Christ (1 Cor. 10:16). According to John 6:53-58 Jesus told His disciples that unless they eat His flesh and drink His blood, they will not have eternal life. At the same time, neither Justin Martyr nor his contemporaries taught that the bread and wine were literally the body and blood of Christ. They believed that Christ was in some sense present in the Eucharist, but they also distinguished between the signs (bread and wine) and the reality signified by the signs (communion with Christ). It was not until the fourth century that the bread and wine first became identified with the body and blood of Christ.

The Roman Catholic Doctrine of Transubstantiation

Ambrose, Bishop of Milan from 374 until his death in 397, was apparently the first to identify the bread and wine with the actual body and blood of the Lord. "As often as we receive the sacramental elements, which by the mysterious efficacy of holy prayer are transformed (*transfigurantur*) into the Flesh and the Blood we do show the Lord's death" (*On the Faith* 4.10). His contemporary, Augustine, whom Ambrose baptized into the Christian faith, took a less literal view, insisting that "the sacrament is one thing; the virtue of the sacrament, another" (*On John's Gospel* 26.11).[19] In this way Augustine distinguished between the signs and that which they signified.

The Western Church eventually followed Ambrose's lead, however. In 1215 the Fourth Lateran Council stated:

> In this Church the priest and sacrifice is the same Jesus Christ Himself, whose body and blood are truly contained in the sacrament of the altar under the figures of bread and wine, the bread having been transubstantiated into His body and the wine into His blood by divine power, so that, to accomplish the mystery of our union, we may receive of Him what He has received of us (Canon 1).[20]

The term *transubstantiation* presupposes the distinction made in Greek philosophy between the "substance" of something and its "accidents." The substance is what a thing truly is; the accidents are properties not necessary to the true nature of that thing. A wooden chair, for example, has wood as its substance, and the properties of a chair as its accidents. Thomas Aquinas defined transubstantiation as meaning that the elements consecrated by the priest maintain their accidental properties of bread and wine (their outward appearance does not change), but undergo a change of substance into the body and blood of Christ (*Summa Theologiae* 3. 75. 2-5). In this way the sign and the thing signified become one.

The Eucharist was also defined as a "sacrifice" by the Fourth Lateran Council. The New Testament says that "Christ, our Passover lamb, has been sacrificed" (1 Cor. 5:7), and makes a connection between the Lord's Supper and the concept of sacrifice (1 Cor. 10:18). The fact that transubstantiation identified sign and thing signified implied that Christ not only "has been sacrificed," but continues to be sacrificed every time the Eucharist is celebrated. It was this notion of the Eucharist as a repetition of Christ's sacrificial death, along with the doctrine of transubstantiation, which led the Protestant Reformers to oppose the Catholic doctrine of the Lord's Supper.

Protestant Alternatives to Transubstantiation

Martin Luther and Consubstantiation. In his *Treatise on the New Testament* (1520) Luther rejected transubstantiation, and opposed the notion of the Eucharist as sacrifice on the grounds that it violated the New Testament's clear teaching that Christ's sacrifice was accomplished once and for all on the cross (Heb. 10:12-14) and thus cannot be repeated. As he did with baptism, Luther saw faith as essential for the efficacy of the Eucharist, thereby rendering inoperative the *ex opere operato*.

Luther nonetheless continued to regard the Eucharist as a sacrament. His view, known as *consubstantiation*, taught that while the consecrated bread and wine undergo no change of substance, the Eucharist is nevertheless "the true body and blood of our Lord Jesus Christ, under the bread and wine, given to us Christians to eat and to drink." The presence of Christ is literal, not merely spiritual. This presence of Christ is not brought to the Christian in the bread and wine, however, but by the Word of God which promises that Christ is given "for you" and "for the forgiveness of sins." Belief in that promise brings Christ, the forgiveness of sins, life and salvation (*Luther's Small Catechism*, "The Sacrament of the Altar").[21]

One other item deserves mention here. In Luther's day the Catholic priest often celebrated Eucharist during the Mass without congregational participation. In other words, Christ was "sacrificed," but there was no communion (Church members were required to take communion at least once a year; *Fourth Lateran Council* Canon 21).[22] Luther took strong exception to this practice, arguing that the priest could not partake of the Eucharist as communion on behalf of individual Church members. In *The Babylonian Captivity of the Christian Church* he asked rhetorically: "Who can receive or apply, in behalf of another, the promise of God, which demands the personal faith of each one individually?"[23] (It is interesting to note in passing that Luther did not apply this same logic to infant baptism.)

Zwingli's memorial view of the Supper. Unlike Luther, Zwingli rejected not only transubstantiation but also a literal interpretation of the words "this is my body" and "this is my blood." His treatise *On the Lord's Supper* (1526) argued that these New Testament statements must be interpreted spiritually rather than literally. For Zwingli, the Lord's Supper represents what Christ did for us. It is a memorial, not an actual imparting of the body and blood of Christ, either literally or spiritually.

Zwingli nevertheless viewed the Lord's Supper as a sacrament and thus a means of grace. The bread and wine set Christ before our eyes and on our tongue, as it were, so we can see and taste as well as hear the Gospel. Like Luther, Zwingli viewed the Supper as being of no value to those without faith. To eat spiritually is to trust "with heart and soul upon the mercy and goodness of God through Christ" (*Exposition of the Faith*).[24]

This memorial view of the Lord's Supper was adopted by the Anabaptists of Zwingli's day, and later by Baptists in England and North America. Unlike Zwingli, however, Baptists refer to the Supper as an ordinance rather than a sacrament. The bread and wine "commemorate together the dying love of Christ" (*New Hampshire Confession* 10; see also *Abstract of Principles* 16).[25]

Calvin and the Reformed view of the Supper. Zwingli's memorial view of the Lord's Supper did not satisfy Luther. Neither did it prevail in the Reformed Churches of Europe, including Zwingli's native Switzerland. Instead, John Calvin's doctrine of the spiritual presence of Christ in the celebration of the Eucharist became the doctrinal stance of Reformed theology (*Westminster Confession* 29), as well as that of the Church of England (*Thirty-Nine Articles of Religion* 28) and Methodism (*Twenty-Five Articles of Religion* 18).

Calvin's doctrine of the Lord's Supper was an attempt to mediate between the Lutheran and Zwinglian views. In so doing Calvin ended up satisfying neither. He agreed with Zwingli that the words "this is my body" should not be interpreted literally, as Luther had done. At the same time, Calvin viewed the Supper as more than a memorial. It is given "to seal and confirm" Christ's promise that His flesh and blood are food and drink to eternal life. Through the sacred Supper we become partakers of Christ's benefits by faith (*Institutes* 4.17.4-5).

Calvin rejected Luther's doctrine of consubstantiation while affirming, over against Zwingli, that Christ's body is truly present in the Lord's Supper through the power of the Spirit. He cited Paul's reference to the Supper as "participation [*koinonia*] in the body of Christ" (1 Cor. 10:16) as evidence of this (*Institutes* 4.17.10, 19). This is only the case for those who partake of the Supper by faith, however.

Like Luther before him, Calvin rejected the practice of offering the Eucharist as a sacrifice without congregational participation in communion. He argued that individuals should take communion "frequently," though he did not specify how often. He also condemned the Catholic practice of "communion of one kind," wherein the cup was withheld from the laity so that they partook only of the bread (*Institutes* 4.17.43-50). This latter practice was connected with the doctrine of transubstantiation, and probably arose from the fear that the laity might spill the actual blood of Christ while passing the cup.

We noted above that Calvin's view of the Lord's Supper attempted to offer a mediating position over against the Lutheran and Zwinglian views. This was typical of Calvin, who often tried to mediate between opposing points of view (his doctrine of predestination is an exception to this general rule). A good example of Calvin's taking a middle position between extremes is his view of Church government. This is the subject which we shall examine next.

Four Views Of The Lord's Supper

View	Summary of Main Points and Scripture References
Roman Catholic	The Lord's Supper (Eucharist) is a sacrament wherein the consecrated bread and wine are changed in substance (*transubstantiation*) into the literal body and blood of Christ. Baptized persons who receive the Eucharist receive spiritual food for the soul (John 6:55). Christ is sacrificed in the Eucharist to atone for the sins of the recipient (1 Cor. 10:18). Like baptism, the Eucharist is efficacious *ex opere operato*.
Lutheran	The bread and wine do not become the body and blood of Christ, but Christ's body is literally present in, with, and under the elements (*consubstantiation*). The sacrament brings Christ to us not in the elements, but by the Word of God which promises that Christ's body is "for you" (1 Cor. 11:24) and "for the forgiveness of sins" (Matt. 26:28). Faith in these promises is necessary for the sacrament to be efficacious.
Reformed	Christ is spiritually present in the celebration of the Lord's Supper. It is a memorial done "in remembrance" of Christ's sacrificial death (1 Cor. 11:24-25), but is more than a mere memorial. The Lord's Supper confirms the faith of the one partaking of it, and is a "participation in the body of Christ" (1 Cor. 10:16). This is only true for those partaking in faith, however.
Baptist	The Lord's Supper is an ordinance, a symbolic act of obedience whereby members of the Church, through partaking of the elements, memorialize the death of Christ and anticipate His second coming (1 Cor. 11:26). Christ is not present in the elements of the Lord's Supper either literally or spiritually. The Supper is thus not a sacrament or a means of grace.

Church Organization

The New Testament Pattern

The first Christians in Jerusalem learned quickly that some form of organization would be necessary for them to operate effectively as a community. In Acts 6 we read of a dispute between Hebrew-speaking and Greek-speaking Christians regarding charitable ministry to widows in the Church. The apostles realized that they could not oversee every detail of congregational administration. For this reason they instructed the fledgling Church to appoint deacons to take charge of the ministry of food distribution to the poor, while the apostles continued to minister through prayer and preaching.

The office of *deacon* is one of only two ongoing offices mentioned in the New Testament. The other office is that of *elder*. The apostolic office was not ongoing, but ceased following the death of the last apostle.

Elders (Greek *presbuteroi*) were placed in charge of local congregations (Acts 20:17). The apostle Paul appointed elders in the Churches he planted. Their primary duties were teaching and spiritual oversight. For this reason Paul also refers to them as "overseers" or "bishops" (*episkopoi*; 1 Tim. 3:1) or "pastors and teachers" (Eph. 4:11), who were called to be shepherds of the Church (Acts 20:28; 1 Pet. 5:2; the word "pastor" means shepherd).

Deacons (Greek *diakonoi*) were in charge of ministries which dealt with temporal needs of the Church, such as described in Acts 6. It appears that deacons were accountable to elders (1 Tim. 3:8-11), who in turn were accountable to the apostles.

The apostles of the Church in Jerusalem had a *de facto* authority over doctrinal matters until the destruction of that city in A.D. 70. After that the Christian Church had no central authority for several centuries. Instead, a system developed where all the congregations in a single locale were under the authority of a bishop.

In addition, the office of priest was a post-apostolic development not found in the New Testament. The apostolic writers spoke of the Church as a collective priest (1 Peter 2:9; see chapter 13, p. 288). Later on pastors would sometimes be referred to as priests (e.g. Tertullian, *On Baptism* 17), though the New Testament idea of the corporate priesthood of believers was also set forth by post-apostolic writers such as Irenaeus (*Against Heresies* 4.7.3), Justin Martyr (*Trypho* 66), and even Tertullian himself, who stated that laypersons as well as priests may be permitted to administer the sacraments (*Exhortation on Chastity* 7).

The Hierarchy of Roman Catholicism

The governing structure of the Latin Church was modeled after the political hierarchy of imperial Rome. The Bishop of Rome thus eventually became the ecclesiastical counterpart to the Roman Emperor. The Church of Rome claimed primacy over the entire Christian Church as early as the fourth century. It was not made official until 445, however, when Emperor Valentinian III decreed that Leo I, Bishop of Rome, had final authority over the Church. This law was binding only in the West, however. The Eastern Church continued to operate with a decentralized government of several archbishops, as it does to this day. The Western Church eventually came under the jurisdiction of the Bishop of Rome, known as the Supreme Pontiff or the Pope.

The Protestant Reformers were united in their rejection of papal authority. Among themselves, however, they could not reach a consensus as to what constituted the proper form of Church government. Protestant denominations today therefore fall under three main categories of Church polity: episcopalian, congregational, and presbyterian.

Episcopalianism

This term comes from the Greek *episkopos*, "one who oversees," a New Testament term sometimes translated "bishop." Episcopalian polity consists of three levels of leadership: bishops (regional leaders), priests (mainly local clergy), and deacons (who are lay people). All three of these are ordained offices in the Church. The priests are not chosen by members of the congregation they serve, but appointed by their respective bishops. Denominational issues are decided by the bishops, who meet from time to time (usually every other year). This form of government is found in Anglican, Episcopalian, Lutheran, and Methodist Churches (though Methodists generally avoid the term "priest" for local clergy). Some Pentecostal Churches use episcopal government, though others are more nearly congregational.

This threefold division of ministry can be traced back to the early post-apostolic period. At the same time, its division between bishops and local clergy does not square with New Testament terminology, which views bishops and local Church leaders (elders) as the same office.

Congregationalism

Under the congregational form of government, the local congregation is the basic governing unit. No denominational official or group of ministers may exercise political authority over the local Church. Who may or may not be ordained into local Church offices is entirely up to the individual congregations. This form of government is practiced, sometimes in modified form, by Congregationalists (including the United Church of Christ), Baptists, Restorationists (Christian Churches and the Church of Christ), some Pentecostal Churches, and various independent Churches.

According to congregational government, local Churches elect their own officers. The pastor is called to serve the local Church by the entire congregation, which also has the sole authority to dismiss the pastor. Baptists and many other congregational Churches consider the words *bishop*, *elder*, and *pastor* as synonyms that refer to the same office.

Presbyterianism

This form of government was devised by Calvin and the Scottish Reformer John Knox, and is found in modern-day Reformed and Presbyterian denominations. It may be seen as a "half-way house" between episcopalian and congregational polities. It gets its name from the Greek word which means elder. The governing board of the local Church, which is comprised of elders elected by the congregation, is called the session. The session has authority similar to that of the governing boards of congregational Churches.

A second governing body or judicatory in the presbyterian system is the presbytery. It is composed of pastors and local Church elders. Pastors are always members of the presbytery, never of the local congregations they serve. Local Church elders are elected to presbytery membership for specified terms. In theory, the presbytery is designed to function as a sort of corporate bishop. As such, the presbytery ratifies each local Church's call of its pastor, as well as intervening when necessary to mediate and even settle disputes within and among congregations.

The highest judicatory of presbyterianism is the general assembly, which meets periodically (usually once a year) to deal with matters of denominational faith and order. A fourth judicatory, the synod (consisting of several presbyteries), is found in some Presbyterian denominations. The presbyterian form of government, with its structure of political checks and balances, provided a model for the framers of the Constitution of the United States.

The Protestant Quest for Unity

The differences among Protestants in matters of faith and order in the Church are significant. In recent times several major Protestant denominations have sought organizational unity. These efforts, labeled the Consultation on Church Union (COCU), have thus far failed to produce a unified Church which includes such diverse elements as Episcopalians, Methodists, Presbyterians and Congregationalists. The history of Protestantism indicates that should such success eventually be forthcoming, dissidents within each denomination will simply split off and begin new ones.

More promising efforts at Christian unity have centered upon cooperative efforts to accomplish the evangelistic mission of the Church rather than on efforts to smooth over doctrinal and organizational distinctives. The Billy Graham Evangelistic Association has been particularly effective in this regard. Its ministries have united Christians not only in North America but also worldwide, as demonstrated by the 1974 Lausanne Conference on Evangelism and the international missions conferences held every three years in Urbana, Illinois.

A visible organizational unity of Christ's worldwide Church, on the other hand, appears to be something which awaits the return of Christ at the end of this present age. This "blessed hope" of Christ's second coming is the central theme of Christian eschatology, which is the subject of our final chapter.

Points To Ponder

1. What were the basic activities of the early Church in Jerusalem?

2. What is the difference between "preaching" (*kerygma*) and "teaching" (*didache*) in the New Testament?

3. Why did Luther and Calvin feel the need to place the sermon at the center of Protestant worship services?

4. Why did Calvin refer to prayer as "the chief exercise of faith"?

5. What are the various meanings of baptism in the New Testament?

6. In what three ways does baptism testify to the universality of Christ's saving grace?

7. What were the similarities and differences between the Eastern and Western interpretations of infant baptism from the fifth century onward?

8. How do the Catholic, Lutheran, Anabaptist, and Reformed positions on baptism differ from one another?

9. What were the two meanings assigned to the Lord's Supper in primitive Christianity? What was the result when these two traditions became intermingled in the post-apostolic Church?

10. What is the Catholic doctrine of *transubstantiation*? Contrast this with Luther's doctrine of *consubstantiation*, and the views of Zwingli and Calvin.

11. Identify and define the two ongoing Church offices mentioned in the New Testament. What third office was added by the post-apostolic Church?

12. Compare and contrast the organization of the Roman Catholic Church with the episcopalian, congregational, and presbyterian forms of government.

15

The Doctrine
of the Last Things

The Scope of Eschatology

The term *eschatology* comes from the Greek *ta eschata*, "the last things." It refers to the final events of human life and God's history of redemption. The last two phrases of the Apostles' Creed comprise its eschatological component: "the resurrection of the body, and the life everlasting."

The subject of eschatology has been the source of both fascination and embarrassment throughout the history of the Church. Ancient and modern Christians alike have at times attempted to pin down the date of the second coming of Christ or to find the hermeneutical key to unlock the mysteries of the book of Revelation. In nineteenth-century North America a Baptist preacher named William Miller predicted Christ would return in 1844. Jesus never showed, but the modern Adventist movement was born. More recently, the present writer has just finished reading a news account of a man who predicts Christ will return in September of 1994. The fact that you are now reading this book testifies to the failure of this latest modern-day prognostication.

It would be a mistake, however, to minimalize the importance of eschatology because some have become obsessed with it. For as we saw in chapter 10, the meaning of Christianity's central event, the resurrection of Jesus, can only be understood within the framework of Jewish and Christian eschatology. Indeed, from a biblical stand-point the meaning of all human history can only be understood in light of what has not yet happened. One cannot interpret the signif-icance of individual events until one has seen the overall picture.[1]

Christians confess that the resurrection of Jesus has given us a basic outline of this overall picture, in that the Kingdom of God has already manifested itself in human history prior to the final con-summation of that history. Biblical prophecy nonetheless testifies that the meaning of human history still awaits its full manifestation (Rom. 8:22). For this reason even those who possess the Spirit of Christ have only partial understanding of God's plan for the ages (1 Cor. 13:12). Partial understanding is not necessarily erroneous understanding, however. It thus behooves us to deal with the sub-ject of eschatology with both confidence and caution: confidence in what God has revealed in Scripture; caution that we avoid unwar-ranted extrapolations from the biblical witness.

Throughout history the Church has viewed the return of Christ as but one of the "last things." Following the overall consensus of both Protestant and Catholic theology, we shall deal with the fol-lowing subjects under the heading of eschatology: physical death, the intermediate state, the Second Coming of Christ, and human destiny.

Physical Death

The Universality of Death

Death comes to all. "Man is destined to die once" (Heb. 9:27). It is the last thing we experience in our earthly sojourn. The notion of reincarnation is foreign to the biblical worldview.

The Meaning of Death

Death has been defined as a termination of physical life by sepa-ration of body and soul.[2] It is not a total annihilation of individual human life. The animating principle of human life, the soul, con-tinues to live on. The body, however, becomes inert, lifeless.

Jesus spoke of death as "sleep" (John 11:11, 14), as did Paul (1 Thess. 4:13; 1 Cor. 15:51). For this reason some Christians believe that the soul is unconscious, or "asleep," between the time of death and the return of Christ. This doctrine of "soul-sleep" runs counter to the overwhelming historical Christian consensus that the human soul remains conscious after death separates body and soul. The human *being*, on the other hand, is not alive in the full biblical sense of the word. This is because biblical theology, unlike Greek philosophy, defines human nature as a unity of body and soul. When this unity is broken, it is called death. Eternal life in its fullest sense is not the disembodiment of an immortal soul, but the resurrection of the body (John 11:21-26).

The Significance of Death

Modern secular materialism sees death as having no significance. It leads to no afterlife; it is the end of each individual's story. Biology is the whole story. When you're dead, you're dead. Period.

Such a view of death betrays a similar attitude towards human life on the part of secular materialism. For if death has no significance, neither does life. A Christian worldview, on the other hand, views death as significant for several reasons.

Death is a punishment for sin. God warned Adam that disobedience to the divine will would result in death (Gen. 2:17). When Adam and Eve disobeyed, the sentence of punishment was pronounced: "Dust you are, and to dust you shall return" (Gen. 3:19). Death is a result of the Fall, and together with sin spread throughout the entire human race on account of Adam's first disobedience (Rom. 5:12, 17). Death is the recompense we receive for sin (Rom. 6:23).

Death is therefore not merely a natural part of human existence. Pelagius and Socinus believed that it was, but that was because they did not believe in sin. They would not have objected to poet Dylan Thomas's portrayal of death as "that good night."[3] For Paul, however, death is an enemy. It is the "last enemy" which God will do away with after He has fully dealt with sin (1 Cor. 15:26).

Death gives meaning to life. Ironically, it is this enemy which gives meaning to our earthly existence. This is because death ends the probationary period wherein human beings choose to accept or reject the way of eternal life offered by God in Christ. The moral choices we make in this life are therefore ultimately meaningful, whether to our well-being or our detriment. Were there no death, there would be no ultimate seriousness to our moral decisions, for we could put off such decisions indefinitely. This is not an option for us, however, because judgment comes after death (Heb. 9:27).

A few Christians throughout history have held that people will have a second chance to repent after death prior to the final judgment. Some point to 1 Peter 4:6, where the writer speaks of the gospel being preached to the dead, as evidence of this. The doctrinal consensus of Christianity has opposed this view, however. Like Augustine, historic Christian belief holds that a person cannot obtain after death that which he has not secured in this life (*Enchiridion* 110).[4]

Death is not final punishment. For those who reject the grace of God, physical death is but a prelude to what the writer of Revelation calls the "second death" (2:11, 20:6, 21:8). This second death is also characterized as "everlasting punishment" (Matt. 25:46) and "everlasting destruction . . . shut out from the presence of the Lord" (2 Thess. 1:9). Jesus said physical death was only the destruction of the body; the thing people should fear is the destruction of both body and soul (Matt. 10:28).

Death is the final step in the believer's sanctification. No one escapes all the infirmities of this life prior to death. Even John Wesley, who spoke of the possibility of entire sanctification in this life, saw death as ushering in a freedom from sin not experienced in one's earthly life (*Forty-Four Sermons*, Sermon 35, "Christian Perfection" section I). Wesley is thus in accord with the Reformed tradition that physical death is the final step in the Christian's sanctification.

Paul, imprisoned in Rome, wrote of his desire to "depart [die] and be with Christ, which is better by far [than remaining on earth]" (Phil. 1:23). On another occasion Paul said he "would prefer to be away from the body and at home with the Lord" (2 Cor. 5:8). Ignatius of Antioch, on his way to being martyred in Rome around the year 115, set forth the classical Christian attitude of a believer facing death when he wrote to the Church of Rome, "I fear lest your very love should do me wrong. [Because] for me it is difficult to attain unto God, unless you spare me [by refusing to intervene to save my life]" (*To the Romans* 1.2).[5]

While death ushers in final sanctification, the glorification of which Paul spoke in Romans 8:30 awaits Christ's return and the resurrection of those who are in Christ. "The intermediate state" is the term used in Christian theology to describe what happens to humans between death and the return of Christ.

The Intermediate State

Between Death and the Age to Come

The doctrine of the intermediate state addresses the question, "Where shall I be five minutes after I die?" Christians find themselves in less agreement on this doctrine than on the doctrines of death and the final judgment.

Roman Catholics, for example, believe that the righteous and the wicked go directly to their final respective destinies of heaven and hell immediately after death. Some Protestants concur, while others believe that the righteous and wicked will go to their final destinies of Heaven and Hell only after Christ returns. This latter group of Protestants uses the names "Hades" and "Paradise" of the intermediate realms where the wicked and the righteous dwell prior to the final judgment. Catholics also believe in an intermediate realm, which they label "purgatory."

For the purposes of our discussion here we shall describe the intermediate state as consisting of three realms: Hades, Purgatory, and Paradise. This threefold division reflects the three books of Dante's *Divine Comedy* (*Inferno*, *Purgatorio*, *Paradiso*). In actuality, it is a composite of Catholic and Protestant views. Protestants do not believe in purgatory, while Catholics see purgatory as the only intermediate state.

Hades

The title of Dante's *Inferno* is the same Latin word used in Jerome's Vulgate New Testament to translate both the Greek *gehenna* (Matt. 23:33) and *hades* (Luke 16:23). Protestants and Catholics agree that *gehenna* should be translated "hell" and refers to final judgment. Those who believe in an intermediate state for the wicked see *hades* as something different from hell.

The word *hades* is found over one hundred times in the Septuagint, usually to render the Hebrew *sheol*. The Greeks used *hades* as the name of the god of the underworld, and as the realm of all the dead, righteous and wicked alike (Homer, *Iliad* 15.188, 23.244). In the Old Testament, however, *sheol* does not refer to an underworld where both the righteous and wicked dead dwell. Rather, it is where the wicked go after death (Job 21:13; Ps. 9:16f.). The word can also mean simply "the grave," that is, physical death which comes to all (Gen. 42:38; Eccles. 9:10). Even in these cases, however, it carries a negative connotation (see Ps. 16:10; 49:14, 15).[6]

Hades is used eleven times in the New Testament. Twice it is translated "the grave" (Acts 2:27 [quoting Ps. 16:10]; 1 Cor. 15:55). At other times it refers to the power of death ("the gates of Hades," Matt. 16:18; see also Rev. 1:18). In Luke 16:23, 28 Jesus refers to Hades as a realm where only the wicked dead are found, as opposed to the "bosom of Abraham" (v. 22) where the righteous dwell. No one in Hades can cross over to Abraham's side, and vice-versa (v. 26; C.S. Lewis's *The Great Divorce* notwithstanding). The wicked await their final destiny in Hades, fully aware of their fate.

The idea of an intermediate prison or "holding-cell" for the wicked awaiting final judgment is also found in 2 Peter 2:9, as well as in the third-century Christian apologist Hippolytus (*Against Plato* 1). Augustine likewise held that the destiny of each individual soul is known immediately after death, though the sentence is not carried out until the end of the age (*The Soul and Its Origin* 2.4).

Purgatory

Catholic dogma teaches that "the souls of the just which, in the moment of death, are burdened with venial sins or temporal punishment due to sins, enter Purgatory."[7] There venial sins are purged by the cleansing fire (*purgatorium*) of God, which is a temporal (not eternal) penalty which purifies Christians of venial sins. Mortal sins cannot be so purged. A Christian who dies in mortal sin goes directly to hell.

The doctrine of purgatory has its origins in intertestamental Judaism. The apocryphal book of Second Maccabees, which is part of the Roman Catholic Old Testament, contains a passage which states that the Jews "made atonement for the dead, that they might be delivered from their sin" by offering prayers and monetary sacrifices (2 Macc. 12:45). The text provides a precedent for the Catholic practices of prayers for the dead and indulgences.

Catholics also believe Jesus presupposed the existence of purgatory when He stated that "anyone who speaks a word against the Son of Man will be forgiven, but anyone who speaks against the

Holy Spirit will not be forgiven, either in this age or in the age to come" (Matt. 12:32). In the fourth century, for example, the Eastern Church theologian Gregory the Great saw this text as implying that many sins can be remitted not only in this world, but also in the world to come (*Dialogues* 4.39). Augustine also believed in purgatory (*City of God* 21.13, 24). The doctrine was not defined authoritatively, however, until 1274 at the Second Council of Lyons.

In addition to purgatory, medieval Catholic theology spoke of two other realms distinct from heaven and hell. One of these, the *limbus patrum* ("Limbo of the Fathers"), is where the Old Testament saints were detained until Christ set them free during the interval between His death and resurrection. This is the doctrine of the "harrowing of Hell" mentioned in chapter 9 (p. 214). The second realm, *limbus puerorum* (or *limbus infantium*), is the abode of all unbaptized children. They remain there without receiving any punishment, but are excluded from the blessings of heaven.[8]

Paradise

Aside from the few who believe in "soul-sleep," Christians generally speak of deceased believers as having "gone to heaven." This reflects the aforementioned conviction of Catholics and some Protestants that the righteous go directly to heaven without an intermediate dwelling place prior to the return of Christ and the resurrection of the body. Such people view "paradise" and "heaven" as synonyms. Others see paradise as an intermediate state, the positive counterpart of Hades. These people would view Jesus' reference to the bosom of Abraham (Luke 16:22) as another expression for paradise.

As Jesus was dying on the cross He promised a penitent thief, "today you shall be with me in paradise." This clearly implies that paradise is a realm of conscious life rather than soul-sleep. Paul spoke of a vision of paradise which he experienced even prior to death (2 Cor. 12:4), in which he "heard inexpressible things," again indicating consciousness rather than sleep. The faithful martyrs of Revelation 2:7 will "eat from the tree of life, which is in the paradise of God." This also rules out an unconscious interval of soul-sleep between physical death and the return of Christ.

While Catholics and Protestants agree that the righteous enter paradise, they disagree on who the "righteous" are. Catholicism defines the righteous as those whose souls at the moment of death are free from all guilt of sin and punishment for sin. Immediate entry into paradise is based on actual righteousness imparted via the sacramental order of salvation.[9] Most Protestants define the righteous as those who possess "the righteousness of God in [Christ]" (2 Cor. 5:21). According to this view, entry into paradise is based not upon the believer's actual righteousness, but upon the imputed righteousness of Christ.

Whatever differences exist among Christians regarding the intermediate state, the consensus of Christian belief throughout history affirms that Christ will return to pronounce final judgment upon both the righteous and the wicked, whose bodies will be raised from the dead. This will mark the end of the present age of evil, and the beginning of the future age of righteousness.

The Second Coming of Christ

The Question of the Millennium

The Nicene Creed's affirmation that Christ "will come again in glory to judge both the living and the dead" is confessed by all branches of Christendom. Jesus foretold His return prior to His crucifixion (Matt. 24:30, 25:31-46). The New Testament authors reaffirmed it (1 Thess. 4:13-17; 2 Thess. 2:1; 1 Cor. 11:26, 15:51; James 5:7; Heb. 9:28; 1 John 3:2; 2 Pet. 3:1; Rev. 19:11). No significant Christian thinker throughout history has denied it.

This unanimous affirmation *that* Christ will return stands in marked contrast to the diversity of opinion as to *when* Christ will return. We noted at the outset of this chapter that setting dates for Christ's return is risky business. Jesus Himself said that prior to His crucifixion even He did not know the day and hour of His return (Mark 13:32). Early in his ministry Paul may have expected Christ to return prior to his own death (1 Thess. 4:17). He never tried to set a date, however. The one clue the New Testament gives as to the timing of Christ's return comes from Jesus Himself. "This gospel of the kingdom will be preached in the whole world as a testimony to all nations [people groups], and then the end will come" (Matt. 24:14; see chapter 10, p. 235).

Given that Christians should not be setting dates for Christ's return, the question remains as to whether Scripture reveals a general pattern of events surrounding Jesus' second coming. Jesus spoke of signs of His return, which include war, famine, earthquakes, and persecution of Christians (Matt. 24:4-10). Paul seems to reinforce this in 2 Thessalonians 2 and 2 Timothy 3. The book of Revelation paints a similar picture.

Perhaps the most controversial issue surrounding this topic is the doctrine of the *millennium*. This doctrine teaches that Christ will rule on earth together with His Church for a thousand-year period prior to the final judgment. The thousand-year reign of Christ is mentioned only in Revelation 20. Due to the writer's use of symbolic numbers in other parts of the book (such as the number 666 in Rev. 13:18), many view John's half-dozen references to a "thousand years" as symbolic rather than literal. Others see Revelation 20 as part of a narrative which foretells future events using symbolic language, but which nevertheless speaks of a literal earthly reign of Christ (Rev. 20:1-6) prior to the final judgment (Rev. 20:11-15).

We shall make no attempt here to decide which of these views is correct. Instead, we shall briefly summarize the four major views of the millennium which have been set forth in the history of the Church. These are, in order of their antiquity, historic premillennialism, amillennialism, postmillennialism, and dispensational premillennialism.

Historic Premillennialism

The earliest form of millennialism interpreted the thousand-year reign of Christ as a time between His return to earth and the final judgment. According to this view the time between Christ's first and second advents will be one of ongoing conflict between the followers of Christ and those who follow the ruler of this world, Satan. Suffering and persecution, which characterize the Church's existence on earth, will intensify as the time draws near for Jesus' return.

When Christ returns, He will save His followers from annihilation and apostasy (Matt. 24:24, 31). He will defeat the forces of evil on earth, who have been led by one Paul calls the "man of lawlessness" (2 Thess. 2:4) and who elsewhere is called the Antichrist (1 John 2:18) and the Beast (Rev. 13, 20). Christ will then establish a thousand-year era of peace upon earth, during which time the power of Satan will be held in check and the Church will rule together with its Lord (Rev. 20:1-6). Following this Satan will be permitted by God to deceive the nations for one last time. Satan will be defeated and judged, after which the final judgment of humanity will take place (Rev. 20:7-15).

This view was held by theologians in both the East and West during the second century. These included Irenaeus (*Against Heresies* 5.28, 33), Justin Martyr (*Dialogue with Trypho* 80, 81), and Tertullian (*Against Marcion* 3.24). Papias (c. 60-130), whom Irenaeus identified as a student of the Apostle John (*Against Heresies* 5.28), also held a premillennial position. Origen, on the other hand, opposed premillennialism strongly (*First Principles* 2.11), which is not surprising considering his love for allegory.

Many early Christians interpreted the references to the judgment of "Babylon" in Revelation to refer to Rome, which persecuted the Church from time to time between the first and fourth centuries (17:5, 18:2; note also the reference to "seven hills" in 17:9, which most interpreters see as an allusion to Rome, the city built on seven hills). Such identification of Babylon with Rome in turn meant that the Beast of Revelation was none other than the emperor. By implication, the millennium would arrive when Rome and the emperor had been defeated by Christ at His second coming.

Amillennialism

A funny thing happened on the way to the millennium, however. The Antichrist became the defender of the Church. This happened in 313, shortly after the last great imperial persecution of the Church, when the Emperor Constantine was converted to Christianity. That same year he issued the Edict of Milan, which gave legal protection to the Christian Church. Christianity eventually became the state religion of the empire.

This rapid change in the Roman Empire's attitude towards Christianity appeared to falsify the premillennial interpretation of Revelation. Rome was not Babylon, and the emperor was not the Antichrist. This situation, combined with the increasing influence of Origen's allegorical hermeneutical method, opened the door to the amillennialism. According to this view there will be no thousand-year reign of Christ on earth between His second coming and the final judgment. The "thousand years" of Revelation 20 are to be interpreted symbolically, not literally.

Augustine formulated the classical amillennial position which was to reign within the Church for the next thousand years. He identified the millennium as having begun with the *first* coming of Christ. The rule of Christ in the Church between His first and second advents is what the writer of Revelation means by his symbolic reference to a thousand years.

> It is then of this kingdom militant [the Church], in which conflict with the enemy is still maintained, and war carried on with warring lusts, or government laid upon them as they yield, until we come to that most peaceful kingdom in which we shall reign without an enemy, and it is of this first resurrection in the present life [the new birth], that the Apocalypse speaks in the words just quoted (*City of God* 20.9).[10]

In this way Augustine made peace with the historical link between Church and empire which existed in his day.

Amillennialism was supported by both Luther and Calvin, despite their opposition both to Rome and to the allegorical hermeneutic Augustine used to articulate his perspective. The fact that some sixteenth-century Anabaptists embraced premillennial views as a pretext for disobeying civil governments probably had something to do with this (see for example Calvin's *Institutes* 3.25.5). In the seventeenth century some Reformed Protestants in Germany and England did return to historic premillennialism. At the same time, the theological diversity ushered in by the Reformation opened the door to yet a third view of the millennium.

Postmillennialism

Postmillennial eschatology, like Premillennialism, holds that the world will experience a golden age of earthly peace in the future. This golden age will be the millennium (though it need not last a thousand years; the number may simply signify a long period of time). The overall structure of postmillennialism, however, is in marked contrast to both historic premillennialism and amillennialism, as shown in the diagrams on p. 346.

Both premillennialism and amillennialism set forth what may be called a cataclysmic view of history, in that the Church will experience a time of great tribulation preceding the return of Christ. Postmillennialism, on the other hand, takes what may be called a gradualist or evolutionary view of history. Despite setbacks along the way, the Church will gradually convert the world through the preaching of the gospel.

Postmillennial doctrine may be outlined as follows:

- Christianity will eventually permeate the entire world, despite setbacks along the way. Not every individual will be converted, but the gospel of Christ will be recognized as true by worldwide consensus.

- When this finally occurs, a long period of unprecedented peace will be established on earth. It will not be without sin and death, but it will be a significant improvement over anything experienced up to this point in human history. It will be, for all practical purposes, a Christian world.

- Most postmillennialists hold that the Jews will be converted at the beginning of, or sometime during, this period.

- At the end of this period Christ will return, the dead will be raised, the final judgment will be pronounced, and the new heavens and the new earth will be revealed.

Some postmillennialists also hold that just prior to Christ's return there will be a brief apostasy and conflict between the forces of Christ and the forces of evil. This view is not held by all postmillennialists, however.

Postmillennialism has been criticized by some as having too optimistic a view of human nature, and thus succumbing to modern notions of the evolutionary progress of the human race. It should be noted, however, that the strongly-Calvinist Puritans in eighteenth-century North America were postmillennialists. Jonathan Edwards, who held as strong a view of human depravity as anyone mentioned in this book, was a postmillennialist.[11] Edwards predicated his postmillennialism not upon human ability, but upon the all-powerful sovereign God whom he worshiped.

During the nineteenth century postmillennialism flourished in North America, particularly among those of the Reformed persuasion. The cataclysm of World War One caused many Christians to rethink their postmillennial perspective, and the view enjoys less popularity today than it did a hundred years ago.

Dispensational Premillennialism

Even as postmillennialism was in its heyday in the English-speaking world, a variation of historic premillennialism was born in nineteenth-century England. Known as dispensational premillennialism, or simply dispensationalism, this eschatological perspective combined a strictly-literal hermeneutic with an absolute distinction between God's dealings with Israel on the one hand and with the Church on the other.

The name of this movement comes from the King James Version's use of the word "dispensation" to translate the Greek *oikonomia* in 1 Corinthians 9:7 and elsewhere. A dispensation is a way of administering matters in a society. Biblically speaking, it is a period of time during which human beings are tested to see if they will obey God's revealed will. C. I. Scofield, editor of the widely-read *Scofield Reference Bible*, identified seven dispensations in God's plan for the ages: innocence (before the Fall), conscience (from the Fall to Noah), human government (from the Fall to Abraham), promise (from Abraham to Moses), law (from Moses to Christ), grace (the Church age), and the kingdom (the Millennium). The close of the Millennium brings the final judgment and humanity's final destiny.

The principal difference between the historic and dispensational varieties of premillennialism concern the fifth and sixth dispensations, those of law and grace. The nation of Israel is the object of the former and is God's earthly people. The Church is the object of the latter and is God's heavenly people, since Christians are not identified with any one nation on earth. The Old Testament promises given to Israel must therefore never be applied to the Church. Furthermore, the hermeneutics of dispensationalism demand that the word "Israel" never be used symbolically of the Church, but only literally of God's earthly people. Dispensationalists call this "rightly dividing the word of truth" (2 Tim. 2:15, KJV).

It is here that one finds the origin of dispensationalism's most glaring difference with historic premillennialism: the doctrine of the *pre-tribulation rapture*. The term "rapture" refers to the event described by Paul in 1 Thessalonians 4:13-17, when Christ will return and take His Church out of the world. Historic premillennialism foresees a "post-tribulation" rapture which will occur at the

A FUTURE RESTORATION OF
THE NATION OF ISRAEL?

In Romans 11 Paul addresses what must have been a sticky question wherever he preached: "Did God reject His people [the nation of Israel]? To which he replies: "By no means!" (Rom. 11:1). He goes on to say that the nation of Israel has indeed "stumbled," but not so as to "fall" (Rom 11:11). To the contrary, when the "fullness of the Gentiles has come in" to God's salvation, "all Israel will be saved" (Rom. 11:25-26).

Paul's answer raises yet another question, one which has divided Christians since the second century. To whom or what does Paul refer when he speaks of "all Israel" being saved in Romans 11:26? Is he talking about a future restoration of the nation of Israel, in fulfillment of promises made by the Old Testament prophets? Or does "all Israel" refer to a spiritual Israel which consists of both Jews and Gentiles, depicted by Paul as an olive tree in Romans 11:17-24?

Advocates of historic premillennialism have tended to adopt the former view. Justin Martyr, for example, believed that God had made an unconditional covenant with the nation of Israel which could not be superseded by the Gentile mission. When the Church has fulfilled this mission,

God will restore the nation of Israel and rebuild Jerusalem. At the same time, Justin admitted that many Christians did not agree with him on this point (*Dialogue with Trypho* 80). Modern-day dispensationalists, with their radical distinction between Israel and the Church, likewise hold to a national restoration of Israel. Some believe that a third temple will be built in Jerusalem, and will follow the design described in Ezekiel 40-48.

Amillennialists and most postmillennialists believe that Paul's metaphor of the olive tree in Romans 11 demonstrates that there is but one people of God, the Church, which consists of both Jews and Gentiles. This is the "Israel of God" (Gal. 6:16). Some postmillennialists believe that a final great ingathering of Jews will precede the return of Christ. They tend to interpret this ingathering not as a national restoration of Israel, however, but a sharp increase in the number of ethnic Jews who place their faith in Jesus as their promised Messiah.

It is unlikely this question will be resolved prior to the Second Coming. Despite this lack of consensus, Paul's emphasis on the organic link among Israel and the

Church in Romans 11 should be a point of accord between all Christians. "Salvation is of the Jews" said Jesus (John 4:22). The Church's failure throughout the centuries to keep Paul's vision of the Jewish-Gentile "olive tree" in the forefront of Christian theology has led to doctrinal waywardness into Greek dualism and the unfortunate spectacle of Christian anti-Semitism. As one modern writer put it:

How odd of God
To choose the Jews.
But not so odd
As those who choose
The Jewish God
And hate the Jews.*

---

* Cited in Edith Schaeffer, *Christianity Is Jewish*, 8.

---

close of that final period of tribulation which precedes the return of Christ. Dispensationalists, on the other hand, divide the return of Christ into two phases: the coming of Christ *for* His Church (the rapture), which occurs just prior to the seven-year great tribulation, and the coming of Christ *with* His Church following the tribulation (see charts on p. 346.

Who, then, are those "elect" whom Jesus said will go through the tribulation prior to His return (Mark 13:18-22)? They are the "servants of God" whom John identifies as "144,000 from all the tribes of Israel" (Rev. 7:3-4). Dispensationalism does not interpret this as a symbolic reference to the Church, as does historic premillennialism (which identifies the 144,000 with the "great multitude . . . from every nation, tribe, people and language" mentioned in Rev. 7:9). Following its rigorously-literal hermeneutic, dispensationalism identifies the 144,000 as regenerated Jews who are converted to Christ during the tribulation. During the tribulation, then, God once again deals with His earthly people, as He did during the dispensation of law prior to the dispensation of grace (the Church age). The pre-tribulation rapture is thus a theological necessity, from the standpoint of dispensationalism, in order to maintain the necessary distinction between Israel and the Church and thus to rightly divide the word of truth.[12]

FOUR VIEWS OF THE MILLENNIUM

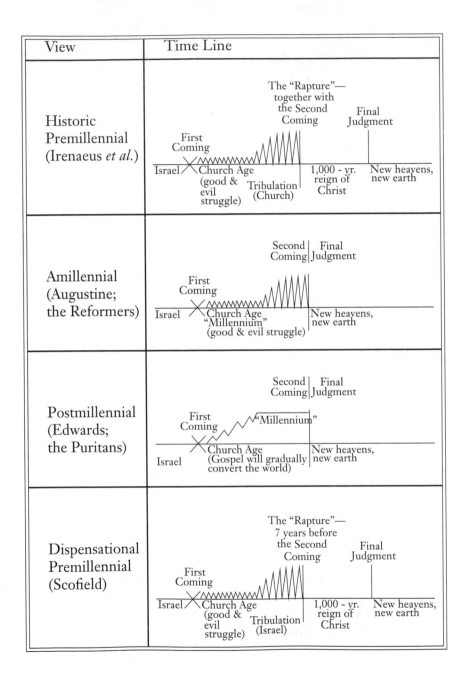

Unity Amid Diversity

For all of their differences, the four millennial views we have examined join together in confessing the following historic beliefs:

- Christ will return bodily to earth for a second time.

- At that time God will raise bodily from the dead those who have trusted in Christ as Lord and Savior.

- Following Christ's return all people who ever lived will face final judgment, where God will pronounce their ultimate destinies.

In the words of the Nicene Creed, Christians "look for the resurrection of the dead, and the life in the world to come." These are the subjects of our final two sections.

The Resurrection of the Body

Resurrection of Both Righteous and Wicked

We saw in chapter 10 that Christianity shares with its Jewish heritage the conviction that salvation consists not merely in the ongoing immortality of the soul, but also in the resurrection of the body to everlasting life. This conviction finds expression in some of the later writings of the Old Testament (Isa. 26.19; Ezek. 37:12), and indirect hints may be found as early as the book of Job (19:26). In the New Testament it is central to the message of the gospel of Christ. Jesus affirmed it over the denials of the Sadducees (Matt. 22:29-32 and parallels). Paul affirmed it not only in his writings (1 Cor. 15; 1 Thess 4 et al.) but also when he was on trial before the Sanhedrin (Acts 23:6) and before Felix (Acts 24:21). Peter refers to the resurrection as the Christian's "living hope" (1 Pet. 1:3).

The Bible also teaches that even the wicked will be raised from the dead prior to the final judgment. The idea that both the righteous and the wicked will be resurrected is first found in the book of Daniel, one of the latest writings in the Jewish canon. "Multitudes who sleep in the dust of the earth will awake: some to everlasting life, others to shame and everlasting contempt" (Dan. 12:2). Jesus reaffirmed this when He said "a time is coming when all who are in their graves will hear his voice and come out—those who have done good will rise to live, and those who have done evil will rise to be condemned" (John 5:28-29). Paul likewise endorsed this belief as he stood trial before Felix (Acts 24:15).

The writer of Revelation goes a step beyond Daniel and Jesus when he separates the resurrections of the righteous and the wicked. "[The dead in Christ] came to life and reigned with Christ a thousand years. (The rest of the dead did not come to life until the thousand years were ended.)" (Rev. 20:4-5). The significance of this thousand-year interval is not clear. Premillennialists interpret it literally, while amillennialists and postmillennialists see the first resurrection as spiritual (Christ's people experience the new birth) and the second resurrection as physical (all people, including Christians, will be raised bodily).

The Nature of the Resurrection Body

The nature of the resurrection body is a mystery which will not be revealed until Christ returns (1 John 3:2). Paul speaks of the present human body as "perishable," the resurrection body as "imperishable" (1 Cor. 15:42), and contrasts the present "natural" body with the future "spiritual" body. Christian doctrine does not interpret the word "spiritual" to mean immaterial, since Jesus insisted that His resurrection body was not merely a spirit, but consisted of flesh and bone (Luke 24:39). In the fourth century Macrina the Teacher, sister of Basil the Great, described the resurrection body as "the re-constitution of our nature in its original form" (Gregory of Nyssa, *On the Soul and the Resurrection*).[13]

Christians further confess that the resurrection body is not a different body from the mortal body, but a different form of the same body (John of Damascus, *On the Orthodox Faith* 4.27; *Westminster Confession* 32). This insistence on the ultimate identity of the pre- and post-resurrection body is tied to the Judeo-Christian anthropology which views human beings as a unity of body and soul. A soul which obtained an entirely new body would be a different person.

Human Destiny

No Probation at the Judgment Seat

Hell is the term used to describe the final destiny of the wicked, while heaven is the final destiny of the righteous. There is no indication in Scripture that the unrighteous dead who have been raised will have a second chance to decide for God prior to being judged.

Hell

The word *gehenna* is on the lips of Jesus when He speaks of hell in the New Testament. The name is apparently a Greek transliteration of a Hebrew *ge hinnom*, which refers to the Valley of Hinnom just outside of Jerusalem. In Jeremiah 7:31 we read that Hinnom was a place where Judah practiced the pagan rite of sacrificing children by fire. Later Hinnom became a rubbish heap where the fires burned day and night. In this way Hinnom, or Gehenna, became a symbol for the punishment of the wicked.

Jesus spoke of Gehenna as a place where the wicked suffer eternal punishment: "Their worm does not die" (Mark 9:48, quoting Isa. 66:24). He also spoke of the judgment of the wicked as "outer darkness" where there shall be "weeping and gnashing of teeth" (Matt. 22:13; 25:30). Such judgment is not remedial but punitive, and is not temporary but unending. The word Jesus uses to speak of "eternal" destruction or hell in Matthew 25:46 is the same word He uses to speak of "eternal" life.

The orthodox doctrine of hell, then, is one of everlasting conscious torment. The metaphor of fire need not be taken literally (after all, how can fire also be darkness?). But Jesus obviously meant for it to be taken seriously. He fully intended to strike the fear of God into the hearts of His audience: "Fear [God] who, after the killing of the body, has power to throw you into Hell" (Luke 12:5). Jesus also spoke of some of the ungodly being beaten with many stripes, and some with few (Luke 12:47-48). This has been interpreted as teaching different degrees of punishment in hell. The nine circles of hell depicted in Dante's *Inferno* reflect this idea.

Throughout the history of Christianity a minority of theologians have attempted either to deny or redefine the orthodox doctrine of hell. Three such alternatives to hell are reincarnation, universalism, and annihilationism.

Reincarnation teaches that the human soul goes through a series of embodiments in order to earn its salvation. This view is part of the worldview of many Eastern religions, including Hinduism. In recent years it has gained popularity in the West through the writings of Edgar Cayce and various forms of the so-called "New Age

Movement" (which is really a term which encompasses many beliefs, some at cross purposes with one another). Reincarnation has been consistently rejected by all branches of the Christian Church, both on the basis of Hebrews 9:27 and the fact that it is based upon a radical dualism of body and soul which runs counter to biblical anthropology.

Universalism is the teaching that everyone will ultimately be saved. Origen wrote that over "countless ages" God would eventually reconcile every creature to Himself. Even the most disobedient, the devil himself, would eventually cease to be the enemy of God (*First Principles* 1.6.1-4; 3.6.5-6). Any mention of the fires of judgment was viewed by Origen to be a form of purgatory, in order to "assist the sinner to health" (*First Principles* 2.10.6).[14] Origen's views on this and other matters were condemned at the Council of Alexandria (400), and the fifth general council at Constantinople (553) listed Origen among ancient heretics. Universalism has nevertheless remained an option for some throughout the centuries, most recently for many within mainline Protestant denominations.

Annihilationism teaches that the wicked will not suffer eternal conscious punishment, but will be annihilated by God and thereby cease to exist. This view is held by the Jehovah's Witnesses and Seventh-Day Adventists, among others. More recently it has been adopted by some prominent Protestant Evangelicals[15] and at least tolerated by others under the label of "conditional immortality."[16] On the other hand, Jesus' statement that it would have been better for Judas never to have been born (Matt. 26:24) seems to indicate that even the wicked will remain immortal, and will not find that to be a pleasant experience.

The principle objection to hell throughout the centuries has been that it seems excessive. If it be true that the punishment should fit the crime, how can any sin committed by finite human beings within a limited period of time, no matter how heinous, merit infinite punishment?

Perhaps the best reply to this objection was given by Jonathan Edwards in his sermon "The Justice of God in the Damnation of Sinners." Edwards argued that the severity of a crime is determined not only by the nature of the act, but also by taking into account against whom it is committed. The more glorious the one against whom the crime is committed, the greater the degree of guilt. (For example, the law recognizes a threatening letter to the President of the United States as a more serious crime than a threatening letter to an average citizen). On this basis, said Edwards, "Sin against God, being a violation of infinite obligations, must be a crime infinitely heinous, and so deserving infinite punishment. . . .The eternity of the punishment of ungodly men renders it infinite . . . and therefore renders it no more than proportionable to the heinousness of what they are guilty of."[17]

In other words, Edwards insisted that *only* an infinite punishment is proper for the infinite crime of violating the infinite glory of God, since all sin is ultimately against God. "Against you, you only [God], have I sinned," said David (Ps. 51:4). Were God not to punish sin eternally, He would in effect be denying the supreme and infinite worth of His own glory, which is something God cannot do.[18]

Heaven

The word "heaven" is used in common speech to refer to both the intermediate state and the final state of the righteous. We have already discussed "heaven" as paradise, the intermediate state. We shall now conclude our survey of historic Christian belief with a brief examination of what Paul refers to as "the glory to be revealed to us" (Rom. 8:18), and what John calls the "new heavens and the new earth" (Rev. 21:1, quoting Isa. 65:17).

In his gospel and epistles John speaks of the destiny of the righteous as "eternal life." More than any other New Testament writer, John speaks of eternal life as a present possession as well as a future hope. Eternal life is already enjoyed (John 3:36), even as it awaits the return of Christ to be manifested in its fullness (1 John 3:2).

Paul uses the word "glorification" (Rom. 8:30) to describe the hope of the Christian, which he also calls the "revelation of the sons of God" (Rom. 8:22). This is a future reality which nevertheless is already experienced in some measure by those who have the Spirit of Christ (Rom. 8:4-27). Like John, Paul views this present experience of the Spirit as merely a first installment or deposit of things to come (2 Cor. 1:22; Eph. 1:14). Until the perfection of our heavenly destiny comes, even those who have the Spirit are limited in their knowledge of God (1 Cor. 13:10, 12).

The writer of Hebrews speaks of the Christians, ultimate goal in life not as any earthly reward, but as a "heavenly country" (Heb. 11:16). For this reason Jesus urged His disciples to lay up treasure in Heaven and not treasure on earth (Matt. 6:19-20). The reason heavenly treasure is so much more valuable than earthly treasure is because it lasts forever. It is not subject to decay and cannot be taken away.

Heaven is the future manifestation of the already-inaugurated Kingdom of God (1 Cor. 15:24). Even though Christians already have a "foretaste of glory divine" (to quote Fanny Crosby's hymn *Blessed Assurance*), it is also true that "no eye has seen, no ear has heard, no mind has conceived what God has prepared for those who love Him" (1 Cor. 2:9). For this reason "we walk by faith, not by sight" (2 Cor. 5:7).

This last statement brings us full circle to where we began our study of historic Christian belief. The first text we quoted in chapter one was Hebrews 11:1: "Faith is the assurance of things hoped for, the conviction of things not seen." The study of Christian doctrine has as its ultimate goal the attainment of the heavenly city, to use the language of the book of Hebrews as well as John Bunyan's classic *Pilgrim's Progress*.

Yet as the Bible closes its pages on God's history of redemption, we see a startling vision in Revelation 21:1-3:

> Then I saw the new heaven and the new earth. . . . I saw the Holy City, the new Jerusalem, coming down out of heaven from God, as a bride beautifully prepared for her husband. And I heard a loud voice from the throne saying, "Now the dwelling place of God is with men, and He will live with them. They will be His people, and God Himself will be with them and be their God."

With these words John tells us that the heavenly city is not an attainment after all. It is, in the end, a gift. And this gift does not consist so much in God's bringing us up to Himself as it does in God's condescending to come live with us. The divine condescension first revealed in the incarnation (John 1:14) will become the reality of both God's existence and ours throughout eternity. This is platonic dualism turned on its head. The material world is not cast off, but remade and inhabited by God Himself.

Such a promise defies description. For this reason the author of Revelation uses brilliant metaphor upon brilliant metaphor to disclose the inscrutable, so that we might be motivated to embrace that which we cannot see. To call heaven the "final state" does not do justice to the vision of the apostle. He portrays heaven not so much as a final state as a pulsating eternity of joyous activity in the presence of God and His people. There is no temple; there are no priests. God's people have immediate access to their Redeemer. Even if Thomas Aquinas was right when he said that people cannot have immediate knowledge of God by divine illumination in this present evil age, that will not be the case in heaven. The curse which has separated humanity from the divine presence shall at last be lifted. The tree of life will no longer be off limits (Rev. 22:19; Gen. 3:24).

The various colors of stones which adorn the heavenly city (21:18-21) reflect a diversity which belies popular notions of heaven as a dull place whose inhabitants sit on clouds and strum harps. It may also reflect the New Testament's indications that there will be differences in heavenly rewards (Matt. 25:21-23; Luke 19:16-19; 1 Cor. 3:12-15), a view echoed by Papias the disciple of John (*Fragments of Papias* 5)[19] and the great fourth-century preacher John Chrysostom (*Letters to the Fallen Theodore* 1.19).[20] Yet despite this diversity there will be no envy among the citizens of the celestial city. It would appear that every person's cup will be full, even while their cups are of different sizes. No one shall sense a lack of the joy of the Lord (Augustine, *City of God* 22.30). For God has promised that He will wipe every tear from their eyes. There will be no more death or mourning or crying or pain, for the old order of things has passed away. And He who is seated upon the throne says, "I am making everything new" (see Rev. 21:4–5).

The End
and
The Beginning

Soli Deo Gloria

Points To Ponder

1. List and expound on four aspects of the significance of death from a Christian perspective.

2. How do the Septuagint and the New Testament use the Greek word *hades*?

3. What is the function of purgatory in Catholic doctrine?

4. What do Catholics mean by *limbus patrum*? *limbus puerorum* (*limbus infantium*)?

5. How do Catholics and Protestants differ in their definitions of the "righteous" who will enter paradise?

6. How does historic premillennialism interpret the thousand-year reign of Christ mentioned in Revelation 20?

7. Why did the conversion of the Emperor Constantine lead to the decline of historic premillennialism and the rise of amillennialism?

8. How did Augustine interpret the thousand-year reign of Christ mentioned in Revelation 20?

9. How does postmillennialism's view of history differ from both amillennialism and historic premillennialism?

10. What are the differences between historic premillennialism and dispensational premillennialism?

11. How did Jonathan Edwards argue for the justness of an eternal hell?

12. What is the significance of the biblical vision of the "New Jerusalem" coming down out of heaven so that "the dwelling place of God" shall be with human beings (Rev. 21:1-3)?

Notes

Introduction

Complete publication data for all works cited in this book is found in the bibliography.

1. Cited in Tony Lane, *Harper's Concise Book of Christian Faith*, 88.

2. C. S. Lewis, *God in the Dock*, 200f.

3. Stephen Neill, *A History of Christian Missions*, 14f.

4. Useful summaries of these schools of thought, as well as a number of other modern expressions of Christianity, may be found in David L. Smith, *A Handbook of Contemporary Theology*.

5. See for example the declaration "Evangelicals and Catholics Together," *First Things* (May 1994), prepared by fifteen leading Catholic and Protestant scholars and endorsed by twenty–five others, including such diverse figures as Cardinal John O'Conner of New York and Dr. Bill Bright, president of Campus Crusade for Christ International.

6. Numerous studies, both scholarly and popular, have documented the rising tide of secularism in the West. For scholarly historical treatments see John Senior, *The Death of Christian Culture*; Paul Johnson, *Modern Times: The World from the Twenties to the Nineties*; and Herbert Schlossberg, *Idols for Destruction: The Conflict of Christian Faith and American Culture*. Concerning the secularist drift of certain elements in the historic Protestant denominations see K. L.

Billingsley, *From Mainline to Sideline: The Social Witness of the National Council of Churches.* The historic shift from a Christian to a secular ethos in American universities has recently been examined by George Marsden, *The Soul of the American University: From Protestant Establishment to Established Nonbelief.*

7. Any reader tempted to believe that communism in the former Soviet Union was not all that bad may refer to Aleksandr Solzhenitsyn's massive three–volume *Gulag Archipelago* for the facts.

8. Michael Novak, "Awakening from Nihilism," *First Things* 45 (August/September 1994), 18–22.

9. For the historic Christian consensus on abortion see Michael Gorman, *Abortion and the Early Church.* The sensitive subject of suicide was treated at length, and with compassion, by Augustine in *The City of God*, Book One, chapters 16 through 28.

Chapter 1

1. Rudolf Bultmann, "What Does it Mean to Speak of God?" *Faith and Understanding*, vol. 1.

2. Augustine of Hippo, perhaps the most influential theologian in the history of Christianity since the Apostle Paul, spoke of the relationship between faith and knowledge as one of faith in God seeking understanding of God. For example, Augustine noted that:

> . . . in matters of great importance, pertaining to divinity, we must first believe before we seek to know. Otherwise the words of the prophet would be vain, where he says: "Except ye believe ye shall not understand [Isa. 7:9 LXX]." Our Lord himself, both in his words and by his deeds, exhorted those whom he called to salvation first of all to believe. And no one is fit to find God who does first believe what he will afterwards learn and know. (*On Free Will*, Book 2; see *Library of Christian Classics* vol. 6, 137)

This notion that faith and knowledge are indivisible has more recently been set forth by the twentieth–century philosopher of science Michael Polanyi in his book *Personal Knowledge*, especially chapters 9 and 10.

3. See Edward John Carnell, *Christian Commitment*, 91f.

4. C. S. Lewis, *Mere Christianity*, rev. ed., 19.

5. Ibid., 19f.

6. See Calvin, *Institutes of the Christian Religion* 1.3.1, ed. John T. McNeill, trans. Ford Lewis Battles 43 n. 2. All translations of Calvin's *Institutes*, unless otherwise noted, are from the McNeill/Battles edition.

7. Translated by J. G. Pilkington in *Basic Writings of Saint Augustine*, vol., 1 3.

8. Pascal's *Pènsees*, 113.

9. Francis Schaeffer, *Death in the City*, 112f.

10. Saint Anselm, *Basic Writings*, 2d ed., 7.

11. See Winfried Corduan, *Reasonable Faith: Basic Christian Apologetics*, chapter 6 for a useful summary and evaluation of Thomas Aquinas's five arguments for the existence of God.

Chapter 2

1. Wesley's precise words were: "Let me be *homo unius libri.*" Cited in Colin W. Williams, *John Wesley's Theology Today*, 24.

2. Lawson, *Introduction to Christian Doctrine*, 184.

3. Karl Barth, *Church Dogmatics*, 4 vol. References to *Church Dogmatics*, both here and throughout this book, will be included in parentheses within the text. For example, (*CD* 1/2, 118) refers to page 118 of Volume One, Part Two.

4. Barth, *Evangelical Theology: An Introduction*, 29.

5. James Smart, *The Creed in Christian Teaching*, 163.

6. Translation from the Latin of Rufinus by Frederick Crombie in *The Ante–Nicene Fathers*, vol. 4, 357.

7. Ibid., 362.

8. For an extended scholarly survey of the Alexandrian and Antiochean schools of interpretation see David Dockery, *Biblical Interpretation Then and Now*, chapters 3 and 4.

9. Luther, *Pagan Servitude of the Church* (also known as *The Babylonian Captivity of the Church*), cited in John Dillenberger, *Martin Luther: Selections from His Writings*, 266.

10. See W. G. Kümmel's discussion in *The New Testament: The History of the Investigation of Its Problems*, 103.

11. Kähler, *The So–Called Historical Jesus and the Historic, Biblical Christ*, 65.

12. Gordon Wenham, *Christ and the Bible*, 9.

Chapter 3

1. Erich Auerbach, *Mimesis: The Representation of Reality in Western Literature*, 15.

2. C. S. Lewis, *Mere Christianity*, Book Four, "Beyond Personality: or First Steps in the Doctrine of the Trinity", 133–90.

3. Cited in John Leith, *Creeds of the Churches*, 23.

4. Cited in *The Ante–Nicene Fathers*, vol. 3, 598.

5. See J. N. D. Kelly, *Early Christian Doctrines*, 132.

6. C. S. Lewis, *Mere Christianity*, 138.

7. Ibid., 150.

8. Translation by A. W. Haddan in *Basic Writings of Saint Augustine*, vol. 2, 787.

9. Cited by Cornelius Platinga, Jr. in "Trinity," *International Standard Bible Encyclopedia*, vol. 4, rev. ed., 920.

10. "An Unpublished Essay of Edwards on the Trinity," 80f.

11. Ibid., 80.

12. Ibid., 93.

13. *Mere Christianity*, 152.

Chapter 4

1. For a fuller discussion of Gnosticism see J. N. D. Kelly, *Early Christian Doctrines*, 22–28.

2. John Piper, *Desiring God*, 14.

3. Translation by David L. Mosher in *Fathers of the Church*, vol. 70, 54.

4. "Dissertation concerning the End for Which God Created the World," in *The Works of Jonathan Edwards*, vol. 1, 102.

5. Ibid., 101.

6. See A. A. Hodge's discussion in *Outlines of Theology*, rewritten and enlarged edition, 237.

7. George Marsden has chronicled the secularization of academia in North America in his recent book *The Soul of the American University: From Protestant Establishment to Established Unbelief.*

8. Monod, *Chance and Necessity*, 112f. Cited in Francis Schaeffer, *Back to Freedom and Dignity*, 11f.

9. Monod, *Chance and Necessity*, 172, 145; cited in Schaeffer, *Back to Freedom and Dignity*, 12.

10. For example, see C. F. Keil and F. Delitzsch, *Biblical Commentary on the Pentateuch*, vol. 1, 48.

11. See for example Howard J. Van Till, "Is Special Creationism a Heresy?" *Christian Scholars Review* 22:4 (June 1993), pp. 380–395.

12. See for example Stanley Jaki, *The Road of Science and the Ways of God* chapter 3.

13. From the title of a book by Billy Graham, *Angels: God's Secret Agents.*

Chapter 5

1. As cited by the Scottish Enlightenment philosopher David Hume in his *Dialogues Concerning Natural Religion.* See Hume, *On Religion*, 172.

2. See for example C.H. Dodd, *The Epistle of Paul to the Romans.*

3. Cited in Ludwig Ott, *Fundamentals of Catholic Dogma*, 87.

4. Cited in Philip S. Watson, ed. *The Message of the Wesleys* 68f.

5. Ibid. p. 67f. Emphasis added.

6. Albert Outler, *Who Trusts in God*, 82. Emphasis added.

7. Edwards, *Remarks on Important Theological Controversies* chapter three, "Concerning the Divine Decrees in General, and Election in Particular" section 8. See *The Works of Jonathan Edwards*, vol. 2, 527.

8. Sophocles, *Oedipus Rex* lines 1. 1178–81. Translation by Albert Cook in *Ten Greek Plays in Contemporary Translations*, 144.

9. The quote from Augustine is cited in John Leith, *Basic Christian Doctrine*, 82.

10. Gottfried Wilhelm von Leibniz, *Monadology and Other Philosophical Essays*, 122.

11. Harold Kushner, *When Bad Things Happen to Good People.* Subsequent page references to Kushner's book appear in our text in parentheses.

Chapter 6

1. For example, the Mormon *Journal of Discourses* VI.4 states, "God Himself was once as we are now, and is an exalted man."

2. Mark Cosgrove, *The Amazing Body Human: God's Design for Personhood*, chapters 1, 3, 5, 7 and epilogue.

3. Thomas Jackson, ed., *The Works of John Wesley*, A.M., vol. 6, 244.

4. *Racovian Catechism*, sect. 2, chapter 1.

5. See for example the discussion in Millard J. Erickson, *Christian Theology*, one-volume ed., 524ff.

6. See the discussion in G. Kittel, ed., *Theological Dictionary of the New Testament*, 298ff.

7. Pascal's *Pènsees*, 113.

8. See for example Michael Gorman, *Abortion and the Early Church*.

Chapter 7

1. Reinhold Niebuhr, *The Nature and Destiny of Man*, vol. 1, 261.

2. See Geoffrey Bromiley, "Karl Barth" in *Creative Minds in Contemporary Theology*, Philip E. Hughes, ed., 53.

3. Mortimer Adler, ed., *Great Books of the Western World*, trans. Charles S. Singleton vol.19, 124.

4. Martin Luther, *Three Treatises*, 285. The translation is by W.A. Lambert.

5. Cited in William G. T. Shedd, *A History of Christian Doctrine*, vol. 2, 28 note 1. See also Shedd's extended discussion of the Greek and Latin anthropological traditions, 26–92, from which the translations in the rest of this section are taken.

6. Cited in ibid., 41.

7. Cited in ibid., 39. The translation from the original Greek (*asphragistous men, aponerous de*) is my own.

8. Translations of Pelagius taken from Gustave F. Wiggers, "The Pelagian View of Original Sin" in Millard Erickson (ed.), *Readings in Christian Theology*, vol., 2, 153–57.

9. Francis A. Schaeffer, *Escape from Reason*, 11.

Chapter 8

1. John Lawson, *Introduction to Christian Doctrine*, 49.

2. Cited in *An English Translation of the Epistles of St. Ignatius*, 39.

3. Cited in John Leith, *Creeds of the Churches*, 21–23. Emphases mine.

4. The *Ante-Nicene Fathers*, vol.3, 358.

5. Translation by J.F. Shaw in *Basic Writings of Saint Augustine*, vol. 1, 683.

6. See Karl Barth, *Church Dogmatics* IV/2 pp. 91f. and Millard Erickson, *Christian Theology*, 756.

7. Oscar Cullmann, *The Christology of the New Testament*, 1.

8. Ibid., 3f.

9. See bibliography for publishing data.

10. Irenaeus (*Against Heresies* 3.3.4) relates a story he attributes to Polycarp, who was a disciple of the apostle John. According to Polycarp the apostle was relaxing in a public bathhouse when he received word that Cerinthus was also there. At that point John rushed out without bathing, exclaiming: "Let us flee, lest the bathhouse fall down, because Cerinthus, the enemy of the truth, is within!"

11. *An English Translation of the Epistles of St. Ignatius*, 27.

12. See M.R. James, ed. and trans., *The Apocryphal New Testament*, 91.

13. References to Tertullian's *Against Praxeas* found in *The Ante-Nicene Fathers*, vol. 3, 598 and 623.

14. Cited in Jack Rogers, ed. *Case Studies in Christ and Salvation*, 22.

15. Henry Bettenson, *Documents of the Christian Church*, 45.

16. Cited in Rogers, *Case Studies in Christ and Salvation*, 33. See also Jaroslav Pelikan, *The Christian Tradition, Volume 1: The Emergence of the Catholic Tradition* (100–600), 251.

17. This translation is taken from Paul K. Jewett's unpublished Christology syllabus, which was to have been part of the three-volume systematic theology which he did not live to complete. A thorough documentary account of the Third Ecumenical Council is found in Volume 14 of *The Nicene and Post-Nicene Fathers Second Series*, xxff.

18. The situation among Eastern Orthodox Christians has changed since these words were first written. In late 1993 the Chalcedon branch of Orthodoxy agreed to recognize the non-Chalcedon (Monophysite) branch. The two sides stated that "the Councils and fathers previously anathemized or condemned [including Cyril of Alexandria] are Orthodox in their teaching . . . . [Both branches of Orthodoxy] have loyally maintained the authentic orthodox christological doctrine and the unbroken continuity of the apostolic tradition, though they have used christological terms [such as 'person' and 'nature'] in a different way [the Chalcedonians distinguished be-

tween these two terms; the Monophysites did not]." Once this statement has been ratified by individual churches of both branches of
Orthodoxy, the Monophysites will be granted joint communion
with the rest of the Orthodox Church for the first time in over fifteen hundred. See *Christianity Today* January 10, 1994, 51.

19. Translation from Paul K. Jewett, unpublished Christology syllabus.

20. The Reformed wing of Protestantism has also used the word
communicatio; see Calvin, *Institutes* 2.14.1 and Bullinger, *Second Helvetic Confession*, section 11. But the theological differences between
the Lutheran and Reformed traditions are best distinguished by using *communicatio* of the former and *communio* of the latter.

21. Herder, *Christliche Schriften*, cited in W. G. Kümmel, *The New
Testament: The History of the Investigation of its Problems*, 103.

22. Cited in Kümmel, op. cit., 183.

Chapter 9

1. See C.H. Dodd, *The Bible and the Greeks*.

2. See Leon Morris, *The Apostolic Preaching of the Cross*.

3. Cited in Gustav Aulén, *Christus Victor*, 24. See *The Ante-Nicene
Fathers*, vol. 1, 524.

4. Cited in Aulen, op. cit, 26. See *The Ante-Nicene Fathers*, 527.

5. Jasper Hopkins and Herbert Richardson, ed. and trans., *Treatises of Anselm of Canterbury*, vol. 3, 49. From an offprint by the Edwin
Mellen Press, n.d. Subsequent references to Anselm in this section
are from this translation.

6. Cited in John Dillenberger, *Martin Luther: Selections from His
Writings*, 122, 132, 136.

7. Henry Beveridge, trans., in *Great Books of the Western World*, vol.
20, 239.

8. Cited in William G. T. Shedd, *History of Christian Doctrine*, vol.
2, 376 n. 1.

9. *Defensio Fidei cahtolicae*, cited in Thomas C. Oden, *The Word of
Life*, 408.

10. Barth, *Dogmatics in Outline*, 101.

11. Barth, *Church Dogmatics* IV/1, 257.

Chapter 10

1. Oscar Cullmann, *Christ and Time*, 85.
2. Ibid., 84.
3. Thomas Oden, *The Word of Life*, 464.
4. Translated by Marcus Dods in *Basic Writings of Saint Augustine*, vol. 2, 225.
5. Ibid., 654.
6. Cited in *The Nicene and Post-Nicene Fathers, First Series*, vol. 8, 266.
7. John Stott, *Basic Christianity*, 49.
8. John Lawson, *Introduction to Christian Doctrine*, 107.
9. John Warwick Montgomery, *The Suicide of Christian Theology*, 263.
10. Louis Berkhof, *Summary of Christian Doctrine*, 101.

Chapter 11

1. Cited in Henry Bettenson, *The Early Christian Fathers*, 315.
2. *The Journal of John Wesley*, 8 volumes.
3. See *Nicene and Post-Nicene Fathers, First Series*, vol. 12, 168.
4. See Benjamin Warfield, *Miracles: Yesterday and Today*.
5. Francis Schaeffer, *The Mark of the Christian*, 14.

Chapter 12

1. The New International Version and the Revised Standard Version both translate the Greek present participle *tois pisteuousin* of John 1:12 as "those who believed." The Authorized (King James) version, like the NASB, translates it "those who believe."
2. John Lawson, *Introduction to Christian Doctrine*, 211.
3. Carl Bangs, *Arminius: A Study in the Dutch Reformation*, 350.
4. Traditional Catholic dogma, as articulated prior to the Second Vatican Council (1962–1965), is found in the creed and the canons of the Council of Trent (1563), which itself was a response to the Reformation doctrines of Luther and Calvin. The creed and canons of Trent may be found, among other places, in John Leith's *Creeds of the Churches*, 400–42.

5. Ludwig Ott, *Fundamentals of Catholic Dogma*, 326. Ott's discussion of the five sacraments of the order of salvation, found on pages 325–450, is the main source of our discussion here.

6. Ibid., 329.

7. Cited in Thomas Oden, *Life in the Spirit*, 125. See also *Catechism of the Catholic Church*, 481 ff.

8. Ludwig Ott, *Fundamentals of Catholic Dogma*, 479.

9. Augustine forcefully yet compassionately articulated the Catholic view of suicide as homicide in *The City of God, Book One*, chapters 16 through 28.

10. Cited in Richard P. McBrien, *Catholicism*, 684.

11. Citation from English translation published by Robert Carter, 525.

12. Luther speaks of "passive" righteousness in his *Commentary on Galatians*, ibid. xxiv, and of "alien" righteousness in his sermon "Two Kings of Righteousness," cited in John Dillenberger, *Martin Luther*, 86.

13. See Martin Luther, *Three Treatises*, 285.

14. Ibid., 298.

15. See Dillenberger, *Martin Luther*, 86.

16. Cited in Luther's *Works*, vol. 27, 230. Recently John Gerstner, a Presbyterian, has argued that Thomas Aquinas did believe in the concept of *justificatio impii* ("justification of the ungodly"), but that his viewpoint was rejected by Rome along with Luther's at the Council of Trent in 1563. See Gerstner, "Aquinas Was a Protestant," *Table Talk* 8:5 (May 1994), 13–15, 52.

17. *The Writings of James Arminius*, D.D. 3 vols.; hereafter *Writings*. vol. 1, 253. A concise summary of Arminius's theology is found in Carl Bangs, *Arminius*, 332–55.

18. Arminius, *Writings*, vol. 1, 526.

19. Ibid., 253.

20. Carl Bangs, *Arminius*, 343.

21. Ibid. chapter 15; see also 347–49.

22. "Minutes of Some Late Conversations between the Rev. Messrs. Wesley and Others," Friday, August 2nd, [1745] (sic). Cited in John Leith, *Creeds of the Churches*, 378.

23. Sermon entitled "Predestination Calmly Considered" in *The Works of the Rev. John Wesley*, A.M., vol. 10, 229.

24. The text of this 1784 Methodist confession may be found in John Leith, *Creeds of the Churches*, 354–60.

25. John Wesley, *Forty-Four Sermons*, 130. Wesley regarded the forty-four sermons as the most concise summary of his teaching.

26. "Minutes of Some Late Conversations between the Rev. Messrs. Wesley and Others," Conv. 1, Monday, June 25, 1744. Cited in John Leith, *Creeds of the Churches*, 375.

27. Wesley, *Forty-Four Sermons*, 53.

28. Ibid., 53.

29. Albert C. Outler, *Theology in the Wesleyan Spirit*, 33.

30. John Wesley, *A Plain Account of Christian Perfection*. See especially page 112 for a summary of Wesley's doctrine of Christian Perfection.

31. Wesley, *Forty-Four Sermons*, 457. References in the text are to part (Roman numeral) and paragraph (arabic numeral).

Chapter 13

1. See Lovett H. Weems, *John Wesley's Message Today*, 48.

2. See John Piper, *Let the Nations be Glad!* chap. 1.

3. For a thoroughly-documented treatment of Augustine's role in the Donatist controversy see Vernon J. Bourke, *Augustine's Quest for Wisdom*, chap. 9.

4. Translated by Henry Bettenson in *The Early Christian Fathers*, 246.

5. See *Nicene and Post-Nicene Fathers*, Second Series, vol. 11, 132.

6. Oscar Cullmann, *Peter: Disciple-Apostle-Martyr*, 214.

7. Oscar Cullmann, "The Tradition: the Exegetical, Historical, and Theological Problem," trans. A.J.B. Higgins in Oscar Cullmann, *The Early Church*, 94.

Chapter 14

1. See John Leith, *Creeds of the Churches*, 571.

2. See G. R. Beasley-Murray, "Baptism" in Colin Brown, ed., *New International Dictionary of New Testament Theology*, vol. 1, 144–54.

3. Oscar Cullmann, *Baptism in the New Testament*, 26.

4. See J.N.D. Kelly's discussion in *Early Christian Doctrines*, 430.

5. Ibid., 431f.

6. See John Leith, *Creeds of the Churches*, 426.

7. Luther's *Works*, vol. 35, 23–44.

8. Martin Luther, *Three Treatises*, 197.

9. See G.H. Williams, ed., *Spiritual and Anabaptist Writers*, vol. 25 of the *Library of Christian Classics*, 80.

10. See Geoffrey Bromiley's discussion in his *Historical Theology: An Introduction*, 274.

11. See G.W. Bromiley, ed., *Zwingli and Bullinger*, vol. 24 of the *Library of Christian Classics*, 130.

12. "A Treatise on Baptism" in *The Works of the Rev. John Wesley, A.M.*, vol. 10, 192.

13. The text of the 1859 Baptist *Abstract of Principles* is found in John Leith, *Creeds of the Churches*, 340–43. For a Baptist perspective on baptism see Stanley J. Grenz, *Theology for the Community of God*, 677–91.

14. See Peter Lampe, "The Eucharist: Identifying with Christ on the Cross," *Interpretation* January 1994, 36–49.

15. Oscar Cullmann, "The Meaning of the Lord's Supper in Primitive Christianity," in Cullmann and F.J. Leenhardt, *Essays on the Lord's Supper*, trans. J.G. Davies, 6.

16. The earliest non-canonical reference to the Eucharist, found in the Didache (around A.D.100), has no reference at all to the body and blood of Christ. See Bettenson, *The Early Christian Fathers*, 69f. An extended discussion of the historical development of the Lord's Supper is found in *The New Schaff-Herzog Encyclopedia of Religious Knowledge*, vol. 7, 24–40.

17. Cited in Henry Bettenson, *The Early Christian Fathers*, 87.

18. Ibid., 85f.

19. Cited in *The New Schaff-Herzog Encyclopedia of Religous Knowledge*, vol. 7, 33.

20. John Leith, *Creeds of the Churches*, 57.

21. Ibid., 123.

22. Ibid., 59.

23. Martin Luther, *Three Treatises*, 167.

24. G.W. Bromiley, ed., *Zwingli and Bullinger. Library of Christian Classics*, vol.,24, 257.

25. John Leith, *Creeds of the Churches*, 338, 342.

Chapter 15

1. Wolfhart Pannenberg, *Systematic Theology*, vol. 1, 16.

2. Louis Berkhof, *Summary of Christian Doctrine*, 181. This definition comes from Augustine's *City of God*, Book 13, chapter 6.

3. This phrase comes from the title and first line of Dylan Thomas's poem "Do Not Go Gentle into That Good Night."

4. *Nicene and Post-Nicene Fathers First Series*, vol. 3, 272.

5. *An English Translation of the Epistles of St. Ignatius*, 29.

6. See William G.T. Shedd's article "Intermediate State" in his *Dogmatic Theology*, 610–40. A reprint is found in Millard Erickson, ed., *Readings in Christian Theology*, vol. 3, 443–61.

7. Ludwig Ott, *Fundamentals of Catholic Dogma* op. cit., 482.

8. Ibid., 191, 476.

9. Ibid., 476.

10. *Basic Writings of Saint Augustine* vol. 2, ed. Whitney J. Oates, trans. M. Dods , 524.

11. See Jonathan Edwards, *The History of Redemption* in *The Works of President Edwards*, vol. 5, 167ff. Edwards spoke of four comings of Christ: (1) the incarnation; (2) the christianization of Rome under Constantine; (3) the future Millennial Age and the triumph of the Gospel; (4) the end of history and the final judgment.

12. For an in-depth examination of the origins and theology of Dispensationalism see Clarence Bass, *Backgrounds to Dispensationalism* (Grand Rapids: Eerdmans, 1960).

13. See *The Nicene and Post-Nicene Fathers, Second Series*, vol. 5, ed. Philip Schaff and Henry Wace, 467.

14. Cited in Henry Bettenson, ed. *The Early Christian Fathers* ,356.

15. Clark Pinnock, "Fire, Then Nothing," *Christianity Today* March 20, 1987, 40.

16. See for example David Edwards, *Evangelical Essentials, with a Response from John Stott.*

17. *The Works of President Edwards*, vol. 1, 669.

18. See also Daniel P. Fuller, *Unity of the Bible*, chapter 13, "The Justness of an Eternal Hell."

19. Cited by Irenaeus in his *Against Heresies*. See *The Ante-Nicene Fathers*, vol. 1, 154 ("Fragments of Papias" V) and 567 (*Against Heresies* 5.36).

20. *Nicene and Post-Nicene Fathers, First Series*, vol. 9, 111.

Glossary

A Posteriori: Methods of argumentation based upon observed facts. Chapter 1

A Priori: Methods of argumentation based not on observed facts, but upon ideas or propositions regarded as self-evident. Chapter 1.

Adoption: Legal term signifying that all who are justified enjoy the privileges of the children of God. Chapter 12.

Adoptionism: Christological heresy which teaches that Jesus Christ was not truly God, but was "adopted" by God in order to fulfill the divine plan of salvation. Chapter 8.

Anabaptism: Sixteenth-century theological movement which split off from the Protestant Reformation by rejecting infant baptism. Chapter 14.

Antilegomena: Greek word meaning "spoken against." Refers to several Christian writings which had difficulty getting into the Christian canon (including Hebrews and Revelation) or, after much controversy, were not included in the New Testament (Epistle of Barnabas). Chapter 2

Apollinarianism: Fourth-century christological heresy taught by Apollinarius, who believed Christ had a fully divine nature while possessing a human nature which excluded a rational human soul. Chapter 8.

Apostles: From the Greek apostello, "I send." Refers to followers of Jesus who were eyewitnesses to the risen Jesus and were commissioned by Christ as agents of divine revelation. Chapter 2.

Arianism: Fourth-century christological heresy taught by Arius of Alexandria, who believed Christ had a fully human nature but was not co-equal and co-eternal with God the Father in His divinity. Chapter 8.

Arminianism: Theological tradition, based upon the teachings of the sixteenth-century Dutch Protestant theologian Jacobus Arminius and later developed by the eighteenth-century English evangelist John Wesley, which affirms human free will and denies predestination. Chapter 12.

Atonement: Theological term which refers to the saving work of Christ, which has brought reconciliation ("at-one-ment") between the holy God and sinful human beings. Chapter 9.

Augustinianism: Theological tradition based upon the thought of the fifth-century North African theologian Augustine of Hippo, who emphasized the sovereignty of God and the total depravity of fallen humanity. Chapter 3.

Baptism: From the Greek baptizo, "to dip; to immerse." Rite of initiation into the Christian Church, wherein the person being received into the local congregation is immersed in or sprinkled with water. Some Christian groups baptize only those old enough to profess faith in Christ; other Christian groups baptize infants as well as adults. Chapter 14.

Barthianism: Theological tradition based upon the thought of the twentieth-century Swiss theologian Karl Barth, who emphasized the fundamental discontinuity between God and humanity and the centrality of Jesus Christ as God's sole self-revelation. Chapter 2.

Calvinism: Theological tradition based upon the thought of the sixteenth-century French Protestant Reformer John Calvin, who combined Martin Luther's emphasis on justification by faith with Augustine's emphasis on the sovereignty of God and the total depravity of fallen humanity. Chapter 5.

Canon: From the Greek kanon, "reed; measuring rod; standard of measure." A collection of books considered sacred by adherents of a particular religion. The Christian canon consists of the Old Testament and the New Testament. Chapter 2.

Catholic: The word has two meanings. In its broader sense it means "universal," and refers to the entire Christian Church and/or the principal doctrines believed by all Christians. The word is also used to refer to the Roman Catholic Church.

Cerinthianism: First-century christological heresy attributed to Cerinthus. This heresy taught that the man Jesus received the Spirit of

Christ when John baptized him, but that the Spirit left Jesus when he was crucified. Chapter 8.

Christology: Branch of Christian theology which deals with the doctrine of the person and work of Jesus Christ. Chapter 8.

Christus Victor: Latin for "Christ is the victor." Theory of the atonement which views the death of Christ as a triumph over the power of the devil. Chapter 9.

Communicable Attributes: Those attributes, or characteristics, of God which are also present to some degree in human beings (for example, personality). Chapter 3.

Communication of Attributes: Lutheran christological teaching that Christ's human nature participates in the divine attributes by virtue of the union of His deity and humanity, so that there is an interpenetration of the human nature of Christ by the divine nature. Chapter 8.

Communion of Attributes: Fifth-century christological teaching that Christ's divine attributes may be applied to the man Jesus, and that His human attributes may be applied to His divine Person. Chapter 8.

Confirmation: In the Roman Catholic Church, the sacrament wherein a baptized Catholic receives the laying on of hands by a duly ordained priest for further spiritual empowerment. This is usually done after a prolonged period of instruction in the teachings of the Catholic faith. Chapter 14.

Congregationalism: Form of church government in which the local congregation has final authority on matters of Christian faith and conduct. Chapter 14.

Conscience: Inward human moral faculty which evaluates a person's own attitudes and actions towards others. Chapter 1.

Consubstantiation: Martin Luther's doctrine of the Lord's Supper, which teaches that the substance of Christ's body and blood are present alongside the substance of the bread and wine partaken in the Eucharist. Chapter 14.

Creationism: Theory of the human soul's origin which teaches that God has directly created each individual human soul, either at the moment of biological conception or following conception. Chapter 6.

Creed: From the Latin credo, "I believe." A formal summary of the Christian faith, held in common by all Christians, or by Christians within a particular tradition. The Apostles' Creed and the Nicene Creed are the two most important universal creeds. Introductory chapter.

Deism: Theology which grew out of the seventeenth-century Enlightenment philosophical tradition. Deism recognizes God as the Creator of the universe, but rejects the idea the God continues to be involved in governing the world. Chapter 5.

Dispensationalism: Nineteenth-century perspective on biblical interpretation which views God as dealing with human beings in different ways during different periods of times or "dispensations." Dispensationalism tends to make a radical distinction between Israel (God's earthly people) and the Church (God's heavenly people). Chapter 15.

Docetism: From the Greek dokeo, "to appear" or "to seem." Early christological heresy which denied that Christ was a true human being, teaching instead that He was a spirit-being who only seemed to be human. Chapter 8.

Dualism: Worldview which depicts reality as divided into two mutually exclusive realms, the material (sometimes called phenomenal) and the spiritual (sometimes called noumenal). Chapter 2.

Ebionitism: Early Jewish-Christian form of adoptionism, which viewed Jesus not as God incarnate but as a supernaturally-empowered human being. Chapter 8.

Ecclesiology: Branch of Christian theology dealing with the doctrine of the Christian Church. Chapter 13.

Election: Biblical term referring to God's activity of choosing a people for Himself, that they might experience the joys of salvation. Chapter 12.

Enlightenment: Philosophical movement of seventeenth- and eighteenth-century Europe which emphasized the autonomy and capabilities of human reason. Chapter 1.

Episcopalianism: From the Greek word episkopos, "overseer; bishop." Form of church government in which bishops have theological and governing oversight of groups of local churches. Chapter 14.

Eschatology: Branch of Christian theology dealing with the doctrine of the last things in history, including death, the return of Christ, and eternal life. Chapter 15.

Eucharist: From the Greek eucharisto, "I give thanks." The partaking of bread and wine (or unfermented grape juice) in remembrance of the death of Christ, in celebration of His presence within His Church, and in anticipation of His return. Also known as Communion or the Lord's Supper. Chapter 12.

Evangelical: In North America and Western Europe, this word refers to Protestants who are not theological liberals, but who affirm the authority of Scripture and the need for salvation by faith in Jesus Christ. In historically Catholic countries such as those in Latin America, the word "Evangelical" refers to any Protestant. Chapter 1.

Evidentialism: Methodology which seeks to confirm the truth of Christianity by means of evidences and criteria of verification agreed upon by everyone, Christians and non-Christians alike. The opposite of fideism. Chapter 2.

Exegesis: From the Greek ex ago, "I bring out." The attempt, by means of grammatical and historical data, to "bring out" or articulate the message which the biblical writers intended to convey. Exegesis is one branch of hermeneutics, the science of literary interpretation. Chapter 2.

Extreme Unction: Roman Catholic sacrament whereby a sick or dying believer, by the anointing of oil and the prayer of the priest, receives the grace of God for the supernatural salvation of the soul, and sometimes also for the natural healing of the body. It is sometimes referred to as "last rites," since it is the final sacrament one receives prior to death.

Faith: The word has two meanings in Christian theology. Objectively, it refers to doctrine, or that which is believed ("The Faith"). Subjectively, it refers to the act of placing one's confidence in God's promises. Chapter 1.

Fideism: From the Latin fides, "faith." Methodology which seeks to confirm the truth of Christianity by appeal to grounds which are unique to Christianity. The opposite of evidentialism. Chapter 2.

Functional Christology: Study of Jesus Christ which focuses on His function, or work, in God's plan of salvation in history. Chapter 8.

General Revelation: What God has revealed of Himself to all people everywhere through His creation, whether or not they know anything of Christ or the Bible. Chapter 1.

Glorification: Refers to the resurrection of the body to everlasting life when Christ returns. Chapter 12.

Gnosticism: From the Greek gnosis, "knowledge." Philosophical or religious perspective which assumes a radical dualism, or separation, between the material and spiritual realms, and attempts to bridge the gap between the two by means of hidden knowledge and secret rituals. Chapter 8.

Hermeneutics: Study of the principles of interpreting texts. Chapter 2.

Homoousion: Greek expression meaning "of the same substance." Refers to the teaching that Christ was both fully divine and fully human, homoousion with both God and humanity. Chapter 8.

Hypostatic Union: Doctrine of the union of divine and human natures in Jesus Christ. Chapter 8.

Imago Dei: Latin for "image of God." Chapter 3.

Imputed Righteousness: Reformed Protestant teaching that the actual righteousness of Jesus Christ is credited, or imputed, to sinners as the basis for forgiveness of sins. It refers to legal righteousness, not ethical righteousness. Chapter 12.

Incommunicable Attributes: Those attributes, or characteristics of God, which are not shared by human beings (for example, infinity). Chapter 3.

Infused Righteousness: Roman Catholic teaching that the actual righteousness of Christ is given to, or infused within, Christians so that they are not merely considered legally righteous by God (i.e., pardoned), but actually made ethically righteous. Chapter 12.

Judicial Sentiment: Inward human moral faculty which judges the acts of other people towards oneself. Chapter 1.

Justification: The word has two meanings in the historic Christian tradition. In Roman Catholic thought, justification refers to the actual imparting of ethical righteousness to the Christian as well as to forgiveness of sins. In Protestant thought justification refers to the pardon of sins based upon the imputed righteousness of Christ. Chapter 12.

Kenosis Christology: From the Greek kenosis, "act of emptying." Based on Paul's remarks in Philippians 2:7 that Christ "emptied Himself," a set of various theories which seek to determine of what Christ emptied Himself. Chapter 8.

Liberal Theology: Post-Enlightenment Protestant tradition which emphasized a fundamental continuity between God and humanity, tended to deny miracles, and viewed Jesus not as the savior of sinners, but as the model Christian. Chapter 8.

Limited Atonement: Calvinist doctrine which teaches that Christ died for His chosen people (the "elect"), and no others. Chapter 9.

Lutheranism: Theological tradition associated with the sixteenth-century German Reformer Martin Luther, who emphasized justification by faith in Christ and the authority of Scripture above Church tradition. Chapter 12.

Modalism: Second-century trinitarian heresy which taught that the divine names Father, Son and Spirit do not refer to three Persons within the godhead, but instead are simply three different labels for three divine functions or "modes" of operation (such as creation, redemption, and sanctification) performed by the one divine Person who is God. Chapter 8.

Monergism: From the Greek mono ergo, "work alone." The teaching that God alone works out a human being's salvation, since the human will is not free, but in bondage to sin. Chapter 7.

Monophysitism: From the Greek *mono physis*, "one nature." Fifth-century christological heresy which taught that Christ had but one nature, a mixture of the divine and human. Chapter 8.

Mortal Sin: Roman Catholic term referring to grievous sins such as murder, adultery and denial of Christ. Such sins, if not absolved by a priest prior to one's death, preclude even a baptized Catholic from entering heaven. Chapter 12.

Nestorianism: Fifth-century christological heresy attributed to Nestorius, bishop of Constantinople, which teaches that Christ not only had two natures but was also two persons, divine and human. Chapter 8.

Orthodoxy: The word has several meanings. The two most prominent are (1) the doctrines which characterize the Eastern Orthodox Christian tradition, and (2) "right belief" or "true doctrine," as opposed to heresy. Chapter 2.

Pantheism: From the Greek pan theos, "all [is] God." The Hindu teaching that the world is a part of, or emanation from, God. Also referred to as monism (as opposed to dualism). Chapter 4.

Patripassianism: Another name for modalism, from the Greek words pater ("father") and pascho ("suffer"). Since modalism taught that the names Father and Son referred to the same divine Person, it could be said that the Father was crucified. Chapter 8.

Pelagianism: Theological tradition based upon the thought of the fifth-century British monk Pelagius, who opposed Augustine's doctrine of total depravity and taught that human beings were basically good. Chapter 7.

Penance: In the Roman Catholic Church, the sacrament which secures temporal forgiveness of post-baptismal sins. Chapter 12.

Pentecostalism: Twentieth-century theological tradition which emphasizes the miraculous gifts of the Spirit and the manifestation of speaking in tongues as a sign of being filled with the Spirit of God. Chapter 11.

Perseverance of the Saints: Calvinist teaching that all who have been truly regenerated by God's Spirit will persevere in faith and not fall away from Christ. Chapter 12.

Predestination: In the Augustinian-Reformed tradition, God's sovereign choice of some individuals within the fallen human race to receive salvation through Jesus Christ. Sometimes called "particular election." Chapter 12.

Providence: From the Latin pro videre, "to see beforehand." The doctrine which teaches that God not only created the world, but also continues to govern His creation. Chapter 5.

Purgatory: In Roman Catholic doctrine, the intermediate state between physical death and final judgment where baptized Church members are purged of temporal punishment of venial sins which were not absolved by penance or extreme unction prior to death. Chapter 15.

Reformed: Term which refers to the theological tradition based upon the writings of John Calvin and his successors. Chapter 12.

Regeneration: God's gift of new life to the sinner by means of the indwelling Spirit of Christ. Also called the "new birth." Chapter 12.

Sacrament: From the Latin sacramentum, "sacred thing" or "mystery." In Roman Catholic doctrine, a sacrament is an effective sign of grace instituted by Christ which gives grace. For Reformed Protestants, a sacrament is an outward and visible sign on an inward, invisible grace. Roman Catholics identify seven sacraments; Reformed Protestants, only two (baptism and the Lord's Supper). Chapter 12.

Sanctification: From the Latin sanctus, "holy." Refers to the process whereby a Christian grows in actual, ethical righteousness. In Roman Catholicism sanctification is part of the larger process of justification. Protestants, on the other hand, sharply distinguish between justification and sanctification. Chapter 12.

Semi-Pelagianism: Medieval theological tradition which sought a middle ground between Augustinianism and Pelagianism. Chapter 7.

Sensus divinitatis: Latin for "sense of God." Refers to the idea that all human beings have an innate sense of who God is and a felt need to worship God. Chapter 1.

Sola Fide: Latin for "faith alone." The principle of Reformed Theology which teaches that sinners are justified solely by faith in Christ, and not by good works. Chapter 12.

Sola Scriptura: Latin for "Scripture alone." The principle of Reformed Theology which teaches that the Bible is the sole final authority in all matters of Christian faith and conduct. Chapter 2.

Soli Deo Gloria: Latin for "to God alone be the glory." The principle of Reformed Theology which teaches that the final purpose of the Christian life, and indeed of the entire creation, is the glory of God. Chapter 15.

Soteriology: From the Greek soteria, "salvation." That branch of Christian theology which deals with the doctrine of salvation. Chapter 12.

Special Revelation: What God has revealed of Himself to a limited number of people through the events of redemptive history. The two principal components of special revelation are Jesus Christ and the Bible. Chapter 1.

Synergism: From the Greek sun ergo, "work together." The teaching that human free will must cooperate, or work together, with God in the attainment of salvation. Chapter 7.

Temporal Punishment: In Roman Catholic theology, a penalty assigned to undo the temporal (not eternal) effects of sin, and to purify the sinner. Penance and purgatory are examples of temporal punishment. Chapter 12.

Theodicy: Theological justification of the goodness of God amid a world which includes great evil. Chapter 5.

Thomism: Theological tradition based upon the writings of the Roman Catholic medieval theologian Thomas Aquinas. Chapter 1.

Total Depravity: Doctrine which affirms that Adam's sin has affected every aspect of the human race, leaving people entirely incapable of delivering themselves from divine judgment. Chapter 7.

Traducianism: Theory of the human soul's origin which teaches that each individual's soul is inherited from one's parents, along with one's bodily traits. Chapter 6.

Transubstantiation: Medieval doctrine of the Eucharist according to which the bread and the wine are changed in their inward substance into the body and blood of Christ, while retaining their outward accidental characteristics. Chapter 14.

Bibliography of Works Cited

Anselm of Canterbury. *Why God Became a Man (Cur Deus Homo)*. Off-print from *Treatises of Anselm of Canterbury*, vol. 3. Translated by Jasper Hopkins and Herbert Richardson. The Edwin Mellen Press, n.d., 49-137.

————. *Saint Anselm: Basic Writings*. Translated by S.N. Deane. 2d edition. LaSalle, Ill.: Open Court Publishing Co., 1962.

Arminius, James. *The Writings of James Arminius*, D.D. 3 vol. Grand Rapids: Baker, 1956 (reprint).

Auerbach, Erich. *Mimesis: The Representation of Reality in Western Literature*. Translated by Willard R. Trask. Princeton University Press, 1953.

Augustine of Hippo. *Basic Writings of Saint Augustine*. 2 vol. Edited by Whitney J. Oates. New York: Random House, 1948.

————. *Augustine: Earlier Writings*. Translated by John H.S. Burleigh. Vol. 6 of *The Library of Christian Classics*. Philadelphia: Westminster, 1953.

————. *Eighty-Three Different Questions*. Translated by David L. Mosher. Vol. 70 of *Fathers of the Early Church*. Washington, D.C.: Catholic University of America Press, 1982.

Aulén, Gustav. *Christus Victor*. New York: Macmillan, 1969.

Bangs, Carl. *Arminius: A Study in the Dutch Reformation*. Nashville: Abingdon, 1971.

Barth, Karl. *Church Dogmatics.* 4 vol. Edited by Geoffrey W. Bromiley and Thomas F. Torrance. Translated by G. W. Bromiley et al. Edinburgh: T. & T. Clark, 1956-1975.

———. *Evangelical Theology: An Introduction.* Translated by Grover Foley. Garden City, N.Y.: Anchor Books, 1964.

Bass, Clarence. *Backgrounds to Dispensationalism.* Grand Rapids: Eerdmans, 1960.

Berkhof, Louis. *Summary of Christian Doctrine.* Grand Rapids: Eerdmans, 1938.

Bettenson, Henry. *Documents of the Christian Church.* London: Oxford University Press, 1963.

———. *The Early Christian Fathers.* London: Oxford University Press, 1956.

Billingsley, K.L. *From Mainline to Sideline: The Social Witness of the National Council of Churches.* Washington D.C.: Ethics and Public Policy Center, 1980.

Bourke, Vernon J. *Augustine's Quest for Wisdom.* Milwaukee: Bruce Publishing Co., 1945.

Bromiley, Geoffrey W. *Historical Theology: An Introduction.* Grand Rapids: Eerdmans, 1978.

———, ed. *Zwingli and Bullinger.* Vol. 24 in *The Library of Christian Classics.* Philadelphia: Westminster, 1953.

Brown, Colin, ed. *New International Dictionary of New Testament Theology.* Vol. 1. Grand Rapids: Zondervan, 1986.

Bultmann, Rudolf. "What Does It Mean to Speak of God?" *Faith and Understanding.* Vol. 1. Edited by Robert W. Funk. Translated by Louise Pettibone Smith. London: SCM Press, 1969: 55-61.

Calvin, John. *Institutes of the Christian Religion.* Edited by John T. McNiell. Translated by Ford Lewis Battles. Vol. 21 and 22 of *The Library of Christian Classics.* Philadelphia: Westminster, 1960.

———. *Institutes of the Christian Religion.* 2d ed. Vol. 20 in *Great Books of the Western World.* Edited by Mortimer J. Adler. Translated by Henry Beveridge. Chicago: Encyclopaedia Britannica, Inc., 1990.

Carnell, Edward John. *Christian Commitment.* New York: Macmillan, 1957.

———. *Catechism of the Catholic Church.* Mahwah, N.J.: Paulist Press, 1994.

The Constitution of the Presbyterian Church (U.S.A.), Part I: Book of Confessions. Includes texts of the Apostles' Creed, Nicene Creed, Scots Confession, Heidelberg Catechism, Second Helvetic Confession,

Westminster Confession of Faith, Westminster Shorter and Larger Catechisms, Theological Declaration of Barmen, and Confession of 1967. Published annually by the General Assembly of the Presbyterian Church (U.S.A.), Louisville, Ky.

Corduan, Winfried. *Reasonable Faith: Basic Christian Apologetics.* Nashville: Broadman & Holman, 1993.

Cosgrove, Mark. *The Amazing Body Human: God's Design for Personhood.* Grand Rapids: Baker, 1987.

Cullmann, Oscar. *Baptism in the New Testament.* Translated by J.K.S. Reid. Philadelphia: Westminster, 1950.

————. *Christ and Time.* Translated by Floyd Filson. Rev. Ed. Philadelphia: Westminster, 1964.

————. *The Christology of the New Testament.* Translated by Shirley C. Guthrie and Charles A. M. Hall. Philadelphia: Westminster, 1963.

————. *The Earliest Christian Confessions.* Translated by J.K.S. Reid. London: Billing & Sons, Ltd., 1949.

————. *The Early Church.* Edited by A.J.B. Higgins. Philadelphia: Westminster, 1953.

————. *Peter: Disciple-Apostle-Martyr.* Translated by Floyd Filson. London: SCM Press, 1953.

————. and F.J. Leenhardt, *Essays on the Lord's Supper.* Translated by J.G. Davies. Atlanta: John Knox, 1958.

Dante Alighieri. *Paradiso. Book Three of The Divine Comedy.* Vol. 19 in *Great Books of the Western World.* Edited by Mortimer J. Adler. 2d Ed. Chicago: Encyclopaedia Britannica, Inc., 1990.

Dockery, David. *Biblical Interpretation Then and Now.* Grand Rapids: Baker, 1992.

Dodd, C.H. *The Bible and the Greeks.* London: Hodder and Stoughton, 1935.

————. *The Epistle of Paul to the Romans.* Moffatt New Testament Commentary. London: Hodder and Stoughton, 1932.

Edwards, *David. Evangelical Essentials, with a Response from John Stott.* Downers Grove, Ill.: InterVarsity, 1988.

Edwards, Jonathan. "Dissertation Concerning the End for Which God Created the World" in *The Works of Jonathan Edwards.* 2 vol. Revised and corrected by Edward Hickman. Carlisle, Pa.: Banner of Truth, 1974.

————. *Freedom of the Will.* Library of Liberal Arts edition. Edited by Arnold S. Kaufman and William K. Frankena. Indianapolis and New York: Bobbs-Merrill, 1969.

————. *The History of Redemption,* in *The Works of President Edwards.* Vol. 5. Reprint of 1817 London Edition. New York: Burt Franklin, 1968.

————. *An Unpublished Essay of Edwards on the Trinity.* Edited by G.P. Fisher New York: Charles Scribner's Sons, 1903.

Erickson, Millard J. *Christian Theology.* One-volume edition. Grand Rapids: Baker, 1985.

————. *Readings in Christian Theology.* 3 vol. Grand Rapids: Baker, 1974-1979.

Fuller, Daniel P. *The Unity of the Bible.* Grand Rapids: Zondervan, 1992.

Gerstner, John. "Aquinas Was a Protestant." *Table Talk.* Volume 8 Number 5 (May 1994), 13-15, 52.

Graham, Billy. *Angels: God's Secret Agents.* Garden City, N.Y.: Doubleday & Company, 1975.

Grenz, Stanley J. *Theology for the Community of God.* Nashville: Broadman & Holman, 1994.

Gorman, Michael. *Abortion and the Early Church.* Downers Grove, Ill.: InterVarsity, 1982.

Guthrie, Donald. *New Testament Theology.* Downers Grove, Ill.: InterVarsity Press, 1981.

Hodge, A.A. *Outlines of Theology.* Rewritten and enlarged edition. New York: Robert Carter and Brothers, 1878.

Hughes, Philip E. *Creative Minds in Contemporary Theology.* Rev. ed. Grand Rapids: Eerdmans, 1969.

Hume, David. *On Religion.* Edited by Richard Wollheim. Cleveland: Meridian Books, 1963.

Ignatius of Antioch. *An English Translation of the Epistles of St. Ignatius.* Translated by J.H. Srawley. London: S.P.C.K., 1954.

Jaki, Stanley. *The Road of Science and the Ways of God.* Washington D.C.: Regnery-Gateway, 1988.

James, M.R., ed.. *The Apocryphal New Testament.* Translated by M.R. James. Oxford: Clarendon Press, 1924.

Jewett, Paul K. "Unpublished Christology Syllabus." Fuller Theological Seminary, 1970.

Johnson, Paul. *A History of Christianity.* New York: Atheneum, 1977.

————. *Modern Times: The World from the Twenties to the Nineties.* New York: HarperCollins, 1991.

Kähler, Martin. *The So-Called Historical Jesus and the Historic, Biblical Christ.* Edited and translated by Carl Braaten. Philadelphia: Fortress Press, 1964.

Keil, C.F. and F. Delitzsch. *Biblical Commentary on the Pentateuch.* Vol. 1. Grand Rapids: Eerdmans, 1951 (reprint).

Kelly, J.N.D. *Early Christian Doctrines.* Rev. ed. San Francisco: Harper & Row, 1978.

Kittel, Gerhard, ed. *Theological Dictionary of the New Testament.* Vol. 6. Translated by Geoffrey W. Bromiley. Grand Rapids: Eerdmans, 1968.

Kümmel, Werner Georg. *The New Testament: The History of the Investigation of Its Problems.* Translated by S. MacLean Gilmour and Howard Clark Kee. Nashville: Abingdon, 1972.

Kushner, Harold. *When Bad Things Happen to Good People.* New York: Avon Books, 1981.

Lampe, Peter. "The Eucharist: Identifying with Christ on the Cross." *Interpretation.* January 1994, 36-49.

Lane, Tony. *Harper's Concise Book of Christian Faith.* San Francisco: Harper & Row, 1984.

Lawson, John. *Introduction to Christian Doctrine.* Grand Rapids: Zondervan, 1980.

Leibniz, Gottfried Wilhelm von. *Monadology and Other Philosophical Essays.* Translated by Paul Schrecker and Anna Martin Schrecker. Indianapolis: Bobbs-Merrill, 1965.

Leith, John. *Basic Christian Doctrine.* Louisville, KY: Westminster/John Knox Press, 1993.

———. *Creeds of the Churches.* 3d ed. Atlanta: John Knox Press, 1982.

Lewis, C.S. *God in the Dock.* Grand Rapids: Eerdmans, 1970.

———. *Mere Christianity.* Revised and enlarged edition. New York: Macmillan, 1952.

Luther, Martin. *Commentary on Galatians.* New York: Robert Carter, 1845.

———. *Luther's Works.* Fifty-four volumes to date. Edited by Jaroslav Pelikan and E. Theodore Bachmann. Concordia and Fortress Press, 1958-.

———. *Martin Luther: Selections from His Writings.* Edited by John Dillenberger. Garden City, N.Y.: Anchor Books, 1961.

———. *Three Treatises.* Philadelphia: Fortress Press, 1960.

Marsden, George. *The Soul of the American University: From Protestant Establishment to Established Nonbelief.* New York: Oxford Press, 1994.

McBrien, Richard. *Catholicism*. San Francisco: HarperCollins, 1981.

Milton, John. *Paradise Lost*. Volume 29 of *Great Books of the Western World*. Edited by Mortimer J. Adler. Chicago: Encyclopedia Britannica, Inc., 1990.

Monod, Jacques. *Chance and Necessity*. New York: Alfred A. Knopf, 1971.

Montgomery, John Warwick. *The Suicide of Christian Theology*. Minneapolis: Bethany Fellowship, 1971.

Morris, Leon. *The Apostolic Preaching of the Cross*. Grand Rapids: Eerdmans, 1955.

Neill, Stephen. *A History of Christian Missions*. Baltimore: Penguin, 1964.

Neuhaus, Richard John et al. "Evangelicals and Catholics Together." *First Things*, No. 43. May 1994, 15-22.

Niebuhr, Reinhold. *The Nature and Destiny of Man*. 2 vol. New York: Charles Scribner's Sons, 1941, 1943.

Novak, Michael. "Awakening from Nihilism." *First Things*, No. 45. August/September 1994, 18-22.

Oden, Thomas C. *Life in the Spirit*. San Francisco: HarperCollins, 1992.

———. *The Living God*. San Francisco: HarperCollins, 1987.

———. *The Word of Life*. San Francisco: HarperCollins, 1989.

Ott, Ludwig. *Fundamentals of Catholic Dogma*. 2d Ed. Rockford, Ill.: Tan Books and Publishers, 1974.

Outler, Albert. *Theology in the Wesleyan Spirit*. Nashville: Discipleship Resources, 1975.

———. *Who Trusts in God*. New York: Oxford University Press, 1967.

Pannenberg, Wolfhart. *Systematic Theology*. Vol. 1. Translated by Geoffrey W. Bromiley. Grand Rapids: Eerdmans, 1991.

Pascal, Blaise. *Pascal's Pènsees*. Translated by W.F. Trotter. New York: E.P. Dutton, 1958.

Pelikan, Jaroslav. *The Christian Tradition, Volume One: The Emergence of the Catholic Tradition* (100-600). University of Chicago, 1971.

Pinnock, Clark. "Fire, then Nothing." *Christianity Today*. March 20, 1987, 40.

Piper, John. *Desiring God: Meditations of a Christian Hedonist*. Portland: Multnomah Press, 1986.

———. *Let the Nations Be Glad!* Grand Rapids: Baker, 1993.

Platinga, Cornelius Jr. "Trinity" in *The International Standard Bible Encyclopedia*. Rev. ed., Vol. 4. Grand Rapids: Eerdmans, 1988.

Polanyi, Michael. *Personal Knowledge*. University of Chicago, 1962.

Rees, Thomas S., ed. *Racovian Catechism*. Translated by Thomas S. Rees. Lexington, Ky.: American Theological Library Union, 1962.

Roberts, Alexander and James Donaldson, eds.. *The Ante-Nicene Fathers*. 10 vol. Grand Rapids: Eerdmans, 1979 (reprint).

Rogers, Jack, ed. *Case Studies in Christ and Salvation*. Philadelphia: Westminster, 1977.

Schaeffer, Edith. *Christianity is Jewish*. Wheaton, Ill.: Tyndale House, 1975.

Schaeffer, Francis. *Back to Freedom and Dignity*. Downers Grove, Ill.: InterVarsity Press, 1972.

———. *Death in the City*. Downers Grove, Ill.: InterVarsity Press, 1969.

———. *Escape from Reason*. Downers Grove, Ill.: InverVarsity Press, 1968.

———. *The Mark of the Christian*. Downers Grove, Ill.: InterVarsity Press, 1970.

Schaff, Philip, ed. *The New Schaff-Herzog Encyclopedia of Religous Knowledge*. New York and London: Funk and Wagnalls, 1910.

———. and Henry Wace, eds. *A Select Library of the Nicene and Post-Nicene Fathers*. First Series, 14 volumes. Second Series, 14 vol. Grand Rapids: Eerdmans, 1983 (reprint).

Schlossberg, Herbert. *Idols for Destruction: The Conflict of Christian Faith and American Culture*. Rev. ed. Chicago: Crossway Books, 1993.

Senior, John. *The Death of Christian Culture*. New Rochelle, N.Y.: Arlington House, 1978.

Shedd, William G.T. *Dogmatic Theology*. Grand Rapids: Zondervan, 1888.

———. *A History of Christian Doctrine*. 2 vol. New York: Charles Scribner, 1863.

Smart, James. *The Creed in Christian Teaching*. Philadelphia: Westminster, 1962.

Smith, David L. *A Handbook of Christian Theology*. Wheaton, Ill.: Victor Books, 1992.

Solzhenitsyn, Aleksandr. *The Gulag Archipelago*. 3 vol. Translated by Thomas P. Whitney (Vol. 1 and 2) and Harry Willetts (Vol. 3). New York: Harper and Row, 1973-1978.

Sophocles. *Oedipus Rex.* Translation by Albert Cook in L.R. Lind ed., *Ten Greek Plays in Contemporary Translations.* Cambridge, Mass.: The Riverside Press/Houghton Mifflin Company.

Stott, John R.W. *Basic Christianity.* Downers Grove, Ill.: InterVarsity Press, 1971.

Torrance, Thomas F. *God and Rationality.* London: Oxford, 1971.

Thomas Aquinas, *Summa Theologica (Summa Theologiae).* 2d ed. Vol. 17 and 18 in *Great Books of the Western World.* Edited by Mortimer J. Adler. Chicago: Encyclopaedia Britannica, Inc., 1990.

Van Till, Howard J. "Is Specal Creationism a Heresy?" *Christian Scholars Review* XXII:4 (June 1993), 380-95.

Warfield, Benjamin B. *Miracles: Yesterday and Today.* Grand Rapids: Eerdmans, 1953 (reprint).

Watson, Philip, ed. *The Message of the Wesleys.* Grand Rapids: Zondervan, 1984.

Weems, Lovett H. *John Wesley's Message Today.* Nashville: Abingdon, 1982.

Wenham, Gordon. *Christ and the Bible.* Downers Grove, Ill.: InterVarsity, 1973.

Wesley, John. *Forty-Four Sermons.* London: Epworth Press, 1944.

———. *The Journal of John Wesley.* 8 vol. Edited by Nehemiah Curnock. London: Epworth Press, 1938.

———. *A Plain Account of Christian Perfection.* London: Epworth Press, 1952.

———. *The Works of the Rev. John Wesley, A. M.* Edited by Thomas Jackson. London: John Mason, 1829-31.

Williams, Colin. *John Wesley's Theology Today.* Nashville: Abingdon, 1960.

Williams, G.H.,ed. *Spiritual and Anabaptist Writers.* Vol. 25 in *The Library of Christian Classics.* Philadelphia: Westminster Press, 1957.

Names Index